Current Economics and Politics of (ex-) Czechoslovakia

Current Economics and Politics of (ex-) Czechoslovakia

Edited by

J. Křovák

Nova Science Publishers, Inc.

Art Director: Christopher Concannon
Graphics: Elenor Kallberg and Maria Ester Hawrys
Book Production: Michael Lyons, Roseann Pena, Casey Pfalzer, June Martino, Tammy Sauter, and Michelle Lalo
Circulation: Irene Kwartiroff, Annette Hellinger, and Benjamin Fung

Library of Congress Cataloging-in-Publication Data

Current economics and politics of (ex-)Czechoslovakia / J. Krovak, editor
p. cm.
Includes bibliographical references and index.
ISBN 1-56072-147-2 : $69.00
1. Czechoslovakia -- Economics policy -- 1989-1992. 2. Czechoslovakia -- Economics conditions -- 1945-1992. 3. Czechoslovakia -- Politcs and government -- 1989- . 4. Czech Republic -- Economic policy. 5. Czech Republic -- Economic conditions. 6. Czech Republic -- Politics and government. I. Křovák, Jiří.
HC270.283.C87 1993 93-21515
338.9437 -- dc20 CIP

6080 Jericho Turnpike, Suite 207
Commack, New York 11725
Tele. 516-499-3103 Fax 516-499-3146
E Mail Novasci1@aol.com

Printed in the United States of America

CONTENTS

CHAPTER 4.

CHAPTER 5.

CHAPTER 6.

CHAPTER 7.

CHAPTER 8.

CHAPTER 9.

CHAPTER 10.

CHAPTER 11.

CHAPTER 12.

CHAPTER 13.

CHAPTER 14.

CHAPTER 15.

CHAPTER 16.

LIST OF CONTRIBUTORS*

1. Brada, Josef; Professor
Department of Economics, College of Business,
Arizona State University, Tempe, AZ 85287-3806, U.S.A.

2. Buchtíková, Alena (Staff Member) and Flek, Vladislav (Staff Member)
The Institute of Economics, State Bank of Czechoslovakia,
Politickych veznu 7, CS-111 73 Praha 1, Czechoslovakia

3. Capek, Ales; Head of Department
The Institute of Economics, State Bank of Czechoslovakia,
Politickych veznu 7, CS-111 73 Praha 1, Czechoslovakia

4. Frydmanova, Marie (Staff Member) and Zelenkova, Hana (Head of Department)
The Institute of Economics, Czechoslovak Academy of Sciences
Politickych veznu 7, CS-111 73 Praha 1, Czechoslovakia

5. Hejnák, Miloslav; Head of Department
The Institute of Economics, Czechoslovak Academy of Sciences
Politickych veznu 7, CS-111 73 Praha 1, Czechoslovakia

6. Hlaváček, Jiří; Head of Department
Department of Economics, Faculty of Social Sciences,
Charles University, Smetanovo nabrezi 995/6, CS-110 01
Praha 1, Czechoslovakia

7. Hrnčíř, Miroslav; Head of Department
The Institute of Economics, State Bank of Czechoslovakia,
Politickych veznu 7, CS-111 73 Praha 1, Czechoslovakia

---

* The List of Contributors lists affiliations, positions and addresses of each author at the time of the writing of the contribution.

8. Janáček, Kamil; Deputy Minister
Ministry of Labor and Social Welfare of the Czech Republic,
Na poricnim pravu 1, CS-120 00 Praha 2, Czechoslovakia

9. Janáčková, Stanislava, Staff Member
The Institute of Economics, State Bank of Czechoslovakia,
Politickych veznu 7, CS-111 73 Praha 1, Czechoslovakia

10. Jonas, Jiri; Assistant to Executive Director
International Monetary Fund, 700 19th Street N.W.,
Washington, D.C. 20431, U.S.A.

11. Klvačová, Eva; coeditor
Ekonom weekly economic journal, Na porici 30, CS-112 86
Praha 1, Czechoslovakia

12. Stepanek, Vit; Advisòr to the Minister,
Ministry of Economic Policy and Development of the Czech
Republic, Vrsovicka 65, CS-101 60 Praha 10, Czechoslovakia

13. Šujan, Ivan; President
Federal Statistical Office, Sokolovska 142,
CS-186 13 Praha 8, Czechoslovakia

14. Yancis, Lisbeth
The University of Texas at Austin
Rue de Nalinnes 7, B-5651 Thy-le-Chateau, Belgium

15. Zamrazilova, Eva; Deputy Head of Department
The Institute of Economics, Czechoslovak Academy of Sciences
Politickych veznu 7, CS-111 73 Praha 1, Czechoslovakia

16. Zemplinerová, Alena (Staff Member)
The Institute of Economics, Czechoslovak Academy of Sciences
Politickych veznu 7, CS-111 73 Praha 1, Czechoslovakia

1

TRANSITION TO THE MARKET: INTERACTION OF MACROECONOMIC AND SOCIAL POLICY

Kamil Janáček
Deputy Minister
Ministry of Labor and Social Welfare

The initial conditions in Czechoslovakia were - at the end of 1989 - different from those of other transforming economies, particularly Poland and Hungary (with whom Czechoslovakia is usually compared). First, Czechoslovakia had some advantages:

1) There was a long tradition of tight monetary policy. Not only was Czechoslovakia an island of monetary stability in the hyper-inflationary Central Europe of the Twenties; it even managed to retain this tradition during the long decades of central planning. The financial discipline of the government and enterprises was relatively strict, state budgets were balanced and the balance of payments showed no big deficits or surpluses.

2) Inflation, both open and suppressed, was low. According to recent analysis (see Drábek - Janáček - Tůma, 1992), the overall annual inflation rate did not exceed 5 % in the 1980s.

3) Czechoslovakia's external debt was low by all international standards.

4) The country has well-educated and relatively skilled labour. In this respect, the gap vis-a-vis advanced economies is probably lower than in other transforming economies.

On the other hand, there were some disadvantages:

1) The system of command economy was very complete; there was no private sector, almost everything being socialised.

2) Almost all prices were centrally controlled. Only in the second half of the eighties did some slow and half-hearted steps toward decontrol of prices

take place. Enterprise managers were also tightly controlled by government planning organs, and they had little autonomy in decision-making.

3) Exports were predominantly aimed at C.M.E.A. markets (more than 70 % in the second half of the eighties). Especially high was the share of the Soviet Union (almost 40%). A considerable part of these exports are not saleable in western markets.

In light of these initial conditions, the following major measures were chosen as the pillars of economic transformation:

1) Massive and rapid privatization. Privatization is a top priority in all truly transforming economies, and it has special importance in Czechoslovakia. A massive shift of property rights from state (e.g. government) to private hands is essential if the economy is to become a market economy. There is a real effort being made to privatize as much as possible as fast as possible. Privatization must be done quickly, because it is the only way to fundamentally change the behaviour of economic agents, expose them to the pressures of the market, and initiate the structural changes that will prevent the prolongation of the post-socialist, hybrid economy, that is highly prone to economic collapse.

2) Price liberalization - a necessity for a functioning market economy, and for efficient allocation of resources. The atrophied price structure which had become totally distorted by forty years of central planning had to be liberalized immediately, since attempts at gradual change would simply lead to a prolongation and deepening of the distortions.

3) Opening of the Czechoslovak economy to the world, i.e. liberalization of external trade and the introduction of internal convertibility of the Czechoslovak crown. These are the most effective ways to create a competitive environment. The establishment of a monetary market and providing of free access to foreign currency bring domestic prices closer to world prices. A realistic exchange rate reduces pressure on the balance of payments (which is threatened by the collapse of traditional markets and by the low competitiveness of exports).

4) Restoring and preserving macroeconomic equilibrium is a conditio sine qua non for progress. Tight macroeconomic policy, based on a state budget surplus and prudent monetary policy, is absolutely necessary; otherwise, a vicious circle of inflation and stagnation would evolve, and direct controls would have to be reintroduced.

5) Maintenance of social consensus, i.e. sufficient support by the population, is of prime importance to successful transformation. Transformation is inevitably accompanied by an increase in unemployment, increased poverty in certain social groups, retraining needs etc. For this reason it is necessary to create a social safety net which would provide an adequate safeguard against unrest and - simultaneously - motivate the people to take initiative in solving their economic problems. It requires continuous testing of the feasibility - from the social point of view - of the transformation process. So far, transformation in Czechoslovakia has been very successful in avoiding social unrest, strikes etc., while taking steps

which adversely affect the standard of living of the population. Czechoslovakia is an exception among East European countries in this respect.

1. MACROECONOMIC PERFORMANCE IN 1991 - 1992

The present stage of transformation of the Czechoslovak economy is characterized by largely conflicting trends. Production and gross domestic product fell significantly. Main causes of this fall were:

- the breakdown of markets in former C.M.E.A. countries, and, mainly, of the Soviet Union market. The loss of these "soft" markets is all the more serious that part of products previously sold here are unsalable on other markets;

- a sharp decline of domestic demand for consumer goods and investment, as a result of price liberalization, of the pre-privatization climate in state-owned enterprises, and of a disruption of traditional links among the enterprises;

- the starting decrease of material intensity of Czechoslovak production, resulting in a fall of internal demand for some raw materials and intermediate products.

On the other hand, in some sectors, industries and enterprises, the start of an economic revival can be observed, thanks to:

- the growth of the private sector, mainly in trade and services. One can infer that faster progress of the private sector in the Czech Republic is one of the reasons of the less adverse impact of transformation here, as compared to Slovakia.

In the Czech Republic, private sector`s share in the gross domestic product was almost 10 % in 1991, compared to 4 % in Slovakia. As a result, the contribution of the private sector to new job creation is different in both republics, too. It is estimated that private sector has created one million of new jobs in the whole Czechoslovakia; hence the different unemployment rates in the two republics are, among other factors, also due to the differing dynamics of the private sector.

- the growth of exports to advanced market economies. Devaluation of the Czechoslovak Crown, and the loss of Eastern markets, have forced numerous producers to seek new markets in advanced economies, mainly in the E.C. countries. After a 10 % increase in 1991, the growth of exports to this region went on at a higher rate in the first half of 1992 (18 %). One can conclude that this has in some (though, so far, smaller) part compensated for the loss of the C.M.E.A. markets. An indisputable comparative advantage of Czechoslovakia - as different from some neighbouring transforming economies - is the level of the exchange rate, and the wage level;

- keeping inflation under control. Since the second half of 1991, the quarterly inflation rate has not exceeded 2 - 3 %. Inflation expectations of both households and entrepreneurs have been low, household savings have been increasing, as have the deposits of enterprises. This can partly explain the increase of investment activity in some segments of the economy - as low inflation has enabled longer horizons in decision-making.

- the fact that the fall of consumer demand stopped in the first quarter of 1992. In view of a moderate growth of real incomes, some increase of consumer demand can even be registered against last year - though not in the whole demand structure.

Conflicting and highly differentiated trends are characteristic also for individual industries. On the whole it can be said that the dividing line between the winners and losers runs across individual industries, rather than between them. Enterprises that have high exports, links to foreign capital, or good management, are far ahead; at the moment, it does not even matter so much whether the enterprise is already privatized, or waiting for privatization.

With the necessary time-lag, the positive effect is now being felt of the partial write-off of enterprise debts, and the recapitalization of commercial banks. Among other things, this has enabled to direct, in the first quarter of 1992, more than the whole increment of credits into the private sector. Gradually, other measures of government support of the private sector will be felt as well, such as the founding of the Guarantee Bank, the possibility of government coverage of part of interest payments for private firms participating in some selected programs, etc.

The impact of transformation has been different in agriculture than in industry. The differences become obvious if one compares agriculture with food-processing industries, or with the other sectors of the economy. They are manifested mainly in a completely different dynamic of prices of agricultural products since the price liberalization. This, together with other impacts of transformation, has resulted in a critical income situation in agriculture. Negative effects of this state will complicate the process of privatization of state-owned farms, and of transformation of agricultural cooperatives; some risk even arises that the level of sufficient food supply may be jeopardized.

Indeed, the price dynamics of agricultural products have differed substantially from industrial producer prices, and from consumer prices. If one takes the average price level for 1991 against 1989, producer prices in industry grew by three quarters, prices in construction by almost three fifths; consumer prices grew almost by three quarters (foodstuffs prices by more than three fifths, other consumer goods by 90 %). Only prices of agricultural products stagnated; their average level in 1991 was only 3.8 % higher than in 1989, and they did not increase against 1990.

The cumulated effect of falling demand, stagnating prices of agricultural products, significantly rising prices of inputs,
cuts in subsidies, and worse credit conditions, was of such an extent that even pushing costs down could not prevent large losses (which, in sum, reached 10 billion Crowns in 1991). On the whole, 73 % of agricultural cooperatives and 87 % of state-owned farms are operating at a loss.

The situation in agriculture has also been negatively influenced by the fact that government economic policy paid much less attention to agriculture than to other sectors. The slower progress of transformation in agriculture, compared to the rest of the economy, is a potential source of tensions and serious economic problems.

As was mentioned above, trends in external economic relations have been relatively positive. The trade balance shows a surplus of 10.2 billion Crowns. The whole surplus has been achieved by exports from the Czech Republic. The positive trade balance has led to a surplus of the current account balance in convertible currencies, amounting to 826 million dollars in the first half of 1992. In the same period, convertible currency reserves reached 5 billion dollars - the level of roughly eight-months` imports. At the same time, gross indebtedness rose from 9.4 billion dollars to 9.8 billion. Especially positive is the fact that the inflow of foreign direct investment was 443 million dollars in the first half of 1992.

As to the trends in the labour market, unemployment went down during the nine months of 1992, in both republics. More factors contributed to this change:

- stricter conditions for the payment of unemployment allowances led to higher activity of the unemployed in seeking new jobs;
- creation of new jobs in the growing private sector, and public job creation policies of both republic governments. Especially successful has been the policy of employing fresh secondary school leavers and university graduates in so-called assistant jobs, with wages paid by the labour offices. Unemployment in this category fell below 10 % (which is very low in comparison with West European countries);
- the pre-privatization climate in most state-owned enterprises, characterized now no more by the endeavour to maintain the volume of production, but by the striving to maintain the employment levels. The task to shed unneeded workers is passed to the new management, after privatization.

In the labour market, regional and structural differences persist which appeared in 1991. Unemployment rate in Slovakia is roughly four times higher than in the Czech Republic; the share of unemployed without secondary education is growing, the share of university graduates in unemployment goes down. Women`s share in unemployment is significantly higher than their share in total labour force. Regional programs which are under preparation will only show in the labour market in a longer time horizon.

The share of unemployed undergoing retraining fell to 2 %. One reason is insecurity as to the structure of future demand for labour. Another is the absence of other than governmental subjects in the organization of retraining programs. In this respect, making broader use of the experience of West European countries would be highly beneficial.

Regions with a one-sided production structure (be it industry or agriculture) are more hit by unemployment. Changes in agriculture (mainly, the breakdown of large state-owned farms) have significantly influenced unemployment in some regions.

Regional differences in unemployment are not exclusively connected with varying production structures, and uneven demand situation. They stem also from differences in the age and qualification structure of the population. From recent trends, it is obvious that regional aspects must play an important role in economic policy. In areas hit hard by unemployment, solutions must be sought in cooperation of central government with local organs and local enterprises.

Labour and social incomes, too, show in the first half of 1992 some new trends. In 1991, wage incomes slowed down, incomes from agriculture fell, while social incomes grew quickly. Thus, the share of social incomes in total money incomes increased, and that of labour incomes went down. As an example, while total real incomes fell by 26 %, the real value of old-age pensions decreased only by 19 %. Social policy was aimed at compensating the price growth after price liberalization (e.g., the average old-age pension in 1991 reached 73 % of the average net wage - the highest ratio since 1954). This policy contributed significantly to the social feasibility of the first stage of transformation of the Czechoslovak economy.

In the first half of 1991, the dynamics of both nominal and real incomes changed. Nominal incomes grew by 20.3 %, real incomes by 6.9 %; real wages grew by more than 8.9 %. The fall of real incomes stopped; the share of labour incomes in total money incomes is again growing.

Differentiation of incomes is going on. At present, this is connected with wage differentiation, with the growth of private enterprise, and with the extra-court rehabilitations. One of the key questions is how the Czechoslovak society, with a long tradition of equalized incomes and property, will absorb the new situation. Though equalized incomes have often been criticized, and most people see the necessity of linking income closer to performance, sizable income differences provoke aversion. This is a similar phenomenon as when people accept the necessity of a radical economic reform, but, at the same time, insist on maximum social security. Such inconsistencies are typical for the present Czechoslovak society. Moreover, the present income and property differentiation is accompanied by a loss of social comfort, and growing social insecurity. Under such conditions, its impact on social climate will be significant; and its economic dimension will be very important for social feasibility of transformation.

The behaviour of households already in 1991 was characterized by renewed thriftiness, restraint in purchases and a positive savings rate; these trends seemed to be of longer-lasting character. Households were showing a clear tendency to learn from their past mistakes. The horizon of their decision-making was getting longer, and they were diversifying economic activities securing their financial funds.

Developments in the first half of 1992 show the same trends. Household expenditures tripled within this period, in comparison to the same period of last year; yet the growth of expenditures remained well below the growth of incomes.

The fact that incomes grow faster than expenditures shows a positive turn in household behaviour - a preference of savings, and a tendency to create reserves for entrepreneurial activities, as well as for increased regular financial payments. The population has begun to react to economic insecurity in ways characteristic for a market economy - by creating financial reserves, not reserves in goods (as was usual previously). A new pattern of household behaviour is crystallizing, with demand and consumption stabilizing in a new structure. On the other hand, the price shock was of such an extent that full adaptation of households probably could not be achieved yet, and one must still expect that there will be a mixture of adaptation and inertia in consumption. This can provoke tensions (documented by the negative evaluation of own living standards signalized by opinion polls), and lead to revival of old habits - e.g., return to traditional Christmas and New Year shopping and consumption upsurges, as it happened in December of last year.

On the whole, the present situation and trends in the Czechoslovak economy show a highly conflicting picture. That increases the need for economic analysis identifying the causes of different trends, and providing starting points for economic policy.

2. TRENDS IN THE LABOUR MARKET

Transformation of the economy was accompanied by falling employment, and rising unemployment till the end of 1991. Decisive for employment trends in that year was the state sector. The emerging private sector has growing influence on total employment since the start of 1992.

Unemployment has a very differentiated internal structure. It is differentiated as to republics and regions. With federal unemployment rate 6.6 % at the end of 1991, the unemployment rate in Czech republic was 4.1 %, while in Slovakia the respective figure was 11.8 %. The gap between unemployment rates in both republics was widening throughout the whole year 1991. In 1992, unemployment has decreased (at the end of September 1992, the unemployment rate for the Czech Republic was 2.6 % and for Slovakia 10.6 %).

Unemployment is varying strongly in different regions, depending on the structure of production. Regional differences which arose in the first half of 1991 are persisting also in 1992. The relation between the shares of both republics in unemployment (40 % for the Czech republic, 60 % for the Slovak republic) is inverse to the relation of their shares in total employment (which is 68 % in the CR and 32 % in the SR).

These trends resulted partly from a different accent laid in the two republics on active employment policy. In the Czech republic, some 157 000 new jobs were created by public policies in 1991 (of these, 50 000 assistant jobs, paid by the labour offices, for fresh school graduates). In Slovak republic, such activities began with a delay, and there were only 24 000 new jobs created by public policies.

Differences in unemployment in regions and districts are connected with gradual restraint of some types of production, and with starting structural change. For example, unemployment rate in Prague fell in September 1992 to 0.3 %, while in some districts in Northern and Eastern Slovakia, it approaches 20 %. No significant changes of these trends can be expected in the short time horizon. Growing regional differences prove also the absence of a regionally specified employment policy.

In Czechoslovakia as a whole, only about 2.5 % of registered unemployed were being retrained at the end of 1991. This figure has not significantly changed in 1992. Regions with the highest unemployment rate have the smallest share in retraining. One of the reasons for this situation is the endeavour of labour offices not to retrain without some reasonable hope that the retrained person can indeed find a new job. Solutions are to be sought in a broader concept of retraining, in its substantial decentralization, and in participation of more institutions in retraining programs. These are economic policies that are promoted now in the Czech republic.

As for the age structure, the most productive age groups (20 to 40 years of age) are most hit by unemployment. These groups represent almost 60 % of total unemployment. This is significantly different from, e.g., the West European economies (where, in addition to fresh school leavers, the oldest groups within the labour force have the highest unemployment rates). The situation in Czechoslovakia is probably influenced by the fact that there are - till the moment - no economic reasons to lay off the older workers (no substantial modernization was taking place). The existing social climate at most workplaces shifts the burden of unemployment rather on the younger workers who are not yet so firmly integrated in the collectives within the enterprises. One reason can lie also in a lower level of knowledge and experience of the young workers.

Unemployment of fresh graduates from universities and secondary schools is a very serious problem. Some estimates say that up to 60 % graduates have problems with finding their first job. On the other hand, establishment of the possibility to employ them as assistants (paid by the labour offices) has been one of the few really successful measures of active job-creation policy.

Women are more hit by unemployment than men. In September 1992, the share of women in total unemployment was about 55 % (women's share in total labour supply is 46.5 %). Also the unemployment of Gypsy population has been growing during 1991 and 1992. It is estimated that the unemployment rate is about 20 % within the Gypsy population. Almost 80 % of the Gypsy unemployed are in the Slovak republic (e.g., in the East-Slovakian region, Gypsies have a 40 % share in unemployment). In the Czech republic, the North-Bohemian region has the highest Gypsy unemployment (16.5 % share in the total figure for the region). Growing Gypsy unemployment brings big social risks, and it probably has partly a racial background.

Positive is the fact that only about 3 % unemployed are without job for more than one year. However, the possibility which existed in 1991, to get full unemployment allowance for as long as a year, destimulated some groups of unemployed from seeking a new job (unskilled workers, Gypsies, young people). According to an analysis completed by the labour offices in the Czech republic, about 35 % unemployed have no serious interest to find a new job. Owing to their requirements and possibilities, a number of these people are prone to enter the group of long-term unemployed.

Not only the above-mentioned possibility to get unemployment allowance for one year destimulated some groups of unemployed from re-entering the labour market; also the fact contributed that (in contrast to advanced countries) the amount of allowance was not limited by additional conditions. Situation was further complicated by a high level of minimum income and minimum wage.

For this reason, from January 1, 1992, Federal government severed the conditions. Unemployment allowance is limited to six month, and supplementary conditions were imposed to rise the individual effort to seek a new job. These measures have brought some positive results in cutting down unemployment.

According to opinion polls, the population regards the solution of the unemployment problem as one of the main tasks of government economic policy. With some simplification one may say that fears of unemployment are expressed mainly by those groups that are at present most vulnerable (the least skilled, the older, and women). The highest level of apprehension was felt by cooperative farmers and blue collar workers, the lowest by employees of the service and public sector.

63 % of the respondents were of the opinion that unemployment allowance should be of a minimum amount, to force the unemployed to accept a less qualified job, to undergo retraining, to move to another city or region, etc. A relatively high percentage (e.g., 30 % of all the women respondents) were ready to accept a worse-paid job in case of unemployment (14 % of women were ready to work for less than the minimum wage).

Readiness to accept a worse-paid job goes down with growing education and qualification, changes with age (being lowest for the middle-age group), is lower in agriculture and higher in the service sector. It is also generally lower in the Slovak republic. Around 25 % of the respondents feared that they themselves could become unemployed (this percentage exceeds all official and unofficial estimates of expected unemployment - see below).

On the whole, however, liberalization of the labour market is finding a positive support among the population, although the support differs in both parts of Czechoslovakia.

3. INCOME DIFFERENTIATION

Growing wage differentiation is a new phenomenon in the Czechoslovak economy. A key question is whether it goes in the direction of rectification of distorted wage relations, and of forming a wage structure characteristic for advanced economies.

The difference between average wages in production and services has diminished, thanks to a fast wage growth in some services (banking, insurance). But many other activities which in advanced economies stand at the top of the wage hierarchy (medical care, justice, scientific research) still are at or below the average. In the fuel industries, wages are 75 % higher than in culture, 55 % higher than in education, 42 % higher than in medical care. The wage of a physician is at the same level as that of a worker at a state-owned farm - and more of similar examples could be found. In some industries, wages have grown out of proportion thanks to their monopoly structure. In 1992, wage differentiation can be expected to grow further - both across and among industries.

Higher **differentiation of incomes** is caused not only by the proceeding wage differentiation; it also results from the growth of the private sector. Another contributing factor is restitution of property; this, however, causes mainly property differentiation, which is always higher than income differentiation. It is hard to predict the future income and property distribution which will emerge as a result of the transformation of the economy. But it is highly probable that both income and property distribution will be more skewed to the left than in the past.

The long tradition of equalized incomes and property constitutes a serious obstacle of the transformation process. Adaptation to a more differentiated income structure will be the more difficult, the less will the changes be felt as contribution to social justice. According to sociological polls, more than half of the population at present see the ongoing changes as just, i.e., as change from unjust equality to fair (or at least more legitimate) inequality. But at the same time, the citizens find it hard to accept the growing differentiation of property. The confrontation of income and property differentiation with the distorted visions of social justice as egalitarian equality can bring serious problems.

4. HOUSEHOLD BEHAVIOUR

According to analyses of consumer behaviour, most consumers recovered from the first shock caused by liberalized prices, adapted to the new situation and began to behave rationally, with increasing thriftiness. After April 1991, the propensity to save began to grow. By the end of 1991, it had reached 9.3 %, which was the highest level since 1954. In the first half of 1992, the propensity to save reached 10.6 %.

Thriftiness and self-restraint in demand and consumption are gradually becoming durable traits. Fewer households are eager to spend all their money immediately. The decreasing propensity to consume results, on the one hand, from this changed behaviour of households, whose preference of savings is growing and on the other hand, it reflects the decline in purchasing power. Purchases are also being delayed, as consumers expect prices of goods of Czechoslovak make to fall.

This is in sharp contrast to the behaviour of households under a command economy characterized by shortages in consumer markets. A common characteristic of Czechoslovak consumers under the shortage economy was an extremely high propensity to consume in times of recession and severe shortage of consumer goods. Such consumer behaviour reflected the fact that those periods were always characterized by increased inflation - open or hidden - which dampened the propensity to save. This reaction differs significantly from consumer behaviour in a market economy, where the propensity to save usually rises in times of recession, as households try to cope with the growing uncertainty of future incomes.

Under the command economy, the typical consumer reaction to economic recession aggravated inflationary pressures. Moreover, inflation was also fed by high inflationary expectations based on past experience: the government usually sought a solution for growing shortages in centrally-made price increases.

Despite the fact that consumer habits show a high degree of inertia, consumer and saving behaviour already began to change in 1991. Nevertheless, the unprecedented price rise of foodstuffs and industrial goods constituted a shock that, given the low growth of nominal incomes (mainly wages), exceeded the capacity of long-term adaptive mechanisms. And the conflict between adaptability and inertia in consumer behaviour may cause some tension in the future.

Opinion polls organized by the Research Institute of Social Development and Labour and the Statistical Office show that only 7 % of households in the Czech Republic, and 6 % in the Slovak Republic, saw their living standards in 1991 as higher than in 1990; 69 % in the CR, and 79 % in the SR, saw it as lower. As to present living standards, only 46 % of respondents in the CR and 25 % in the SR see them as good. Negative expectations prevail for future: only 22 % of Czech households, and 9 % of Slovak ones, expect an improvement within 5 years - 44 % and 57 %, respectively, expect a deterioration of their situation.

The test of the market situation also confirms that in spite of some improvement in the Spring of 1992, against Winter 1991, the living standards are still the critical point of public opinion. Neutral responses constituted 49.4 %, but negative responses were given in 27.8 % of cases. Only 22.8 % of households saw their economic situation and living standard as good.

But the evaluation of the living standards is no more deteriorating, which suggests that Czechoslovak citizens have already adapted to the new situation and became oriented in it. Scepticism, and fear of the future, are getting less frequent.
Also the fact that inflationary expectations are relatively low speaks for a renewed trust in a stabilized economy.

Households are diversifying their economic activities, as well as their financial and other assets (crown savings, hard currency savings, securities, real estate, and goods as a store of value). Such behaviour as a response to insecurity is showing many characteristics proving an (often unconscious and intuitive) application of the portfolio theory, diversification of economic activities which secure financial means for the household, and spreading of the risks posed by a deteriorated economic situation.

It can be expected that positive trends in household behaviour will continue throughout 1992 (higher savings rate, better coordination of expenditures with incomes). But old habits inherited from the past system are not forgotten; this heritage, together with increased necessity to adapt to higher income differentiation, can again bring some lability into the behaviour of households.

5. SHORT-TERM OUTLOOK

The year 1992 has been, and will continue to be, influenced by past and present trends, by the social and political climate, and by the political business cycle. This is a decisive period in which the Czechoslovak economy will go through the most critical phase of transition toward the market. In 1992 the economy will, with high probability, reach the bottom of the decline connected with transformation (with both its external and internal aspects). Much will depend on flexible reaction of economic policy, on its success in respecting the main building blocks of economic transformation and, at the same time, using all potential ways to stop economic decline and to revive the economy.

For the whole of 1992, it can be expected that Gross Domestic Product will fall by 3 to 6 %; but the analysis shows that trends will be highly differentiated in individual sectors of the economy. On the whole, the microsphere can be expected to react more rationally to government economic policy - thanks, mainly, to privatization and the positive change in enterprise behaviour it is to induce. Privatization should also help to stop the present myopic behaviour of managers, force the enterprises to form more long-run strategies of development, and to adapt production to the requirements of exacting world markets. But it has to be kept in mind that the effects of privatization will probably be uneven, and that the first positive results can only be expected by the end of 1992, or in 1993.

The fact that the fall of consumer demand has stopped will help to decelerate the decline of industrial production: its further decline by 10 - 12 % has nevertheless to be expected, owing to continuing fall of investment. Decline will be highly differentiated as to single industries. Sharpest decline is to be expected in electronics and heavy engineering, lowest in energy production, building materials, and in some consumer goods industries. Demand for investment will grow only gradually, starting from demand for reconstructions, repairs, and public investments. A sizable turn in enterprise investment activity can only be expected after privatization - i.e., not before the end of 1992.

Efforts will go on to replace stagnating domestic demand (and falling demand in former C.M.E.A. countries) with exports to advanced market economies. Further revival of external trade can be expected in 1992, increasing exports to this area by at least 10 % against 1991 (i.e. by roughly one billion dollars). Positive effects of the government export-supporting program can come in the second half of the year. The pro-export effects of currency devaluation will still be felt in this year, supposing that inflation can be kept under control. There will be a turn in import trends - demand for imports will grow with the expected restructuring of privatized firms.

Imports of machinery and equipment will increase against 1991, with stagnating level of imports of consumer goods.

Positive effect of foreign investment on the economy could increase in 1992, thanks to privatization. Direct foreign investment can help to revive the internal investment demand which is now very low. Total sum of foreign investment which is needed in the economy is several billion dollars. But developments in the first half of 1992, and the overall political situation, lead to the estimate that the inflow of foreign capital in 1992 will only be slightly higher than in last year, and will reach 0.8 - 1.0 billion dollars. At the same time, there will be an outflow of roughly 100 million dollars in repayments of joint ventures in hotels.

Trends in the labour market in Czechoslovakia often go in opposite directions, but till the end of 1992, there will be no critical fluctuations.

The fall of demand for labour will be only gradual. Here, the main impact of large privatization will come in the first half of 1993, rather than in the second half of 1992. On the other hand, information from a number of enterprises shows that in the second half of 1992, they will have to draw conclusions from the long-term fall of production and decrease employment (up to now, the fall of production has led to falling labour productivity more than to falling employment). Another factor limiting employment can be the relatively fast growth of average wages (not backed by a corresponding increase in labour productivity) which is reducing the comparative advantage of cheap labour.

On the other hand, there will be the positive impact of growing numbers of new small and medium-size private firms. At the end of 1991, this sector already was employing about one million workers; during 1992, it can create another 500 - 700 thousand new jobs.

These facts, as well as the actual development of unemployment in the first half of this year, lead to the estimate that at the end of 1992, there will be 500 - 540 thousand unemployed, which means that the unemployment rate will be below 6 %.

Inflation - provided we have neutral, or only slightly expansive, monetary policy and non-inflationary fiscal policy - will be between 12% and 15 % in 1992. Households will continue their prudent behaviour, preferring to build up savings. Revival of demand for food, non-durables and services will be moderate; demand for durables of domestic make will remain low (with the exception of cars).

Analysis of the trends of economic development leads to the conclusion that government economic policy should concentrate more on a selective support of those promising activities which speed up the transformation process. This includes a more decisive pro-export policy, as well as public investment and a complex support of new small and medium-size private businesses. The task is to find ways of demand support that are compatible with the market principles - and in harmony with the ongoing institutional change - and which do not imply a danger of a new inflation.

Since the start of 1991, trends in the economy have proved that keeping inflation under control is and must be one of the priorities of government economic policy. This increases the importance of monetary policy. The expansion of credit (money supply) must be consistent with short-term potential output: an over-restrictive approach would prolong and deepen the depression; an excessive expansion of credit would revive inflation, undermining price stability and jeopardizing the whole transformation process.

Similar constraints apply to fiscal policy. Attempts to revive the economy through budget deficits are sustainable only if they can stimulate enough growth to cover interest and debt repayments without tax increases. Otherwise, the economy would fall into a debt trap.

The room between an excessively restrictive policy ("restriction trap") and a policy trying to stimulate growth by an overexpansion of money supply ("inflation trap") is very narrow in all transforming economies. In such conditions, it is quite normal to adopt a trial-and-error approach, in which the effects of every single step of economic policy are soberly scrutinized.

At the same time this means that various measures of economic policy must be combined. One cannot lay a one-sided stress, for example, on the interest rate, or on monetary policy only. A decrease of the interest rate cannot in itself bring economic revival; the key problem at present is not the interest rate but the lack of money in a de-capitalized transforming economy. Hence the question how to increase the money supply in a way which is sound economically, is of first-rate importance.

One of the solutions could lie in another partial write-off of the so-called "bad debts" (a write-off which could amount to 50 - 60 billion crowns) - by means of issuing special bonds with low interest rate, guaranteed by the Funds of National Property. Such a measure could not only revive economic activity but also improve the financial position of commercial banks. In combination with a lowered interest rate, it would help to revive economic growth in Czechoslovakia - especially if supported by other measures, such as a more decisive pro-export policy, guarantees for loans to private investors, etc. Only the use of a certain "program mix" can bring a longer-lasting effect.

Such an approach would at the same time enable to keep a reasonable ratio between interest rates on credit, and on deposits - where a positive real interest rate in the longer run is necessary for the growth of credit resources of commercial banks. Also for the emerging private sector, a realistic, positive real interest rate is a necessary parameter for their decisions; otherwise they could get into serious trouble in future.

Keeping inflation under control, promoting active employment policy, and finishing the building of a social safety net are important preconditions of retaining the social consensus, and ensuring social feasibility of the next stage of transformation.

Social peace, however, must not be sought at the cost of permissive income and wage policy. Wages must be kept in line with the present (relatively low) productivity level in order to secure the competitiveness of Czechoslovak products. The example of the former GDR - where, for political reasons, wages were allowed to shoot up irrespective of the productivity gap - is a warning to all transforming economies.

The ongoing division of Czechoslovakia into two states would be economically painful for both sides, but experts from both nations agree that it would be worse for Slovakia. At present, there are already some signs of adverse economic influence of the negotiations about the division of Czechoslovakia:

- Czech and Slovak enterprises are trying to limit their mutual links, and search for suppliers and markets in third countries. This is especially typical of some Czech enterprises with relatively good export prospects toward the EC area. This threatens that economic division could in fact start before political one is agreed upon;

- the banks in the Czech Republic are limiting credits to their Slovak partners (i.e. Slovak banks). This leads to tensions, and relative lack of liquidity, in Slovak banking institutions. The situation in Slovakia is the more serious that the savings rate of the Slovak population is lower than of the Czechs;

- recently, Slovak households are starting to prefer savings in hard currencies, much more than Czech households. This can be seen as a hint that they expect a sizable devaluation of the Slovak currency after possible separation.

In general, the experience of transforming economies shows that the success of transformation depends on several fundamental conditions: low inflation, a stable exchange rate, privatization, price and trade liberalization, hard budget constraints for all economic agents, and the maintenance of social consensus. These conditions are necessary but there is no guarantee that they are sufficient. Much will depend on the ability of economic policy to react flexibly to economic development. In this context, continuous empirical analysis is of vital importance, along with deeper theoretical understanding.

REFERENCES

Aghlevi, B.B. - Borensztein, E. - van der Willigen, T.(1992): *Stabilization and Structural Reform in Czechoslovakia: An Assessment of the First Stage.* IMF Working Paper, Washington 1992

Drábek, Z. - Janáček, K. - Tůma, Z., *Inflation in Czechoslovakia,* 1985-1991, World Bank Research Paper, 1992 (forthcoming).

Hare, P. - Hughes, G.: *Competitiveness and Industrial Restructuring in Czechoslovakia, Hungary and Poland.* European Economy, Special Edition, No. 2, 1991

Janáček, K. et al.: *Transformation of the Czechoslovak Economy: Macroeconomic and Social Problems and Perspectives.* Prague Economic Papers, No.1, 1992.

Janáček, K., et al.: *Macroeconomic and Social Analysis*: Spring 1992, Prague Economic Papers, No. 4, 1992.

Janáčková, S.: *Microeconomic Aspects of Transformation.* Prague Economic Papers No. 3, 1992.

Klaus,V.: *Dismantling Socialism. A Preliminary Report.* Top Agency, Prague 1992.

Kornai, J.: *The Road to a Free Economy - Shifting from a Socialist System: The Example of Hungary.* W.W. Norton, New York, London, 1990.

Managing Inflation in Socialist Economies in Transition. The World Bank, Washington 1991.

OECD: Czechoslovakia. OECD Economic Surveys, OECD, Paris, 1991.

The Economist Intelligence Unit: Czechoslovakia. Country Report No. 1,1992. London, 1992.

2

BREAKING UP IS HARD TO DO: THE ECONOMICS OF CREATING INDEPENDENT CZECH AND SLOVAK REPUBLICS

Josef C. Brada
Department of Economics
Arizona State University
Tempe, AZ 85287-3806, USA

SUMMARY. This paper examines the economic aspects of the breakup of the Czechoslovak Republic. It argues that the economic and technological forces leading to the creation of multi-ethnic states in the 19th and 20th centuries have been considerably weakened, giving greater scope to nationalist movements. In the case of the Czech and Slovak Republics, there appears to be a logic for separation in that the two Republics may both benefit from separate currencies and monetary, fiscal and trade policies. Attempting to retain too much of past ties can only serve to dilute the potential benefits of separation.

1. INTRODUCTION

The separation of Czechoslovakia into two independent Republics represents a traumatic event in the history of the region. Nevertheless, from an economic standpoint, there are a number of advantages, some immediate, others potential, from the dissolution of the old Republic. In this paper the economic forces that led to the creation of multi-ethnic states are examined, and I argue that these forces have, over time, become less compelling. At the same time, in the case of the Czech and Slovak Republics there are important differences in policy objectives and attitudes toward appropriate economic policies that make it very difficult for the Republics to coordinate their policies, either in a unitary state or in some form of customs or monetary union. Thus, given the freedom to formulate policies independently both Republics may be able to follow policies better suited to their needs as the result of the dissolution of the Czechoslovak state.

2. ECONOMIC ORIGINS OF THE MULTI-ETHNIC STATE

The imminent separation of the CSFR into two independent republics is but the latest of such separatist episodes among the formerly-socialist countries. The collapse of the USSR and the de facto demise of its successor, the CIS, is as much evidence of the ability of ethnic-based nationalism to overcome the powerful centripetal forces of history and existing institutional arrangements as the Yugoslav experience is evidence of the destruction that such separatist episodes can bring about. Nor, should it be recalled, are wealthy and democratic market-based societies immune to such separatist tendencies. Belgium and Canada come readily to mind as examples of seemingly functional nation states whose existence is imperilled by ethnic-based separatist pressures.

A question that arises naturally for an economist is why such ethnically-driven separation should now be making itself felt in societies that were created in the nineteenth and early twentieth centuries, and that more or less successfully functioned for an appreciable period of time. While some of the answer may lie in the ability of dominant ethnic groups in these societies to impose unity through political and social pressure, such an explanation clearly lacks much of its applicability in the case of Canada and Belgium, for example, or in pre-World War II Czechoslovakia.

An alternative approach to the emergence of ethnic separatism is that the economic benefits of submerging ethnic identities and interests in a multi-ethnic nation-state have declined and that the economic costs of an independent ethnic identity have declined, thus altering the cost-benefit calculus in favor of independence for many ethnic groups.

The creation of multi-ethnic states has rarely proceeded along spontaneous lines. Rather, the multi-ethnic states created in the nineteenth and early twentieth centuries were forced together to meet economic imperatives of their day. Nations were perceived to need a certain economic size in order to be economically viable. This largely reflected the technology of the middle and late industrial revolution with its emphasis on large firms that were able to create and master new technologies; to capture economies of scale and serial production; and to compete on global markets. Given the competition for global markets, the potential for trade conflicts and the pressures of economic nationalism, it is not surprising that policymakers wanted to create nation-states whose domestic markets would be of sufficient size to permit at least some modern industries to exist on the basis of a sufficiently large domestic market and whose economic size would sustain the institutions of modern commerce and economic policy intervention, including a national banking system, stock exchange, etc. This imperative for sufficient size to ensure economic viability, or, put more positively, the belief that larger countries were economically more viable and, ultimately, wealthier was as much evident among the economic and political imperialists of the West as it was among Lenin and his successors.

The creation of a national culture in the nineteenth and early twentieth centuries was also subject to important scale economies that induced ethnic factions to submerge their animosities in an effort to protect their cultural heritages against foreign domination. In this, technology had a great role to play. The production of newspapers and books was a highly capital-intensive activity whose fixed costs could only be amortized over large press runs. Theater and musical performances and similar cultural activities also involved high fixed costs, and thus needed a relatively potential large audience to amortize these costs. Moreover, not merely the means for disseminating a national culture were subject to high fixed costs. The shortage of indigenous intellectuals in many of these societies made it imperative that authors, newspaper writers and artists be given the widest possible audience to economize on scarce cultural and intellectual inputs. Thus, only by submerging inter-ethnic differences within a multi-ethnic state could a national, though multi-ethnic, culture emerge and thrive.

By the late twentieth century both these factors had lost much of their strength. The opening up of trade through the reduction of tariffs as part of the GATT process as well as the effects of regional economic integration on the movement of goods, services and factors of production have made foreign markets and access to them much more important for economic success than the existence of a large, protected domestic market. The rapid expansion of the role of the multinational firm in global commerce has also strengthened the interactions and exchanges of goods among countries. Thanks to the ability of multinational firms to coordinate complex production among affiliates in various countries, even small countries now find themselves with production units that are specialized to an unprecedented degree and whose scale of production is geared to a global market. Thus a large domestic market is no longer seen as necessary for a viable industrial sector or for economic prosperity.

Indeed, the small country is viewed as having important advantages in that homogeneity of interests, culture and political beliefs make it possible to tailor foreign trade policies toward success in the international marketplace more easily than in a society with diverse interests. Moreover, in many sectors, economies of scale and scope are less important for success than are flexibility, the ability to innovate, etc., features that require less hierarchial, more informal, enterprise organization, which may be more easily achieved in an ethnically and culturally homogeneous society.

The technological changes that have altered the economic imperatives for large nation-states have also revolutionized the production and dissemination of national culture. Computers, desk-top publishing and printing technologies have sharply reduced the volume of newspaper and book production needed for economic viability. In the United States, for example, relatively small ethnic communities in major cities are able to economically sustain a local newspaper in their native tongue due to modern publishing and typesetting technologies. Similarly, the fixed costs of production of books has been sharply reduced through computerized typesetting. Television and radio enable artists to reach a much greater proportion of their co-ethnicists, thus making it possible for a numerically smaller potential audience to become a much larger actual audience than was the case when theatrical and musical performances were limited to the capital and a few large provincial cities.

With the economic and cultural costs of ethnic separatism so sharply reduced, it is no surprise that advocates of ethnic separatism have been able to find a sympathetic audience in many multi-ethnic states. That the greatest sympathy for separatism appears to be found in the countries of the former Soviet bloc is also not surprising. First of all, these totalitarian societies simply submerged ethnic conflicts without resolving them. As a consequence the populations of these countries have been unable to develop mechanisms and modes of discourse through which inter-ethnic conflicts could be articulated and resolved and long-standing ethnic grievances and misunderstandings could be ameliorated. Since the official view was that such conflicts had ceased to exist under Communism, there was no need to for such mechanisms.

At the same time, the economic system tended to exacerbate ethnic tensions. The poor performance of the economic system made ethnic groups less willing to coexist in a state that was clearly dysfunctional. Each ethnic group felt that it would be better off if it could jettison the economic policies and ideology of the central state. The redistributive apparatus of the socialist economy also tended to pit one ethnic group against the other. Since the bulk of economic outcomes was the result of state policies rather than of the relatively impartial workings of the market, each ethnic group tended to see its economic welfare as the direct consequence of state policies, thus inducing ethnic groups to compete against each other for government-directed investments, subsidies and benefits.

Even worse was the fact that the irrational pricing system and resource allocation mechanisms of the centrally planned economy led ethnic groups to suspect that they were being disadvantaged in the allocation of benefits. Since subsidization of enterprises was commonplace and since prices in which investment and other resource flows were denominated were arbitrary, the true economic benefits or costs of government policies toward regions were impossible to measure, thus creating distrust and confusion. Such disputes over who benefitted and how much from inter-ethnic government redistribution have characterized Czechoslovakia, the USSR and Yugoslavia, and in all three cases the available economic data are insufficient to provide convincing answers, even to outsiders.

3. THE COSTS OF SEPARATION

If the long-term costs of separation along ethnic lines appear to be in decline, one must nevertheless consider the short-term costs of separation as well. Of course, depending on the course that the separation process follows, such costs can be tragically high, as the Yugoslav case shows all too clearly. On the other hand, if the separation can proceed in a non-violent manner, then the short-term costs should be associated largely with the losses that accrue from the effects on foreign trade and on inter-regional trade, production and factor movements. In all these cases, however, there are both costs and benefits, and thus whether separation entails heavy costs or not requires further examination.

3.1 The Effects of Separation on Foreign Trade and Investment

The Czechoslovak economy underwent two foreign trade shocks since the collapse of the communist regime, and both of these have had rather different consequences for the Czech and the Slovak Republics. One of these was the collapse of the Council for Mutual Economic Assistance (CMEA) and the consequent sharp decline in trade within East Europe, particularly with the Soviet Union and its successor states. The impact of this trade collapse was a much greater impact on Slovak industries than on Czech industry. The second shock was the sharp devaluation of the koruna, which increased exports to the West, with more of a beneficial effect on Czech exports than on Slovak ones.

Along with the devaluation came a new foreign commercial policy, one that opened Czechoslovakia to foreign investment and to tourism. Both these policies also favored the Czech Republic, if not in their intent, then very clearly in their results. For example, Martin (1992) reports that at the end of 1991 there were 4,735 and 1,186 joint ventures in the Czech and Slovak Republics respectively and that of the approximately $1 billion in foreign investment that had flowed into the country, only 20 percent was directed toward Slovakia. Casual empiricism and the logic of geography suggest that the Czech Republic has enjoyed a tourist boom that has not been matched in the Slovak Republic.

The Czechoslovak government supported this turn toward the West with efforts to join international economic organizations such as the IMF and the World Bank; to, successfully, negotiate stand-by credits to support the convertibility of the koruna; and to gain Associate status with the European Community (EC). Within the East Europe, the Czechoslovak government has sought to promote a revival of intra-regional by participating in the Vysegrad cooperation with Hungary and Poland and by negotiating barter agreements with the successor republics of the USSR.

Whatever the consequences on the existing foreign trade and resource flows a separation of the two Republics might have, it is important to recognize that they might well be different for the two Republics, and, perhaps equally important, that interpretations of developments may differ between the two Republics as well.

Possibly the most serious short term effect on the external economic relations of the successor Republics of the CSFR would be a disruption of the agreements negotiated with the EC, the IMF and the World Bank.[1] One concern is that there would be an interruption of balance of payments support from the West, leading to the suspension of convertibility and a subsequent setback to the entire reform process. The other main concern is that the agreement over Associate status with the EC would have to be renegotiated, and this could somehow prove to be a difficult process.

These concerns seem to me to pose minor difficulties. In the case of the Czech Republic, it seems likely that, vis a vis the West, the Republic's balance of trade must be in surplus, more so than is the case for the entire cSFR. Thus, why currency convertibility would require foreign support or would have to be suspended is not at all clear. Indeed, a Czech koruna might prove so strong as to provoke pressures for revaluation. In the case of the Slovak Republic, it is asserted that its industry is less competitive in Western markets.[2] This suggests that the Slovak koruna, or whatever currency is adopted by that Republic, would come under pressure from balance of trade deficits. However, this last sentence must be qualified by the phrase: at existing exchange rates and under existing commercial policies. If the Slovak Republic finds itself in balance of trade deficit, it will have two options. One is to see whether western lenders and international agencies will extent it credits. My suspicion is that these creditors and donors will have powerful incentives to attempt to minimize economic destabilization in the region, and, thus, with some preliminary negotiations beforehand, the money put in place for the CSFR will be available to the two successor Republics, with perhaps a greater share available for Slovakia. The other option for Slovakia will be to undertake to manage its trade deficit. One way to do so would be to offset its competitive disadvantage by devaluing its currency. A more likely course, given the rather protectionist and etatist attitudes of Slovak politicians, is an increase in trade barriers to control import competition for Slovak industry. The latter is a less desirable way of managing the trade deficit and attempting to reflate the economy, but it is a feasible way none the less.

In terms of relations with the EC, there are clear benefits to the Czech Republic as well. Unemployment in the Czech Republic is quite low, there are growing exports to the West, inflation is under control, western firms are active and the Republic appears to be politically stable and democratic. All these factors should, indeed, make the Czech Republic an almost model East European candidate for EC membership. The case of the Slovak Republic will likely depend more on the direction and success of its economic policy.

---

[1]These, as well as the possible problems raised in this section, are evidently widely shared by politicians and economists in Czechoslovakia. They are gleaned from the comments of Zdenek Drábek in Slay (1992), from Martin (1992), from conversations with Czechoslovak economists and politicians and from an unsystematic reading of the Czechoslovak press.

[2]See remarks of both Zdenek Drábek and Kamil Janáček in Slay (1992) on this point.

Clearly an inward-oriented policy favoring protectionism, import substitution and state support for industry will make it more difficult to comply with EC requirements, but at the same time, relatively open policies supported by a devaluation of Slovakia's currency could lead to improved economic performance and a positive scenario for EC membership in due course.

Trade with the East would probably hold up reasonably well for both successor Republics, although different factors would be at work. In the case of the Czech Republic, good relations with Poland and Hungary would continue, so that market-mediated exchanges would take place under favorable conditions. Slovakia's relations with Hungary may prove problematic over minority issues and over the Danube dam, problems from which the Czech Republic has been eager to distance itself. On the other hand, to the extent that Slovakia adopts a more statist and less market-based economic system, the more appealing it will be, from an institutional point, as a trading partner for Ukraine and other countries to the East. Whether this market will prove to be a useful one remains an open question, but given Slovakia's size and trading capacities, a few successful trade agreements with Ukraine, Russia and other ex-Soviet republics could have a large positive impact on the domestic economy.

Finally, in terms of investment flows, both Republics may benefit from a peaceful separation, the prospects of which have caused a number of western investors to either defer or avoid investing in the country. Both Republics will be free to follow policies that are better suited to their own objectives and circumstances, and each has features that may prove attractive to foreign firms.

3.2 The Effects of Separation on Commerce Between the Success or Republics

In domestic prices of the time, in 1989 about one-third of Slovak industrial output was exported to the Czech Republic; the Czech Republic is less dependent with 10-15 of output directed toward Slovakia (Martin, 1992, p. 34). In some sectors, however, the dependence between the two Republics is greater. For example, 70-80 percent of Slovak electricity comes from the Czech Republic while the Czech Republic is heavily dependent on oil and refined products coming from, or through, Slovakia.

Some observers suggest that trade flows can be maintained by means of a monetary and customs union between the two successor Republics. The first, and more general observation that must be made with regard to such a policy is that attempting to maintain the volume and commodity-structure of trade flows that existed between the two Republics under the communist regime may be both impossible and counterproductive due to the fact that the trade flows decreed by central planners may not be sustainable in a market environment because they are simply not economically rational or profitable under the new circumstances. More important, the old trade flows may simply be irrational, and thus reduce rather than enhance the welfare of the trading partners. To judge the effects of separation negatively because they reduce trade flows between the two Republics that may be irrational and uneconomic would be a serious mistake.[3]

A second problem with the argument for a customs and monetary union between the two Republics is that while it appears to retain as much of the pre-separation trade as possible, a goal whose economic benefits are questionable, it makes it difficult to achieve many of the desirable economic objectives that the two Republics would be able to follow in isolation.

The situation may best be understood by contrasting the macroeconomic conditions of the two Republics. Unemployment stood at 2.85 percent in the Czech Republic and 11.31 percent in the Slovak Republic in May, 1992; at the same time Slovak performance in terms of inflation and output has been marginally worse than that of the Czech Republic. This divergence in economic performance suggests that there are significant differences between the two economies, and that different economic policies, and that different economic policies will be appropriate. In the case of the Czech Republic, there is less pressure to reflate due the lower levels of unemployment. Moreover, low levels of unemployment imply smaller government outlays for unemployment benefits. Thus, the Czech Republic, even without taking into account the ideological preference for conservative monetary and fiscal policy of its government, is in an excellent position to follow conservative macroeconomic policies.

The government of an independent Slovakia, on the other hand, will most likely inherit an economy that will, under current circumstances, face sizeable foreign trade and government-sector deficits, the latter due to both high levels of unemployment and the probable subsidization of state-owned firms. Because the Slovak government is unlikely to be able to put into place either higher taxes or the mechanism to collect them, a resort to monetary expansion to finance at least part of the government deficit seems inevitable. Thus, the likely feasible, and preferred, policy for the Slovak Republic will be one of a more rapid monetary expansion and a higher rate of inflation than are either warranted or desired in the Czech Republic. With higher rates of inflation and a likely trade deficit at the current exchange rate, the Slovak Republic will be forced to opt for some combination of growing import restrictions and devaluation of its currency.

The above macroeconomic and exchange rate scenarios clearly show that the Czech and the Slovak Republics are not good candidates for a partnership in a monetary and customs union. On the issue of customs, the Czech Republic has opted for, and probably will be able to sustain, relatively low trade barriers. The Slovak Republic, on the other hand, will find it increasingly difficult to maintain low tariff and non-tariff barriers in the face of growing balance of trade pressures. Consequently, a common external tariff policy for the customs union would be difficult to achieve. A further hindrance to an effective customs union would be the likely subsidization of large state-owned Slovak enterprises, as the export of their

---

[3]For Further discussion of this point, see Brada (1991).

products to Czech markets is likely to raise demands for countervailing measures on the part of Czech producers of competing goods.

A monetary union would be even more difficult to achieve given the divergent macroeconomic policy objectives of the two Republics. To let the Slovak Republic run a larger government deficit financed in part by money emission would not only represent a subsidy to that Republic paid for by the citizens of both Republics in the form of higher prices, but also yield a higher rate of inflation than desired by the Czech Republic. On the other hand, a more restrictive monetary and fiscal policy that reflected Czech policy objectives would consign the Slovak Republic to a long period of unemployment and economic stagnation.

3.3 The Effects of Separation on Production

A generally voiced fear is that separation will lead to a disruption of production as trade between the two Republics declines. To some extent fears regarding such a trade war are not without foundation, although the mutual reliance of firms in the two Republics on each other as principal suppliers or buyers of each other's goods is likely to install a degree of discipline on rash politicians. No doubt some trade will disappear, to be replaced by suppliers or buyers from third countries, but such changes in trade patterns, based on rational economic calculation, will, in the long run, improve the welfare of the two Republics and eliminate the excessive autarchy that characterized the domestic trade of the communist regime.

More important, separation and the ability to formulate an independent trade and macroeconomic policy, and to set its own exchange rate will be crucial for Slovakia. This is because Slovak firms in a number of sectors of industry are less efficient than their Czech counterparts. Consequently if they calculate costs and revenues in the same currency, then, for a given set of input and output prices, they must be less profitable than their Czech competitors. Therefore, Slovakia must always suffer greater unemployment and lower profits than the Czech Republic unless it can offset this efficiency differential by means of an exchange rate policy that would value its currency below the current value of the Czech koruna.

To demonstrate this point, I estimated a frontier production function for Czech and Slovak enterprises of the form:

Equation 1

$$\ln Y_i = C_i + D_{csi} + \ln W_i + \ln K_i + u_i - v_i$$

where

Y_i = value added by firm i

C_i = constant

D_{csi} = dummy variable equal to 1 for Czech firms, 0 for Slovak firms

W_i = labor time utilized in firm i

K_i = capital stock of firm i

u_i = error term, normally distributed

v_i = technical efficiency, half-normal distribution.

Equation 1 was estimated using data for 1990 for firms in the following sectors: ferrous metallurgy, non-ferrous metallurgy, chemicals and rubber, electrical engineering, building materials, woodworking, metalworking, pulp and paper, glass and ceramics, textiles, foodstuffs, and other industry. A frontier specification was utilized in order to capture the likelihood that firms may be holding excess workers or capital since they have not had an opportunity to respond fully to the general decline in production. Thus firms that are operating at best practice technology would lie on the production frontier but for the random error term ui, while firms that produce less than the best industry practice level of output with their given inputs are below the frontier level of production, reflecting technical inefficiency measured by the half-normal error term v_i.

The estimates of the parameters of Equation 1 are reported in Table 1. The estimates of the capital and labor coefficients are plausible, which is encouraging given the fact that industry was faced with a fall in production in 1990. More important, in five of the twelve sectors of industry the Czech-Slovak dummy in significant and positive. This indicates that, for given input levels, Czech firms in the sector produced more output than did Slovak firms. Note that the frontier specification ought to capture, in the technical efficiency term, the overmanning and excess capital that may have existed in all firms in a sector, and thus such technical efficiency effects are not responsible for the significant inter-Republic differences.

Of course, the lower levels of output per unit of inputs in Slovak enterprises might be offset by lower input costs and an adjustment of input use toward the cheaper input. However, the evidence suggests that there is little difference in the capital to labor ratio of Czech and Slovak firms and that the scope for capital-labor substitution is limited. These conclusions follow from Figure 1 which presents, for each sector, a unit isoquant for one unit of value added and the normalized capital and labor inputs utilized by the Czech and Slovak firms in our sample. If anything, Slovak firms appear to be more capital intensive than their Czech counterparts; see, for example, non-ferrous metallurgy, building materials, woodworking. Therefore it is unlikely that lower wages in Slovakia could serve as an important means of reducing costs in these firms. Note also that the scope for capital-labor substitution is limited in a number of the sectors, making it difficult for firms to respond to changes in input prices.

The systematic difference in factor productivity between the two Republics underscores the problem facing the Slovak Republic. In a single state, or in a monetary union with the Czech Republic, its firms will be less competitive than their Czech counterparts, and therefore some Slovak firms will experience chronic difficulties either in being able to price products competitively or to operate profitably. These chronic problems could be sufficient to have an effect on the economic health of the entire Republic unless remedied by some combination of import restrictions and devaluation of the Slovak currency.

4. CONCLUSIONS

While the separation of Czechoslovakia into two independent Republics is fraught with potential pitfalls, it is critical to understand what economic issues are central to the process. Focusing on maintaining as much of the former economic and trade ties as possible is likely to be shortsighted and to limit the benefits that independence can bring to the two Republics. To an outside observer, it seems clear that the benefits to the Czech Republic of a "velvet divorce" are unambiguous in that it will be able to follow the conservative monetary and fiscal policies and liberal trade policies that have been the hallmark of the Klaus government. Relations with the EC and with Hungary and Poland cannot but be improved by the split, and developments in trade and macroeconomic policy are self-reenforcing.

In the case of the Slovak Republic, there are benefits as well, although these are more in the form of "potential" benefits than those accruing to the Czech Republic. They are "potential" because they will depend on the policies that the Slovak Republic adopts. A statist policy of subsidization of industry supported by government deficits, money expansion and import-substituting trade policies carry with it the danger of inflation and economic stagnation. Thus, whether the freedom to shape macroeconomic and trade policies that independence brings to Slovakia can be used wisely is the key issue facing Slovak leaders.

Table 1. Parameter Estimates for Industry Frontier Production Functions

INDUSTRY AND IDENTIFICATION NUMBER	NUMBER OF FIRMS	PARAMETER ESTIMATES				$\bar{R}^2$
		Constant	Dummy	ln W	ln K	
23 Ferrous Metallurgy	20	-1.215*	0.021*	0.612*	0.297*	0.932
24 Non-ferrous Metallurgy	22	0.880	0.552	0.221	0.552*	0.581
25 Chemical, Rubber, etc.	68	0.611	0.018	0.659*	0.171	0.679
27 Electrical Engineering	90	-0.326	0.069	0.787*	0.073	0.708
28 Building Materials	120	2.320	0.340*	0.565*	0.056*	0.501
29 Woodworking	49	3.822	0.405	0.333	0.253	0.408
30 Metalworking	84	4.512	0.026	0.264*	0.293*	0.495
31 Paper and Pulp	20	7.888*	0.403	-0.130*	0.446*	0.250
32 Glass and Ceramics	38	0.891	0.064	0.777*	0.003	0.371
33 Textiles	80	0.953	1.131*	0.493*	0.232*	0.542
37 Foodstuffs	176	0.681	0.297*	0.782*	0.011	0.522
39 Other	34	3.212*	0.816*	0.153	0.466	0.591

Notes:

* - indicates | t-ratio | ≥2.0
W - hours worked
k - average stock of fixed capital
Dummy - equal 1 for firms in Czech Republic, 0 for firms in Slovak Republic.

Comparison of Individual Firms with Industry Frontier

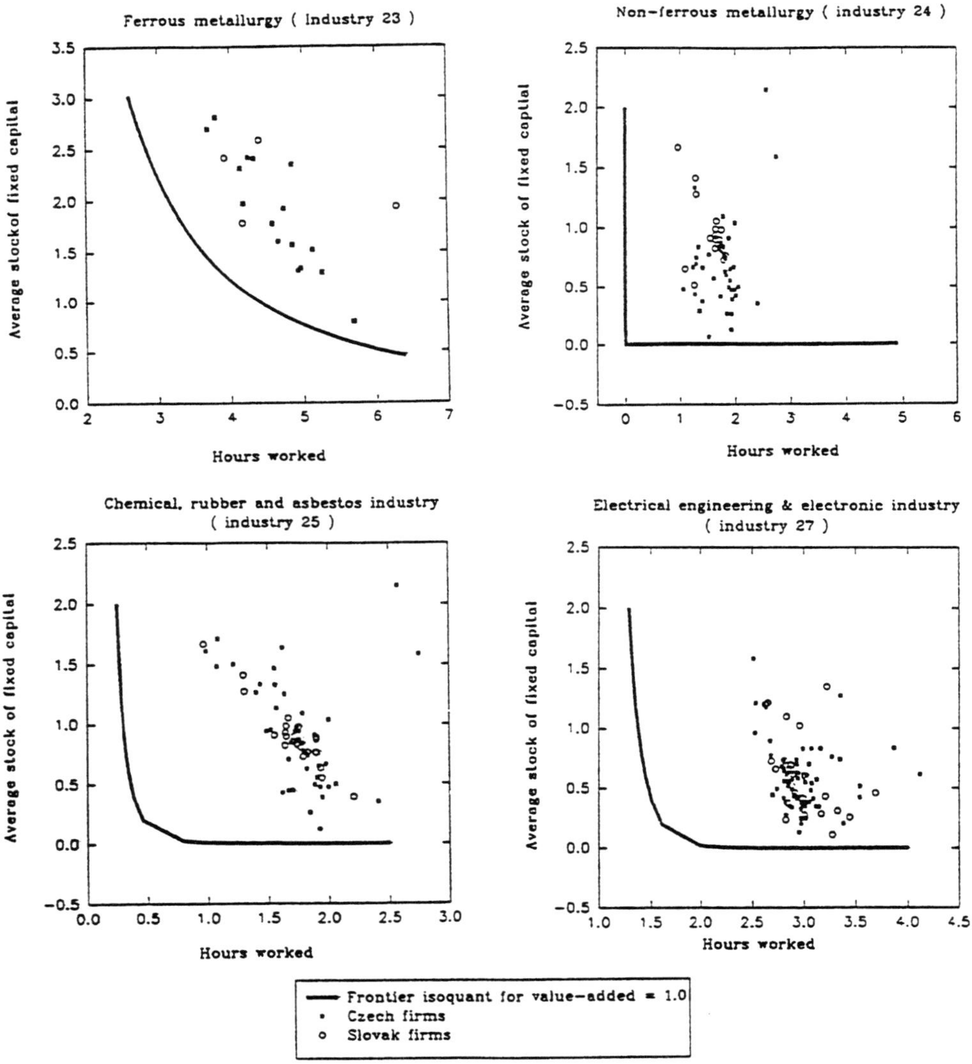

Comparison of Individual Firms with Industry Frontier

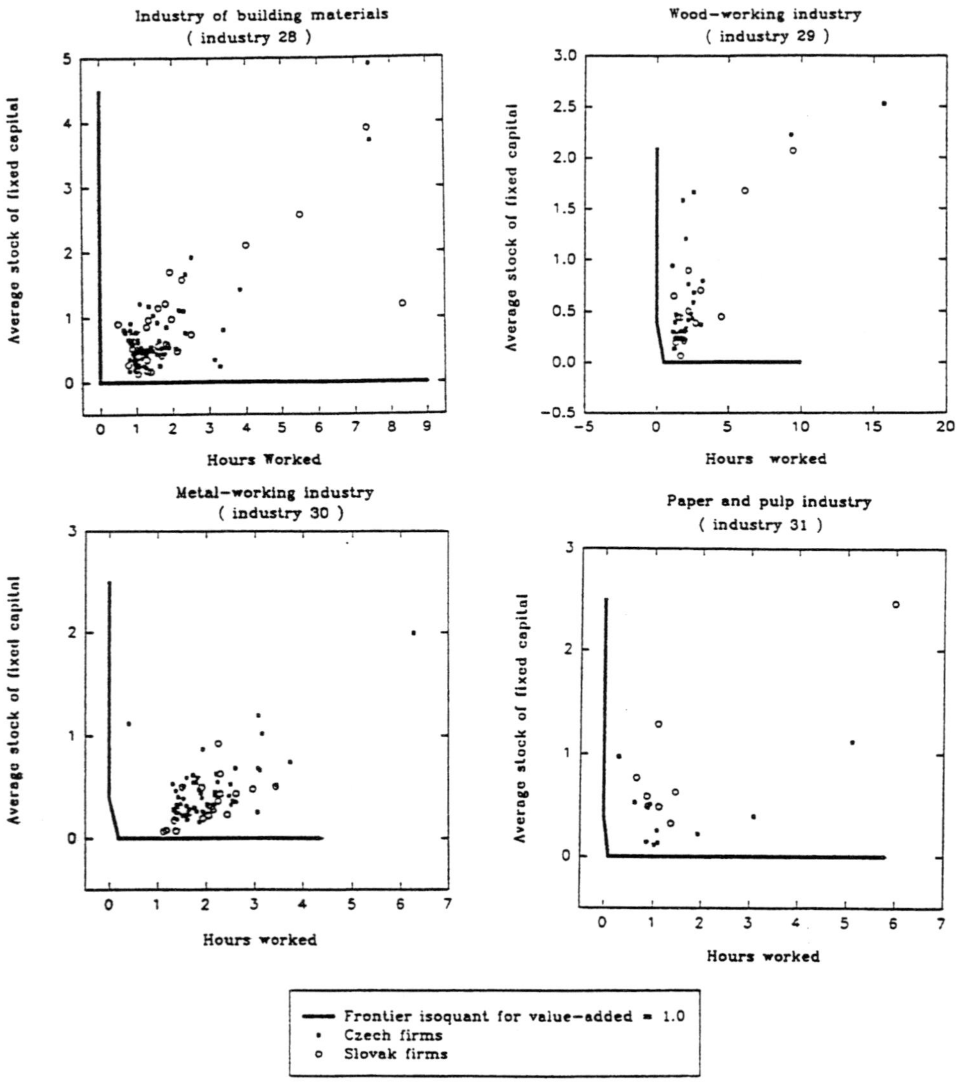

Comparison of Individual Firms with Industry Frontier

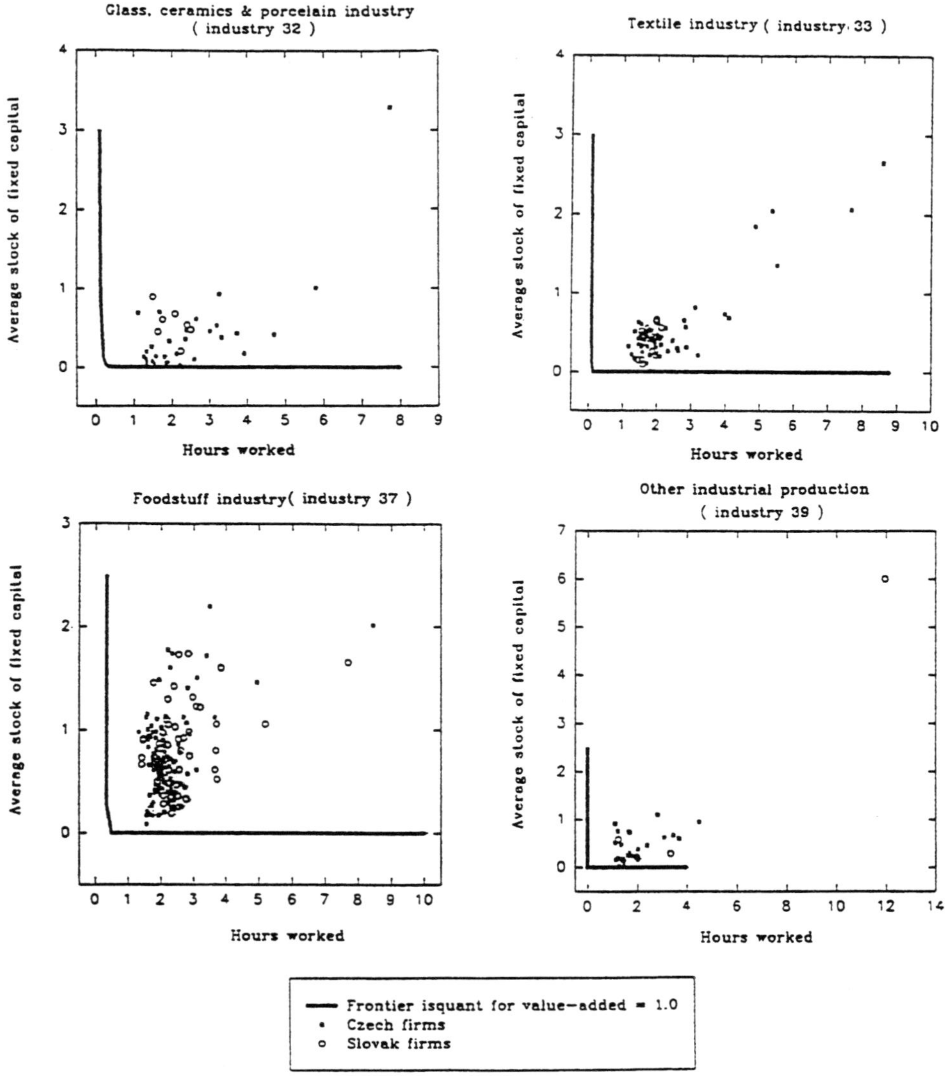

REFERENCES

J.C. Brada, "Okonomische Kosten und ökonomischer Nutzen der Zerfalls der UdSSR," Bundesinstitut für ostwissenschaftliche and internationale Studien. Köln, 1991.

P. Martin, "Slovakia: Calculating the Cost of Independence," RFE/RL Research Report, Vol. 1, No. 12, 1992, pp. 33-38.

B. Slay, "Roundtable: Prospects for Reform," RFE/RL Research Report, Vol. 1, No. 12, 1992, pp. 23-29.

3

THE CZECH AND SLOVAK REPUBLICS: A STARTING POINT

Ivan Šujan
President, Federal Statistical Office,
Sokolovská 142, 186 13 Prague 8, CzechRepublic

SUMMARY—After the disintegration of Czecho-Slovakia on January 1, 1993, an interesting question arises: what is the starting point of two independent economies?

The Czech economy is currently far behind the developed market economies, however, it is undoubtedly the best among the post-communist countries, (except East Germany, which is a special case). Clearly it has the highest per capita GDP, highly positive trade balance, lowest inflation and unemployment rate. The division of the federation will have some negative impacts on the Czech economy causing a one-year delay in economic recovery, but by then the Czech Republic will have even better prospects for macroeconomic stabilization and growth.

The Slovak economy is second best among post-communist countries. However, its separation from the Czech economy will have serious negative impacts, delaying its recovery by at least two years and bringing about the question as to whether its transformation to a market economy might be successful. The starting point of the Slovak economy is much worse, e.g. devaluation of its currency is inevitable. While the Slovak economy is better than that of Hungarian right now, it might become worse.

1. INTRODUCTION

Presently the Czech and Slovak Federal Republic (ČSFR) is divided into two independent states, (as of January 1, 1993). Evaluating the prospects of their further development, contemporary position of both economies, the range of their mutual connection and costs following the division of the joint state must be taken into account.

Some differences and links between Czech and Slovak economies were identified in [1,2]. However, published descriptions of the starting position of both republics and estimations of the inevitable costs of their separation have been rather incomplete so far. The authors' papers [3,4] attempted to contribute to these questions mainly by a more detailed estimation of the impacts of separation.

The major contribution of this paper may be seen in a comprehensive description of the starting point of the Czech and Slovak economies, mainly in terms of macroeconomic performance and stability, extending this description by a comparison with some neighboring countries, (mainly Hungary and Poland), a more complete evaluation of mutual links between Czech and Slovak economies, and an updated estimation of the costs of separation and their reflection in short-term prospects of both economies.

2. THE PRESENT POSITION OF THE CZECH AND SLOVAK ECONOMIES

The pre-war economic level of Czechoslovakia was quite comparable with such countries as Germany, France, Belgium and Austria. According to statistical data on industrial production before World War II Czechoslovakia was one of the 10 most industrialized countries in the world.

However, over the past 40 years, the allocation of resources through central planning rather than market mechanism has resulted in a long-term slowdown in productivity and standard of living, as well as the loss of international competitiveness of Czechoslovak industry. Over the past 20 years, Czechoslovakia's economic performance has been particularly disappointing.

The real power of the Czechoslovak economy can be compared with the underdeveloped economies of West European countries, (e.g. Ireland, Spain, Portugal), and, at the same time, it stands at the head of the group of post-communistic countries in Central and Eastern Europe.

There are some differences between Czech and Slovak economies, (Table 1 and 2). The gross domestic product (GDP) per capita in the Czech

Table 1. Comparison of the economics of the Czech and the Slovak Republics in macroeconomic indicators (data for 1991).

Indicator	Value per capita		Percentages in the ČSFR values		Ratio
	ČR	SR	ČR	SR	ČR : SR
Number of inhabitants	1.0	1.0	66.1	33.9	1.95
Gross domestic product, constant prices, thousands of KCs	41.8	34.2	70.4	29.6	2.38
Industrial production, constant prices, thousands of KCs	49.1	37.8	71.7	28.3	2.54
Private consumption, constant prices, thousands of KCs	18.5	16.3	68.9	31.1	2.22
Investment, constant prices, thousands of KCs	9.1	9.6	64.8	35.2	1.84
Employees (in 1000 inhabitants)	491.9	415.0	69.8	30.2	2.32
Unemployees (in 1000 inhabitants)	21.5	57.2	42.3	57.7	0.73
Exports (incl. services), current prices, thousands of KCs	28.5	20.2	73.4	26.6	2.76
Imports (incl. services), current prices, thousands of KCs	25.8	20.6	71.0	29.0	2.45
Gross profit, current prices, thousands of KCs	13.6	8.1	76.7	23.3	3.30
Expenses of budget of republics, thousands of KCs	23.3	24.1	65.4	34.6	1.89

Table 2. Comparison of the economies of the Czech and the Slovak Republics in natural indicators of production (data for 1990).

Indicator	Value per capita		Perçentages in the ČSFR values		Ratio
	ČR	SR	ČR	SR	ČR : SR
Electric energy, thousands of kWh	6.04	4.54	72.2	27.8	2.60
Coal mining, t	9.80	0.65	96.7	3.3	29.22
Processing of crude oil, t	0.71	1.23	52.9	47.1	1.12
Steel production, t	1.03	0.91	69.1	30.9	2.23
Cotton textile, m	47.00	17.62	83.9	16.1	5.22
Wearing apparel, pieces	2.33	3.98	53.4	46.6	1.15
Car production pieces for 1000 inhabitants	18.12	0.65	98.2	1.8	54.38
Color TV, pieces for 1000 inhabitants	0.58	71.70	1.6	98.4	0.01
Refrigerators, pieces for 1000 inhabitants	0.00	84.76	0.0	100.0	0.00
Grain, t	0.86	0.68	71.2	28.8	2.47
Meat, kg	65.23	54.37	70.1	29.9	2.35

Republic is 21 percent higher than the 1991 GDP in the Slovak Republic. According to Table 1, we see a Slovak economy tends to use higher sources than create them, (relatively higher investment, consumption, imports and Government expenditures against production, exports, profit, incomes, etc). The great disadvantage of the Slovak economy is high unemployment. But it cannot be explained with only the harder impact of economic reform on Slovakia, because the differences in the decrease of production are not that much higher between both republics. In the Slovak Republic, previously higher social unemployment, the less suitable demographic and qualification structure of inhabitants and slower development of private enterprise are in action.

The economy of the Czech Republic keeps its top start position in the first half year of 1992, as well, mainly in lowering unemployment, in a positive balance of trade and in a growing physical volume of retail sales. However, other differences between the Czech and Slovak Republics are insignificant.

The present dissimilar economic conditions in the Czech and the Slovak Republic are closely connected with historical developments. Bohemia and Moravia, before the Second World War, were among the industrialized countries of Europe. They inherited a large portion of industry from the Austrian part of the Austro-Hungarian Monarchy, while Slovakia, which had belonged to the Hungarian part of the Monarchy, was an underdeveloped agrarian country. After the Second World War when the communists had come to political power, Slovakia was given the "benefit" of preferential industrialization in line with the traditional Stalinist pattern. The enormous financial means for this transformation were made available within the framework of budgetary redistribution, at the cost of the Czech Republic. In this process, an over-proportional share of new industries, partly in basic and arms production, has been established in Slovakia.

Whereas the Czech Republic produces and exports mostly finished products, a much more important role is played by the production and export of semi-finished products and weapons in Slovakia. This puts Slovakia in a less favorable position in its product and export structure, although in a short-term perspective some semi-finished products could be more competitive in Western markets than lower-quality goods. Besides, Slovakia's economic development and productivity level is lower than that in the Czech part of the country.

As recently as 1987, Czechoslovakia produced 29 billion Kčs worth of armaments representing a 3% share in total industrial output. Two thirds of the country's armaments production, worth 19 billion Kčs, were produced in Slovakia. The share of armaments in Slovak industrial production has been four times higher than in the Czech Republic.

With the easing of political tensions, weapons production and exports have decreased since 1988; this process has been accelerating, especially since the revolution of November 1989.

This curb on weapons production and exports, concentrating on heavy armaments, (such as artillery, tanks and armored vehicles), has mainly hit

Slovak state enterprises, where it has cost more than 35,000 people their jobs. A number ofconversion projects exists for the desired conversion from weapons production to civilian goods production, but there is hardly enough money for these projects.

3. A COMPARISON WITH OTHER CENTRAL EUROPEAN ECONOMIES

As a major indicator of economic development, real GDP per capita in US currency is commonly used. In Central European economies, the purchasing power parities (PPP's) may be more appropriate convertors than official exchange rates (Table 3 and 4). According to such indicators, the economic level in the Czech Republic in 1991 was 21% higher than the Slovak Republic, 36% higher than Hungary and almost twice higher than Poland's. On the other hand, the economic level of the Czech Republic was just 45% of the level of Austria and 38% of West Germany, (i.e. without the former GDR). For the Czech Republic, a comparison with East Germany, (the former GDR), is most relevant. While both economies were almost equal in per capita GDP in 1991, 1992 and 1993 the East Germany economy will be better than that of Czechoslovakia by 9% and 14%, respectively, mainly due to enormous subsidies from West Germany.

The economic level of the Slovak economy in 1991 measured by per capita GDP, while substantially lower than in the Czech Republic, was 13% higher than in Hungary and 64% higher than Poland. On the other hand, it was just 38% of Austrian and 32% of West German levels. For the Slovak economy, a comparison with Hungary is most important. According to recent forecasts, the priority of the Slovak economy against Hungary will decrease from 13% in 1991, to 8% in 1992 and just 1% in 1993, while in 1994 the Slovak economy will be even 2-3% below the Hungarian economy, mainly as a result of the division of the ČSFR.

As seen in Table 3, private consumption per capita in both Czech and Slovak Republics is even lower than Hungary, it decreased much more during the past two years and comprises much lower proportion of GDP. This share is also lower than in Poland. On the other hand, gross fixed investment per capita in both Czech and Slovak Republics is much higher than in Hungary or Poland and despite the much sharper decrease over past two years, (especially in the Czech Republic), its share in total GDP is still larger. In addition to this, per capita savings in both Czech and Slovak Republics are greater than in Hungary or Poland and are greater than per capita foreign debt.

Table 3. Comparison of the Central European Economies: Selected National Accounts Indicators.

Indicator	Czech Republic	Slovak Republic	Hungary	Poland
Values for 1991 per capita in US currency1				
Gross domestic product[2]	7 197	5 958	5 291	3 624
Private consumption [2]	3 278	2 785	3 727	1 974
Gross fixed investment[2]	1 514	1 519	970	701
Exports [3]	809	564	1 002	390
Imports [3]	755	603	1 149	412
Trade Balance[3]	+54	-39	-147	-22
Gross foreign debt[4]	601	601	2 190	1 265
Savings of households[4]	2 273	1 933	1 065	612
Percentage change between 1989 and 1991				
Gross domestic product[2]	-15.7	-17.5	-13.3	-18.4
Private consumption[2]	-20.2	-24.3	-2.6	-20.0
Gross fixed investment[2]	-32.7	-23.2	-15.6	-17.4
Shares in real GDP in percent, 1991				
Private consumption	45.5	46.8	68.3	54.5
Gross fixed investment	21.0	25.6	17.8	19.3
Shares in exports in percent, 1991				
Trade balance	+6.7	-6.9	-14.7	-5.6
Gross foreign debt	74.3	106.6	218.6	324.4

[1] GDP, consumption, investment and savings converted to US currency according to purchasing power parities (PPP), other indicators according to official exchange rates.

[2] In 1990 constant prices.

[3] Without services

[4] End-of-period values.

Table 4. Comparison of the Central European Economies: Other Selected Macroeconomic Indicators.

Indicator	Czech Republic	Slovak Republic	Hungary	Poland
Absolute values, 1st half of 1992				
Population, 1000 persons, middle-period	10 316	5 295	10 328	38 336
– change between January 1 and June 30	+6	+10	-14	+54
Unemployment rate, percent, end-of-period	2.7	11.3	10.1	12.6
– change between January 1 and June 30	-1.4	-0.5	+1.6	+0.8
Monthly average wage in US currency[1]	412	398	382	324
Monthly retail turnover per capita, US currency[1]	245	187	173	80
Average official exchange rate of US currency[2]	28..76	28.76	78.68	13 050
Average purchasing power parity of US currency[2]	10.43	10.43	50.80	8 163
Ratio of official exchange rate to PPP	2.76	2.76	1.55	1.60
Annual percentage changes between 1st halfs of 1991 and 1992				
Consumer price index	+11.5	+12/5	+24.2	+40.9
Nominal wage rate	+23.2	+19.7	+33.4	+59.1
Real wage rate	+10.5	+6.4	+7.4	+12.9
Official exchange rate of US currency	-1.8	-1.8	+7.7	+31.4
Purchasing power parity of US currency	+8.8	+8.8	+20.8	+37.1

[1] Converted to US currency according to PPP's.
[2] Expressed in local currency units (Kčs Ft, Pzl).

Foreign trade and debt values in Table 3 are expressed in US currency according to official exchange rates. The highest per capita exports in 1991 was reached in hungary, followed by the czech republic, while per capita exports of slovakia and poland were significantly lower. On the other hand, Hungary also reached the highest per capita negative trade balance and foreign debt. A positive trade balance, (6.7% of exports), was only produced in the Czech Republic. The current foreign debt of Czechoslovakia is supposed to be proportionally shared by the Czech and Slovak Republics among their population, i.e. Their starting per capita foreign debt is equal, (601 US dollars at the end of 1991), and much lower than Hungary or Poland. However, in terms of its ratio to annual exports, it is lower for the Czech Republic, (about 74%), than the Slovak Republic, (almost 107%). In poland the foreign debt per capita is lower than Hungary, ($1265 against $2190 US dollars), but its ratio to annual exports is higher (324% against 219%)

As seen in Table 4, the population of the Czech Republic is almost equal to that of Hungary (10.3 million), however, there is some growth in the Czech Republic and a decline in Hungary. The population of Slovakia, (5.3 million), is about half that of the former countries, but its growth rate is even higher than Poland, which seems to be overpopulated.

The unemployment rate in the Czech Republic is in a surprising decline and very low, even lower than all the EC countries, (except Luxembourg). The updated value at October 31, 1992, is just 2.5% and is 1.6 points lower as of January 1. The unemployment rate in 1992 is also declining in Slovakia, from 11.8% on January 1 to 10.4% on October 31, however, it is still similarly quite high in Hungary or Poland, where unemployment is raising.

The differences in average wages between 4 countries in Table 4 are not significant, except the lower wages in Poland. The differences in per capita retail trade turnover are much greater, the level in the Czech Republic being even three times higher than in Poland, but this may also reflect some statistical discrepancies. It should be noted that the level of average wages in US currency, (converted using the PPP's), in all four Central European countries is about 10 times lower than advanced market economies. The growth of real wages in the first half of 1992 was clearly slower in Slovakia than the Czech Republic. In Hungary and Poland the growth of wages is somehow inflationary.

While the annual rate of inflation in the Czech and Slovak Republics in the first half of 1992 was still within acceptable limits, (about 12%), it was much higher in Hungary and Poland (24% and 41%, respectively). The growth rates of the PPP's of the US dollar were similar. However, changes in the official exchange rates were smaller by about 10 points, i.e. all the Central European currencies were in fact revaluated. The change in the Czechoslovak exchange rate reflected only the fluctuations of the dollar value against other convertible currencies, while Hungary and, in particular, Poland made some official devalutations of their currencies, well below the rate of inflation expressed with consumer price index. The ratio of the official exchange rate to the PPP remained almost twice as high in

Czechoslovakia as in Hungary and Poland, indicating that the Czechoslovak crown (KCs) is undervaluated.

Summarizing a comparison of the four Central European economies, it is obvious that the Czech Republic has the best starting position at the beginning of the second stage of transition to a market economy; it has the highest level of per capita GDP and savings, positive trade balance, relatively low foreign debt, very low unemployment, lowest inflation and still very low wages contributing to the competitiveness of Czech products. The position of the Slovak Republic is significantly worse, but still somehow better than that of Hungary. Clearly Poland has the weakest economy in this region.

4. THE MUTUAL LINKS BETWEEN CZECH AND SLOVAK ECONOMIES

The substantial mutual connection of both economies has been documented in Table 2. The production of some important products in the one of both the republics is almost completely absent and is substituted with a delivery from the second one. The delivery from the Czech Republic to the Slovak Republic, (also after corrections based on a real evaluation of production and territorial displacement of productive units), are higher than the delivery in opposite direction.

According to the business surveys of the Federal Statistical Office, the Slovak Republic is more dependent on mutual trade with the Czech Republic than vice versa. From the industrial production of the Slovak Republic more than 32% is exported to the Czech Republic, while from the industrial product of the Czech Republic only 15% is exported to Slovakia. However, due to 2.5 times greater volume of the Czech industrial production, even this small share is greater in its absolute value than the opposite flow, creating a surplus of the Czech Republic estimated to more than 13 billion KCs in 1992 (about 0.5 billion US currency).

Whereas finished products constitute the main share of Czech Republic deliveries to the Slovak Republic, the latter exports primarily raw materials and semi-finished products to Bohemia and Moravia. Since the Czech Republic exports a higher share of its own production to the West in particular, Slovakia is more dependent on the Czech market than vice versa. But Slovakia could more easily redirect part of its exports to the West instead of supplying it to the Czech Republic than vice versa. Needless to say, there are common transport and communication networks, (especially oil and gas pipelines), as well as an integrated electricity grid.

In machine building, cooperation between the two republics is concentrated in various semi-products, automotive industry and agro-technique. Among finished products, primary motorcars, lorries and trucks, tractors and locomotives are supplied to the Slovak Republic by the Czech Republic. Slovak deliveries to the Czech Republic are insignificant in that sector.

In the energy sector, the mutual dependence of both republics is extremely high. Czechoslovakia's total crude oil imports in 1991 amounted to 11.2 million tons; 9.4 million tons of which were imported to the Slovak Republic via the "Druzhba" pipeline from the CIS countries and 1.8 million tons by the Adria pipeline. More than half of these inflows, (6.3 million tons), were "re-exported" from there to the Czech Republic. Speculations have been voiced on whether the Slovak Republic might perhaps use the Czechs dependence as an economic weapon. It is an unlikely proposition from an economic point of view, since the Slovak Republic is itself interested in making full use of the pipelines capacities because of its earning from transit fees. And besides, full Czech dependence would only last till 1994, when a pipeline from Ingolstadt, (Germany), to Litvinov and Kralupy, with an annual capacity of 10 million tons, is scheduled to come into operation.

Because of high processing capacities in the Slovak Republic, the Czech Republic is also receiving some of their crude oil products. If the Slovak Republic were to suspend deliveries, this would mean an unwelcome low capacity utilization of the expensive processing capacities for the Slovak Republic. Besides, the Czech Republic would be able to compensate these losses by imports from the West.

As far as the natural gas is concerned, the situation is even simpler. Czechoslovakia is seen to be one of the most important transit routes for natural gas deliveries from the CIS countries to Western Europe. A total of almost 70,000 million cubic meters are transported through Czechoslovakia, and about 80% of these are routed on to the West, constituting an important source of income. It is completely unthinkable, for political and economic reasons, that these deliveries would be suspended. However, the issue of transit fees will certainly be one of the key points of discussion in the current negotiations.

The Slovak Republic, in turn, imported 2.8 million tons of hard coal, 4.3 million tons of soft coal and 0.4 million tons of coke, as well as 3,173 kWh in 1991 from the Czech Republic. For this dependence, the Slovak Republic could only compensate by other imports from other countries.

On this basis, it can be stated that any suspension of mutual energy deliveries in consequence of an impending separation of the two republics is improbable. On the other hand, price increases for energy supplies and transport may well be in the offing.

In mutual agriculture dependence only exists in the field of plant production. The Czech Republic imports mainly grain and fruit and vegetables from the Slovak Republic while delivering potatoes and barley.

5. THE IMPACTS OF THE CZECH AND SLOVAK REPUBLICS SEPARATION

Using various partial estimations, direct calculations and model simulations, we tried to estimate the possible impacts of the division of ČSFR on the GDP of both republics and on the components of its use (consumption, investment), on exports, imports and balance of payments, on unemployment, inflation and state budget. The mutual dependence of these macroeconomic indicators has been considered and secondary (indirect) impacts have also been taken into account. The mutual partial exchange of the impacts on the both republics has also been considered, because of their high initial economic mutual connection.

In Table 5, the estimations of the main impacts on GDP, balance of payments and the state budget of both republics are presented. These and other influences have been later projected into model prognoses for 1993 and 1994 in Table 6.

The first group of influences in Table 5 comprises costs for new banknotes, state documents and valuables, etc. In this group we have also calculated all costs connected with the division of state administration, army, common properties, representative offices abroad, with the renovation of international agreements, with the probable decreased number of tourist visitors from abroad and with other impacts following the loss of the international position of the ČSFR, and last but not least with the slowdown in international capital flow and, coherently, the reduction of increase of export ability. The last mentioned influences would be worse for Slovakia, which is considered to be politically and economically less stable.

The further group of influences is connected with mutual trade between the Czech and the Slovak Republics. After a supposedly different economic policy, (mainly finance and monetary), it would be impossible to keep the joint currency longer than half a year. This would mean a transition to an international standard of payments and probably to world prices. In many cases the prices would become higher, (prices which are presently valid and partially regulated are mainly disadvantageous to the Slovak Republic), which, with the harder payment conditions, would mean the decrease of demand for mutual deliveries. This fact would not result in a trade war but instead only a natural reaction of economic subjects to the changed conditions. The negative impacts of these influences would be higher in the Czech Republic, (except in the balance of payments, considering the supposed better possibility to shift its deliveries to other markets).

Table 5. Estimation of the impact of division of the state on economies of the Czech and Slovak Republics macroeconomic indicators (data for 1991)

Indicator	Impact in Czech Republic			Impact in Slovak Republic		
	GDP	BP	SB	GDP	BP	SB
New banknotes, passports, identity cards, stamps, costs for property division, completing of state representation abroad, renovation of international agreements, decrease of traveling, decrease of foreign capital flow, etc.	-6.0	-3.2	-4.8	-7.8	-3.1	-5.3
Impact of reduction of mutual deliveries after transition to the world prices and international payment standard	-10.7	+2.8	-6.9	-7.7	-1.9	-2.8
Impact of deficit financing of programs for development, slowing down of armament production conversion in the Slovak Republic	+3.0	+2.3	+1.7	+6.0	+2.1	-3.1
Transition of account of payment balance in mutual deliveries to that of payment balance, separation of state budgets and profits of joint enterprises	–	+16.7	+13.4	–	-16.7	-13.4
Impact of arrangements to moderation of passive payment balance and of deficit in state budget in the Slovak Republic	-3.7	-2.9	-2.0	-11.2	+12.5	+14.1
Total impacts in bil. KCs	-17.4	+15.7	+1.4	-20.7	-7.1	-10.5
Contribution of total impact to the GDP, exports or budget revenues of the Czech or Slovak Republic, in percent	-2.1%	+5.3%	+.04%	-5.7%	-6.7%	-5.7%

Explanations: GDP-gross domestic product, BP-balance of payments, SB-state budget

Table 6. Short-term prognosis of macroeconomic indicators of the Czech and the Slovak Republics – with projection of the impacts of division of the state

Indicator annual growth rates in per cent		Actual			Prognosis			
					joint state		divided states	
		1990	1991	1992	1993	1994	1993	1994
Gross domestic product (GDP) in constant prices	ČR	-1.9	-14.5	-5.6	2.9	4.4	0.7	3.3
	SR	-1.3	-16.4	-6.3	2.4	4.1	-3.4	1.2
Private consumption in constant prices	ČR	2.9	-22.8	9.3	2.4	2.9	-0.3	1.6
	SR	3.0	-26.4	2.8	1.9	2.6	-7.7	-2.2
Investment in constant prices	ČR	-1.6	-32.2	-2.5	7.9	11.0	2.0	8.1
	SR	11.8	-31.0	-2.0	6.5	9.6	-5.2	3.7
Rate of unemployment (in percent of disposable labor force) 1) 2)	ČR	0.8	4.1	2.6	5.0	5.1	6.8	6.0
	SR	1.5	11.8	10.7	12.2	11.0	17.3	13.6
Consumer prices	ČR	9.9	55.7	10.9	11.9	7.7	13.9	8.2
	SR	10.3	60.8	10.3	12.0	7.2	19.2	10.8
Exports (incl. services, current prices)	ČR	2.5	44.1	-1.7	6.2	8.4	6.4	8.5
	SR	-2.8	62.1	-3.3	5.4	7.7	-10.6	-0.3
Imports (incl. services, current prices)	ČR	14.2	33.8	3.9	15.4	15.5	9.1	12.4
	SR	14.2	26.5	-0.2	11.2	10.2	2.4	5.8
Balance of payments (netto exports+services) bill. KCs	ČR	+5.2	+27.8	+11.5	+15.2	-3.7	+30.9	+5.2
	SR	-20.3	-2.3	-5.8	-7.6	-11.1	-14.7	-14.6
Account of inter-republics transfers (netto exports of the Czech Rep. to the Slovak Republic) bill. Kčs 1)	ČR	+3.3	+7.7	+13.5	+16.7	+18.6	x	x
	SR	-3.3	-7.7	-13.5	-16.7	-18.6	x	x

1) Absolute values in corresponding units
2) State at the end of period

In the third group of influences, the supposed deficit financing of some development programs should be taken into account in the Slovak Republic, directed at the support of investment and exports and at production and employment as well. The supposed slowdown in the conversion of armament production in the Slovak Republic belongs to these programs. Compensated with higher expenses from the state budget, this arrangement would temporarily improve the production of the GDP, employment and balance of payments. Paradoxically, these positive impacts would also be reflected in the Czech Republic as a recovery of demand, among others, for deliveries from the Czech Republic.

The fourth group of influences expresses the widening of payment balances for both the republics after the division of state by the amount of balance in mutual deliveries, (estimated for 1993 as a surplus of 16.7 billion KCs for the Czech Republic). It also means the separation of state budgets. The redistribution for the benefit of the Slovak Republic would be finished, in a volume of 18.4 billion KCs in 1993. The supposed profits of the joint enterprises, (the transit oil and gas pipelines etc.), may be estimated for the benefit of the Slovak Republic 5 billion KCs, which should be subtracted from the sum.

The last group expresses the impacts of supposed inevitable actions of the Slovak government directed at the moderation of the negative balance of payments, (probably by an increasing of import surcharge), and of the deficit in state budget, (partially by the emission of state bonds or bank credits, which would take away the free money and would reduce demand; and also partially by inflationary emission of money, which would go to the similar result in consequence of induced inflation). These actions would not only improve the balance of payments and state budget deficit but would also reduce the GDP production in consequence of increasing inflation and lowering of demand, which would also be partially transferred to the Czech Republic.

In case of a complete separation of the two republics, economic sectors such as, banking (money, foreign exchange), finance (prices, customs duties), the energy and transport sectors, employment policies and foreign trade, in particular, would have to be newly delimitated at very short notice. Whereas the Czech Republic would probably continue the course of radical economic reform, a change in the direction of a gradualist economic policy may be expected in the Slovak Republic. Undoubtedly, in the event of a complete split, both republics would, in the short run, be losers in the economic field. The expected break-up of the federation is already having negative effects on the cooperation of enterprises in the two republics. Price increases are already being registered in bilateral material flows. And foreign investors have switched to a very cautious pace in negotiations with Czechoslovak enterprises, while some of them, losing interest, have withdrawn. Negotiations about dividing joint assets, liabilities and the property of state enterprises could be protracted; it could slow down the speed of economic reform even in the Czech Republic.

6. SHORT-TERM ECONOMIC PROSPECTS OF THE CZECH AND SLOVAK REPUBLICS

From the last lines of Table 5 it follows that the complete impact of the division of the state would be substantially negative for the economy of the Slovak Republic in 1993. As Table 6 shows, the initially prognosed increasing of the GDP, consumption and investment in 1993 would decrease. The unemployment rate would increase about 5 points to 17.3 percent, inflation about 7 points to 19.2 percent. However, all these impacts would be moderated in 1994 with the exception of the high negative balance of payments which would increase the external public debt of the Slovak Republic by about 15 billion KCs or 0.5 billion US dollars per year despite the expected arrangements. This fact would probably evoke the devaluation of the Slovak currency no later than in 1994, according to our estimation, by about 30 percent, from 28,-Kčs to 26-Ks per US dollars.

In the Czech Republic the balance of payments would be better by approximately 15 billion KCs after division of the state, that is in substance the active account of the trade balance against the Slovak Republic after mutual compensation of other influences. The finishing of budgetary redistribution for the benefit of the Slovak Republic would basically not be shown in the state budget of the Czech Republic because it would be almost fully superimposed by other, (mainly negative), influences after the division the state. The impacts on GDP and its use would also be negative in the Czech Republic, though relatively less than in the Slovak Republic. However, it is not negligible if GDP will increase about 2.9 percent in the Czech Republic or about 0.7 percent in 1993, if the consumption will increase about 2.4 percent or decrease about -0.3 percent, if the increase of investment is 8 or 2 percent. In 1994 all these influences, as well as unemployment and inflation, would be moderated substantially.

Despite some temporary negative consequences of the ČSFR division on the Czech economy, the positive balance of payments and relatively well conditions for increasing foreign capital inflow may create favorable prerequisites for eventual revaluation of the Czech currency. If it takes place in 1994, it may decrease the present basic exchange rate of the US dollar by 10-15%, i.e. from 28 Kčs to 24-25 Kč. Along with the expected devaluation of the Slovak currency it would mean that the exchange rate between the Czech and Slovak currencies would be at least 1 Kč=1.50 Ks.

As far as industrial production is concerned, it reached its bottom in both republics in the fourth quarter of 1991. In 1992, a moderate recovery began and in the fourth quarter of 1992 industrial production in both republics is expected to be about 5-8% higher than in the fourth quarter of 1991. However, the total annual industrial production in 1992 will be about 11% lower than in 1991.

In the first half of 1993, a moderate recovery of industrial production may continue. But in the second half of 1993, after the expected separation of the joint currency, the decrease in mutual trade and other impacts of the division of the ČSFR will take place and will be strengthened by the inevitable bankruptcies of some large non-profit firms. This will cause a new decline in industrial production, which would be deeper in Slovakia. The development of GDP may be similar.

Continuous privatization, as well as a decline in production, will increase unemployment in both republics, especially in the second half of 1993. While the expected unemployment rate at the end of 1993 in the Czech Republic may be acceptable, (less than 7%), in the Slovak Republic, (more than 17%), it may cause serious social problems.

Consumer prices in 1992 have stabilized at a 10-11% annual inflation rate in both republics. In the first quarter of 1993, an increase of prices by about 6% is due to the introduction of the tax reform (VAT, income tax, etc.). In the second half of 1993, the impacts of the division of the CSFR may be expected. Moreover, the separation of joint currency and the supposed devaluation of the Slovak currency will considerably speed inflation in Slovakia, while in the Czech Republic it may have some deflationary impact.

Summarizing the economic prospects of both republics for 1993, it is obvious that they are much more favorable for the Czech Republic. Freed from the burden of national conflicts, the Czech Republic could, in a relatively short time, compensate the costs of separation by increased economic dynamics. The Czech Republic would also be rid of co-responsibility for the more difficult restructuring of the Slovak economy and the financing thereof.

In the short run, there is no doubt that, in both republics, the economic transformation, as well as the recovery of production, would be delayed even under the optimistic scenario of a Velvet Divorce. However, the possibility of a "trade and currency war" cannot be excluded. To keep the costs of the impending split low for both sides, it will be important to agree on an economic policy that would maintain past, intensive economic cooperation between the enterprises in the two republics, for instance, a trade and customs union would be highly desirable. In the transition period it is a question of the search for coexistence of the Czech and the Slovak Republic in the European region, where a process of integration is going forward in West Europe. The future European Economic Region could serve as a model for cooperation between the two republics – that body, into which both the Czech and the Slovak Republic, as independent states, wish to eventually become integrated.

7. CONCLUSION

This analysis of the contemporary position of the Czech and Slovak economies, evaluation of their mutual links, estimation of different impacts of their separation and the resulting short-term economic prospects for both republics may give relevant information on their true economic situation in the near future when both republics will start their independent economic development. Such information may be interesting for potential foreign investors, as well as for international institutions like UN, OECD, EC, IMF, WB, etc.

Of course, this type of analysis may only provide approximate information which may be subject to certain assumptions and estimates. However, substantially different actual development can hardly be expected, namely in obvious advantages in the position of the Czech economy before Slovakia, Hungary and Poland. On the other hand, further precision and updating of the presented results, taking into account all the new information, will be highly desirable.

REFERENCES

1. Z. Lukas, *ČSFR: Standing of Both Republics and Effects of a Separation,* Vienna: WIIW, 1992, p. 24.
2. ČSFR v mezinárodní ekonomice (*ČSFR in International Economics*), Prague: VÚVEV, 1992, p. 113.
3. I. Šujan, "Estimation of Consequences of the Czecho-Slovak Divorce, a paper prepared for the meeting of the Project A.C.E." *Modeling Economies in Transition,* Santa Sofia, Italy, October 19-23, 1992, p.13.

4

THE SPLIT OF CZECHOSLOVAKIA AND THE SPECIFIC FEATURES OF THE SLOVAK ECONOMY

Ales Capek
The Institute of Economics
State Bank of the Czech Republic

1. INTRODUCTION

The first best solution of the arrangement of the economic relations between the Czech and Slovak republic, which I once called the "functioning federation", is at present obviously not possible. Rather than a "non-functioning" federation accompanied by increased uncertainty and failures of economic policy, it is now desirable that the second best solution - the economic separation is implemented in a reasonable civilized manner with lowest possible costs.

In this paper I made an attempt to identify some specific features of the Slovak economy which might have some importance in the process of separation. These specificities were often used as an argument for the adjustment of economic reform to the specific conditions of Slovakia. I argue however that whereas some of the economic specificities of Slovakia mentioned generally in the literature may be statistically illustrated others are overestimated or even clearly do not get the support of the data.

2. THE SPECIFICS

The structural specificities of the Slovak economy are the result of past formation of the Slovak economic potential and resulting integration of the Slovak economy into the Czechoslovak economy and international economic relations. It is reasonable to expect that these specificities influence the economic transformation of the region and that certain developments in external environment affect the Slovak economy in a different way compared with the economy of the Czech lands.

What are actually the specific features of the Slovak economy? Up till now they were formulated in a rather vague way. It is usually mentioned that:

a) The Slovak industries usually operate in the initial stages of the production process; they produce intermediate goods to be further manufactured in the Czech republic. The Czech industry on the contrary produces more final goods;
b) The Slovak economy is more import oriented; the imports from former CMEA countries and especially Soviet Union play an important role in the structure of Slovak imports; in the form of intermediate goods supplied by Slovak producers these imports flow to the Czech economy;
c) Production of traditional arms is an important industry in Slovakia;
d) The market of former CMEA is for Slovakia more important as compared with Czech lands with regard both to imports and exports;
e) In spite of the achieved level of economic equalization the efficiency of production and exports in Slovakia is lower as compared with the Czech economy.

Let's try to verify the above mentioned specificities.

3. LEVEL OF FINALIZATION

First we shall analyze the level of finalization of produced goods. The differences in this respect between the CR and SR are very often mentioned. However if we use the available data we shall find that these differences are not so easy to prove and some data even indicate that the differences are just opposite to the general belief.

Using the data of table 1 we cannot unambiguously say that the industries producing for further manufacturing are more predominant in Slovak economy as compared with Czech economy. It is true that the share of such industries producing for production use as construction materials or paper industry is higher in Slovakia as compared with CR. However in the CR the share of other intermediate goods producing industries is higher as e.g. metallurgy. The data from table 2 in the Appendix further show that in many cases of Czech and Slovak industries the Czech industries are oriented more to the production of intermediate goods. This difference is significant especially within chemical and rubber industries and within the production of construction materials. In the aggregate in 16 from 30 industries in the table the share of production for producers' use was higher in the CR as compared with SR. The total share of supplies for final use in the above industries represented 48.2 percent in the CR as compared with 48.9 percent in the SR. These data indicate that the very often repeated argument about low level of finalization of Slovak output is not valid.

Another piece of interesting information is further provided by the data on the flows of Czech goods to Slovakia and vice versa Slovak goods to Czech lands. The data are in sharp contrast with the assertion about higher finalization of Czech output. Full 64 percent of Czech supplies to Slovakia are goods for further use in production whereas in the case of Slovak goods supplied to the CR the corresponding number is 52.4 percent.

Table 1

The Industrial Structure of the Czech and Slovak Economy in 1989
[in %]

Industry	CR	SR
Total	100.0	100.0
A. Production of Means of Production	70.2	70.1
B. Production of Consumer Goods	29.7	29.9
of which:		
Fuels	6.1	1.1
Energy	4.0	3.7
Metallurgy: iron	8.8	7.5
non iron	2.2	2.0
Chemical and Rubber Industry	9.7	16.1
Machinery	22.0	17.0
Electrical and Electronics Industry	3.9	5.6
Metalworking (inc.plastics)	3.2	6.1
Construction Materials	3.0	4.0
Wood and Furniture	2.9	3.8
Paper Industry	1.8	2.7
Glass, China and Ceramics	1.6	0.8
Textile Industry	4.8	3.4
Apparel	1.2	2.0
Leather	2.2	2.9
Printing Industry	0.4	0.5
Food and Beverages	16.6	17.5
Tobacco, Cooling Plants, Mineral Springs Exploitation	0.4	0.7
Other	3.9	2.6

Source: Calculated from 3, p. 362

Table 2

The Supplies for Production Use and Final Use from Selected Industries in the CR and SR in 1987

[in %]

Industry	CR Product. Use	CR Final Use	SR Product. Use	SR Final Use
Agriculture	84.9	13.2a)	79.0	18.6
Forestry	89.6	10.5	86.5	13.6
Water Supplies	83.9	15.1	65.2	33.9
Fuels	57.7	43.0	134.0	-33.9
Energy Industry	61.1	43.7	71.6	36.6
Metallurgy: iron	79.1	21.3	79.2	25.2
non iron	83.0	0.3	76.9	24.6
Chemical, Rubber and Asbestos Industry	80.8	17.6	53.4	46.6
Machinery	36.6	63.8	45.2	56.4
Electrical and Electronic Industry	56.9	42.3	57.7	41.7
Construction Materials	90.4	11.9	73.8	26.2
Wood and Furniture	55.9	43.3	50.0	48.8
Metalworking Industry	68.3	30.9	52.6	47.4
Paper Industry	77.0	24.5	67.9	31.2
Glass, China and Ceramics	41.7	57.1	65.8	32.0
Textile Industry	43.6	55.5	69.7	28.6
Apparel	8.6	88.5	8.0	89.4
Leather	41.2	57.3	34.0	63.0
Printing Industry	50.0	53.7	55.5	50.0
Food and Beverages	23.2	74.6	23.1	74.3
Tobacco, Cooling Plants, Mineral Springs Exploitation	17.4	67.4	25.7	65.1
Other Industry	70.4	35.4	67.8	42.6
Construction	14.5	83.7	11.4	87.0
Geological Exploration	54.4	45.6	77.4	22.6
Technical Design Activity	7.9	95.4	8.4	96.4
Transport	51.2	47.7	57.5	41.5
Table 2 continued				
Telecommunications	48.7	52.5	48.5	52.6
Internal Trade, External Trade, Public Catering	0.9	99.1	1.6	98.4
Material Technical Supplies	68.9	31.1	100.0	- 0.8
Buy up of Agricultural Products	57.3	42.7	50.8	49.2

a) Losses and Statistical Discrepancies add up to 100

Source: 1, pp. 91, 170.

Table 3

The Structure of Flows of Goods between the Republics
(in %)

		Sales of Czech Enterprises in Slovakia	Sales of Slovak Enterprises in the Czech lands
Total Sales		100	100
of which:	Investments	7.1	4.6
	Domestic Trade	14.7	13.0
	Nonproduction Use	1.8	6.6
	Sales Organizations	9.9	16.0
	Other	66.6	59.9
Share of Sales for Production Use		64.1	52.4

Source: Calculated from 5, pp. 27, 28, 37, 38

4. IMPORT INTENSITY

Let's analyze the other specificity of Slovak economy which is its higher import intensity. The data from the input-output table really indicate, that for Slovakia the imports are more important as compared with CR. The share of imports in total supplies for 30 industries in the economy represented in the SR 14.9 percent as compared with 13.2 percent in the CR. The share of previous socialist countries in total imports was at the same time higher in Slovakia as compared with CR. The data show that in 1987 72 percent of Slovak imports were from socialistcountries as compared with 66 percent in the case of Czech lands.[Calculated from 1, pp. 99, 105, 186, 192.]

The input-output table data further indicate that the imports for producers' use especially from previous socialist countries (i.e. mainly Soviet Union) were more important for Slovakia. The share of import for producers' use in total imports in 1987 in Slovakia was 73.5 percent and the share of imports for final use 26.4 percent. The corresponding data for the CR are 65.8 percent and 34.2 percent. The share of socialist countries in the case of imports for production use was 75 percent in Slovakia and 67 percent in the CR. Thus the data say that raw materials, intermediate goods and other commodities used in production which come to Slovakia especially from the Soviet Union represent a considerable item in the structure of Slovak imports.

A more detailed analysis would show differences among industries. Our attention was attracted especially by the extent of Slovak imports within the fuels industry, which represent some four fifths of Czech imports within this industry. Their share in total Slovak imports for production use was full 43 percent as compared with 28 percent in the CR [calculated from 1, pp. 99, 105, 186, 192]. Almost all of these imports were from USSR. At present the territorial restructuring of imports of oil is underway and the share of USSR, which in the past was the monopoly supplier of oil to Czechoslovakia, is diminishing. The Slovak economy is nevertheless supposed to be still vulnerable to the disturbances in imports within this industry.

5. PRODUCTION OF ARMS

Further often mentioned specific feature of the Slovak economy is the high share of arms industry which became a problem after the decision to reduce the industry considerably. Due to the character of this industry detailed data are not available. The data which we have found scattered in the literature however enable to draw the following conclusions. The production of arms culminated in Czechoslovakia in 1987, when its share in total industrial output represented some 3 percent and the employed labor force within the industry amounted to some 100 thousand. In accordance with the estimates the share of Slovakia represented at least 60 percent of the production capacity. It means that whereas in the CR the share of arms production in total industrial output represented less than 2 percent, in Slovakia it was between 5-6 percent. The production of arms should be reduced considerably. Especially in Slovakia this process should be very rapid. Its share in total Czechoslovak output of arms should drop to less than 40 percent [2, p. 8]. The restructuring would thus mean that some 50 thousand labor places in Slovakia would be affected.

We are however of the opinion that rather than a problem of the republics the restructuring of arms industry is a problem of regions. Besides central Slovakia where some 30 percent of Czechoslovak labor force within the arms industry are employed, the reduction of the production of arms will affect souther Moravia employing roughly 20 percent of the labor force in the industry and Prague where some 17 percent of the total labor force within the arms industry are employed.

Table 4

The Structure of Imports to the CR and SR According to their Final Use in 1987
[in %]

	CR	SR
Total imports	100.0	100.0
of which:		
production use	65.8	73.5
personal consumption	7.1	6.5
social consumption	8.7	7.7
investment	13.5	11.6
change in inventories	1.1	- 0.6
exports	3.8	1.3
final use	34.2	26.5

Source: Calculated from 1, pp. 99, 186

6. TERRITORIAL STRUCTURE OF SALES

Other structural specificity of the Slovak economy is the role which the former CMEA countries play in Slovak external economic relations. We have already mentioned the role of imports from these countries to Slovakia. Let's now look at the exports. The input-output table data for 1987 indicate small difference between the share of exports to these countries in total flows of goods in the Czech and Slovak economy. The share of exports to the CMEA countries in total output was 13 percent in Slovakia and 11.8 percent in the Czech lands [calculated from 1, pp. 91, 170]. The structural balance of sales data show similar slight difference with regard to the importance of the external markets for the CR and SR. Thus similarly like in the case of imports the Slovak economy is more vulnerable in connection with disturbances in external trade flows affecting its exports to the east.

It would be interesting in this connection to analyze the real impacts of the disintegration of eastern markets on both the Czech and Slovak economics. The available data gave us however only the opportunity for a very simple analysis of the reduction of the former soviet market and of the trade reorientation of the CR and the SR on other markets. Table number % shows that in 1991 total sales in 19 industries decreased in the SR roughly by 28 percent compared with 25 percent in the CR. The share of decrease in sales to the former Soviet Union in this total drop represented in the SR 8.27 percent and in the CR 5.65 percent even though in absolute terms the decrease in the case of Czech lands was higher. (The real impact on the economy would be of course much more extensive when taking into account the multiplicative affect on the chain of suppliers to the exporters.)

In different industries however the situation was very different. Among industries with the biggest share of the loss of the markets of the CIS in total decrease of sales belong in both republics apparel, leather, shoes and fur industries, glass, china and ceramics, wood working industry, machinery, electrotechnical industry and metallurgy. In the SR moreover the printing industry. Within the apparel industry which was obviously most affected by the loss of the Soviet marker, this drop represented nearly 60 percent of the decrease in total sales in both of the republics. In absolute terms the biggest decrease in exports to the CIS was in machinery. In most industries the impact of the loss of the Soviet market was bigger in the SR compare with the CR.

Very interesting and rather surprising (due to the general belief about the lower flexibility of the Slovak enterprises) is at the same time a further conclusion which can be drawn, i.e. the conclusion about a fast reorientation of Slovak exporters on other markets. In a number of Slovak industries, as documented by table 4 a remarkable shift of exports to the former Soviet Union towards other markets occurred. Noticeable is this trend e.g. in the case of Slovak metallurgy or production of glass, china and ceramics. In the Czech industry this reorientation was slightly slower. As a result whereas total real exports from the CR in 1991 decreased by more than 5 percent in the SR it increased more than by 2 percent.

This development contrasts to a certain degree with the general belief about lower export performance of the Slovak enterprises. which are documented by various indicators. The data from the structural balance of sales e.g. slow that in the end of 1980s the difference coefficient of Slovak exports to the former socialist countries was 104.3 as compared with 115.9 in the CR and the same indicator with regard to the exports to western countries was 97.4 in Slovakia compared with 101.4 in the Czech lands. [5, pp. 27, 28, 37, 38] The situation differs of course across industries and table 5 shows that there are some industries where Slovak exporters perform better compared with their Czech counterparts.

Table 5: Impact of the Decrease of Exports to CIS from Industrial Sales in 1991

CZECH REPUBLIC

Industry	Growth in 1990-91 in 1990 prices						B/A	C/A	(C-B)/A
	Total sales	%	Exports to CIS	%	Total exports	%	%	%	%
	(A)		(B)		(C)				
Fuels	-11025525	-15.71	-1704	-100.00	1854762	58.91	0.02	-16.82	-16.84
Energy	-4855583	-8.41	-6019	-9.51	-272471	-41.53	0.12	5.61	5.49
Metallurgy- Iron	-16196129	-25.93	-1005098	-32.76	1231057	9.37	6.21	-7.60	-13.81
Mettalurgy- non Iron	-8622846	-47.24	-986	-100.00	316363	59.36	0.01	-3.67	-3.68
Chemicals	-17820050	-25.44	-448302	-40.67	-1708978	-14.24	2.52	9.59	7.07
Machinery	-46665344	-30.77	-3357469	-25.23	-5784377	-14.29	7.19	12.40	5.20
Electrotech.	-11588886	-36.13	-740146	-28.80	-1741549	-27.56	6.39	15.03	8.64
Construction Materials	-4736566	-28.88	-105581	-77.90	832311	65.54	2.23	-17.57	-19.80
Woodworking	-4250170	-26.89	-306138	-41.95	-17720	-0.47	7.20	0.42	-6.79
Metal Working	-7068167	-33.49	-219229	-83.97	-48804	-1.82	3.10	0.69	-2.41
Pulp and Paper	-2747392	-21.38	-24333	-99.38	206597	10.33	0.89	-7.52	-8.41
Glass, China, Ceramics	-3608496	-28.26	-652841	-86.31	-555045	-11.22	18.09	15.38	-2.71
Textile	-12095007	-34.39	-849893	-53.56	-226459	-2.72	7.03	1.87	-5.15
Apparel	-2377320	-41.10	-1352734	-98.02	-579547	-27.10	56.90	24.38	-32.52
Leather	-4164386	-32.83	-1165318	-47.66	-1094900	-27.17	27.98	26.29	-1.69
Printing	-1684909	-40.77	-13168	-100.01	-70042	-28.61	0.78	4.16	3.38
Foodstuffs	-22884762	-18.77	-52930	-16.41	1205318	17.42	0.23	-5.27	-5.50
Tobacco, Cooling	-709504	-21.60	0	********	-27401	-79.62	0.00	3.86	3.86
Other	-2090961	-21.45	-159865	-96.76	433677	28.32	7.65	-20.74	-28.39
Total	-185192003	-25.23	-10461754	-37.45	-6047208	-5.29	5.65	3.27	-2.38

(Table 5 continued on next page)

(*Table 5 Continued*)

SLOVAK REPUBLIC

Industry	Growth in 1990-91 in 1990 prices						B/A	C/A	(C-B)/A
	Total sales	%	Exports to CIS	%	Total exports	%	%	%	%
	(A)		(B)		(C)				
Fuels	-5724004	-45.48	-9062	-100.00	30301	53.49	0.16	-0.53	-0.69
Energy	-4074703	-16.91	0	********	30902	9.49	0.00	-0.76	-0.76
Metallurgy-Iron	-1961299	-8.90	-384147	-59.26	3346677	53.57	19.59	-170.64	-190.22
Metallurgy-non Iron	-2116847	-36.65	-19957	-94.97	419352	67.40	0.94	-19.81	-20.75
Chemicals	-11028479	-23.71	44481	3.40	230002	3.09	-0.40	-2.09	-1.68
Machinery	-19087041	-38.65	-3335404	-50.94	-2278623	-19.56	17.47	11.94	-5.54
Electrotech.	-6661953	-40.41	-590329	-54.87	-764031	-38.09	8.86	11.47	2.61
Constructive Materials	-3853669	-39.60	-245467	-77.28	-281482	-23.30	6.37	7.30	0.93
Woodworking	-2579914	-28.68	-349502	-31.05	-93205	-4.00	13.55	3.61	-9.93
Metalworking	-4787096	-34.97	-89569	-67.06	-118751	-9.74	1.87	2.48	0.61
Pulp and Paper	-1406601	-18.11	-6749	-47.63	566003	36.66	0.48	-40.24	-40.72
Glass, China, Ceramics	-404137	-17.28	-89903	-89.42	219172	32.00	22.25	-54.23	-76.48
Textile	-3962709	-41.16	-350963 -	43.50	114686	5.61	8.86	-2.89	-11.75
Apparel	-1627308	-40.04	-962797	-78.92	-542296	-27.67	59.17	33.32	-25.84
Leather	-2944666	-41.44	-589673	-43.34	-478691	-22.79	20.03	16.26	-3.77
Printing	-5116	-0.25	-5257	-99.21	111524	48.34	102.76	-2179.91	-2282.66
Foodstuffs	-9717739	-19.07	91918	82.81	318030	10.26	-0.95	-3.27	-2.33
Tobacco,Cooling	-506220	-27.63	0	********	28604	67.05	0.00	-5.65	-5.65
Other	-834173	-40.40	676	********	152142	443.85	-0.08	-18.24	-18.16
Total	-83283674	-28.03	-6891704	-46.54	1010316	2.25	8.27	-1.21	-9.49

Source: Calculated by A. Buchtíková

Table 6

The Difference Coefficient with Regard to Exports from the CR and SR Capitalist and Former Socialist Countries in 1989
[in %]

	CR		SR	
Industry	SC	CC	SC	CC
Coal Mining	76.0	98.9	150.1	111.4
Gas Industry	57.8	126.7	59.0	67.9
Production of Heat and Electricity	80.3	85.9	79.6	82.1
Ores Mining	112.8	98.8	105.3	116.0
Metallurgy: Iron	71.2	116.9	90.5	132.0
Non Iron	145.9	161.9	106.2	145.0
Chemical and Oil Industry	102.3	113.2	79.7	94.7
Rubber, Plastics, Asbestos	115.6	107.5	103.6	106.5
Production for Medical Use	184.0	94.3	230.3	77.2
Heavy Machinery	125.1	119.0	125.2	395.9
General Machinery	137.6	106.8	121.8	106.5
Electrical Industry	154.3	86.0	143.0	92.4
Construction Materials	110.8	147.3	112.0	106.0
Wood and Furniture	78.9	104.8	69.8	84.5
Paper Industry	90.0	117.9	71.1	119.7
Glass, China, Ceramics	113.0	130.0	97.8	103.1
Textile Industry	90.9	87.6	81.0	82.5
Apparel	69.6	87.8	66.5	88.5
Leather, Shoes, Furs	94.9	86.4	99.7	83.8
Printing Industry	123.6	74.7	126.7	82.6
Food and Beverages	57.4	58.5	59.4	49.7

Source: Calculated from 5, pp. 19-23, 29-34

7. THE TRADE FLOWS BETWEEN THE REPUBLICS

Interesting are not only data concerning Czech and Slovak exports. Even more important are probably data with regard to total sales including domestic markets. They provide the information for which markets and in which extent each of the republics produces. In other words on which markets and to what extent each economy depends. Thus we may hypothesize more precisely how important may be the reduction or even loss of a certain market for each of the economies.

The data in table 7 illustrate a small difference in the importance of external markets (both of the western and eastern countries) between the CR and SR. The biggest difference however consists in the fact that for the

Czech producers the Czech market is far more important than the Slovak market for Slovak producers. In other words the Slovak economy depends on the sales in Czech lands much more than the Czech economy on the sales in Slovakia. This fact constitutes one of our main arguments supporting the assertion that the possible split of Czechoslovak economy accompanied by a break of economic links between the republics would have different consequences in both republics. The impact of this development would be much more dramatic in Slovakia as compared with the Czech lands.

8. CONCLUSIONS

Summing up the above:

1. We did not succeed to prove that the Slovak economy is more oriented towards the production of less finalized goods as compared with the CR.
2. The Slovak economy is slightly more import intensive in comparison with the Czech economy. The former CMEA countries and especially USSR play decisive role in Slovak imports. At the same time imports for production use are more important in the case of Slovakia in comparison with the CR.
3. The share of industries producing arms in higher in Slovakia and the reduction of arms production might affect some 50 thousand labor places. However rather than a problem of the whole Slovak republic it is a problem of certain regions.
4. The main difference between the CR and SR with regard to the territorial structure of their sales is the fact that for Slovak economy the Czech market is far more important than the Slovak market for the Czech economy.
5. Lower general efficiency and lower export performance as compared with the Czech economy characterize the Slovak economy as well. It is however remarkable how the Slovak exporters succeeded to shift their exports from the markets of the CIS to other markets.

Table 7

Territorial Structure of Sales of Czech and Slovak Producers in 1989
[in %]

Industry	Location of Enterprise	CR	SR	Socialist Countr.	Western Countr.
Total Sales	CR	75.8	11.5	7.1	5.7
	SR	26.9	59.2	8.1	5.9
Selected Industries:					
Coal Mining	CR	81.2	10.4	3.9	4.5
	SR	0.0	99.6	0.3	0.0
Gas Industry	CR	70.9	29.1	0.0	0.0
	SR	9.1	90.6	0.1	0.1
Heat and Electricity	CR	96.2	2.1	1.0	0.7
	SR	2.8	93.6	2.0	1.6
Ores Mining	CR	67.5	12.6	15.2	4.8
	SR	36.9	29.5	26.7	6.9
Metallurgy - Iron	CR	69.9	15.6	8.5	6.1
	SR	47.9	24.2	15.4	12.5
Metallurgy - Non Iron	CR	79.1	18.3	1.4	1.2
	SR	65.7	25.2	4.1	4.9
Chemical and Oil	CR	67.6	20.3	3.7	8.4
Industry	SR	33.3	50.6	6.1	9.9
Rubber, Plastics,	CR	73.4	14.8	5.3	6.4
Asbestos	SR	53.6	32.3	6.4	7.7
Production for	CR	81.1	8.7	5.3	5.0
Medical Purposes	SR	53.9	30.4	5.0	10.8
Heavy Machinery	CR	55.8	15.1	23.3	5.9
	SR	57.0	20.3	21.8	0.8
General Machinery	CR	62.3	16.2	14.7	6.8
	SR	42.5	38.4	15.4	3.8
Electrical	CR	67.1	16.6	12.3	4.1
Industry	SR	45.7	40.4	11.5	2.4
Construction	CR	88.7	6.5	2.6	2.2
Materials	SR	13.2	83.8	2.4	0.6
Wood and	CR	70.7	6.3	6.2	16.8
Furniture	SR	13.6	66.2	10.7	9.5
Paper Industry	CR	76.0	11.0	1.6	11.4
	SR	32.3	48.5	3.5	15.6
Glass, China,	CR	48.4	11.1	14.0	26.5
Ceramics	SR	28.5	37.4	11.7	22.4
Textile Industry	CR	60.0	16.2	8.8	16.0
	SR	28.9	49.7	11.2	10.2
Apparel	CR	43.7	18.5	28.8	9.1
	SR	31.9	23.7	28.6	15.7
Leather, Shoes,	CR	67.1	10.6	14.0	8.4
Furs	SR	23.3	54.2	15.1	7.4
Printing Industry	CR	85.4	5.8	1.6	7.1
	SR	4.7	85.1	1.2	9.0
Food and Beverages	CR	90.7	3.7	1.1	4.5
	SR	9.1	84.0	1.7	5.2

Source: Calculated from 5, pp. 19-26, 29-34

REFERENCES

[1] *Bilance mezioborovýh vztaů CSSR za rok 1987* (The Input-Output Table of CSSR), Federâlnî statistický úřad, Prague. 24.8.1989

[2] Ježek, M.: *Konverze zbrojní výroby*. (The Conversion of the Arms Industry), Národnî hospodářství 8/1991

[3] *Statistická ročenka CSFR 1990*. (The Statistical Yearbook of CSFR), SNTL - Nakladatelstî technické literatury, Praha, 1990

[4] *Stratégia ekonomického rozvoja Slovenska*. (Strategy of economic development of Slovakia), VP č. 81, Ekonomicý ústav SA, September 1990

[5] *Strukturální bilance odbytu v hodnotovém vyjádřeí za 1. - 4. čtvrtletí 1989* (Structural Balance of Sales for 1989), Fedeálnî statistický úřad čj. 1789/90

5

ECONOMIC RECOVERY AND FOREIGN EXCHANGE RATE REGIME IN THE TRANSITION ECONOMIES: THE CASE OF CZECHOSLOVAKIA

Miroslav Hrnčíř
The Institute of Economics
State Bank of Czechoslovakia

1. INTRODUCTION

In 1992, the key issue facing Czechoslovakia, as well as some of the other transition economies in Central Europe, was the initiation of economic recovery.

The transition economies suffered a rather severe decline in economic activity and in real incomes. Czechoslovakia, despite its relatively stabilized initial macroeconomic conditions, experienced a 16% decrease in its GDP and 24% decrease in real wages in 1991. Along with the drop in consumer demand, estimated at 33%, aggregate demand was substantially depressed due largely to the fall in investment activities. The volume of investment decreased by 33.8% in 1991 from the previous year (data includes investment activities of private and small firms). Such a deterioration in macroeconomic performance exceeds by far the worst recession recorded in any comparable market economy over a period of several decades.[1]

---

[1]It does not apply, however, to the level of unemployment. In spite of a substantial increase from almost zero unemployment rate in 1989 (according to the official figures) to 6.6% rate at the end of 1991, it remained fairly below in the course of 1992, to 5.5% in the mid-year.

The rather divergent trends in the level of economic activity and in the level of unemployment are evidently mostly conditioned by the delayed institutional changes: The

The figures for the mid-1992 signaled certain stabilization of the level of economic activity, however not yet the reversal of the underlying trends.

In contrast to market economies, the current recession in transition economies is predominantly of a structural nature, with cyclical factors playing a less significant role. This points to the limitations of traditional anti-cyclical policies in the context of transition economies.

Table 1
Main macroeconomic indicators (in %)

	1989	1990	1991	I-II/1992+
GDP (annual growth rate)	1.4	-0.4	-15.9	-13.0
Inflation rate (CPI, annual charge)	1.4	10.0	58.7	11.8
Unemployment rate (end of period)	...	1.0	6.6	5.5
Real wages (annual growth rate)	0.9	-5.6	-24.0	8.9

\+ Compared to the first half of 1991 Source: Statistical Bulletin, Federal Statistical Office

A reversal of "downward" expectations, reflected by an extremely sharp decline in investments, is hindered not only by demand side constraints, but also by perseverance of institutional rigidities interrelated with policy flaws in promotion of supply side adjustment.

Under a rather imperfectly competitive environment in the domestic economy the incentives to invest and the prospects for any investment to turn profitable are conditioned by the parallel behaviour of other investors. A reversal of existing expectations could evidently take place more likely and more timely provided a positive solution of the implied coordination problem is achieved. R. Dornbusch identified this coordination problem in the context of the IMF model and the lessons from Latin America as an "economy wide" externality, solution of which could be hardly left to market forces only (R. Dornbusch, 1990).

The effects of domestic environment on expectations of economic agents became also in transition economies increasingly interrelated with those of external environment. Given the achieved stage of openness to the outside world and desirable continuation of this process, any recovery of domestic activities in Czechoslovakia could be made sustainable only if an adequately growing export potential matches the increasing import over the medium-

impacts of both the large-scale privatization and of the full implementation of bankruptcy law are still forthcoming.

term horizon. Economy wide privatization process initiated, along with hoped-for increased inflow of FDI, should make this desired outcome more probable.

Legacy of the past development under the virtually closed economy framework represents, however, another "externality" in transition economies. To cope with it, an export oriented strategy, including export promotion schemes and support of related services, institutions and infrastructure seems necessary to correct for the inherited drawbacks.

In this context, the paper examines the role of foreign exchange rate in transition and in economic recovery of Czechoslovakia: options of foreign exchange rate regimes which could be resorted to, and how these options could affect the development path of the economy.

2. FOREIGN EXCHANGE RATE IN CZECHOSLOVAKIA: PAST AND PRESENCE

2.1 Changed Institutional Setting

Despite "nominally" in existence, foreign exchange rate had negligible importance under the centrally planned economy framework, maintained in Czechoslovakia up to the end of 1980s. The "official" exchange rate was kept overvalued, while on the other hand various black and parallel market rates tended to depress unrealistically the external value of the currency. Moreover, the "implied" exchange ratios were widely diversified across both trade and non-trade flows.

With the start of the transition at the beginning of 1990, an unified exchange rate was introduced, eliminating the duality of so-called commercial and tourist rates. A radical move towards opening of the Czechoslovak economy, including the changeover to limited (internal) currency convertibility and foreign trade liberalization at the beginning of 1991, was paid for "in advance" by the three consecutive devaluations of the unified exchange rate of koruna (CSK) vis-a-vis convertible currencies in the course of 1990.[2]

Since the beginning of January 1991, the nominal effective exchange rate of CSK (NEER) has been pegged to the basket of five currencies.[3] The aim was to use the fixed exchange rate as an instrument of macroeconomic stabilization. This approach followed the suit applied elsewhere in stabilization programmes, reflecting that foreign exchange rate is a special

[2]CSK was devalued by 16.6% on January 8, by 55.3% on October 15, and by 15.98% on December 28. Though it could be argued that the initial ratio hardly represented an exchange rate proper, the cumulative depreciation in the course of 1990 was substantial: after the third devaluation at end-December 1990, the exchange rate changed to CSK 28 per USD, as compared to CSK 14.29 per USD end-December 1989.

[3]Both the composition of the basket and the relative weights of individual currencies are, however, revised on an annual basis. The respective shares in 1991 were as follows: DEM 45.52%, USD 31.34%, ATS 12.35%, CHF 6.55%, GBP 4.24%. The revised composition of 1992: USD 49.07%, DEM 36.15%, ATS 8.07%, CHF 3.79%, FRF 2.92%.

"macroeconomic" price, with substantial impact across the entire national economy. Though advancing along this strategy of "nominal exchange rate anchor", the Czechoslovak authorities did not commit themselves, however, to any pre-announced period of keeping the given exchange rate unaffected.

In reality, the peg has been kept since January 1991. The changes in the CSK's exchange rate in this period only reflected the development in the cross-rates of the basket currencies.

Given all the upheavals accompanying the start of transition, the untouched peg for almost two years now may appear surprising. It has been made possible by an unexpectedly favourable development of foreign exchange flows in the mentioned period. Both trade balance and current account in convertible currencies have substantially recovered after a sharp deterioration in 1990. In 1991, a surplus of USD 0.3 billion on current account was achieved instead of an envisaged deficit of USD 2.5 billion. And again in 1992, a predicted deficit of USD 0.6 billion has been revised at mid-year to an expected surplus of USD 1 - 1.5 billion.

This outcome is to be viewed as a coincidence of two factors which worked in the same direction in the given period:

- the first "programmed" one was a wide margin between the current exchange rate and the domestic purchasing power (PPP) of the currency, which was on purpose further widened by three devaluations of the domestic currency in the course of 1990,

- the second one, a deep protracted recession in the domestic economy, represented on the other hand both unpredicted and unwelcomed phenomenon. The extent of the recession in reality substantially outrun not only the government forecasts, but also "the black vision" of the sceptics.

2.2 Divergent Foreign and Domestic Purchasing Power of the CSK

A wide gap between the domestic and external values of their currencies was a common feature of the former centrally planned economies. In the case of Czechoslovakia, the gap widened further in nominal terms at the very beginning of the transition as a result of the devaluations effected in the course of 1990.

Most expert studies identified the domestic PPP of CSK at the beginning of 1990, i.e. at the start of the transition, in the range of CSK 7-8 per USD. Using the mid-point of the interval, i.e. 7.50 CSK/USD, as a benchmark, the resulting development of the PPP in the course of the transition is presented in the chart 1 (for data see table 2).

The identified decrease in the implied purchasing power of the CSK with respect to the USD from CSK 7.50 in January 1990 to CSK 12.46 in April 1992 reflects Czechoslovakia's inflation differential as measured by ratios of CPIs for the given period.

As follows from data in table 2, the disparity between the PPP and the CSK's exchange rate culminated towards the end of 1990 (after effected devaluations and a sweeping liberalization of domestic prices only forthcoming). In December 1990 the implied exchange rate/PPP ratio amounted to 2.93, since then it decreased continuously to the level of 2.33 in April 1992.

The study by PlanEcon (PlanEcon Report 16-17,18,1992) evaluated the PPP of the CSK at the beginning of 1990 even more favourably, 6.20 CSK/USD in January 1990 and 10.30 CSK/USD in May 1992. While diverging from the initial level, the resulting rate of change for the examined period coincides with the above estimates.

The exchange rate/PPP ratio this study gave for the Hungarian forint was 2.15 in January 1990, decreasing to 1.62 in May 1992. For the Polish zloty the corresponding figures were 3.88 and 1.70 respectively.

Comparing these findings for Hungary and Poland with the above results for Czechoslovakia, the following conclusion may be drawn:

- while at the beginning of 1990 the extent of the disparity in all three reforming countries appeared to be significantly wider than in comparable market economies,[4] the implied exchange rate/PPP ratio for the CSK fell only modestly up to mid-1992, unlike in Hungary and Poland,
- this implies that the CSK has been kept relatively undervalued with respect to convertible currencies, and in the course of the recent period this has become the case with respect to the Polish zloty and the Hungarian forint.

2.3 The Impact of Transition on Nominal and Real Exchange Rates

In the period January 1990 - May 1992 the NEER of the CSK depreciated to 56% of its value, as a result of devaluations vis-a-vis convertible currencies in October and December 1990. However, the real effective exchange rate (REER)[5], calculated on the basis of the CPI, depreciated as well despite a high inflation differential against the countries of basket currencies. Though only by 6 percentage points, the level of the REER was in May 1992 still below its January 1990 base. (See Chart 2a, data in Table 3).

Parallel calculations for Hungary and Poland indicate REER appreciation of both forint and zloty in 1990 and 1991. Between January 1990 and May 1992 forint's REER appreciated by 32%, while the zloty's appreciation was much sharper, by 140%.

---

[4]According to Summers-Heston, the respective ratios (ERDI coefficient) for comparable European countries in 1985 were as follows: Spain 1.81, Ireland 1.34, Greece 1.70, Portugal 2.28, Turkey 2.99. (Summers R., Heston A., 1988).

[5]Greater value than 100 signifies appreciation and less then 100 depreciation.

Chart 1

Purchasing Power Parity Rate, Nominal Exchange Rate and Parallel Market Exchange Rate of CSK in 1989-1992
(CSK per USD, average per period)

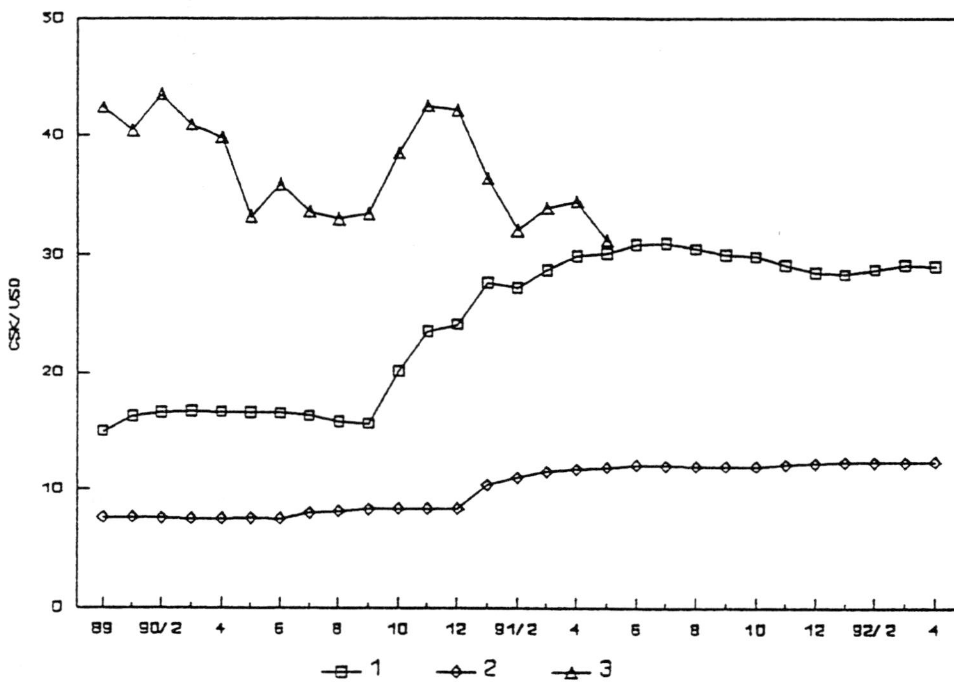

1 = Exchange Rate
2 = Purchasing power parity
3 = Parallel market rate

Table 2

Exchange Rate, Purchasing Power Parity Rate and Parallel Market Exchange Rate of CSK in 1989-1992
(CSK per USD, average per period)

	1	2	3	4
1989	15.05	7.50	2.01	42.39
1990/ 1	16.29	7.50	2.17	40.39
2	16.60	7.46	2.22	43.46
3	16.72	7.42	2.25	40.88
4	16.67	7.44	2.24	39.81
5	16.64	7.45	2.23	33.20
6	16.58	7.43	2.23	35.88
7	16.37	7.88	2.08	33.55
8	15.89	8.05	1.97	32.99
9	15.71	8.23	1.91	33.42
10	20.18	8.26	2.44	38.52
11	23.63	8.26	2.86	42.45
12	24.19	8.27	2.93	42.10
1991/ 1	27.65	10.34	2.68	36.34
2	27.24	11.04	2.47	32.02
3	28.74	11.54	2.49	33.88
4	29.94	11.75	2.55	34.43
5	30.12	11.96	2.52	31.19
6	30.89	12.13	2.55	..
7	31.00	12.11	2.56	..
8	30.53	12.06	2.53	..
9	30.03	12.05	2.49	..
10	29.89	12.02	2.49	..
11	29.15	12.17	2.39	..
12	28.55	12.31	2.32	..
1992/ 1	28.36	12.42	2.28	..
2	28.78	12.44	2.31	..
3	29.16	12.40	2.35	..
4	29.06	12.46	2.33	..

1 = Exchange rate
2 = Purchasing power parity (PPP rate)
3 = Exchange rate/PPP rate ratio (1:2)
4 = Parallel market rate

Chart 2

Effective Exchange Rates of CSK

Chart 2a. January 1990 = 100

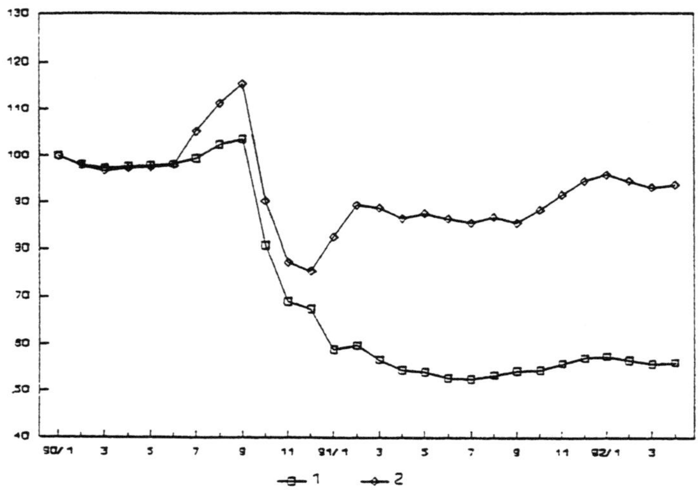

Chart 2b. May 1990 = 100

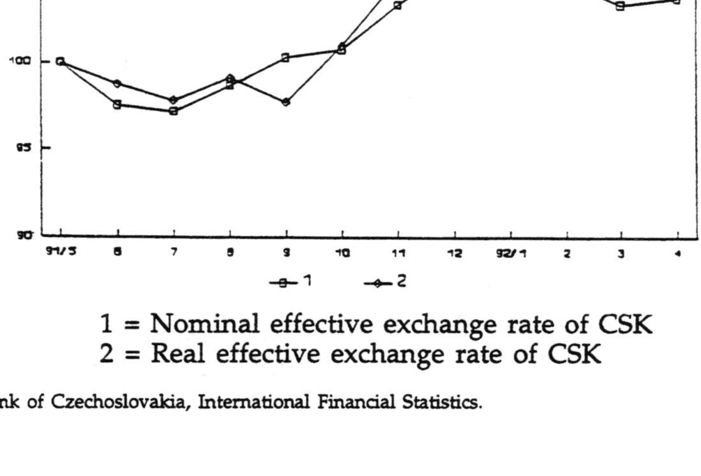

1 = Nominal effective exchange rate of CSK
2 = Real effective exchange rate of CSK

Source: State Bank of Czechoslovakia, International Financial Statistics.

Table 3

Effective Exchange Rates of CSK

Indexes (January 1990 = 100)

	CSK/USD*	1	2	3	4
1990/ 1	16.29	100.00	100.00	100.00	100.00
2	16.60	98.13	100.00	100.43	97.71
3	16.72	97.43	100.00	100.69	96.76
4	16.67	97.72	100.40	100.87	97.26
5	16.64	97.90	100.70	101.09	97.52
6	16.58	98.25	101.00	101.35	97.91
7	16.37	99.51	107.50	101.52	105.37
8	15.89	102.52	110.90	102.07	111.39
9	15.71	103.69	114.30	102.64	115.47
10	20.18	80.72	115.50	103.31	90.25
11	23.63	68.94	115.60	103.26	77.17
12	24.19	67.34	115.70	103.32	75.41
1991/ 1	27.65	58.92	145.60	103.99	82.49
2	27.24	59.80	155.80	104.22	89.40
3	28.74	56.68	163.10	104.24	88.69
4	29.94	54.41	166.30	104.59	86.51
5	30.12	54.08	169.70	104.91	87.48
6	30.89	52.74	172.60	105.39	86.37
7	31.00	52.55	172.60	106.10	85.55
8	30.53	53.36	172.50	106.15	86.71
9	30.03	54.25	173.00	109.80	85.47
10	29.89	54.50	172.90	106.67	88.34
11	29.15	55.88	175.60	107.09	91.63
12	28.55	57.06	177.70	107.18	94.60
1992/ 1	28.36	57.44	179.50	107.50	95.92
2	28.78	56.60	180.40	108.06	94.49
3	29.16	55.86	180.90	108.52	93.12
4	29.06	56.06	181.79	108.73	93.72

(table 3 continues on the next page)

Table 3

Effective Exchange Rates of CSK
(continued)

Indexes (May 1991 = 100)

	CSK/USD*	1	2	3	4
1991/ 5	30.12	100.00	100.00	100.00	100.00
6	30.89	97.51	101.71	100.45	98.73
7	31.00	97.16	101.71	101.06	97.79
8	30.53	98.66	101.65	101.19	99.11
9	30.03	100.30	101.94	104.69	97.67
10	29.89	100.77	101.89	101.68	100.97
11	29.15	103.33	103.48	102.08	104.74
12	28.55	105.50	104.71	102.17	108.13
1992/ 1	28.36	106.21	105.77	102.47	109.63
2	28.78	104.66	106.31	103.01	108.01
3	29.16	103.29	106.60	103.45	106.44
4	29.06	103.65	107.12	103.64	107.13

* Monthly average values
1 = Nominal effective exchange rate of CSK
2 = Consumer prices of Czechoslovakia
3 = Consumer prices of basket countries
4 = Real effective exchange rate of CSK

However, as is apparent from chart 2b, the CSK's REER has tended to appreciate as well recently. Along with a marginal appreciation of the NEER expressed in terms of USD, CSK's REER appreciated by 7% in the year ending May 1992.

The divergent trends in the REERs across the reforming countries were conditioned by substantial differences in their inflation records and to some extent also by the difference in the transition strategies adopted:

> a) In Poland at the beginning of 1990, and in Czechoslovakia a year later, the move to a limited currency convertibility was associated with substantial devaluations. Moreover, the authorities in both cases opted for a deliberate overshooting of devaluation, setting the exchange rate close to a parallel market or a "marginal" rate.[6]

Hungary, on the other hand, followed a more gradual path of liberalization, accompanied by repeated, but relatively modest, devaluations of the forint.

Reflecting these differences, the nominal exchange rate of the Polish zloty depreciated between 1989 and 1992 much more than the CSK rate, while the Hungarian forint, on the other hand, depreciated significantly less in nominal terms.

> b) As for inflation in the respective period, Czechoslovak record was more favourable than that of Hungary, and certainly much more favourable than Poland's (compare table 4). In Czechoslovakia, apart from a price jump in January 1991 following the sweeping price liberalization (CPI increased by 25.8% only in this month), inflation was well under control through the entire examined period, with the monthly average at 0.6% for the year ending May 1992.

---

[6]With the advantage of hindsight, it can be claimed that the extent of overshooting was in both countries unnecessarily large. In the Polish case e.g., the adopted rate "survived" a 250% inflation rate in 1990 (December 1989 to December 1990) without any adjustment necessary. A number of observers criticized the extent of the devaluation as an evident policy mistake. It must be admitted, however, that the authorities faced a considerable degree of uncertainty while setting a new exchange rate. Given the sweeping changes taking place with the start of transition and given the proclaimed target of maintaining the exchange rate as a nominal anchor for a specified period (in the case of Poland) or at least to avoid any further devaluation in the near future (in the case of Czechoslovakia) the selection of a proper rate seemed to be more a question of the "art of policy making" than of rational calculation.

Table 4

Consumer prices in Czechoslovakia, Hungary and Poland in 1986-92
(average annual percentage rates over the previous year)

	1986	1987	1988	1989	1990	1991	1992+
Czechoslovakia	0.5	0.1	0.2	1.4	10.0	58.7	11.8
Hungary	5.3	8.6	15.5	17.0	28.9	35.0	
Poland	17.7	25.0	60.0	251.0	586.0	70.0	

Source: Statistical Bulletin International Financial Statistics

To conclude, due to a substantial devaluation of the CSK's NEER associated with a relatively modest increase in the domestic price level since the start of the transition, the implied exchange rate/PPP ratio decreased much less than in Hungary and Poland. Consequently, in comparative terms the CSK has continued to be undervalued at mid-1992.

2.4 Inflation Differential

Though the inflation record of Czechoslovakia has been relatively favourable in terms of transition economies, the inflation rate experienced was considerably above the "standard " of the European market economies, and is likely to remain so in the forthcoming period as well.

In 1992, the projected inflation rate was 12 - 15%. In reality CPI increased by 6.4% in January-September compared to end-December 1991, and by 10.4% compared to the same period of 1991.

The inflation rate in 1993 is expected again to be in the range of 12-15%. As in 1992, the main "culprits" are increases in still administered prices and institutional changes. While in 1992 those were increases in energy prices and in rents, the shift to VAT regime at the beginning of 1993 and some further increases of energy prices are expected to be the main factors inflating price level in 1993. The changeover to VAT alone is likely to increase the domestic price level by 7%. Moreover, it cannot be excluded that the forthcoming split of the federal state will generate some further inflationary pressures.

Given a "positive" inflation differential vis-a-vis countries of basket currencies which the CSK is pegged to at present, the trend towards a further appreciation of the REER of CSK will persist. It implies a gradual erosion of the gap between the current exchange rate and PPP of the CSK. In the past period, however, the competitiveness of the exchange rate was based on this particular gap.

Along with the impact of inflation differential, any revival of economic growth is to be expected to add pressures on balancing foreign exchange flows. Consequently, both the main factors which worked up to now for increasing current account surplus are then likely to subside or to disappear altogether. Czechoslovakia, though later on than Poland and Hungary, is thus to face the issue what type of foreign exchange rate strategy to adopt in coping with the challenges of competitiveness in the world markets and of balancing foreign exchange accounts.

Both Hungary and Poland have been recently adjusting their nominal exchange rate level to re-establish balance in external accounts.

In 1990, the Polish authorities fixed the nominal exchange rate of zloty as a part of stabilization package to fight existing hyper inflation. The peg was in reality maintained far beyond the pre-announced period, despite considerable deterioration of competitiveness and increasing balance of payments deficit. This development was criticized by some observers as an outright policy mistake.

The growing inflation differential induced ultimately the authorities to resort to repeated devaluations of zloty in 1991 and 1992, which were later on followed by adoption of a crawling peg system, implying continuous pre-announced depreciations of zloty vis-a-vis convertible currencies.

In the less inflationary environment, the Hungarian authorities coped with the ensuing price level differential via repeated discrete devaluations of forint. The policy followed, however, was not to correct for its entire extent, but to press the Hungarian firms for a gradual competitive adjustment.

3. EXCHANGE RATE REGIME OPTIONS

Despite a significant progress towards a market economy framework accomplished within a relatively short time span, the transition economies of Central Europe are still far from being homogenous enough to react sensitively to price and foreign exchange rate developments. It appears therefore justified to claim that given this "state of affairs" the impact of foreign exchange rate level and foreign exchange rate regime must be less significant compared to market economies. "In the dislocated economies of Eastern Europe, the exchange rate is far from the pervasive price that it is thought to be in the West...In other words, the exchange rate can hardly be relied upon to anchor an economy in which competition is limited, marketing nonexistent and communications appalling". (Fry, 1992).

On the other hand, however, just the transition makes the present stage of specific importance: the "code of behaviour" of newly created and restructured agents, including private and privatised firms, trade unions, and government authorities is being forged and "built in". The alternative options of exchange rate regime evidently differ in the requirements and signals sent to economic agents. And given that Czechoslovakia is a small economy, increasingly opened to the outside world, the impact of foreign exchange rate regime adopted at present is likely to co-determine the type of expectations and behaviour of economic agents at least in the medium run.

3.1 Changing Approaches in the Postwar World Economy

Neither the experience from the development of market economies nor the theory on optimal exchange rate systems can suggest an unambiguous answer what should be the foreign exchange rate regime for the transition economies. However, both the experience from elsewhere and theoretical writings on exchange rate systems, based in particular on the "optimal currency area" argument (Mundell, 1961; McKinnon 1964), do provide an useful guidance and lessons to be learnt.

Since World War Two quite differing options of exchange rate systems dominated in the successive stages of the world economy's development: adjustable peg system of the Bretton Woods' framework, implying relatively firmly fixed rates (except for the case of fundamental disequilibrium, Nurkse, 1945), was substituted by mostly floating rates of major currencies in 1970s. The 1980s saw a resurgence of interest in fixed exchange rate options and in international policy coordination, underlying the role of fixed exchange rates in the disinflation process. The disciplining arguments of fixed rates, along with the concepts of credibility and reputation, came to the fore with the revival of the ERM and EMS, and with the projects of EMU and common European currency in particular.

The mentioned stages and their regimes are often evaluated by the observers in an entirely opposite way: it can be argued that Bretton Woods' system functioned quite satisfactorily for a period, on the other hand it is stressed that it was doomed to collapse. Freely floating rates provided a solution at a time, deepening, however, undesirable volatility and misalignments in foreign exchange sphere and, consequently in the entire world economy. In a sense this concept failed in the same way as the Bretton Wood's arrangement. The controversial aspects of ERM and EMS became the hot political and economic issues quite recently.

The experience with the particular type of foreign exchange rate arrangement differs widely also across individual countries. In the case of currency pegs e.g., which is the arrangement relevant for small transition economies, Austria was quite successful in pegging the ATS to the basket and later on to the DEM for two decades, (Hochreiter E., Knobl A.,1991), while the experience of some other small economies was considerably less satisfactory. Finland, e.g. was recently induced to break the peg two times in the course of one year period (Leppanen S., 1992)

Summarizing the experience from the postwar developments in the world economy, two alternative strategies of the exchange rate policy can be distinguished:

(a) External Balance and Employment Oriented Concept of Exchange Rate

In this case the exchange rate is assigned the role of an instrument securing competitiveness of domestic industries on the world markets, working towards maintaining both employment and external balance of the given national economy. Its level is adjusted accordingly, either through floating or by discrete changes. This concept of exchange rate policy reflects the "conventional wisdom" which traditionally associates preservation of competitiveness with adjustments of the exchange rate itself, i.e. as a rule through (competitive) depreciation of the domestic currency.

(b) Stability oriented exchange rate concept

In this approach the exchange rate is expected to be an instrument contributing primarily towards stability and low inflation path of domestic development, and only via this also to external balance. This option, a "hard currency policy", implies a fixed exchange rate pegged to a stable currency. The disciplining and credibility effects of this type of foreign exchange rate regime, i.e. of a nominal anchor, should provide a basis for maintaining its competitive level vis-a-vis other countries.

The identified alternative regimes differ in their priorities and aims and, consequently, in their impact on behaviour and expectations of economic agents.

3.2 Arguments in the Choice of Exchange Rate Regime

Though the literature on optimum currency area cannot give any definite answer as for the concrete type of the foreign exchange regime (e.g. Wihlborg, C.G., Willett T.D., 1992), it does provide a number of relevant arguments and a guidance for the discussion of the issue.

It suggests that there is always a tradeoff between the macroeconomic advantages of flexible exchange rates and the microeconomic advantages of fixed rates. The relative costs and benefits of fixed versus flexible exchange rates vary across countries, depending on their size, structural and institutional characteristics, the nature and source of shocks they face, their objectives and current economic situation. Other dimensions given, the case for a fixed exchange rate regime in a transition economy is evidently much stronger for a smaller country with a higher share of export and import flows on its economic activity. (In an extreme case, with only a few non-traded goods and services, the impact of exchange rate changes would be more or less confined to the changes in domestic price level).

3.3 The Case for "Simple Rules" or "Managed" Type of Exchange Rates?

As more objectives are as a rule aimed at in contemporary economies, with different weights attached to them across countries and periods, and given the existence of various shocks, external as well as domestic, the "simple rule" solution of exchange rate appears to be not smoothly applicable. The experience also suggests that exchange rates tend to be mostly -more or less- managed in the present world economy.

The "simple rule" alternative comprises two extreme options: freely floating rate and firmly fixed rate. After the collapse of the gold standard there were only a few cases of entirely fixed rates in the long run, while on the other hand free float was also mostly confined to several episodes.

In the conditions of transition economies:

a) The Free Float Option was sometimes suggested as a reasonable approach to establish a proper initial value of the currency after the breakdown of the former centrally planned economy framework.

There are, however, severe constraints on its potential merits in the environment of the transition economies: a rather thin currency markets, underdeveloped institutions, lack of forward foreign exchange markets and of short term "arbitrage" and speculative capital flows which could under certain conditions work towards stabilizing the exchange rate (Williamson J., 1991). Consequently, the extent of misalignments and exchange rate volatility would be evidently much greater than in consolidated market economies of a similar type. And even in those stabilized economies the experience with free float was not particularly encouraging. This type of solution seems therefore disqualified for the environment and objectives aimed at in Czechoslovakia.

b) Irrevocably Fixed Exchange Rates

The comparison with developed open market economies seems again to suggest non-viability of this solution for transition economies. Given the profound changes, including institutional, uncertainties and shocks involved in the transition process, it appears unrealistic to attempt to fix an "equilibrium rate" for the long term. Moreover, apart from the issue at what level to set the original fixing, even more controversial appears to make the adopted rate reasonably sustainable in the long run, without inflicting unbearable costs on the economy.

It follows, neither free float nor irreversibly fixed rate options seem to be realistic for transition economies, however attractive the simple rule approach might be given too many complexities involved in the transition. Some type of a compromise "managed" solution, involving more or less of discretion, appears therefore the justified way out.

3.4 The "Managed" Option as Applied in Transition Economies

In Czechoslovakia, a version of adjustable peg system seems to be applied. While maintaining a fixed rate pegged to the basket, the authorities made no commitments as to its duration, not excluding thus its possible adjustment.

In Hungary the solution has been developing along the parallel lines. Discrete adjustments of forint's exchange rate effected aimed at keeping the real rate more or less stabilised.

In the Polish case on the other hand, a crawling peg system was adopted in 1992 to cope with the inflation differential.

A crawling peg implies that the exchange rate is adjusted by small changes at regular intervals (daily, weekly or monthly); in the case of Polish zloty daily base was chosen. The apparent advantage of this type of solution is to avoid abrupt changes in the exchange rate's level, which has certainly some merits in the still relatively inflationary Polish economy. On the other hand, there is an implied danger of embedded inflationary expectations. The crawling peg arrangement may then turn to be an additional source of inflation differential rather than the way of coping with it.

Though in a different way, the" managed" alternatives of exchange rates in Hungary and Poland recently tended by and large to adjust for the differences in relative price performance vis-a-vis their partners. The policy was thus - at least to some extent- developing along the real exchange rate anchor concept, suggested for transition economies by M. Nuti (1991) and Fry and Nuti (1992).

The concept of real exchange rate anchor has certainly some advantages, given the environment of transition economies with "positive" inflation differential. It tends to provide relatively stabilized conditions vis-a-vis the outside world for investors and traders, which may positively affect their activities and expectations. Assuming that the starting point is chosen correctly, it could be expected to yield a medium-term balanced current account.

However, there are some constraints implied as well. Data on price level developments are available with some lags only. Applying them means that real exchange rate is only ex post accommodating the price differential, without exercising any disciplining effect on economic agents. To establish instead real "anchor" ex ante would require some kind of forecasted or targeted data on relative inflation rates, which is by itself open to a considerable margin of misassessment.

To conclude, managed type exchange rates appear the only feasible alternative for the transition economies. The policy of a stabilized real rate, while accommodating for ensuing inflation differential, is likely to work towards balancing foreign exchange accounts and at the same time to provide a stable parameter in real terms for investment and trade activities with respect to the outside.

On the other hand, however, this type of solution is not particularly helpful to restructuring in microsphere and to exercising disciplining role on the behaviour and performance of economic agents. Without doubt, just these microeconomic dimensions are of the key importance, conditioning in fact any economic recovery and revival of sustainable growth in transition economies. Are there other options of foreign exchange rate regime which could be more conducive in this respect without, however, imposing intolerable macroeconomic costs? Under what conditions?

4. STRUCTURAL DEFECT OF CZECHOSLOVAK EXPORTS AND "SOFT" EXCHANGE RATE REGIME

As discussed in section 2, a common feature of the former centrally planned economies, including Czechoslovakia, was a wide gap between the domestic and external values of their currencies.[7] The mentioned disparity was due not only to technical and technological gaps with respect to developed market economies as elsewhere, but also due to the institutional, systemic and policy peculiarities of centrally planned economies.

4.1 Legacy of the Centrally Planned Economy

Czechoslovakia (Czech lands in particular) belonged to the top ten industrial countries before World War II and in the early postwar period. Since then it lost its position in a dramatic way. The gap is particularly large in manufacturing branches, where the productivity level is estimated only at 25-30% of the German standard.

The manifold reasons behind this rather unfavourable trend have a common denominator in almost" perfect" shelter provided to enterprises both domestically, by centrally planned economy framework, and at the same time also from the outside, by CMEA institutions[8].

As a consequence, Czechoslovak manufacturing firms did not experience for decades any real competitive pressure, neither domestically nor from the world markets. Along with the resulting gap in technical and quality standards, their products were loosing western markets and/or experiencing relatively declining prices because of lack of marketing, distribution networks, business contacts and expertise, deficient financial, payment,

[7]The existence of such a gap itself is hardly an exceptional case in the world economy. The countries at a relatively lower level of development inevitably face productivity and efficiency gaps with respect to their more developed partners. B. Balassa developed an argument on "productivity Bias" to PPP, implying that divergent productivity levels lead to systematic trend deviations from PPP (Balassa B., 1964). Nonetheless, the extent of the mentioned gap in the case of the former centrally planned economies tended to be significantly wider than in other countries at a similar level of development.

[8]Czechoslovakia maintained second largest share of CMEA trade among the CMEA members and, unlike Hungary and Poland started to reallocate only in the beginning of 1990s. The detrimental impact of CMEA "shelter" was thus rather high also in comparative terms.

insurance, telecommunication infrastructure and services. These flaws appeared even more detrimental to the competitiveness of the Czechoslovak manufacturing products than their technical and technological shortcomings alone.

According to a survey, exports to market economies did not in 342 cases (of a total of 866 surveyed firms, i.e. in almost 40 per cent) exceed 1 per cent of their total deliveries (Kolanda, Kubista, 1990). This implies that four out of every ten firms had almost no contact with world markets and had no grasp of what real competition actually meant and required.

The phenomena, which were developing under the given institutional and incentive framework, would be entirely paradoxical within the logic of an open market economy:

(i) Various industries and branches as well as individual firms could go on extending their activities at a widely differentiated efficiency level in terms of world markets' criteria. The cases of entire branches with negative value added at world market prices were not exceptional ones (Hare P, Hughes g., 1991). Moreover, the implied concept of "balanced" development required the disposable resources (capital, labour, imports) to be channeled to the arising "bottlenecks", i.e. mostly to the least efficient branches and firms instead, as could be expected, to the prospective ones.

(ii) The relative efficiency of individual firms within the same industry, i.e. under the same institutional and incentive regime, was estimated to be dispersed up to 10 times more compared to the standard of the developed market economies (Kolanda M., 1989).

As the "soft budget constraint" was claimed responsible (Kornai J.,1986), its important component was "soft" exchange rate regime. The implied exchange ratio adjusted ex-post in a freely floating way, without exercising any significant impact on the behaviour of domestic firms.

(iii) The number of manufacturing stages was as a rule negatively correlated with the profitability of sales in world markets. It means,the higher the level of processing, the lower appeared the gains from trade.[9]

---

[9]However anecdotal it may strike, exporting furniture appeared as a rule less favourable than prefabricated parts, these intermediate products were in turn less profitable than timber, and timber less profitable than selling just trees.

This paradox in the terms of a manufacturing economy (which was, however, not confined to Czechoslovakia only) can be explained as a cumulative impact of both "real" and " valuation" factors:

- an increasing gap in productivity, technical and quality standards with respect to the competitors,

- depressed prices of Czechoslovak manufactures in the world markets because of marketing and institutional flaws,

- biased ratios of foreign to domestic prices due to the deficiencies of domestic price setting (not reflecting e.g. land rent), and due to the distortive impact of applied tax and subsidies schemes.

Consequently, the various effectiveness criteria based on ratios of foreign and domestic prices, introduced as an innovative instrument "to enhance the efficiency", provided a rather unreliable and biased information.

The above conditions and institutional peculiarities of the centrally planned economy framework resulted in Czechoslovakia's long-run declining share of the world's exports coupled with the increasing replacement of higher value-added products by lower value-added ones, such as raw materials, intermediate products and standard consumer goods in its exports to the convertible currency markets.

In the period 1975-1989 the Czechoslovak share of imports of OECD countries fell from 0.28% to 0.18%. Its share of machinery imports fell even more drastically, from 0.21% to 0.07% (Data: OECD Trade Statistics).

Simultaneously, a tendency toward a "dual" structure of export flows to the former "socialist" and developed market economies became increasingly pronounced. Manufactures (SITC 6-8) accounted for 87% of exports to former socialist countries in 1990, but for only 66% in exports to market economies (Data: Facts on Czechoslovak Foreign Trade, 1991).

This legacy inevitably affected the initial conditions for transition and, consequently, constrained the rationality of conventional policy schemes and instruments.

4.2 Trade and Balance of Payments in the Transition Period

The previous inertia of both the domestic and external environments ended abruptly at the beginning of 1990s. The impact of external shocks[10] interacted with institutional changes initiated in the domestic economy and with a parallel severe contraction of domestic demand.

a) **The volume of foreign trade** decreased in absolute terms throughout the transition period, thus accelerating a long term decline in Czechoslovakia's shares of world markets. Between 1989 and 1991 its share of world exports dropped from 0.46% to 0.33%.

In 1991 imports were 20% lower than in 1990 (reflecting a deep domestic recession), while exports declined by 7%, recovering in the second half of the year. The level of exports remained stabilized in the first half of 1992 compared to the same period of 1991 (index 99.2), while imports continued to decrease (index 87.8). A certain reversal of this trend, i.e. a recovery of imports is, however, likely to take place in the second half of the year.

b) **Changes in the territorial distribution of Czechoslovak trade:** Whereas up to 1989 the share of former centrally planned economies was dominant in Czechoslovak foreign trade, substantial shifts have subsequently taken place (table 5).

c) **Changes in Commodity Composition of Czechoslovak Trade**

Discontinuities experienced in both the domestic and external environment affected substantially the commodity composition of trade flows in 1989-1992.

According to the data in table 6, the implied changes in the export pattern (as reflected in the aggregate product groups) were unfavourable: the trend towards an increasing share for raw materials and intermediate products in Czechoslovak exports became even more pronounced.

[10]According to M. Landesmann, the CSFR may have been hardest hit by the trade shocks (due to the collapse of CMEA trade and institutions in particular) of all the Central and East European countries (Landesmann, M., 1991).

Table 5

Territorial distribution of Czechoslovak trade
(per cent shares, derived from values in CSK, current prices and foreign exchange rates)

	Exports				Imports			
	1989	1990	1991	1992+	1989	1990	1991	1992+
Former CPEs	60.8	49.0	39.3	23.8	62.3	51.2	42.8	40.2
former CME	54.9	43.4	32.8	23.4	56.1	44.4	39.5	37.8
former USSR	30.5	25.2	19.4	9.4	29.7	21.6	31.8	31.0
Market economies	39.2	51.0	60.6	76.2	37.7	48.8	57.1	59.8
Developed	31.2	42.4	51.9	65.0	31.1	42.6	48.9	54.2
EC	18.2	26.5	40.7	50.6	17.8	23.8	33.0	38.5
Developing	8.0	8.6	8.7	11.2	6.6	6.2	8.2	5.6

+ First half of 1992, Source: Facts on Czechoslovak foreign trade

Table 6

Product Composition of the Czechoslovak Foreign Trade
(per cent shares, SITC classification)

	Exports			Imports		
	1989	1991	1992+	1989	1991	1992+
Food and beverages (0+1)	5.0	8.6	7.7	7.6	6.9	7.6
Crude materials, excluding fuels (2+4)	3.8	5.5	6.7	9.1	9.5	7.7
Fuels (3)	5.2	4.2	4.2	17.3	29.8	29.1
Chemicals (5)	7.6	10.6	10.7	9.3	9.8	10.3
Products classified according to the material (6)	23.4	30.4	37.6	10.4	9.0	8.8
Machinery and transport (7)	44.4	27.9	21.3	37.0	28.1	28.7
Manufactures (8)	9.7	12.7	11.7	6.2	7.0	7.7

+ First half of 1992
Source: Facts on Czechoslovak foreign trade Bulletin, Federal Statistical Office, Prague

According to the data in table 6, the share of relatively higher value-added products in total exports continued to decrease between 1989 and 1992. In particular, the share of machinery & transport equipment (SITC 7) decreased dramatically in the mentioned period: from 44.4% in 1989 to 27.9% in 1991 and to mere 21.3% in the first half of 1992.

On the other hand, the role of raw materials, intermediate products and foodstuffs in total exports kept increasing.

Assuming that the SITC groups 2 - 6 represent raw materials, materials and intermediary products (which mostly applies in the Czechoslovak case), the ratios in export pattern developed as follows:

	Foodstuffs : (SITC 0+1)	Materials : (SITC 2-6)	Finished manufactures (SITC 7+8)
1989	5.0 :	40.1 :	54.1
1991	8.6 :	51.8 :	40.6
1992+	7.7 :	59.4 :	33.0

It may be argued that the recent shift to a higher share of raw materials and intermediary products in total exports only reflects legacy of the "dual" structure of Czechoslovak trade in the past. As the role of lower value-added products was higher in the trade with market economies, given the materialized substantial reallocation of exports to them, the share of materials and intermediary products in total exports was likely to increase accordingly.

It is true that the collapse of CMEA trade, with the former USSR in particular, was the main cause of the mentioned dramatically decreasing share of machinery and transport equipment in total exports. Its increasing role in exports to market economies in 1990-91 (the share of SITC 7 on exports to the EC countries increased from 13.9% in 1989 to 18.1% in 1991) couldn't by far compensate for the losses in CMEA markets.

This is, however, not the whole story. First, despite some increase in the share of finished manufactures (SITC 7+8) in exports to market economies in 1990-91, their relative role remained rather low. Second, the data for the first half of 1992 indicate again decrease in their share compared to 1991 (SITC 7 by 1.2%, SITC 8 by 1.4%).

The shifts in the composition of imports were not particularly encouraging either, when viewed from the point of the future prospects. In imports from both the EC and EFTA countries the share of machinery imports diminished while that of foodstuffs and consumer goods increased in the first half of 1992 compared to 1991.

d) Balance of Payments

Unlike the volume of trade flows, the current account balance in convertible currencies has recovered after a sharp deterioration in 1990, with surpluses steadily increasing in the course of 1991 and the first half of 1992 as well. Correspondingly, the foreign exchange reserves also recovered and reached the highest level in the entire postwar period.

Compared to the past when merchandise trade flows were dominant, a tendency to an increased share of various services, tourist trade and income transfers was clearly surfacing and contributing to favourable changes in the current account (compare table 7). While trade balance is likely to deteriorate once the domestic recovery will be under way, the surplus on non-trade flows can be expected to continue to balance current account at least for some time ahead.

Table 7

Balance of payments in convertible currencies
(in USD million)

	1989	1990	1991	1992+
Current account	439	-1105	356.5	826.3
Trade balance	419	- 785	-447.4	188.4
Service balance	218	37	827.4	432.9
Income balance	-163	- 316	- 65.4	111.5
Transfers	- 35	- 40	41.8	93.5
Capital account	326	326	47.0	- 53.6
Direct foreign investment	256	181	592.4	442.6
Other long term capital	- 53	718	1731.7	520.0
Short term capital	123	-573	-2277.1	-1021.4
Errors and omissions	-197	-324	494.4	28.0
Changes in reserves (increase = -)	-569	1102	-897.9	-800.0

+ first half of 1992 Source: State Bank of Czechoslovakia

4.3 The Case for an Export-Led Recovery?

In the Czechoslovak case, the inflation and balance of payments records were certainly two domains where the results achieved in the course of transition were highly satisfactory.

In the trade sphere, a major reorientation of trade towards the OECD area (to the EC countries in particular) has been accomplished, with exports to OECD rising in 1990 and 1991 by 18% and 35% respectively. Since 1991 export demand and export flows have been developing more favourably than domestic sales, contributing thus to lessen the implied fall in the GDP.

Viewing from the demand side, the recovery of transition economies could be fostered either through the expansion of domestic demand components or through expanding foreign demand. While the possibilities of an across-the-board promotion of domestic demand appear to be rather constrained under the current terms, the prospects of foreign demand expansion seem to be more promising. In the case of Czechoslovakia there is certainly a scope for revival of trade in the area, with neighbouring Hungary and Poland in particular. At the same time there are still unused opportunities to expand also " non-sensitive" exports to the OECD area, especially when the present recession in the main OECD countries is over.

It follows, a continuation of the recent trends towards an export surplus, developing into a type of export-led recovery might be a feasible way out from the current structural depression.

This proposition appears, however, disqualified by standard macroeconomic reasoning. The macroeconomic identities suggest that the export-led recovery implies "by definition" exports of domestic savings. As the transition economies seem to be clear examples of capital deficiency, just the opposite trend, i.e. a net inflow of foreign savings is considered desirable.

The static and dynamic considerations of the issue should be, however, distinguished. It could be argued that

- under the given constraints for domestic demand promotion, an increasing export demand would be a feasible way to unleash domestic investment, generating then increasing domestic savings. The point is that the recovery of development would be made sustainable only providing a domestic investment-saving mechanism is set into motion,

- an export surplus signals a trend toward a strong and a stabilized currency. This would contribute to policy credibility and to a changing expectations of both domestic and foreign investors. Just this change in expectations appears to be crucial for the reversal of present economic downturn. Otherwise, any promotion of aggregate demand is likely to be mostly translated into import and price increases.

It may also be argued that the real impact of relevant macro-variables is conditioned by their composition, which is not, however, identifiable in the terms of macroeconomic identities. As follows from table 7, the recent surpluses on current account were in the Czechoslovak case matched by re-payment of short-term bank liabilities, apart from an increase of foreign exchange reserves. At the same time, an increasing inflow of long-term capital, of FDI in particular, outweighed the surplus on current account. A net increase of savings "earmarked" for productive use could thus be achieved, despite current account surplus.

4.3. "Wrong" Type of Exports ?

The developmental impact of export surplus appears, however, in reality rather "devalued" due to its composition. As discussed in section 2, Czechoslovak exports to the world markets were increasingly shifted towards relatively lower value-added products. This trend got momentum particularly since early seventies, under the re-imposed centrally planned economy framework; it went on, however, in the course of transition as well.

As shown by a recent study, (Bohata M., Fischer M, 1992), in the falling export volume of 1990 and 1991 the stabilized and even increasing exports were those of iron-metallurgy and of basic chemicals. It was so, despite their rather high energy and material inputs, supply of which, moreover, was subject to increasing uncertainties and constraints.

These industries were also at the top in relative export performance expressed as the volume of exports per employee and/or firm.

Table 8
The Relative Export Performance of Selected Industries in 1991

Industry	Average export performance	
	a) per enterprise (mill CSK)	b) per employee ('000 CSK)
Iron-metallurgy	1962.8	272.1
Chemical ind.	466.9	255.1
Engineering	189.2	121.9
Electrotechnics	75.3	63.0
Glass and porcelain	179.7	144.5
Shoe and leather	352.6	126.9

Source: Bohata M., Fischer M.,1992

4.3.1 The Role Of Foreign Exchange Rate Regime

As discussed above, the long-run trend towards less value-added composition of Czechoslovak export flows appears to continue and even to deepen in the recent period. While certain inertia from the past could be predicted, the policies adopted seem to further strengthen the inherited structural defect.

The strategy followed in the trade sphere initially relied almost entirely on the exchange rate adjustment only, leaving aside policies of export promotion, the instruments of commercial and industrial policies in particular. The reasoning behind was to put everybody on "equal footing" and to avoid any "administrative" interference in the production and trade patterns.

The three consecutive devaluations of CSK in 1990 were effected in accordance with this reasoning; they aimed at creating conditions for sustainable trade liberalization and limited currency convertibility via providing a "flat" basis for export expansion.

The devaluation-type approach is expected to lead to an improvement in price and cost competitiveness, given satisfactory price elasticity and provided that the effects of devaluation are not quickly eroded by the follow-up increases in incomes.

Apart from the qualification that these conditions need not be apriori satisfied, the export stimulus of devaluation applies to those items where the cost and price dimensions of competition are substantial, if not dominant. The non-price factors on the other hand tend to be more important with non-homogeneous products, more sophisticated and higher value-added ones, where goodwill, reliability, advertising and marketing, prompt delivery, after-sales service and meeting of individualised customer demands are crucial.

This qualification to the devaluation's export stimulus appears to be highly relevant in the conditions of transition economies. The legacy of the past development and the rigidities of the existing markets, of labour and financial markets in particular, severely constrain reallocation of resources and supply response to the changing price and exchange rate ratios. Even more important, the lack of the established contacts with the world markets, lack of distribution networks, underdeveloped marketing and deficient related services substantially diminishes the impact of price advantages implied in devaluation, in particular in the sphere of non-homogeneous, higher value-added products.

Consequently, as could be expected, the response to the devaluations effected in Czechoslovakia in 1990 was in the short-run rather unequal across individual branches. As a rule, with some notable exceptions, raw materials, intermediary products and construction materials could find new exports markets relatively more easily.[11]

The ensuing shifts in the export pattern have evidently contributed to the divergent performance record of individual industries. Those hardest hit by the present recession are mostly manufacturing ones, while in heavy industry branches the drop experienced was only modest. The energy and fuel industries could even maintain the former level of their output.

4.3.2 Short Term Gains Versus Medium- and Long-Term Costs of the Devaluation Type Approach

Under the environment created by the devaluations at the start of transition, the implied comparative advantages of Czechoslovak exporters

---

[11]An export "boom" in steel and rolled material on the EC markets already led to countermeasures by the EC countries, involving anti-dumping procedure.

were increasingly based on cost advantages, conditioned particularly by the depreciated labour costs in foreign exchange terms.[12]

The impact of this type of development appears rather controversial. To its credit could be claimed that it secured

(i) trade balance and current account surplus in the conditions when
- internal convertibility on current account and trade liberalization were implemented,
- foreign exchange reserves were rather low,
- sustained export-growth to convertible-currency markets was crucial in order to offset at least partially the sharp contraction of trade to the former CMEA,

(ii) more attractive conditions for foreign investors who were ready to exploit the opportunities provided by low labour costs (particularly since the labour force is relatively well educated and qualified), along with prospective capital gains.

On the other hand, however, the implied consequences in the medium- and long-run are hardly favourable:

(i) data on recent trends seem to confirm that the incentives derived from an undervalued currency and "cheap labour" fostered a further shift towards lower value-added branches, and within branches to relatively less sophisticated products, accentuating thus long-run trends to "regressive specialization",

(ii) the negative implications of moving to lower value-added products include the risk of
- a brain-drain and of an increasing gap from the technological standards in the world economy. By contrast, the successful examples of revitalization elsewhere were based on the narrowing of the mentioned gap,
- an increasing cost disadvantage compared to the parallel products of low-income countries, as well as the risk of continued clashes of interest in the "sensitive sectors" with the EC countries,[13]

---

[12] Though the former rather equalized level of wages and salaries began to differentiate substantially in the recent period, the "average" wage of a qualified worker - when expressed in foreign exchange terms - still amounted to less than UDS 200 per month at the beginning of 1992, a rather low level among comparable countries of Western Europe and, apparently even lower than in neighboring Hungary and Poland.

[13] Their share was estimated over 50% of total Czechoslovak exports to the EC markets in 1990, including agricultural products 8.1%, textiles 11.5%, iron and steel 16.3%, coal 2.5%, products with tariff ceilings and quotas 19.2% (Rollo, 1992).

(iii) in the conditions of transition economies the "soft" exchange rate regime is particularly prone to contribute to the vicious circles of devaluation, inflation and moving down on the value-added vertical, as :

- to reverse inertia of the past trends, enterprises must be induced to make all possible effort to innovate, to develop and to market new products of a higher quality and technical standard, to catch up in the marketing and sale-services. As they were accustomed to rely more on the "outside" help and ex-post corrections in the rules rather than on their own internal adjustment, "devaluation type" policies in fact provide for a continuation in the "traditional" behaviour pattern and expectations,
- given the underdeveloped financial and labour markets and existing institutional rigidities, there is an implied inertia in the "given" allocation of resources. While in the past the preferences were mostly given to heavy industry branches, the devaluation-type policies gave a further impetus to their comparatively high "profitability" and "export orientation". As a result, a biased picture of comparative advantages, favouring material and energy intensive branches, is being built into the resource allocation.

A conclusion follows, that the "devaluation-type" approach was able to secure competitiveness of the Czechoslovak exports in the short-run. At the same time, however, due both to the type of signals to economic agents and to the generated pattern of resource allocation it worked in fact against their competitiveness in the medium- and long-run.

5. AN ALTERNATIVE EXCHANGE RATE REGIME FOR CZECHOSLOVAKIA ?

The main challenge of the Czechoslovakia's development in the medium run is to reverse the downgrading trends of its production and export structures which dominated in the past period. Increasing share of low value-added branches and products produced and traded depressed the economic potential of the country relative to the outside world, constraining the scope for productivity increases. Consequently, real incomes were doomed to fall in relative terms, which really materialized in the long-run.

If this trend continues in the medium and long run, a kind of vicious circle is likely to develop. Under the terms of an open economy, the increasing productivity gap with respect to the trade partners would further diminish gains from trade and feed in repeated waves of inflation and devaluations. Such an outcome, widening - instead of narrowing- productivity and income gaps, would imply a further peripherization of Czechoslovakia, and not only in the European terms.

Instead, any sustained recovery and revival of economic growth requires moving upwards on the value added vertical. As argued in section 4, devaluation type policies do not seem to be particularly helpful in that respect, especially under the Czechoslovak conditions. In particular, they are not capable to correct for the legacy of the past, neither in the behaviour pattern and expectations of economic agents, nor for the defected production and export structures.

5.1 Policies to Cope With Microeconomic and Structural Defects

An alternative to exchange rate policies accommodating ex post to domestic cost and price increases via repeated devaluations, is the " hard currency" option. It implies nominal exchange rate being a policy target. Its most demanding version is an irrevocably fixed nominal rate, pegged to a low-inflation "pilot" national or composite (ECU) currency.

The main argument for such an approach of fixing nominal exchange rate is the traditional one: disciplining effects on economic agents. In the case of Czechoslovakia, these effects should contribute to the desirable entire overhaul and re-orientation of their behaviour pattern and expectations. It does not follow, however, the nominal exchange rate anchor could be powerful enough to effect "the job"; other instruments must be applied in a consistent and comprehensive way to make the regime change in the microsphere effective (Portes R.,1990).

Once the policy of nominal exchange rate target is made credible (i.e. after the authorities passed several "tests" of their policies and proceeded differently from what could be otherwise expected), and the enterprises learned that they could not rely any more on "traditional" depreciation of domestic currency as a way out from re-appearing pressures of inflating domestic costs, the microeconomic advantages of the fixed exchange rate approach should begin to materialize. The experience from elsewhere, notably e.g. from Austrian development seems to support this assumption (Marin D.,1985).

In the Czechoslovak conditions, a wide margin for productivity increases is available, provided the changed regime and re-oriented incentives and expectations begin to bite. As a legacy of the past, there is an accumulated potential of efficiency gains in the existing wasteful methods of using inputs and equipment, "organizational slack", overstaffing, outmoded routines. Even more important are potential gains in a dynamic setting, as the centralized framework failed particularly in introduction of new products and technologies.

Along with the microeconomic impact, the policies adopted should be capable to cope with the structural defects of the Czechoslovak economy. As argued in section 4, rather unequal starting conditions across branches and industries resulted from the past development. Consequently, the policy only relying on unified exchange rate and its changes, aiming at "equal footing", works in reality in a discriminatory way. It favours as a rule in the past preferred heavy industry branches, at the cost of most manufacturing ones.

To correct for this and to achieve a real "leveling of the grounds" would require a transitional arrangement, combining exchange rate policies with promotion schemes for those "disfavoured", i.e. for industries with a higher value-added products.

Consequently, there seems to be a legitimate case for such forms of "industrial policies" which - not attempting to pick up winners and losers - would contribute to the development of infrastructure, telecommunications, business, trade and banking services, to the increased mobility of labour and to upgrading of human capital. The flaws just in these spheres placed firms in sophisticated manufacturing branches to rather less favourable conditions with respect to both the foreign competitors and the domestic producers of basic, low value-added products as well.

In a parallel way, the export promotion schemes appear to be warranted to correct for the implied disadvantages of domestic exporters of higher value-added products. These schemes should:

- enable to carry the costs of export reallocation and of penetration of world markets (the extra cost of developing marketing, goodwill, distributional networks, the additional risk implied), and

- provide a "breathing space" for adjustment and restructuring to those which are likely to be viable producers and exporters in the medium run.

These arguments, developing along an infant industry reasoning and which could be baptized " revitalizing industries" arguments given their prior existence in the Czechoslovak case, appear to be fairly powerful ones. They could be claimed necessary to resort to, if the implied, mostly from the centrally planned economy inherited, disadvantages of branches and products where the non-price factors of competition dominate, are to be corrected within a reasonable "transitory" period.

There are, of course, well-known qualifications and difficulties with the infant-industry argument for protection (Baldwin R., 1969; Hillman A.L., 1991). In the context of transition economies, several issues appear to be especially relevant:

- is the protection once extended likely to remain only temporary,
- as the whole manufacturing sector cannot be protected to revitalize, the selection implies moral hazard problem,
- even if temporary only, protection incurs costs,
- infant protection may more or less eliminate foreign competition which, given the absence of workable domestic competition, is only capable to provide effective incentives for restructuring. The " revitalizing" protection may work just opposite to the hoped-for disciplining effects of fixed exchange rate.

5.2 The Potential Role of Foreign Competition

It is true, in the transition scenarios the incentive and disciplining impact of foreign competition was attributed key role in developing competitive environment. It was recognized that the reforming countries of Central and Eastern Europe, unlike e.g. Japan, cannot rely on "workable" and "contestable" competition to be created within the domestic economy only.

However persuasive and unambiguous this claim may appear, the "revitalizing" impacts of foreign competition on domestic firms turned to be in the Czechoslovak case up to now far from expectations and, moreover, controversial ones (Hrncir M.,1992). 1992.

It may be claimed that among the main reasons behind were the adopted policies, relying on "non-discriminatory" exchange rate's changes only, in the inherently unequal conditions for individual industries and branches.

At the start of the transition, the substantial devaluations effectively eliminated foreign competition to most industries. The exceptions were only the least efficient ones, including Czechoslovak consumer electronics, which for the most part could not survive the competitive pressure even at a rather depreciated exchange rate.

In the existing conditions, a dilemma is faced. On the one hand, a more intensive impact of foreign competition would be highly desirable as a driving force for restructuring of domestic firms. On the other hand, however, any profound flat increase in exposure to foreign competition is likely to threaten the very existence of sophisticated, relatively higher value-added branches, while leaving mostly unaffected material- and energy-intensive basic industries.

Unlike the policies adopted at the start of transition, the strategy combining fixed exchange rate target concept with the schemes of industrial and export promotion policies could also allow for a more intensive role of foreign competition.

Under the hard currency approach, the pressure of foreign competition would tend to squeeze the profits across all industries. Contrary to the past, however, the support via industrial policy and export promotion scheme would compensate

However persuasive and unambiguous this claim may appear, the "revitalizing" impacts of foreign competition on domestic firms turned to be in the Czechoslovak case up to now far from expectations and, moreover, controversial ones (Hrncir M.,1992). 1992.

It may be claimed that among the main reasons behind were the adopted policies, relying on "non-discriminatory" exchange rate's changes only, in the inherently unequal conditions for individual industries and branches.

At the start of the transition, the substantial devaluations effectively eliminated foreign competition to most industries. The exceptions were only the least efficient ones, including Czechoslovak consumer electronics, which for the most part could not survive the competitive pressure even at a rather depreciated exchange rate.

In the existing conditions, a dilemma is faced. On the one hand, a more intensive impact of foreign competition would be highly desirable as a driving force for restructuring of domestic firms. On the other hand, however, any profound flat increase in exposure to foreign competition is likely to threaten the very existence of sophisticated, relatively higher value-added branches, while leaving mostly unaffected material- and energy-intensive basic industries.

Unlike the policies adopted at the start of transition, the strategy combining fixed exchange rate target concept with the schemes of industrial and export promotion policies could also allow for a more intensive role of foreign competition.

Under the hard currency approach, the pressure of foreign competition would tend to squeeze the profits across all industries. Contrary to the past, however, the support via industrial policy and export promotion scheme would compensate manufacturing branches for their relative disadvantages, enabling to those viable in the medium run to survive and to expand.

The export promotion schemes, oriented on the higher value-added branches, should be based on ex-ante established rules to avoid administrative discretion and moral hazard problem as much as possible: the support is extended only to those who qualify. The experience from elsewhere (including Far-East Asian countries) suggests the feasibility of such schemes, rewarding volume and/or increasing rates of export sales. Unlike in the past, in this type of promotion schemes the support is oriented on the relatively successful and prospective ones. Consequently, the success in keeping it as a temporary device only is more likely.

To conclude: while the case for an unified exchange rate to be preferred to commercial policy measures holds as a general proposition, under the given distorted conditions a transitory "corrective" departure appears to be desirable. Along the parallel reasoning McKinnon argued for "cascading" tariffs rather than a lower exchange rate (McKinnon, 1991).

5.3 Conditions for Fixed Exchange Rate Regime to be Viable

The microeconomic advantages of the fixed nominal exchange rate policy must be, however, compared with the macroeconomic constraints and costs implied. However attractive its disciplining and behaviour effects might be in the environment of transition economies, it does not follow that the "hard currency" policy of fixed exchange rate could be reasonably resorted to at any conditions and at any time. It would be neither viable nor sensible, if its costs in terms of lost output, increased unemployment and social hardship were likely to outweigh microeconomic and structural benefits.

In the postwar period, a number of European economies (e.g. Nordic countries) adopted a different strategy: promoting macro-economic developments via low interest rates, while repeated adjustments of exchange rates were used to accommodate for domestic costs pressures and to re-establish strong competitive position. And only at a more mature and stabilized phase they mostly shifted to the policy of fixed rates.

If in a "strict" version, i.e. when irrevocably fixed, exchange rate is "lost" as a policy instrument. It implies, the other instruments must be used, and must be capable of securing competitiveness.

In the medium- and long run, maintaining competitiveness is an issue of fundamentals, they must converge with those of the anchor currency's country (countries). At the same time, however, cyclical changes and various external and domestic shocks are arising in the course of time which must be accommodated as well. It follows, the policy of fixed exchange rate is highly demanding on the mechanisms of domestic adjustment: they must be sufficiently effective and flexible both as for the trend and short-run developments.

When assessing the chances of fixed exchange rate policy in a transition economy, what matters most is the potential development of the real rate. Providing that the prospective inflation differential with respect to the anchor country would be either zero or negative, the given nominal exchange rate is likely to be sustained.

The changes in the real exchange rate are related to change in nominal exchange rate and to relative changes in wage levels, in profit rate and in productivity with respect to the anchor countries. The key variable appears to be relative change in productivity. If favourable, i.e. higher or at least matching the increases in the partner countries, wages and profits may rise accordingly, without causing real rate appreciation. This type of favourable constellation materialized e.g. in the postwar Germany. It may be also a challenge for transition economies: could they use the chance of starting at a rather low level and to achieve relatively higher productivity increases while catching up?

The structural and institutional properties of the given economy are evidently decisive in this respect, in particular the degree of effectiveness and flexibility in the functioning of labour and financial markets. It matters whether the disposable savings are increasingly channeled to the "right" users. In a parallel way, a flexible functioning of the labour market is apparently crucial, if the competitiveness is to be maintained via domestic adjustments instead of nominal exchange rate changes. The positive experience of social corporatism and voluntary incomes policies in a number of small European economies at earlier stage of their development could be a good example to follow in the Czechoslovak case (Pekkarinen J., Pohjola M., Rowthorn B., 1992).

However, even with appreciating real exchange rate the given nominal rate could be successfully maintained, provided counterbalancing effects of the improving non-price factors of competition. Particularly these effects are hoped-for to result from the hard currency policy, in the Czechoslovak conditions they would be of vital importance. The Austrian example suggests their feasibility: "Austria has increased her real market share in the OECD area from 0.9 percent in 1970 to 1.08 percent in 1980. This 20 percent increase in Austrian market share took place despite a 18 percent revaluation of the real exchange rate of the schilling vis-a-vis her trading partners in the same period" (Marin D., 1985, p.479)

5.4 In Conclusion

However unrealistic the fixed exchange rate regime may appear under the present conditions of the transition economies, we do suggest that its benefits and costs should be seriously scrutinized, accounting for the specific terms of individual countries. In the Czechoslovak case, we believe, it could be a desirable option in the future.

There are contradictory factors as for the time horizon of its possible adoption. Referring to the arguments in the section 3.3 of this paper, it is evidently not viable in the next period of 1 - 2 years, taking into account all the forthcoming institutional changes in the Czechoslovakia and the uncertainties involved.

On the other hand, a number of factors would call for to avoid any unnecessary delay in the mentioned policy shift:

- one of the lessons from the development of open market economies is that it takes time to build the credibility of the strategy, and it must be " earned" (Hochreiter E., Knobl A., 1991). To implement the changeover becomes increasingly demanding, the more are the opposite expectations embedded in the behaviour of firms, trade unions and various pressure groups. A comparison between Austria and Nordic countries is of particular interest in this respect. Along this reasoning, there is a considerable difference between forward- and backward looking expectations in inflationary tendencies (Barro R.J., 1983), and in the possibilities to be coped with by fixed exchange rate regime,
- while the capital account flows remain mostly regulated, the "complicating" role of interest rate parity and of speculative capital flows is substantially diminished, if not eliminated. It seems therefore advantageous to go through the process of learning in the conditions when the " fundamentals matter".

A reasonably early move to the policy of nominal exchange rate anchor could therefore create a more favourable environment for the future development stages.

Despite all the barriers, Czechoslovakia should have relatively good prospects to succeed with the fixed exchange rate strategy. Along with the comprehensive privatization programme and inflow of FDI, there is a tradition of industrial development and, moreover, of prudent monetary and fiscal policies aiming at a stabilized currency. This tradition dates back to the period after World War I, when the newly created Czechoslovak republic adopted conservative fiscal and monetary policies and, as a result, avoided hyper inflation experienced by all its neighbours, including Germany, Austria, Hungary and Poland (Sargent T.J., 1986).

The hypothesis is that in the given conditions, the policy of the hard currency - instead of devaluations as implied in the conventional wisdom - should be capable to develop a sustained, export-led recovery of the Czechoslovak economy in the medium run.

REFERENCES

Balassa, B.: The Purchasing Power Doctrine: A Reappraisal, *Journal of Political Economy*, December 1964.

Baldwin, R.: The Case Against Infant - Industry Tariff Protection, *Journal of Political Economy*, 1969.

Barro, R.J.: Rules, Discretion and Reputation in a Model of Monetary Policy, *Journal of Monet. Econ.*, 1983.

Bofinger, P.: *The Role of Monetary Policy in the Process of Economic Reform in Eastern Europe, CEPR,* Discussion Paper No. 457, 1990.

Bohata, M., Fischer, M.: Analyza Vyvoje Vykonnosti Prumyslu v Prubehu Tranformacniho Procesu, *UUNV*, Prague 1992.

Dornbusch, R.: *From Stabilization to Growth,* NBER Working Paper No. 3302, 1990.

Fry, M.J., Nuti, D.M.: Monetary and Exchange Rate Policies during Eastern Europe's Transition, *Oxford Review of Economic Policy*, Spring 1992.

Herr, H., Tober,S. Westphal, S.: A Strategy for Economic Transformation and Development in Eastern Europe, *De Pecunia* No. 3, December 1991.

Hillman, A.L.: *International Trade Policy and Transition from Socialism,* Conference Paper, Jerusalem 1991.

Hochreiter, E., Knobl, A.: *Exchange Rate Policy of Austria and Finland, Two Examples of a Peg,* Bank of Finland Discussion Papers, 12/91.

Hrnčíř, M.: *Developing Competition in a Transition Economy,* Conference Paper, Prague 1992.

Hughes, G., Hare, P.G.: Industrial Policy and Restructuring in Eastern Europe, *Oxford Review of Economic Policy,* No.1 1992.

McKinnon, R.: *Liberalising Trade in a Socialist Economy,* Conference paper, Vienna, 1991.

Kolanda, M., Kubista, V.: Costs, Performance and Behaviour of the Czechoslovak Manufacturing Enterprises on the World Markets in the 1980's, The Institute of Forcasting, Prague 1980.

Kornai, J.: The Soft Budget Constraint, *Kyklos,* 1986.

Landesmann, M.: Industrial Restructuring and the Reorientation of Trade in Czechoslovakia, *European Econony*, Special Edition No. 2, 1991.

Leppanen, S.: *Finland and Austria: Two Different Economic Policy Strategies*, Conference Paper, 1992.

MacDonald, R., Taylor, P.M.: Exchange Rate Economics, IMF Staff Papers, 1/92.

Marin,D.: Structural Change Through Exchange Rate Policy, *Welt. Archiv, Heft 3*, 1985.

Mundell, R.A.: The Appropriate Use of Monetary and Fiscal Policy for Internal and External Stability, International Monetary Fund Staff Papers, 1962.

National Economic Development Office: *International Price Competitiveness, Non-Price Factors and Export Performance*, London 1997.

Nurkse, R.: Conditions of International Monetary Equilibrium (1945), in Ellis H.S., and Metzler, L.S.: *Readings in the Theory of International Trade*, 1950.

Nuti, D.M.: Internal and International Aspects of Monetary Disequilibrium in Poland, in: Economic Transformation in Hungary and Poland, *European Economy* 1990.

Pekkarinen, J., Pohjola, M., Rowthorn, B.: *Social Corporatism, A Superior Economic System?*, Clarendon Press, Oxford 1992.

Pick, M.: *Productivity, Purchasing Power Parity, Exchange Rate, Institute of Forecasting*, Prague 1990.

Plan Econ. Report No. 16-17, 18 ed. Vanous, J. April-May 1992.

Portes, R.: Introduction, in: *Economic Transformation in Hungary and Poland, European Economy*, No. 43, 1990.

Sargent, T.J.: *Rational Expectations and Inflation*, Harper and Row, 1986.

Summers, R., Heston, A.: New Set of International Comparisons of real Product and Price Levels, Estimates for 130 Countries, *Income and Wealth* No. 1, 1988

Wihlborg, C.G., Willett, T.D.: Optimal Currency Areas Revisited, in: Wihlborg, C.G., Frantianni, M., Willett, T.d.: *Financial Regulation and Monetary Arrangements After 1992*, Amsterdam, 1991.

Williamson, J.: The Economic Opening of Eastern Europe in Williamson, J. (ed.): *Currency Convertibility in Eastern Europe*, Washington D.C., 1991.

6

THE CURRENT SITUATION OF PRIVATIZATION IN CZECHOSLOVAKIA

Eva Klvačová
Co-Editor - *Ekonom*

1. CHARACTERISTIC FEATURES OF THE CZECHOSLOVAK PRIVATIZATION, THE EXISTING PROBLEMS

The pattern of the Czechoslovak privatization which is one of the key elements and prerequisites of a radical economic reform is not simple. The comparison with the standard procedures applied in the countries which have no experience with centrally planned economy reveals principal differences.

The shape of the Czech privatization is mainly the result of the efforts of the authors of the reform and the state administration to find new owners as quickly as possible thus minimizing losses ensuing inevitably from the transformation of ownership relations.

The speed of the privatization is the basic objective and criterion of its implementation, however of no less importance are such factors like efficiency and legality of the privatization process. Even though the speed and efficiency of privatization are by their substance in mutual contradiction, the Czechoslovak privatization does not resign the efficiency. In fact it cannot afford it with respect to public opinion, the state of the art of economy and state budget. Similarly it cannot allow the existence of unrestrained, unlawful privatization and it strives to reduce its extent to minimum. The prerequisite of the implementation of privatization and one of the most important criteria thereof is a political consensus of all citizens on this issue. The four basic criteria of privatization project is speed - efficiency - legality - political consensus.

The Czechoslovak privatization in principle does not aspire to restructuring of state enterprises. It is based on the prerequisite verified by practice that the State is not by its definition able to put into effect business decisions such as the decision on restructuring of state enterprises prior to privatization or relating to it. It'is also a fact that in post-socialist economy where there are no reliable market signals the decision-making on restructuring of state enterprises would be incomparably more difficult than in market economies. Another problem is the extent of such a task when the State would have to restructure hundreds if not thousands of state enterprises. The task to restructure state enterprises is left in the concept of the radical economic reform unconditionally to the future owners.

However, the question is to what extent this philosophy of privatization will be preserved in case of the split of Czechoslovakia: the Slovak representatives and economists have a substantially stronger inclination to accept state interventions, state paternalism than the representatives of the Czech political scene and the Czech authors of the radical economic reform. It can be anticipated that in case of the split of the State the issue of restructuring of state enterprises would be raised again in Slovakia. Highly probable is also the maintenance of higher state ownership share in Slovakia than in Bohemia. So far, however, the economic reform scenario aims at the privatization of all eligible state enterprises and preserve the state sector only in the traditional (if possible minimized) sphere of public goods and services.

The form of privatization is the resultant of a whole number of factors the most important of which are undoubtedly economic interests and the actual power of individual social strata striving to acquire the national property. At the game are mainly management of state enterprises, the new group of private entrepreneurs coming into being with difficulties, heirs of original owners and last but not least the group of persons who have succeeded in getting rich under the past regime be it as a result of their privileged position in the society, of the trade on black or grey markets or other types of "socialist" business. The Czechoslovak privatization is affected by the lack of domestic capital and at the same time by a certain aversion (manifested mainly by the actual or potential domestic entrepreneurs) to the sale of national property to foreign capital. It is also significantly affected by the state of the art of knowledge, experience, the existing institutions as well as ethical standards. It is a privatization implemented in the post socialist society where the State owned practically 100% of all business property and this fact represents a quality unknown in any other country where private ownership has never ceased to be the fundamental drive of the economic development. It is a privatization implemented in the economy described by Western textbooks of economy in a simplified way as the centrally planned economy. However, the relation between the economic center and state enterprises was in fact based on negotiations and bidding in which the state was mostly a weak partner for state enterprises and it rather hindered their development, their prompt responses to the market signals, the innovations and their business in general than assisting them in achieving benefits to the detriment of other economic entities.

It may be stated that the shape of privatization has been co-determined also by the mentality of the Czech nation. (The philosophy of privatization, its approaches and procedures have been created similarly as the whole economic reform in Bohemia). The willingness to a quick adaptation to the new and changing conditions (occurring innumerable in the history of the nation) on one side and the tendency to seek compromising solution reflecting the interests of individual social strata have found their expression in the adoption of a whole number of privatization laws in a very short period of time. Among them are mainly the following:

1) ACT No. 298/1990 Coll.
on the settlement of some property relations of religious orders and congregations and the Olomouc Archbishopric
2) ACT No. 403/1990 Coll.
on alleviation of consequences of some cases of property-related injustice in the wording of Act No. 458/1990 Coll. and Act. No. 137/1991 Coll.
3) ACT No. 87/1991 Coll.
on extra judicial rehabilitations
4) ACT No. 229/1991 Coll.
on the settlement of ownership relations to land and other agricultural property
5) ACT No. 172/1991 Coll.
on transfer of some property of the Czech Republic to the ownership of communities
6) ACT No. 427/1990 Coll.
on transfer of some state assets to other juristic or physical persons in the wording of Act No. 541/1990 Coll. and Act No. 429/1991 Coll.
7) ACT No. 500/1990 Coll.
on authority of the Czech state administration with respect to transfer of state ownership of some property to other juristic and other persons in the wording of Act No. 541/1990 Coll. and Act No. 429/1991 Coll.
8) ACT No. 92/1991 Coll.
on transfer of state assets to other persons in the wording of Act No. 92/1992 Coll.
9) ACT No. 171/1991 Coll.
on authority of the Czech state administration with respect to transfer of state assets to other person
10) ACT No. 42/92 Coll.
on the settlement of property relations and property claims in cooperatives.

The privatization in Czechoslovakia is a combination of the following forms: returning a property to original owners or their heirs, sale of a property to domestic or foreign investors, free transfer of a property to cities and municipalities and several other entities (including pension and social security funds and foundations) and distribution of a property through a voucher privatization. It consists of a full range of standard privatization methods and amends those methods by including one non-standard method, a voucher privatization.

To understand a process of Czechoslovak privatization in countries with traditionally democratic regime, minimal state involvement defined ex ante by more or less rigid rules, developed market economy, institutional structure being entirely different from countries with command economy, it is crucial to appreciate that even the process of privatization of the state property as a way of reestablishing the private ownership as well as traditional market economy carries along and, by definition, it has to carry the remnants of the past, the remnants of a huge state involvement and bureaucratism of the society.

It is both curious and logical that political and economic structure of the country in the past 40 years is reflected in privatization forms and methods. Since the hierarchical arrangement with several management levels was the typical pattern of a command economy, the similar organization can be viewed in the country's privatization. In a command economy the plan was developed from the bottom level: it was submitted by companies, reviewed by relevant Ministry and approved by the central body - State Planning Commission. The final approval was given by the government. In addition, the communist party bodies - with the same rigid hierarchical structure - were the informal body reviewing the plan and giving approvals while having the unwritten right to get involved in the process anytime, in relation to anything and on any level. Obviously, the post November developments in the Czecho-Slovakia resulted in elimination of communist party bodies. However, the methodology underlying both large and small privatization schemes often conforms to a command economy which brings along peculiarities not understandable in countries with market economy and minimal state involvement.

A privatization project represents a crucial element of the large privatization. Under the Large Privatization Act this project must be filed by each privatized company - this project, however, can be submitted by any legal or physical person. The project is being prepared in compliance with the Binding Principles, the main purpose of which is to standardize the process of drafting and reviewing of each project. The Principles are prepared in great detail and the task of an entity submitting the project is to provide to a decision-making authority a detailed information about the scope and structure of its privatized assets.

In addition, an entity submitting the project must file the business plan as well as propose a privatization method or a combination of those methods.

Privatization projects are submitted to the relevant Founder being the appropriate Ministry or State Administration body. The Founder acts as a first level to sort out and review the projects. Then, the Ministry for Privatization (of the Czech Republic and the Slovak Republic) represents a second level in the decision-making process. This Ministry has the power to

The process of reviewing project

approve the privatization projects of small- and medium-size business provided that the privatization method applied is not direct sale of the business to a buyer determined in advance (the method minimizing the presence of a competitive environment). In respect to privatization projects of any business with number of staff being higher than 3 000 and/or including a direct sale of the business or its part to a buyer determined in advance, the Ministry for Privatization is only entitled to recommend such project for an approval. Such projects are then reviewed by the Economic Council and consequently approved by the Government. As the number of companies with more than 3 000 employees is high and direct sale as a preferred privatization method is proposed in most cases (since the privatization project elaborator is entitled to propose a privatization method and, in the most cases, the elaborator intends to become the owner of the privatized business, then he would have to be out of his mind if he proposed competitive methods of sale i.e. public auction or tender), the majority of privatization projects are being reviewed on four levels as follows: Founder (the decision-making process is often two-tier on this level.) - Ministry for Privatization - Economic Council - Government.

The process of privatization project reviewing and approval split into more levels which results in somewhat more bureaucratic approach and rises concerns of foreign investors in particular, is also inherent to the small privatization.

A proposal to privatize any business (shop, restaurant, service outlet, production plant) can be filed by anyone. There are, however, specific institutions - District Privatization Committees, the task of which is to identify appropriate businesses and obtain all necessary privatization related from companies. These Committees were appointed by the Ministers for Privatization of the Czech and Slovak Republics. (The Privatization Committees in the Czech Republic were appointed for each of the 75 districts and the number of their stall was approximately 20. All members of each Committee were appointed individually by the Minister on the basis of a recommendation provided by relevant local authority). District Privatization Committees reviewed any suggestions obtained from citizens and private entrepreneurs or state and cooperative companies related to including any entity into the small privatization and, in particular, they were actively involved in identifying of such business. They acted as a first reviewing body in the process of the small privatization. In order to sell a business in the auction, its including into the small privatization had to be approved by local authorities, relevant Founding Ministry (Ministry of Trade, Ministry of Industry, Ministry of Agriculture) and eventually by the Ministry for Privatization.

An application of hierarchical decision-making system known from a command economy brings along a number of obstacles. Multi-level approval system should ensure a certain degree of objectivity pertaining to the approval process, however, given its nature this system rather slows down and delays the entire privatization. In addition, it keeps alive the negotiation and bargaining strategies inherent to a dialogue among the individual levels involved in the process of reviewing and approval of privatization projects. Small privatization process involved a lot of bargaining whether to include or not to include a given business into the small privatization scheme. Directors of state enterprises, under whose authority a given privatized business belonged, acted as real owners and tried to negotiate the elimination of that entity from the auction with District Privatization Committee, District Authorities, Founding Ministry and, last but not least, with the Ministry for Privatization. The objective of such bargaining was to retain the business in the company thus increasing the chance for its survival, to avoid a public auction and rent out the business pursuant the Act on Non-residential premises without an obligation to pay a high price for an acquisition of the right to rent out the business, or to sell the business on the basis of an exemption from Large Privatization Act, or to retain this business in the company and privatize the company as a whole entity while using one of the "softer" privatization methods. However, it was not only directors who were involved in the bargaining process which also included Ministry officials, private entrepreneurs, members of professional association etc.

The possibility to negotiate was supported by another traditional pattern inherent to a command economy which is an aversion to generally accepted principles and tendency to their individualization. Small Privatization Act did not lay down an explicit definition of terms under which the business, or its part had to, or did not have to be included in public auction. In this respect, it was the District Privatization Committee responsibility and their ability to determine what is, and what is not a separate business. A separate business could be a shop, department store, restaurant, luxury hotel, small-size service outlet as well as relatively big production plant. The Act does not set forth an exact definition to include the business into the small or large privatizations e.g. according to the number of employees or level of capital, etc. Eventually, a definition was laid down - again in the spirit of a command economy - by preparing a list of companies to be privatized under the large privatization. This list was prepared by the Ministry for Privatization on the basis of information provided by relevant branch Ministries. Again, these Ministries had gained this information from privatized companies. The list was approved by appropriate Republic government.

Negotiations underlying the large privatization are somewhat different. The avoidance of privatization in general is no longer negotiated. Company management has already understood that privatization is a real issue which cannot be avoided. Its strategy therefore focuses on becoming the future owner of the company. Consequently, a hierarchical negotiation has therefore gained a new dimension. This dimension is: a competition. As the law stipulates that privatization project of the company has to be filed by its managements and, simultaneously, any other entity can file a privatization project for a business or its part, decision-making bodies obtain approximately four privatization projects to be reviewed which relate to one company (a record is 128 privatization projects for one attractive brewery). Selection of the best project is a task of the Founder, the Ministry for Privatization, the Economic Council and eventually the Government itself. Aversion to generally binding principles inherent to a command economy is reflected in the Large Privatization by in the law stipulated equal significance of all privatization methods as well as non-existence of a comprehensive system of fixed and determined criteria underlying the project approval process. By its nature, the approval process is a multi-criteria system whilst specific criteria are not explicitly defined and their significance in the entire process is not weighted, as appropriate. It is not by coincidence that privatization project elaborators as well as laic public are raising questions such as: Which of the following methods will be preferred in the privatization of the company X - should it be privatization project A proposing direct sale of the business to the determined private entrepreneur (usually the elaborator of submitted privatization project), or project B, including the tender as a method of privatization of the business, or project C, proposing public auction, or project D, proposing a transfer of the business to a joint stock company the assets of which will be sold through a voucher privatization, or project E which is, again, proposing a transfer of the business to a joint stock company the assets of which will be sold as follows - 20% to a private entrepreneur (e.g. former director of the company), 50% for vouchers and 20% transferred to the National Property Fund and remaining share determined for a free transfer to municipalities? Or project F will be selected as the preferred one, including the proposal to sell majority holding to an international corporation and remaining part through vouchers? Will the decision-making body place the strongest emphasize on quality of the business plan (which, however, is not binding in any way for anyone), formal accuracy of submitted project, the promise to maintain employment levels, solutions related to environmental clean-up issues, or the level of direct payment to the National Property Fund? There is no explicit answer to any of the above questions. Non-existence of strictly defined rules opens the door for actions attempting to influence both reviewing and decision-making bodies for the benefit of their businesses, as well as to get involved in the privatization process through bribing or personal contacts. This, however, leads to the existence of an efficient feedback resulting in improvement and cultivation of the entire privatization process. Elaborators of refused privatization projects (who often tried to influence the decision-making bodies by promising them future benefits or being backed by powerful people) insists on knowing why their project was worse that those of their competitors. Doubts related to the objectivity of the decision-making process resulted in personnel changes, requirement to set forth exact "rules of the game", higher transparency of the privatization process and less paperwork. It appears that in this respect the Czechoslovak privatization is flexible, and it quickly reacts to any criticism.

However, using the established institutions with a long tradition does not involve disadvantages only. While using the established structure of the Founding Ministries the privatization in Czechoslovakia is not required to establish its own extensive administrative network. The Czech Ministry for

Privatization employs about 200 staff and the number of people working at the Ministry for Privatization of the Slovak Republic is about the same. In addition, this system enables to use the extensive experience and knowledge of Founders, their distinctive capacity and expertise related to specific company. The branch Ministries have also been given - although temporarily and for a definite period - raison d'être of their existence. Consequently, the representatives of administration bureaucracy necessary in a command economy have obtained a temporary job before this bureaucracy ceases to exist. One of the remarkable advantages pertaining to the selection of this solution is that their aversion against the privatization is significantly decreased and it comes to the point that they even support it. Benefits of the chosen approach should be higher than its cost associated with the possibility of subjective decision-making and establishment of professional coalitions consisting of representatives of privatized companies and founding ministries.

Czechoslovak privatization does not seek to find ideal owners. Its objective is much more straightforward: to determine first private owners and their rights, duties and responsibilities and therefore establish the first (although not sufficient) assumption for the establishment of an efficient market economy. Despite existing problems and mistakes, all privatization laws as well as all applied privatization methods are heading towards meeting this objective.

2. THE LARGE PRIVATIZATION

2.1 Methods of the Large Privatization in the Czech Republic

There are exactly ten privatization methods (including all the modifications) embodied in the Act on Large Privatization. All of them are legally equal since they strive for the same goal - for finding real private owners. The advantage of so wide a range of privatization methods available is that it enables both the entity drafting a project and its reviewers, both the founder and the endorsers, to select the most convenient method.

However, the equivalency of the privatization methods does not go beyond the identity of target and legal equality. Individual privatization methods differ not only as to their suitability for concrete privatized equities, but also as to the absence of preferential treatment and difficulty to reach the privatized equity, suitability or unsuitability for a concrete social stratum, presence or absence of competition and need for administrative review of business plan.

Public auction's principal advantages are the absence of preferential treatment as to the privatized equity, existence of a single criterion employed to decide upon its acquisition, presence of competition and accordingly higher amount paid by an acquirer, and - last but not least - no need to carry out any complicated administrative review of a business plan.

There is also some guarantee of the acquirers' responsibility for the gained property following from his willingness to pay the price arrived at during the auction. As to the difficulty of acquiring the privatized equity, the public auction method is unambiguously the most strict one, because the possibility to acquire the property is dependent on the sufficiency of the financial means and willingness to accept a great deal of business risks. In the public consciousness it is linked (and thereby handicapped) with the unfair property acquisition and dirty money.

As to difficulty to reach the equity, public bidding stands one level below. Its basic features are similar to those of private auctions, but at the same time this method employs more criteria which brings about on one hand a possibility to approach the equity more sensitively and to respect its non-negligible specifications, but on the other also a larger space for subjectivity and manipulations in decision-making and finally a greater administration demands.

Direct sale to a designated owner (be it of the equity as a whole, of its detachable part or in form of shares) excludes both competition and non-preferential treatment. It causes the decision-making about the prospective owner to be transferred from the impersonal market criteria unto the state establishment and requires the latter to examine the standard of business plans and the ability of prospective owners to put them in practice. And so it asks the state administration to solve the problem for which it is not equipped. This method implies a higher probability of a lower price arrived at, a higher probability the personal connections, acquaintances and corruption will play their role. It is far from being accidental that the direct sale to a designated owner has - from the law - a more "strict" procedure and that it must be approved by the government. It appears, though, that this condition does not discourage the entities drafting privatization projects too strongly and in case they themselves are bidding for the equity, this method is extensively preferred.

Voucher privatization as a privatization method makes it possible to overcome the lack of domestic capital and to arrive at a relative valuation of the privatized equity. It is a method which enables the widest strata of society, including the poorest ones, to take part in the privatization process and it also has an educational role with respect to business activities. It is at arm's length and breaks through the aversion of the existing administration of national property, e.g. company management, against privatization. At the beginning it creates a dispersed ownership and thus enables the company's management to exercise further temporary (though only short-term) control over the equity privatized. The Act entitles each entity drafting a privatization project to propose the proportion of the vouchers in accordance with their views and business plan. The proposed part of equity intended for voucher privatization often indicates well not only the standard of a company but also of its management; and that part's size and the standard stand in inverse proportion.

Moreover, the scale of privatization methods is complemented by share's sale via bank or stock exchange with all the positive features of a market way of sale going along, transfer of equity, its part or shares to the municipalities free of charge, namely to the funds of social benefits and sick allowances, and finally temporary equity retaining at the National Property Fund. The two latter instances should be an exception rather than a rule. The municipalities are not businessmen and they should administer only the property which is of a general benefit to the society; the National Property Fund should not be intended to substitute for the state in its business function. In the face of law, however, even these methods are of equal status.

A law regarding all the privatization methods equal many a time during the review and endorsement of the projects makes the life of those in charge of decision-making miserable. The criteria of decision-making will unquestionably represent a principle preference of the competition forms over those with the competition elements lacking, creating a sufficient offer of the property for the voucher privatization and creation of small-scale and middle-scale business, creation of not only diffused but also concentrated ownerships, financial means gained by the privatization, speed of realization of a business plan suggested within the scope of a project and - last but not least - consensus within the society.

2.2 Non-Standard Method: Voucher Privatization

Usage of non-standard method of voucher privatization is a specific feature of Czech privatization. Every adult Czech person (above 18 years old) can buy a voucher book with 1 000 investment points for a symbolic price of Kcs 1 000 (approximately USD 35). 8,5 million of Czechoslovak citizens (i.e. 77% of Czechoslovak adults) have accepted the opportunity of taking part in the process of voucher privatization.

Bought investment points could be invested by a citizen himself or by means of some of 437 privatization funds that were established in accordance with the process of voucher privatization. In the first case he can get shares of given joint stock companies and in the other case shares of an Investment Privatization Fund. Approximately 60% of participating citizens have given their investment points to funds and so they take part in voucher privatization more or less in a passive way.

It is the evaluation of the privatized property that is probably the most interesting aspect of voucher privatization. Voucher privatization is a special kind of auction where investment points and not money are means of payment and share price is given in these points. Voucher privatization runs in several rounds and prices of offered shares change in each round in accordance with demand and supply. (The number of rounds is supposed not to exceed 5.) The initial rate of shares of all companies participating in voucher privatization was the same in the first round - 3 shares for 100 investments points. It was the same for both highly attractive enterprises of traditional branches of Czechoslovak economy (breweries, enterprises of glass and artificial jewelry industry, china factories etc.) and for monuments of socialist economy - huge machinery enterprises established for needs of the former U.S.S.R.. It was the same for enterprises efficient as well as non-efficient, new as well as outdated, with ensured sales as well as without them, profitable as well as indebted. Considerations of possible division of enterprises into several groups in accordance with expertise and reached efficiency criteria and of setting different initial rates preceded the decision of the same initial rate. The idea that the rate creation in voucher privatization should be directed by demand and supply mechanism from the very beginning has - reasonably - dominated.

The shares demand of which was smaller than supply or equal to it were sold for initial rate in the first round. Remaining shares of enterprises supply of which is higher than demand were offered to the second round for proportionally reduced rate.

In case of supply higher than demand a very simple rule has been used. If the difference is more than 125%, results of the first round will be canceled and new share rates will be set accordingly to the first round demand. (For example demand of 150%a corresponds to the increased rate by 2 shares per 100 points etc.). When the difference is lower than 125%, supply of investment privatization funds will be shortened (so there is a rule of priority of citizens who invest directly into the company before investment privatization funds and shares are being sold for defined rate).

Even the results of the first privatization round have already shown diversity of demand for shares of various companies. Share rates defined for the second round were profoundly differentiated and they ranged from 100 shares for 100 points (yet mentioned giant machinery, i.e. electrical enterprises aimed at export to the U.S.S.R.) to the rate of 1 share for 300 points (international hotels). We can expect further differentiation in next rounds.

Supply is also an interesting matter of voucher privatization. Property supply for voucher privatization is made by mechanism of approving privatization projects. Original assumption taking voucher privatization as the only method of Czechoslovak national economy privatization or at least the only method of large scale privatization has not been accomplished. Voucher privatization is not either a method preferred by law, it is given the same meaning by law as all other methods are (problems - see chapter on methods of privatization). However, it is the method of the most ranged application. The property of Kcs 300 billion will be privatized through it in the first wave. (For comparison - small scale privatization has created private property of the value of Kcs 6 billion). One can say that the voucher privatization has got its way as a very important addition of standard privatization methods. It occurs in proposed and approved privatization projects together with direct sale to a designated owner of foreign or domestic origin, together with sale of shares through bank and stock-exchange with free of charge share transfer to municipal and local authorities. (Along with that shares are then sold - in accordance with approved project - for both investment vouchers and real money for prices defined by particular markets. In fact, for lot of joint-stock companies it represents the only way of privatization when 97% of shares are sold through vouchers and 3% are due to enter the Restitution Investment Fund. After finishing the first round it is possible to watch the statistically important inversely proportional dependence between the percentile portion of shares sold for vouchers and the demand. The lowest demand and the highest fall of rate of shares can be watched at the enterprises fully privatized through voucher method. On the contrary the lower is the share of voucher privatization, the higher is the demand and the more often is the increase of voucher rate. This statistical dependence proves explicitly that voucher method is used as a residual one.

Voucher privatization is assumed to be carried out in two waves. Nowadays the first wave is in force and it should be finished by the end of this year. The second wave should start at the beginning of 1993 and the privatization projects for the second wave have already been submitted. The second wave should be of approximately the same extent as the first wave. Potential changes of the future constitutional arrangement can interfere with implementing the process of privatization. Voucher privatization was drafted as a federal - with a consistent philosophy of approach and with a universal proceeding. In principle it would be possible to realize both privatization waves in this way under the presumption that the law of investment protection will be adopted in time before the eventual splitting of the republic.

It is premature to anticipate future development but it seems that at present there exist signals indicating that the second wave of privatization will be divided into the Czech and the Slovak part when the motivation for splitting is different on both Czech and Slovak sides.

There is no doubt that Czech enterprises are on the average of higher quality and more effective and this fact excites an endeavour to give an opportunity of investing in them only to Czech owners of investment vouchers. On the other hand it is obvious from the declaration of the Slovak government's program that there is the effort to create their own conception of privatization with a greater role of the state with greater state interventions, with restructuring tendencies before the enterprises have been privatized with slow-down of the privatization process. Under these circumstances it is possible to anticipate that division of the second wave of the large-scale privatization is highly presumable.

2.3 Role of Foreign Experts in Czechoslovak Privatization

At present there is a team of 20 advisers at the Czech Ministry of Privatization who have been sent to the CSFR on the request of the government of the CSFR by the Agency for International Development (USAID). They are paid by the US government. The task of the team whose members are mainly investment bankers and specialists in management is to provide technical assistance in analyzing and evaluation of privatization projects. The assistance is concentrated on privatization projects with foreign capital participation. The experts complete the knowledge of the team by their knowledge of market economy, they play the role of an intermediatory in exchange of information and in connection with a foreign investor, they represent and defend the interests of the Czechoslovak state. Their task is to suggest a way of finding potential foreign partners, to choose the best among them, to review the quality of the chosen partner, to provide him with information regarding the privatized enterprise and to guarantee the best possible conditions for a foreign partner's entry into the privatization process from the point of view of the Czechoslovak economy. If the choice has been already done by an enterprise or a founding ministry, the experts review the fairness and benefits of a transaction. The evaluation results in a recommendation whether to carry out or not the suggested transaction.

Evaluation of foreign investors, exchange of information and negotiation the best conditions is on the basis of the rules set in advance, even though not very rigid - methodological procedures of privatization with participation of a foreign investor. One of the fundamental starting points is "a translation" of a privatization project not only into English but also into the language of a market economy. Privatization projects which have been and from the viewpoint of definitions surely must be affected by the existing practice - book-keeping, applied economic indicators, way of thinking (the issue of the business plan) etc. - often constitute a poser for a foreign investors. Often they also are a poser for experts who -according to their own words - are taught practical lessons in post-socialist economy, affected by centrally planned economy in the past that had been stressing, in a monstrous way, the role of state bodies and state interventions.

The actual process of negotiating with a foreign partner has a multi-criterion character. Purchase price represents the first but not the only criterion of decision-making, though the effort to achieve the highest price possible is always a natural personal ambition. Essential efforts is to create a viable enterprise capable of defying keen competition. Therefore emphasis is laid upon commitments regarding future investments that make possible to modernize and reconstruct the enterprise, to improve the quality of production and further technical development.

A very important criteria is considered to be the credibility of a foreign partner and a specific attention is paid to its reliable determination, it is than being verified by number of economic indicators such as the financial situation on the market of the respective type of production and last but not least the political, cultural and historical appropriateness of the partner. The procedure of negotiating conditions for the foreign partner's entry to the Czechoslovak market contains also the possibilities of extending markets for the privatized enterprise and building up of a necessary infrastructure for further business activities. A specific attention is devoted to two especially urgent actual problems: employment and environment. Foreign experts grant higher evaluation to such offers which contain the commitment to create new work posts or to maintain the current employment level or the commitment to professional training and improvement of worker's qualifications. At the same time there is the ambition to choose the offer which contains commitment to eliminate the environmental contamination. Finally the very important criteria of a political and economic character is considered to be the acceptance of the voucher method of the part of the privatized enterprise.

Foreign investors accept as basic positive factors the strategic position of CSFR enabling access to eastern markets, relatively high level of qualification of work force and its relatively low price and a fairly high goodwill of the country arising partly from the historical knowledge with high adaptability to changing conditions partly from the speed with which when compared with other post-socialist countries the economic reform is carried out. Negative factors are political risks connected with geographic position (threat of the development on the territory of the former USSR) on one hand, on the other hand it is the problem of Czech-Slovak relations but it is also the constant tendency to change economic rules and absence of general ones as well as the lack of information of current actions. The technical and moral deterioration of privatized units and the of privatized units and practical absence of technical development over the past 40 years is a negative factor which is thoroughly reflected but the doubts are often cast in concrete cases when the price is being set.

Suggested and in practice implemented conditions of privatization with the help of a foreign investor naturally reflect the reality.

2.4 Results of the Large Privatization So Far Achieved

The first and as to the scale of equity more significant phase of the approval process in the first wave of the large privatization has been finished. At the approval of the last privatization project for the foundation of a joint-stock company intended either wholly or partially for privatization by vouchers, out of the total 11 555 privatization projects, 5 830 have been reviewed. There are 5 725 left for the second phase which will be based on the standard methods of privatization. This mid-point of the endorsement process offers us a good opportunity for first balancing and statistical data monitoring.

The tables numbered 1 and 2 provide us with a basic overview of the privatization methods. They show us clearly that the transformation types D and E put together that means privatization through the joint-stock companies either newly founded (following an approved privatization project) or already existing, have seen the largest use. Out of the total of 2 210 transformations approved the privatization of new joint-stock companies and state equity interest accounted nearly for a half -1 007 cases. The second most largely employed privatization method was that of transfer of equity to municipalities or other economic entities free of charge which has appeared in the approved privatization projects 592 times and thus represents almost 27% of the transformations approved. Direct sale of equity to a designated owner has been approved in 336 cases and represents approximately 15% of all the transformation methods. Public auction and public tender even if put together have not reached the overall level of use of direct sales to designated owners. In average, for each privatization project, a combination of two privatization methods has been employed.

The target of the first phase of the privatization projects' endorsement was mainly to create a sufficient offer of equity for the voucher privatization. Out of the total of the basic capital owned by the 943 already existing joint-stock companies or those newly founded following an approved privatization project in the Czech Republic (equaling Kcs 323 billion), the equity intended for the voucher privatization represents roughly 62% and accounts for the well-known sum of Kcs 200.8 billion. The proportion of the total equity of the joint-stock companies privatized either wholly or partly through the vouchers representing the voucher privatization (Kcs 362 billion) accounts for 55%.

The voucher method as the only privatization method has been applied in case of 375 joint-stock companies with the total equity as high as Kcs 53 billion. In case of 459 joint-stock companies with their equity equaling Kcs 135 billion, the voucher privatization percentile proportion accounts for 50 - 97%, in case of 183 joint-stock companies (equity Kcs 129 billion) for 20 - 50% and in case of six companies the vouchers' use has not reached the level of 20%.

Ministry of Industry of the Czech Republic, the most largely represented branch, shows a similar percentage of the voucher privatization: out of the total of 435, 159 joint-stock companies will be privatized fully through the voucher program (97% for vouchers + 3% for the restitution investment fund), almost as much as a half of the joint-stock companies (219) will show the proportion of the voucher privatization between 50 and 97%, 55 companies between 20 - 50% and only 3 joint-stock companies go under 20%.

What standard methods complement the voucher privatization? 17.5% of the basic capital of the privatized joint-stock companies, that is Kcs 56.5 billion of the book value, will be retained - either temporarily or permanently - in the National Property Fund. The basic capital of Kcs 38 billion will be transferred to the municipalities, social security and sick allowances funds or to other entities free of charge. Direct sale to a designated owner, so frequently discussed and so abundantly written about on the pages of our dailies, will complement the voucher privatization only by 2.8% of equity, that means equity for Kcs 10 billion (Kcs 9 billion of basic capital). One tenth of this amount, that is the equity for Kcs 1 billion, will be purchased by the restituents as an addition to the equity returned to them under the law. The equity which will be purchased by the foreign investors in the scope of direct sales to designated owners, will account for about Kcs 1 billion.

After the voucher privatization, the second most largely used form of the joint-stock companies and state equity interest privatization is that of the transfer of a part of shares to the National Property Fund - be it until a suitable prospective owner is found or permanently. The third form as to the amount of equity involved is the free of charge transfer to the municipalities and funds. Only an insignificant part of the privatized equity has entered a direct sale the private owner in the innermost meaning of the word. The equity sale to a company management and domestic entrepreneurs, so rigidly watched by the public and the even more strictly monitored sale to foreign entrepreneurs, thus represent only a negligible fragment of the Czechoslovak privatization.

The employees shares have appeared both in submitted and in approved privatization projects only to a small extend. Out of the total of 943 joint-stock companies, in case of 722 (almost 77%) they did not appear at all, in case of 124 joint-stock companies their share represents less than 5%, in case of 67 companies it accounts for 5 - 10%, in case of 16 companies it is as much as 10% and in case of 14 companies it exceeds 10%.

The overview of the approved and to some extend also of the submitted privatization projects tells us an interesting story about the representation of the respective entities drafting privatization projects. Out of the total of 1044 privatization projects approved (including a double amount of the privatized entities, that is 2210), the company management involvement accounts for almost 82%, whereas the subsidiary's management only for 5.7% and the bidders without any relationship towards a company management for 7.4%.

It is clear that so far the company management has had much greater portion of the total number of the privatization projects approved than of those submitted. This situation has been evoked by several factors.; But firstly it is, undoubtedly, because of the fact, that the first among the chosen projects were those relevant to the voucher privatization - and these projects were mainly drafted for large companies and were mostly submitted by the company management. The privatization projects of small companies, in which the competition is mostly interested, at the moment wait to be approved.

It is possible to assume that the percentage of competition projects against the total number of projects approved, will be significantly higher in the second half of the reviewed projects. At the same time, we can expect that majority of approved privatization projects will be based on the methods of direct sale without the intermediary of new joint-stock companies' creation and thus the most frequently employed privatization methods will be those of public auction, public tender, internal tender and direct sale to a designated owner.

Table 1

Transformation methods in the process of large-scale privatization (for 1,044 approved projects)

Transformation process	number	in %
A. Public auction	172.0	7.8
B. Public tender	103.0	4.7
C. Direct sale to a designated owner	336.0	15.2
D. Joint stock company	839.0	38.0
E. Privatization of state's property interest in the business of other juristic persons	168.0	7.6
F. Free transfer	592.0	26.8
T o t a l	2.210	100.0

Table 2

Structure of D and E transformation methods

	capital stock (in bill. Kčs)	in %
Vouchers	200.8	62.1
Free transfer	38.1	11.8
Direct sale to a designated owner	9.0	2.8
Broker (bank, stock exchange)	4.8	1.5
National Property Fund (permanently, tempor.)	56.5	17.5
Additional purchase of assest by restituents	1.0	0.3
Others (non specified)	13.0	4.0
T o t a l	323.2	100.0

Table 3

Structure of submitted and approved privatization projects according to authors

Project drafted by	Share in total No of submitted (11,166) projects	Share in total No of approved (1,044) projects (%)
Enterprise management	25.1	81.8
Management of subordinate unit	3.7	5.7
Bidders	39.1	7.4
Restituents	3.6	0.9
Founding ministry	0.2	0.2
Consulting firm	3.0	1.9
District privatization comm.	6.8	0.6
Founder - district authority	3.9	0.2
Trade union organizations	0.2	0.1
Other entities submitting		
projects +	13.0	1.7
Authors not specified	1.4	0.4

\+ This group is very heterogeneous, including private persons, lessees, enterprise employees, liquidators, land owners etc.

2.5 Privatization as the Last Decision of the State

Is the system of privatization projects decision really objective? What criteria is it based on? Do executors have information enough for such considerations and are they true experts? Is national property sold out for an extremely low price? Do foreign consultants follow only their own interest instead of Czechoslovak economy interest? Can decision makers resist attempts at their affecting regardless of whatever form the attempts have?

Approving privatization projects basically means the decision of the state to make the business. It specifies the future owner, allocates sources for his business plan, it rules out unjustified property claimers from the ownership, it prevents from dirty competitive intentions. It comprises and it has to comprise the properties of each business plan carried out by the state.

To be surprised by this fact would mean the similar as to be astonished by the hot weather in the summer time, by falling leaves in autumn and by the snow in winter.

If the decision of the state is to be fair, a large number of information must be provided. The more data is required, the longer time is needed for this decision.

If the state is content with insufficient information, the decision may be subjective. As each account depends on its author, it is distorted according to his interest and getting rid of this distortion is difficult and often impossible. The objectiveness when making decisions requires the knowledge of generally valid rules and it has also been proved that the more detailed rules are, the more difficult and slower decision is. While the decisions based on the market economy are impersonal, decisions taken by the state are personified. This necessarily results in affecting the decision makers. Whilst no one doubts resolutions based on the market economy, that are made ex-post, those taken by state ex-ante are considered to be unverifiable and are easy to be put in doubts. The minimization of the number of faults in this state entrepreneurial sphere is always a matter of finding practical compromise among individual requirements (promptness versus objectiveness) and of developing basic facilities to reach the optimum. There is a whole range of such facilities even when approving privatization projects, especially:

- information scope limited by the law and by the obligatory pattern for the development of a privatization project,
- system of project reviewing and approving by commission,
- application of voucher privatization absent from preferential treatment,
- basic preference of privatization methods based on competition to the methods excluding competition, strict regime for direct sales (governmental approval),
- requirement for setting up the market value in the projects with foreign partnership and the system of independent foreign advisors reviewing adequacy of terms of sale.

All those facilities may minimize faults of state business decision as to competition, though they can't remove it. If they could do that, no privatization would be needed. The best is the fact that privatization project approvals are the last entrepreneurial decisions taken by the state.

3. SMALL PRIVATIZATION

The Act on small privatization was approved on October 25, 1990 and the first auction was held on January 26, 1991. In total 25278 operational units were approved by the Ministry for Administration of National Property of the Czechoslovak Republic prior to their reviewing by founders based on projects elaborated by District Privatization Commissions. By July almost

21.000 operational units were sold and approximately 26 billion crowns obtained through auctions. New private owners having all rights and obligations, obtained the property in extension of 6 billion crowns, since at three quarters of auctions there was just the right to the rise of time limited lease auctioned.

Especially shops have been sold. Common groceries and self-service shops represent 14% of all auctioned ones, stores on hardware and household utilities account for 9&, textile and clothes shops 5%, butcher shops represent 3%, news agent's 9% and shoe-shops, confectioneries, florists and book-shops represent 1% each. Entities providing service were auctioned on the large scale (16% of all sales) and so were restaurants (9%). The small privatization even dealt with hotels (almost 2% of all sales), smaller manufacturing units (almost 2% of all sales as well). Department stores, petrol stations and even computing centers were auctioned though in low numbers.

The average auction price was approximately 50-60% higher than the starting price. The auction price reflected in addition to attractiveness of operational units, the attractiveness of the place where these units could be found and in fact it proved how command prices were absurd. In Prague 1 the average auction price represented 15 times the starting price and it nearly reached five million crowns. In Karlovy Vary, one of the most beautiful spas, the average auction price was twice as higher as the starting price. The average auction price and the average starting price were almost identical in regions less attractive for investing.

So called Dutch auctions fascinated the public. The auction price could drop down to 50% of the starting price in the first and down to 20% in the second run. Apparently evident agreements among bidders could have been proved (in one case the bidders even informed the members of a privatization commission about their interest in the Dutch auction) and absence of effective penalties caused the lack of their sanctions. In most cases the Dutch auctions reflected the low interest in the starting price. It is not by chance that in Prague the Dutch auctions represented 8% of sales (in Prague 1 only 1.5%, in Prague 5 - in the district of shabby tenant houses and factories - 12% and in Prague 6 - the highly attractive district - 4%) while in the Southern Bohemia 14% and in other districts the figure reached nearly one fifth or a quarter of all auctions.

Comparing to large privatization the small privatization dealt with only a small portion of the privatized property though the most apparent part at the same time, and in addition to the basic effect based on determination of the private owners, the small privatization was significantly demonstrative. It proved the practical and evident intention of economic reform endeavouring to establish the private ownership. Consequently, many valuable information were obtained and feedback to the authors of laws related to the privatization and strategy and even to all involved in the privatization process was offered. They informed about the real power of their current managements of privatized enterprises and about their inclination to create barriers against the way of privatization which contradicts the interests of an enterprise and its management.

Especially the claims of the necessity of consensus as to privatization and its methods were extremely important. They pointed out the aversion towards the privatization process giving the property over to the social groups not accepted by the public, they covered the issue on dirty money and urgent need for its solution by means of tax system. They signalized the fact that the aversion of companies' managements is not related to the own privatization process but to that which minimizes their participation.

4. RESTITUTION

Since the second half of the year 1990 the laws were passed proposed by Federal Government and National Governments and by incentive of members of Parliament on property return to the initial owners, and/or their heirs (legally entitled entities). Ministry of National Property Administration and its Privatization of the Czech Republic worked out and Federal Parliament passed the Law No 403/1990 of Cod. (on alleviation of consequences of some cases of property-related injustice in the wording of Act No. 458/1990 Coll. and Act. No. 137/1991 Coll.). The scope of ownership mitigation was then extended by the Law No 87/1991 of Cod. (on extra judicial rehabilitations), having established decisive time for harms rectifying from February 25, 1948 up to January 1, 1990. The Law No 229/1991 of Con (on the settlement of ownership relations to land and other agricultural property) was the legislation to remedy the ownership harms towards agricultural and forest property owners in the time period of 1948 - 1986. The principle of all the above laws is to give the property to legally authorized person. In cases, the nationalized property cannot be given back or when it is degraded to the extend, that does not allow its immediate use without adjustments, the authorized person is entitled to receive financial reimbursement. If the property value has increased, while being state owned property and its price is significantly exceeding the value by the time of nationalization, the authorized person may decide, whether it will claim the property to be issued and pay the price difference or the financial reimbursement. The range of restituents is quite extensive, as the legally authorized persons are (in the stated sequence): heirs from the testament, children and husband and/or children descendants, parents, brothers and sisters and/or their heirs.

Property restitution to the citizens is the principle, essential part of restitution. Besides that though there is also the property restitution to some institutions. It is namely giving the property back to catholic church, handled by Law No 298/1990 of Cod. (on the settlement of some property relations of religious orders and congregations and the Olomouc Archbishopric), to the towns and communities, tackled by the Lax No 172/1991 of Cod. (on transfer of some property of the Czech Republic to the ownership of communities).

While before the restitution laws were passed the extensive discussions took place on whether to return to the past restoring initial proprietor rights is purposeful, effective, honest and justified, at the time being the restitutions appear to represent the most smooth branch of Czech privatization as they are respected by all social levels and property dedicated for restitutions falls out of contest of interests. Also diminishing role of state institutions is playing positive role here. Property is continuously returned by due entities (mostly by state companies), who hold them. Just in case of financial settlement in the relation state - citizen, the central state administration authorities are involved (for inst. financial reimbursement in compliance with the law No 403/1990 of Cod. is tacked by Ministry for National Property Administration of the Czech Republic, reimbursement in compliance with the law No 87/1991 of Cod. is tackled by the Ministry of Finance of the Czech Republic).

To estimate the scope of restituted property is hard at the time being, as the statistic study is just being prepared. Tentative picture on restitution range can be made out of the following data: Involving the Law No 403/1990 of Cod. the Ministry for National Property Administration and its Privatization of the Czech Republic received as of today 10.416 applications to get financial reimbursement for the property, that cannot be given back or is degraded and paid to restituents the sum of Kcs 90 mil. Ministry of Finance received about 44.000 applications related to the Law No 87/1991 of Cod. to get reimbursement. We can suppose the number of applications to physically issue the property addressed to due persons must have been much higher.

Conclusion: Privatization in Czechoslovakia after June General Election

It is quite clear now that the result of June General Election in which Czech voters expressed their will be to the radical transformation of the political and economic system and gave their votes to the coalition of right - wing political parties while Slovaks preferred nationalistic Motion for the Democratic Slovakia, will be two independent states.

As far as privatization is concerned, no basic changes have occurred yet. Restitutions, small privatization and large privatization have continued according federal and republic laws. The splitting of voucher privatization for the second privatization wave is being prepared. Some personal changes were done after General Election. The need for the general rules in large privatization became to be more urgent, it is more stressed than before and the procedure of judging and approving privatization plans is slightly more transparent but its philosophy remained without substantial changes.

It is precocious to express expectations for next development of Slovak privatization. But because Slovak policy - makers and economists are more oriented to state interventions, it is very probable that privatization in Slovakia can slow down.

7

VOUCHER PRIVATIZATION: TARGETS, INTENTIONS AND PRELIMINARY RESULTS

Miloslav Hejnák
The Institute of Economics
Czechoslovak Academy of Science

Motto: "If you deposit your vouchers to the Harvard Investment Funds we can guarantee that, if you wish, after a year and a day, you became our shareholder we will buy out your shares at a minimum price of 10,350 CSK - i.e. at a value 10 times higher than original value of your voucher book.

Nevertheless, by this offer, your chances in voucher privatization do not end. We prepared a super chance for you. If you give your investment points to the Harvard Investment Funds you will be (regardless the number of your points deposited) included in a lottery giving the possibility to win 1 mil. CSK..."
(by Viktor Kožený, president of Harvard Capital and Consulting company.)

1. INTRODUCTION

The motto stated above was used to help understanding the most important breakpoint in thinking of common citizens which were transferred into a role of investment voucher holders (IVHs) i.e. into the role of future shareholders. Even if reasoning, discussions, analyses and educational activities of economists, journalist and ministers concerning voucher privatization were common topic of professional and partly laic public, the interest of spacious public to become shareholders was promoted mainly by the offer to obtain for 1 035 CSK an amount 10 times higher after one year. In addition, the advertising campaign of the Centre for Voucher Privatization activities was not convincing enough and there have been also many unclear circumstances concerning individual privatization waves and rounds themselves (some of them still exist even now, after the third round of the first wave of large-scale privatization was finished).

Shortly after the Harvard Funds' campaign started, many other different investment funds developed strong activities in advertising campaigns in all mass medias as well. They competed among each other in explaining their particular advantages for IVHs. The first results are known: originally distrustful and sceptic general public to voucher privatization was queuing to buy investment books and stamps and than again to their registration. The possibility to became an IVH had each adult Czechoslovak person (above 18 years old) with permanent residence in Czechoslovakia by the date of 1.11.1991. Such a condition fulfilled about 11.4 mil. inhabitants. Final number of IVHs amounting to above 8.5 mil. inhabitants was probable higher than expectations of even strong promoters of the voucher privatization. Still in December 1991 , only 15-20 % of population was interested in investment vouchers, a half of it was fully without interest and the rest was not decided (according to the public opinion surveys). The principal turnover occurred one month later when nearly half of inhabitants bought a voucher book or was decided to buy it.

Originally, a participation of about 2 mil IVHs was presumed, next more precise estimates counted with 4 mil of IVHs at maximum. However, the final number of IVHs exceeded even this estimate and thus the amount of property entering the first wave of large-scale privatization had to be adjusted to the increasing number of participants. Finally, 206 424 410 shares (all in nominal value 1,000 CSK) of 943 joint-stock companies from the National Property Fund (NPF) of the Czech Republic, 90 111 742 shares from 487 joint-stock companies from the NPF of the Slovak Republic and 2 857 121 shares from 61 joint-stock companies from the Federal Fund was determined to the first wave of the large-scale privatization. Altogether, the property above 299 bil. CSK from 1491 joint-stock companies created the supply side of the first wave of voucher privatization. Theoretically, the average value of nominal property per one IVH had amounted to about 35 082 CSK. But it is evident that this amount is a only hypothetical one. Not only each share of the same nominal value will be of a different market value but also a total shift of average market value downstairs can be assumed. Moreover, considerable number of citizens invest by means of an investment fund and each fund deducts a certain amount of a property to cover its administration costs (see in part III.).

On February 17, 1992, the pre-round - (i.e. the period when citizens had possibility to commit their voucher books to investment funds) began and it finished on April 4,1992. On May 18, 1992, the first round of the first wave of large-scale privatization started with 4 month delay contrary to the originally approved time-schedule. The wave of privatization is the period started and finished by the Federal Ministry of Finance in which individual IVHs themselves or by means of investment privatization funds (IPFs) can order shares. During the wave of privatization, the shares are ordered in rounds of privatization - i.e. in the periods from the beginning of orders until the results are announced. The beginning and the end of rounds are again set by the Federal Ministry of Finance. Each round of privatization consists of 4 steps:

- shares rate of individual joint-stock companies announcement
- orders of shares at postal offices
- collection and evaluation of orders
- announcement of results of the round (either purchase of shares or transfer of investment points to the next round in case the demand on shares of particular company exceeds the amount of shares supplied).

The starting rate of shares is a number of shares of the same nominal value (1,000 CSK), which is offered for 100 investment points or other whole multiplier of 100 investment points. In the first round, the unit rate - 3 shares for 100 investment points for all companies was set (the rate is than being changed according to demand and supply on individual joint-stock companies in following rounds). As mentioned above, each IVH could invest 1000 investment points. This unit share rate caused certain lowering of the theoretical property to 30 shares, i.e. to 30,000 CSK per one IVH. The difference compared to original theoretical value 35,000 CSK was explained by several reasons. First, the shares are indivisible (a part of share can not be sold). Second, there was an intentional underestimation with regard to possibility of share value increase and compensations in next rounds, when will be evident which shares are highly demanded and which are nearly unsaleable.

In the following text, the individual interest groups (citizens and investment funds) entering the first wave of voucher privatization with different targets will be monitored separately. Finally, the last preliminary results of the third round will be mentioned.

2. CITIZENS - INVESTMENT VOUCHER HOLDERS (IVHS)

As already mentioned, about 8.53 mil. of Czechoslovak citizens bought and registered their voucher books (according to the report on the final pre-round balance). Even if some other sources published slightly different figures, the number stated above is used in order to assure the consistency of the following text.

Such a large number of persons entering the fist wave of the large scale privatization was among other reasons explained by public broad support and agreement with voucher privatization and with the way of economic transformation in general. The results of registration and number of IVHs - shareholders of investment funds can lead to a more probable conclusion: Czechoslovak citizens became IVHs mostly because of various financial effects (to earn 10 times higher value after one year or to have a possibility of advantageous credits etc.) rather than because of support of the voucher privatization. Surveys of public opinions show that financial benefits were the main motivation for 44 % of IVHs and for next 27 % of IVHs, the motivation was influenced by an effort to help family (this reason was the strongest one in case of older generation). Only 10 % of IVHs (mostly: graduates, employees in a state sector and persons in a middle-age group) explained their active participation in voucher privatization as a support of the state and its transformation policy.

Additionally, a "crowd effect" can be counted as last but not least reason causing such a high final number of IVHs. The growing number of persons which was suspecting to voucher privatization before the end of 1991 changed its opinion and bought the voucher books for themselves, for relatives etc. and so not only unexpected interest in voucher books started but also speculation with them.

Similarly as the Harvard advertisement have started non-precedent advertising campaign of all other investment funds in Czechoslovakia so far, advertisements offering speculative purchases and registration of voucher books became very frequent in many newspapers. The advertisement beginning as follows: 'I will sell a registered voucher book worth... ' was certainly the most common type in an advertisement offer. The fact that supplies of voucher books' sales exceeded the demand enormously leads again to a conclusion of prevailing IVHs' motivation: making a rapid profit. A relatively great part of citizens bough the voucher books in order to sell them immediately.

In the following text, we analyze motivations, possibilities, expectations and some predicted impacts of IVHs behaviour in a greater detail. As mentioned in the introductory section, there was only low interest in investment vouchers in December 1991 even if estimates of the privatized property in the first wave of the large scale privatization per one IVH ranged between 80 - 100,000 CSK. According public opinion surveys, such an amount did not convicted citizens that investment of 1,035 CSK (1,000 for voucher stamp, 35 for voucher book) is advantageous enough.

There were more reasons of general public distrust, the insufficient level of advertisement campaign of the Centre of Voucher Privatization was evidently among the most important. Actually, an average citizen did not know what is the voucher privatization about. This conclusion is supported by results of socio-demographic public surveys. In the beginning of the campaign (September 1991), the highest interest in groups of citizens in middle-age and graduated ones prevailed (education belonged to the most significant socio- demographic differential factors). The lowest interest occurred in the group above sixty and in the group with the lowest education. In the beginning, the interest was higher mostly in cities above 100 000 inhabitants. In February 1992, the all differential factors were nearly equalized.

High increase in demand on voucher investment can be explained and/or summarized mainly by following reasons:

- particular financial offers and behaviour of some IPFs
- possibility of speculative purchases and selling of investment books
- consequent crowd effect i.e. participation of persons which were originally not interested in voucher privatization at all.

It can be derived from preceding reasons, that relatively high increase in supply side of security papers can be expected when the conditions of stock market will be clear. Thus we must mention one of the basic negatives of the voucher privatization for IVHs : persistent uncertainty concerning possibility of selling their shares. Even now, after the fourth round was started (October 1992), the Act on Securities has not been approved yet.

A citizen could find out how to become an IVH, how to use his vouchers and much other information in acts, numerous advertising materials, handbooks etc. But he still does not know the basic information - how to turn his shares into money in time when more than 90 % of points are invested (from the number of investment points which remain to IVHs).

The approval of the Act on Securities will be one of the very important steps of the economic transformation as a whole. Undoubtedly, the supply of securities and particularly of shares will exceed the demand due to motivations of the most of IVHs described above. Moreover, dividends will be probably rather low in several following years. It is very difficult to presume an amount of supplied securities since the conditions of their sales are still not known nowadays. According to some estimates, the total supply of securities (not only of shares from the voucher privatization but also other securities and bonds) will amount to 1,000 bil. CSK. Estimates of the number of shares offered and of the average market value per one share bought in the first wave of the large-scale privatization will depend on many other factors, certainly mostly on the demand.

The voucher privatization itself is monetary neutral but if e.g. one third of IVHs sold their shares (and immediately asked for paying promised amounts from various investment funds) it would cause additional supply of shares amounted to about 100 bil. CSK in the first half of 1993. If such an amount were paid to citizens, a considerably increased demand on some consumption goods would arise (e.g. imported high-tech and durable goods). That could start not only inflation but also affect the balance of payments and than consequently cause the CSK devaluation.

In the end of this section, IVH's basic possibilities of obtaining shares for investment points are mentioned.

1. Each IVH can independently order shares. He will do it in case he is convinced that selected company will be profitable in future (by the form of dividends or share valorization) or in case the voucher privatization is just a game to verify his capabilities.
2. If an IVH has no necessary information concerning individual company or he wants to minimize risk of his bad decision, he usually select one of the numerous investment funds. In this case he mainly looses the possibility to became a shareholder of particular joint-stock companies.
3. If an IVH intends to be an owner of shares of particular companies but he is not interested in investing by himself he can be deputed in decision making and investment by means of an investment club (possibilities (2) and (3) will be discussed in the following section).

(1) In case of individual decision making, the IVH uses either his personal knowledge of the particular company or external information. All brochures or directions concerning evaluation of companies in the first wave of the large-scale privatization were mostly sold very quickly regardless their professional level and real information value. For example, some figures about firms in the "List of Joint-stock Companies Privatized by Voucher System" - which were also supposed to help voucher investors in their decision making - did not include the necessary information. It is true however that, in this case, the distribution of further information about privatized companies may simply be misleading because of the broad inexperience of the public.

In spite of these shortages, the indicators in the above-mentioned "List of Joint-Stock Companies" are more representative and more helpful for future investors than some other handbooks or advices of consulting firms. Unfortunately, the list was published on May 13, 1992 - after the pre-round finished (and at many post offices it was available even later). I.e. it was available when IVHs had no other possibility than individual investment.

Lists of privatized units published before this term were not representative enough and did not conclude most of necessary figures.

3. THE INVESTMENT PRIVATIZATION FUNDS (IPFS)

In general, existence of IPFs is common in the market economies. Their basic function consists of free financial means collecting in order their effective allocation and profit making. The origination of investment funds of a particular sort is the specific feature in conditions of the voucher privatization. In Czechoslovakia, the IPFs do not work with free monetary means but with investment vouchers. They try to gather vouchers from citizens in the pre-round and to allocate them in particular companies (in individual rounds of privatization). Their activities are thus feasible even with minimal financial capital of their own. Undoubtedly, this fact led to foundation of such a number of IPFs which is compared to similar countries out of common rule.

Basically, the targets of most of IPFs' foundation are clear enough: to regulate considerable properties and to make profits both from the possibility of influencing companies and from the administration of shares of their share holders with minimal capital. Original motivation of many IPFs aspired to achieve dominant position in one or more selected companies. In case that this motivation was the main reason for the IPF foundation, we again face one of the basic problems of the voucher privatization as a whole: insufficiency in legislation. The deadline of the IPFs' application was set on 16.12.1991. The activities and performance of IPFs were solved by the Amendment of The Governmental Regulation of the CSFR No. 383/1992 from 30.1.1992 and the Act on Investment Companies and Investment Funds did not become valid until 28.4.1992 (after the pre-round of the large-scale privatization finished). According to these documents, an individual IPF can not own more than 20 % of a privatized company's property and this amount can not exceed 10 % of the IPF's property in the same time. The IPFs founded by one founder can not own together more than 40 % of a company property. This regulation led to higher interest in smaller companies (mostly in case of smaller IPFs) on the one side and to collusion among some IPFs on the other side.

Individual IPFs used different practices to maximize the number of IVHs - besides pointing out their professional background, "venturous" targets and guaranteed profits, they often promised certain financial amounts (as stated above). Such techniques were used not only by private IPFs but also by those ones founded by banks, saving institutes or insurance companies. E.g., the Saving Privatization Joint-Stock Company offered a loan amounted to 1 000 CSK to cover registration costs immediately and in April 1992, it offered a credit covered by purchased shares till a value of 11,000 CSK. The First Investment Joint-Stock Company originated by the Investment Bank offered the loan of 1,000 CSK as well and immediately after the IVH deposited the whole 1,000 investment points, it provided next credit amounted to 15 000 CSK or it promised to buy shares at minimum for 11,000 CSK after one year. The First Privatization Investment Fund founded by the Czech Insurance Company offered to buy IVH's shares at minimum for 15,000 CSK after 1.5.1993, etc. The analysis of the pre-round results shows, that similar promises of financial earnings were the main motives of a substantial number of participants of the voucher privatization and the funds with such offers gathered the greatest number of IVHs.

The IPFs founded by banks offered in addition banking information concerning individual companies in their advertisement campaign. This offer involved not only information about financial situation of particular clients but also information resulting from privatization projects which were in many cases elaborated by banks. Related to this fact, the question concerning abusing of information was discussed. Unfortunately, the relevant governmental regulation No. 383/1991 did not take into account this problem. It only says (in &16 a) that a member of any board must not be employed in the Czechoslovak State Bank or in the institution of state administration. These problems have not been solved yet but it is evident that the IPFs having access to such information had an evident comparative advantage.

One of the most crucial problems expected after the Act on Securities will be approved is that an considerable number of IVHs will require the financial amount promised. That will cause not only a general problem probably impacting financial and monetary policy but also a problem for several IPFs. Basically, the IPFs will have two possibilities in case of high financial demands of their shareholders. First, they can sell their shares to other subjects or they can borrow money from banks. Supposing supply of securities will exceed demand, their price will drop and reduce a property which could be a guarantee for banking credits available to IPFs. That is why individual IPFs must already nowadays prepare a strategy solving such a situation.

Already at present, the Harvard Investment Funds allow term limited sell and purchase of shares covered by assets acquired in the framework of privatization for investment vouchers. In order to that purpose, they founded the Harvard Stock Exchange Company. When the shares of Harvard Investment are sold, the IVH will obtain the promised amount of 10,350 CSK time discounted and further reduced by an administration fee in case he will sell his shares earlier than in December 1993. This reduction is derived from the number of days till the end of December and from the discount rate plus 5 %. In case of sale in November 1992 for example, the sale price would amount to about 9,000 CSK.

On the contrary in case of buying Harvard Investment shares, the minimum price is set to 10.7 CSK per one investment point - i.e. to 10 700 CSK for 1,000 investment points. If the market price is higher than 10.70 CSK, the buyer can determine the maximum price of one point for which he is willing to buy investment points in an amount stated ahead.

Originally, there were 438 IPFs registered in the CSFR for the first wave of the large-scale privatization. In fact, 429 of them entered the first wave (some of them did not fulfill all necessary regulations or gave up their activities). The number of IPFs is not stable, because during the first and second rounds, several IPFs merged or closed mutual contracts and some other IPFs finished their activities till the end of the third round.

There were 8.53 bil. investment points (corresponding to 8.53 mil. IVHs) in the beginning of voucher privatization from which 6.13 bil. (72 %) was committed to IPFs while only 2.4 bil. investment points remained in individual hands of voucher holders. 2.22 mil. voucher holders (26 %) did not participate in the pre-round at all, i.e. they kept the whole voucher book for individual investment. The structure of investment by means of IPFs was as follows: 5.81 mil. IVHs deposited total amount of 1,000 investment unit in several IPFs, 4.7 mil. IVHs committed total amount of 1,000 investment points to one particular IPF only and 0.5 mil. IVHs kept at least 100 investment units for their own direct investment.

Individual IPFs differ considerably as far their capital strength is concerned. The "strongest capital group" including roughly 10 IPFs gathered over 100,000 IVHs what means a theoretical possibility of disposing with property above 3 bil. CSK of its book value. A half of the strongest investment funds can dispose with a property even above 10 bil. CSK. The theoretical book value of property is derived from unit share rate set in the first round and from the average nominal value of 30,000 CSK per one IVH. The "middle capital group" consisted of 50-60 investment funds gathered 10-100,000 IVHs. The "weakest capital group" amounted to above 300 investment funds assembled less than 10,000 IVHs. The structure of investment fund property just has a form similar to the normal distribution expressed by the Gauss curve.

The other possibility of IVH's investment in the voucher privatization will be briefly discussed in the end of this section : the deputing in purchase of particular shares by means of investment club.

The deputing has had various forms. We will not deal with the family and/or friend help, when e.g. one member of a family deputies the others mostly the old ones family members. Nevertheless, there are many types of official or semi-official associations which (besides providing a help to those IVHs which do not know where to allocate investment points and from various reasons do not trust the IPFs) follow their private objectives. Such types of associations are in the following text called investment clubs (IC). Even if they differ in many aspects, some common features can be identified.

As stated in the previous text, each IVH can order shares individually. He makes it in case he is perfectly informed about the selected company or he is sure to find optimal allocation of his investment points.

In case the IVH does not have the necessary information concerning individual companies, he usually chooses investment by means of IPFs. By this choice, he bears a lower risk connected with investment into particular company. What is that risk like? First, the IVH does not know particular company, second, he has no possibility to use voting law derived from only a negligible part of shares owned by him in an active way, and third, he has no possibility to divert ownership to different industries or sub industries.

These arguments were also broadly used by IPFs in their advertising campaigns (apart from financial promises and announcement of famous persons from cultural or sport life supporting respective funds). But evaluating these IPFs' arguments seriously, the validity of the only one of is evident: possibility of a relatively broad portfolio creation. But this fact itself does not mean an advantage in all cases. On the contrary, several IPFs buy only minimal number of shares almost of all companies, and thus they no doubt reduce a risk of bankruptcy of one or more companies but it does not necessary cause the rationale and effective allocation of investment vouchers.

Even if the arguments concerning the IVH's insufficient knowledge of a particular company and/or the limited possibility of using the voting law are sound in general, they are valid in case of investment by means of IPFs as well. In average, each IVH had information about approximately 100 companies from all 1,491 companies entering the first wave. He knew some of them better (he or his relatives or friends worked there) some of them worst (from newspaper, TV sets etc.), but nearly each IVH had a general overview about considerable number of companies at least. As already mentioned, the IPFs originated in the end of 1991 and in the beginning of 1992. IVHs could learn about them during about three month (till the beginning of the pre-round). Even if the advertising campaign has been the greatest one in the CSFR so far, its information value was (besides the financial promises) rather low. The detailed information concerning particular IPFs and their prospects was not available to individual IVHs from the simple reason - IPFs could not do anything but the advertisement campaign to present themselves to broad public. The fact that many of them used the names of known financial institutions or of "socialist companies" with a good performance meant that these institutions were the founders of independent legal entities - IPFs only. Such institutions can earn some fees from IPFs but they do not undertake their liabilities.

Similarly, the argument concerning no possibility of voting law while buying shares of particular company does not benefit to IPFs, because mainly the larger of them concentrate much bigger capital than an average company and that is why an IVH has no considerable chance to use his voting law derived from ownership of IPFs' shares.

Because of reasons stated above, the origination of investment clubs can be evaluated as a compromise between IVH's independent allocation of investment points and investment by means of IPFs.

If the greater number of IVHs is associated in the IC, the possibility of voting law application derived from ownership of shares can be achieved. The IVH will remain an owner of shares of particular company and he will have a law of decision making concerning these shares (in case he is interested he can use an professional help of the IC). The dividends will be paid directly without additional taxation.

The target of ICs is very closed to the general objective of the voucher privatization: the division of part of national property among broad public with regard to minimal capital means of Czechoslovak inhabitants and mainly the transfer of anonymous people property to real owners which will take care of this property.

Voucher privatization itself fulfills the first part of the objective but the second part concerning origination of particular owners is achieved only partially. Due to usual effort of state companies to keep their posts also in future (after privatization) by form of partial direct sale of shares, by effort to gather necessary amount of voucher books or by foundation of a IPF as well, the particular IVH has absolutely no possibility to administer his property himself.

The IC institution enables to associate voting laws derived from ownership of particular companies for different groups of citizens (no matter if this club gains majority or only an important share of votes).

There are big differences among particular ICs, some of them works as 'broaden family boards' having only 10-50 members. Others originated by some informal associations gathering "friends and friends of friends" with hundreds, at maximum thousands of members. The number of ICs is difficult to estimate, because they mostly do not perform as independent legal entities and they are not reported by statistical publications. Even if most of ICs is not financially profitable nowadays (the fees connected with their activities usually cover overhead costs and future profits are not guaranteed), they can build up a strong position in some smaller company. For example, when a company with assets amounting 50 mil. CSK is privatized by the voucher scheme and offers 97 % of its shares (48 500 shares), the IC with 250 numbers can require 50 % of shares (in course 10 shares for 100 points) of a relatively large company. Contrary to IPFs, there are no legislative limitations for ICs. Previous example is mostly an exceptional one in case of "family or friend" based club. But such a technique is evident in case of ICs with very ambitious objectives and advertisement. Two of them are be mentioned as an illustration: the American Exchange and the Ost-West Agentur.

The American exchange does not look like an investment club according its advertisement. It presents itself as a "free advisory service for Czechoslovak citizens in voucher privatization". The free service is explained by the fact, that it does provide commercial-investment advisory activity for Czechoslovak companies on a commercial basis. That is why it does need any fees from future shareholders and on the contrary, it can use its own experience with Czechoslovak companies to help IVHs. This offer looks as fully disinterested one from the first view. But there is a contract including authorization of the owner of voucher book (of the IVH cooperating with the American Exchange) which enable not only unlimited deputing while selection of shares for investment points but also deputing in an assembly. Actually, the contract enables full transfer of IVH's voting law derived from ownership of shares.

In the advertisement paper, this fact is listed as an advantage for the IVH, what can be true in some cases but in reality it means, that the American Exchange will have laws of all owners - IVHs, which let themselves to be deputed in the assembly and consequently in all top authorities of particular companies. Each IVH also pledges, that in case of any other purchase or selling shares, an additional charge will be paid amounted to 10 % of capital value of a particular transaction. In case the IVH will want to sell its shares which can be of a market value e.g. 8 000 CSK, the amount of 800 CSK will be gained by the American Exchange. Thus finally, only 7 200 CSK remains to the IVH: a bit less than one half of the amount offered by numerous IPFs.

On the other hand, such a company also wants to earn some financial effect from its activity and a certain per cent from purchases and sales is in similar investment clubs in market economies common.

The offer of the Austrian OST-WEST AGENTUR was the second most frequent mode of deputy investment by means of an investment club in Prague. This company, presented as a company "for trade and mediating contracts offered the most advantageous possibility to enter voucher privatization in all privatization waves". There is one different argument in their advertising campaign besides the usual ones. The company counts with the fact, that after the fourth round of the first wave will be finished, it will be evident which companies can be bought really cheaply (those ones which were considered to be without prospects mainly because of lack of production and/or sales programs). Just in this moment, IVHs should apply to some of the OST-WEST AGENTUR representatives for information. The OST-WEST AGENTUR offers services to these "bad" companies and it is ready to negotiate efficient production programs with Germany and Austria. These conclusions are derived only from information in press, because the author is not fully acknowledged about detailed conditions of this company and in the time the paper is written, the fourth round has not been finished. Author does not know the number of IVHs intending to use services of this company as well but according to official figures, about 50,000 IVHs did not invest to the third round any investment point. However, waiting with investment seems to by risky from the nowadays viewpoint when accelerated finishing of the fifth wave is possible. The fifth round might be the last one and the investment points which were not used could disappear.

Nevertheless, even if targets and techniques of particular ICs are various, a principle of ICs probably mostly corresponds to global objectives of the voucher privatization.

4. PRELIMINARY RESULTS AFTER THE THIRD ROUND OF THE LARGE-SCALE PRIVATIZATION WAS FINISHED

Voucher privatization was started by the Act No. 92/91 on Conditions of State Property Transfer to Other Subjects. This act solves questions of the large-scale privatization of which the voucher privatization is a part. It divides responsibility concerning performance of voucher privatization between the Czech and Slovak Ministry for Privatization and the Federal Ministry for Finance (FMF). The former one assures selection of companies and their transformation into joint-stock companies, whose shares create the supply side of voucher privatization. The later one takes care of organizational and technical affairs of voucher privatization (press and distribution of voucher books, stamps, booklets, start and finish of pre-round and the other rounds, setting of voucher courses in individual rounds, establishment of register places, computer network etc.) - i.e. it guarantees the demand side of the process. The FMF founded a specific organization - The Centre of the Voucher Privatization which assures particular tasks by means of contracts with other suppliers.

The Act No. 92/91 mentioned above, authorized the federal government (after agreements with republic governments) to regulate the way of investment vouchers issuing and using by The CSFR Governmental Regulation on Issue and Use of Investment Vouchers No. 383/91 from September, 1991 amended in January, 1992. This regulation defined some basic terms related to the voucher privatization (including performance of the IPFs).

In the first round of the first wave of large-scale privatization, the property amounted to 299,393,282,000 CSK, represented by 299,393,282 shares of 1491 companies entered from the Funds of National Property (Czech, Slovak and federal). The number of investment points amounted to 8.53 bil. investment points which would correspond with the nominal value of 35,082

CSK per one IVH and thus with the theoretical share rate 3.5 shares for 100 investment points. Finally, the starting rate of shares 3 shares for 100 points was set equally for all companies.

In the first round, the shares for 2.98 bil. investment points were bought. Thus, the property amounted nearly to 90 bil. CSK, i.e. 89.4 mil. shares (30 % of offered property) was sold. 48 of companies was sold totally, mainly because of possibility of IPFs' bids shortening. The shortening is derived from the Governmental regulation No. 383/91 in order to maximize a number of shares and companies sold. The regulation enables to shorten the IPFs' orders in each round if the total demand on shares of particular company will not exceed 25 % and in the same time none of IPFs will be shorten in its order more than by 20 %.

In the second round, the offer of 210 mil. shares of 1443 companies entered. 78 mil. shares was sold and 132 of remained for the third round. There were 74 companies sold completely again owing to shortening of IPFs' bids in this round. The disposable number of investment points amounted to 5.55 bil. (what corresponds to theoretical rate 3.8 shares for 100 points), but only 4.88 of points was really used. Shares were bought for 3.41 bil. points and 2.14 remained for the third round. On the contrary to theoretical share rate 3.8 shares for 100 points, the shares were bought in the rate 2.3 shares for 100 points finally. It means that more expensive shares were preferred (of higher rate). The share rate set for the second round ranked from 10 shares for 100 points to 1 share for 400 points. Originally unit share rate thus reached the ratio 1:40 between the cheapest and the most expensive shares.

69 % of shares was offered by the Czech republic and the 31 % by the Slovak republic from the total offer amounted to 209.95 mil. shares. Czech IVHs asked for 99 % in the CR and for only 1% in the SR while Slovak IVHs asked for 82 % in the SR and for 18 % in the CR. Czech IPFs ordered 98 % in the CR and 2 % in the SR and the Slovak IPFs ordered 54 % in the SR and 54 % in the CR. Slovak investors (both IVHs and IPFs) bought in the first two rounds 13.5 mil. shares in the Czech republic while Czech investors bought only 3.5 mil. shares in Slovakia.

In the third round, the total offer of 1369 companies reached 132.1 mil. shares. 32.4 mil. shares was sold and 99.6 mil. of them remained for the fourth round. 52 of companies was sold completely in this round. The number of disposable investment points amounted to 2.14 bil.(corresponding theoretical rate was 6.2 shares for 100 points) from which 1.99 bil. was really used. Shares were bought for 1.02 bil. points and 1.12 bil. points was postponed in fourth round. Similarly as in the second round, the theoretical share rate 6.2 shares for 100 points was different than the real one. Finally, shares were bought in share rate 3.2 for 100 points. The shares bought were thus about two times more expensive than theoretical average share rate was set.

The official share rate was set in range from 97 shares for 100 points to 1 share for 800 points in the third round. The ratio 1:776 between the cheapest and the most expensive shares meant that it was possible to order 776 times higher number of the worst (the least demanded) shares than the best (the most demanded) ones for the same amount of investment points.

The number of shares really sold in the third round did not confirm this large range of share rates and for the fourth round, the range was reduced on 60 shares for 100 points to 1 share for 1,000 points (i.e. on 1:600 ratio between the best and the worst companies).

64.5 % of shares was offered by the CR and 35.5 % of shares by the CR from the total offer amounted to 132.13 mil. shares. Czech IVHs asked for 98 % in the CR and for 2 % in the SR while the Slovak ones asked for 81 % in the SR and for 19 % in the CR. Czech IPFs ordered 96 % in the CR and 4 % in the SR and Slovak IPFs ordered 60 % in the SR and 40 % in the CR. Slovak investors bought after first three rounds 15.9 mil shares (2.4 mil in the third round) in the CR and Czech investors bought only 4 mil. shares (0.5 mil. in the third round) in the SR. This evident disproportion in demand on shares led to different average share rates in the Czech republic (2.55 shares for 100 points) and in Slovakia (5.59 shares for 100 points) in the third round.

As the preliminary republic results of voucher privatization show, the strong separatistic tendencies in Slovakia do not correspond with the national trust in Slovak companies' future prospects, since a considerable part of Slovak investors is oriented to Czech companies. Consequently, Czech share holders are in a disadvantageous position, because the Slovak demand on Czech companies make the shares in the Czech lands "more expensive" . The low interest of Czech investors in Slovak companies confirms that the lowest trust in Slovak economy is common in both republics.

5. CONCLUSION

Evaluating the situation in the third round, some other conclusions can be derived. First, the IPFs invested more quickly than the IVHs. The IPFs' share in all point which have not been invested is slightly lower than 50 % so far . Totally, 1.12 bil. points (13 % of original number) entered the fourth round, 0.57 bil. of them remained in hands of IVHs. Second, 200 mil. shares of a book value 200 bil. CSK was sold, i.e. 67% from total offer for the first wave. But concerning the number of sold companies, only 174 (11.7 %) was completely sold from 1491 companies entering the first wave. Third, the theoretical average share rate reached 8.9 share for 100 points. It means that mainly more expensive shares were bought and in the fourth round, the theoretical book value per one IVH (in case he had not invested so far) thus amounted to about 89,000 CSK. Nevertheless, it is probable, that a great part of remaining shares will be less salable and their market value will not be very high.

It is preliminary to evaluate the voucher privatization from the first results. In any case it is an interesting experiment which helped de-nationalize a considerable amount of property relatively quickly. It can be also concluded that the privatization process partially loses its velocity. The corresponding authorities react both by shortening of the next round and by lowering of share ranking. It is very probable, that the first wave will be finished sooner than 95 % of shares will be sold as it was intended (even if not officially reported) before.

The underdeveloped legislation belonged evidently to the greatest problems related to the voucher privatization. It is also difficult to anticipate future performance of the IPFs as biggest owners of shares of companies privatized by the voucher scheme. With regard to fact, that IPFs will merge (formally or informally) also in future, a considerable concentration of decision making in a relatively few hands can be expected. The federal character of the first wave of the large-scale privatization is problematic as well, since Czech investors are in evidently disadvantageous position. However, any interruption of the first wave would bring many problems (legal, economic and technical) with. But on the other hand, it has been already evident that the split of federation would happen during the first wave . Undoubtedly, the second wave of the large-scale privatization will process in both republics separately.

8

FOREIGN TRADE POLICY

Vit Stepanek
Advisor to the Minister
Ministry of Economic Policy and
Development of the Czech Republic

The transformation of the Czechoslovak economy from a centrally directed command model to a market oriented one is an extremely complex process consisting of set of reforms the run of which is not always easy to interpret. One of the essential elements of reform strategy is the rapid integration of Czechoslovakia in to the world economy. In analyses of the achievements in this particular area it is difficult to differentiate between the intensity of the impacts of various influences on the development of the economy as a whole, and on the development of Czechoslovakia's external economic relations, what the consequences of domestic environment and reformed foreign trade policy are and to what extent the present development is also influenced by external factors. However it is incontestable that Czechoslovakia's foreign trade operates in a world which is rather different from the past conditions.

This chapter analyses the development of Czechoslovak external economic relations in the reform process. First part characterizes briefly the role of foreign trade under the past conditions of centrally planned economy. With regard to this second part summarizes reform measures in this area and new foreign trade policy. In the end some open issues are mentioned.

HISTORICAL OVERVIEW OF FOREIGN TRADE POLICY

As well as the whole economy subjected to the centrally planned regime, foreign trade was closely regulated, too, in the past. The domestic economy was almost completely separated from the world market. Exports was seen only as a vehicle of financing of imports, which was seen as a factor that facilitates the surmounting development bottlenecks and elimination of disproportion in the formation and implementation of national economic plans.

The foreign exchange plan specified overall target for exports and imports with individual targets for branch ministries and before 1989 the foreign exchange plan also specified exports and imports for enterprises. All foreign trade was organized by some 50 to 60 foreign trade organizations under the direction of the Ministry of Foreign Trade.

All foreign exchange earnings had to be surrendered to the authorized banking institution which administered it on behalf of the State Bank and the Government. Enterprises with no or insufficient export proceeds were dependent on central allocations of foreign exchange which were typically made available to them through branch ministries.

Already at these times trade flows were rather extensive. They however were not based on the achievement of global competitiveness, maximization of scientific technological progress and the like. Trade occurred primarily in those branches, where the primary decision making factor were those of the dimensions of material needs.

Price changes in the world markets did not affect domestic prices, because complicated system of taxes and subsidies isolated domestic prices from the world market price changes, price changes in the CMEA (Council of Mutual Economic Assistance = Comecon) market as well. Influence of changes in demand in the world markets was similarly paralysed by elaborated system of licence regulations and foreign exchange allocations.

Consequently variables and information on price and demand changes from the external economic environment had no bearing on domestic producers at all levels. The domestic criteria were the decisive ones and all the implications resulting from foreign trade were accommodated by the state. The national frontier was completely unpenetrable in this respect. This made it possible for the national economy to develop independently from its external environment. In spite of the relatively high share of exports in GDP (roughly 27.0 percent in 1990) Czechoslovakia was rather a closed economy.

Trade with CMEA countries was exercised on the basis of bilateral intergovernmental trade agreements. Trade protocols, signed every year, specified volumes and prices of traded commodities, payment was carried out in non-convertible accounting monetary units - transferable rubles, trade balance of mutual trade flows were recorded and settled down in for this purpose established banking institution.

The Czechoslovak participation in the trade system of CMEA resulted in territorial and commodity structure of Czechoslovak foreign trade which was rather different from those of pre-war situation. In its climax trade with CMEA countries represented roughly 80.0 percent of total volume of Czechoslovak foreign trade. In 1989 CMEA foreign trade amounted 60.0 percent of total volume and trade with former Soviet Union reached 39.0 percent. If Czechoslovakia had developed as other market economies in

Western Europe, it could be expected, that the share of Czechoslovak foreign trade with CMEA countries would be hardly half of the volume of this trade in 1989.

Since the year 1989 the share of trade with former CMEA countries has been declining: In 1990 represented less than 50.0 percent and in 1991 such a development went on. The main reason of this fact was radical decrease of exports into the former Soviet Union, loss of another important market - former GDR. Imports from the USSR decreased, too.

Czechoslovakia paid for its closed state-directed trade system and its orientation to the CMEA markets. The price was the loss of competitiveness in the world markets and rather difficult starting position with regard to necessary adaptation of foreign trade flows to new economic conditions.

REFORM APPROACH IN TRADE POLICY

Starting in 1991, Czechoslovakia's foreign trade operates in a world which is rather different from the past conditions. External economic relations play an important role in reform strategy and measures accepted on January 1, 1991 mean radical change in Czechoslovak foreign trade.

Foreign trade is no longer considered as an appendix of the domestic economy and the past conditions, distinctions between convertible and non-convertible currency areas lost their meaning. Enterprises subject no longer to quantitative controls and Czechoslovakia's trade with former CMEA countries is quite similar to trade with market economies. It is conducted in hard currency, and firms are able to take advantage of arbitrage opportunities. Firms are no longer obliged to surrender total export proceeds to the banks, and are therefore able to import from their retained export proceeds without any foreign exchange license.

Foreign trade was radically liberalized. The main aim of this liberalization was to draw the price relations of the world market into the national economy. This measure was in accordance with the implementation of the domestic price reform. International prices, intermediated by export and import flows together with stable exchange rate had to serve as a bias for liberalized domestic prices. Liberalization of imports was used as a mean of demonopolization of national economy, too, which helps Czechoslovak enterprises to accommodate to the new conditions. At the same time direct foreign investment is seen as a mean of modernization of domestic production base, mean of inflow of necessary managerial and technical know-how.

For the purposes mentioned above a set of reform measures was accepted as a ground for new foreign trade policy. The reform strategy in this area stands on following principals:

1. Devaluation of the Czechoslovak crown and the fixing of a firm rate of exchange rate against a basket of five selected convertible currencies with the greater share in the country's balance of payments,

2. Internal convertibility of the crown for all firms in the register of corporations,

3. Deregulation of foreign trade operations,

4. Liberalization of export and import conditions, with negligible non-tariff restrictions,

5. Introduction of an import surcharge.

Deregulation of foreign trade activities (for which, from January 1, 1991, all the firms in the register have the right without any licence to exercise foreign trade activities) mean the abolition of trade monopoly of foreign trade organizations. To the same date, introduction of so called internal convertibility of the Czechoslovak crown (convertibility in the area of current account of balance of payments) enabled practical abolishment of foreign trade monopoly. This measure grants to enterprises the access to foreign exchange necessary for their imports.

Roughly 100.0 percent devaluation of the Czechoslovak crown harmonized the demand for and the supply of foreign exchange and preserved the balance of payments equilibrium. The new exchange rate is kept relatively stable around the level of 28.0 USD for 1 Czechoslovak crown. At the same time, devaluation was the main pro-export measure of the new foreign trade policy. Quantitative restrictions were almost abolished and export licences were radically diminished. The present day level of import tariffs is very low in average (5.0 percent, weighted average tariff 5.7 percent) and has very limited differentiation.

Although Czechoslovakia radically liberalized its trade system, several regulatory measures preventing sharp increase of imports and preserving balance of payments equilibrium in the period of transition were implemented:

1. Temporary and decreasing percentage surcharge on imported consumer goods (at first 20.0 percent in 1990, then 18.0 percent and in the second half of 1991 to recent 15.0 percent).

2. There is no general licensing requirement for imports and exports. Nevertheless for 4 categories of imports is license required (oil, natural gas, narcotics, weapons, ammunition and explosives). For

some 15.0 percent of export items is licence required, too. These are the ones, which are either

(i) in short with the domestic market or
(ii) which subject to limitation from partner states, e.g. iron and steel, textile and clothing etc., or
(iii) which are "sensitive" as weapons etc.

While the former regulation represents typical temporary measure valid in the period of transformation, the two latter are similar to those of market economies practice.

3. Generally the trade between Czechoslovakia and former CMEA is carried on the same conditions as the trade with market economies. In spite of this the Czechoslovak government, having in mind the aim to diminish the negative impacts of breakdown of CMEA market, signed bilateral agreements with these countries. The most important is with Russia, which defined the possibilities of transformation of mutual trade and stipulates conditions of repayment of the Russian debt to Czechoslovakia (Russian past trade deficits). Besides the commitment of Russia to deliver certain amount of oil, the part of this agreement are so called indicative lists, which stipulates the commodities available for barter trade.

4. While the access to the foreign currency for imports is generally free, under the decree of the State Bank import value exceeding a certain amount subjected to regulation under which these imports had to be financed through commercial credits. This regulation was by the end of 1991 abolished.

5. In connection with the situation in Czechoslovak agriculture certain measures were adopted for the purpose of protecting the domestic market. Federal government approved a system of non-tariff regulations for exports a imports of some agricultural commodities, especially meat and butter.

All the measures mentioned above were implemented in a situation of domestic and external sales crisis (limited domestic demand because of reduced purchasing power of the population, reduced investment activity, loss of a large part of the former markets in the USSR and in a number of other former Comecon countries, the end of exports to Iraq, and considerable reductions in armament exports in consequence of worldwide disarmament initiatives).

The situation was aggravated further by the fact that in consequence of a restrictive financial policy, indispensable for maintaining stability in the transitional period and because of the impact of devaluation it was very difficult to finance the necessary export credits, especially for exports of machinery and complete plants.

In this situation, one of the main tasks of the state in the sphere of foreign trade was to create conditions for diversification of trade into new regions and the best possible trade conditions for Czechoslovak exports to all parts of the world, and to secure to the maximum degree existing markets in the former Comecon countries, even under worse economic and legal conditions, as well as to create gradually elements of a goal-oriented pro-export policy. Let us now consider some of the measures which have been taken in this respect.

The first group of measures involved negotiations with a number of countries and integrative groups, on the granting of tariff preferences, which considerably reduce duties on certain categories of products, thus improving the competitiveness of Czechoslovak goods in the markets of these countries. Closely connected with these negotiations were talks on the abolition or at least raising of various limits and quotas which restricted exports of Czechoslovak goods to some countries.

In parallel, negotiations were conducted on the opening of new markets. The steps in this field included the lifting off the embargo on trade with South Africa and the signing of a very advantageous trade agreement with this economically most advanced African country. Trade agreements with American, other African, Asian countries were signed or at least initiated, too.

Extraordinary attention was given to measure designed to overcome the loss of markets in the former USSR and in the trade region very important for Czechoslovakia in neighbouring Poland and Hungary. The complex of these measures deserves special analysis which the extent of this chapter does not permit.

The main pro-export measure of radical economic reform was the devaluation of the Czechoslovak crown. Gradually, as the effects of this measure get exhausted, new tools will have to be implemented. For instance, later on, devaluation was followed by other indispensable prerequisite of exports on the institutional basis. The Export Guarantee and Insurance Corporation (as a state joint stock company) was established for the purposes of necessary partial support the differences between the interest rates on credits extended by Czechoslovak banks and rates usual in the world for exports, handling the insurance against export and credit risks as well, etc.

Extremely important negotiations on association with the European Communities which resulted in Interim Agreement covering the whole trade part of Association Agreement for the period till the end of 1992, talks on agreement on a free trade zone with the EFTA countries and negotiations on restructuring Czechoslovak tariffs so as to make them more suited to the present requirements of the Czechoslovak economy were carried out, too.

MAJOR ACHIEVEMENTS

It is difficult to evaluate to what extent the trade liberalization affected results of Czechoslovak foreign trade, what could be the consequences of the performance of the whole economy and what could be subscribed to external influences outside of Czechoslovakia.

Nevertheless the efforts towards the liberalization of trade has affected concrete results of Czechoslovak Foreign trade. Without exaggeration we can say that Czechoslovakia carried out the largest structural transformation up to date.

After registering a significant trade deficit in 1990, Czechoslovakia achieved a surplus in 1991 and in the first half of 1992. The shift within the territorial structure towards the trade with countries with advanced market economy has been realized. The trade with the former CMEA socialist economies accounted for more than 60.0 percent of total trade in 1989, in 1990 dropped to about 50.0 percent and 40.0 % in 1991. Figures for first six months of 1992 indicates that this share dropped to 32.0 percent. Trade in non-convertible currency basically disappeared and Germany replaced the former Soviet Union as Czechoslovakia's main trading partner, accounting for almost a quarter of Czechoslovakia's foreign trade (more than 30.0 percent of total exports and 24.0 percent of total imports), followed in the area of market economies by Austria, Italy and France.

At the same time the commodity structure of exports got deteriorated. Czechoslovakia does not succeed without introduction of further incentives to support the export of goods with higher stage of finalization. Despite of this fact it is necessary to point out that main watershed between successful and less successful exporters does not lie between industrial branches, but inside of them.

A major controversy surrounds the question of whether trade contracted or expanded during the transition. Official estimates suggest that the physical volume of exports and imports shrunk considerably in 1991. Latest development indicates that at least in terms of exports turnaround appears to be achieved in the end of 1991 and first six months of 1992. Moreover the real effective exchange rate suggests relatively stable competitiveness of Czechoslovak production.

The Czechoslovak foreign trade figures for 1991 and first half of 1992 show that in the first 18 months of the ongoing economic reform the national economy opened itself to the world considerably, and that exports and imports were diversified territorially, which also increased the share of Czechoslovakia's trade with advanced market economies. A great decline in exports a imports was experienced in this field, which is certainly a negative fact in the period under review. On the contrary a positive facts the overall relative and absolute increase in Czechoslovak exports to countries with advanced market economies, as well as the fact that despite very serious difficulties on the markets of the former Comecon countries, Czechoslovak total exports fell considerably smaller than the overall decline in industrial output in the same period.

DIRECT FOREIGN INVESTMENT

Czechoslovakia besides liberalization of foreign trade exercises active policy for attracting of foreign capital, although it is still in the process of creating the necessary legal a economic environment. Until now, experience has shown that participation of foreign capital in the Czechoslovak economy was not only negligible in comparison with the average level in European market economies, but that it was also lower so far than such participation in other comparable countries undergoing the transformation process, such as Hungary and Poland.

At the same time, Czechoslovakia is for a number of reasons attractive for foreign investors, in comparison to the other post-communist countries in Eastern and Central Europe. Indisputable advantages include its position in the centre of Europe, its experience with democracy and the capitalist system acquired in the period between the two world wars, its culture and way of thinking closely related to those in the West, relatively high overall qualification of the labour force, a comparatively developed and reliable infrastructure, a relatively stable macroeconomic situation and until now cheap labour.

The level of foreign investor's willingness to enter with their capital, an economy undergoing a transformation process depends undoubtedly on the degree of political stability in the country concerned. Political stability in a majority of the post-communist countries is threatened, above all, by disputes among nationalities, evident not only in differing views of the various republics with respect to constitutional law issues and the structure of the state, but also in essentially inconsistent views regarding the methods to be used in the national economy.

Such disputes also appear in Czechoslovakia with respect to Slovak nationalist movement. Czechoslovakia is facing now division into two sovereign, internationally recognised states. Political instability related to this development should not be conducive to foreign capital inflow in the near future. Yet the potential foreign capital investors should look beyond the near future and take into account many other longer-term factors as mentioned above. Moreover, the manner in which the splitting up process in Czechoslovakia is regulated guarantees that the principles of democracy, the route of transformation process and economic liberalism will be preserved.

In the process of transformation, a change of ownership relationships through privatization is an absolutely dominant goal for Czechoslovakia, the Czech Republic respectively. In order to expeditiously achieve such objectives, both standard and non-standard approaches based on legislative regulations have been chosen, and practically cover at present the whole area of transformation of ownership rights.

The possibility of foreign investor's participation in the privatization of small businesses has been limited to second round auctions but arrangements with Czech partners cannot be excluded. The "large-scale" privatization of state enterprises which has now been started and is incomparably more important for the privatization process offers foreign investors substantially broader possibilities for capital investment. Numerous Czechoslovak enterprises have been actively discussing foreign capital participation and can include their plans involving foreign partners in their privatization projects.

Foreign partners may enter the Czechoslovak economy through direct acquisition of privatized units in cases of auctions, through the purchase of shares in privatized enterprises, and by means of capital investment and establishment of joint ventures. Until now, joint ventures have been the most frequent method of foreign capital investment because as such they may enjoy so-called national treatment regime, i.e. pursuant to the new Commercial Code those joint ventures enjoy the same legal rights and assume the same legal obligations as any other Czechoslovak legal entity. Foreign persons may establish a wholly-owned Czechoslovak firm, may become partners in either an existing firm or in a new one. A legal entity may even be founded under the law of another country.

Over 4,000 joint ventures were established till December 31, 1991. Three quarters are located in the Czech Republic, the rest in the Slovak Republic. Almost half of them are seated in Prague. Most of the joint ventures , however, are small enterprises with capital investment of 100,000 crowns or less, and capital exceeding 1.0 million crowns was registered only in about 400 cases. Total foreign capital subscribed in the existing joint ventures reached roughly 27.0 billion crown, foreign capital roughly 12.0 billion crowns. Most of the foreign partners in joint ventures are from Germany (around 50.0 percent), followed by Austrians and French investors.

OPEN ISSUES

Although Czechoslovakia has reached relatively good results as for the integration into the world economy, the country still facing several open issues, which have to be solved. It is e.g. necessary to abolish temporary protectionist measures (mentioned above), improve conditions for foreign investment etc.

Protectionist regulations in form of import surcharge, export and import licences etc. as mentioned above were declared as temporary measures. These trade policy instruments play in the transition period an important role of stabilizator of stable exchange rate and balance of payments equilibrium. From the point of view medium and long time horizon it is necessary further develop the competitive role of imports and keep the trade policy transparent. These temporary regulations as e.g. the import quotas for agricultural products have to be more and more abolished.

As for the export licences implemented on the basis of partner countries demand, these instruments cannot be so easily canceled. On the other hand system of administrative allocation of these licences could be changed in favour of auctions. Such a mechanisms would enlarge the access of new producers to exports of goods under licence.

The regulation of foreign trade was based on licences and quantitative quotas in the past. Tariffs existed, but their role was very limited. The structure of tariffs is very flat. In spite of partial restructuralization, the import weighted average tariff is roughly 5.7 percent. The tariff protection is therefore insufficient not only absolutely, but also with compare to foreign trade partners. The tariffs in EC are higher than those in Czechoslovakia. The same is valid as for Hungary and Poland. The restructuralization of tariff system is necessary from both foreign trade reasons and from the point of view of inflow of foreign investment. The low level of tariffs discourages potential investors in locating their funds in Czechoslovakia. The restructuralization of tariff system should take into account the principles of industry policy, too. Nevertheless the restructuralization should not mean the departure from present day liberal attitude to foreign economic matters.

As it was mentioned above, the legal and economic environment helping to attract foreign capital is still in the process of creation. The issue under discussions is, whether and to what extent joint ventures should enjoy advantages in comparison with domestic entrepreneurs. The limitation is, that government cannot implement such measures, which would damage natural regulation of market economy, measures which would represent protectionism and evoke the possibility of different conditions for different investors. Prevailing opinion in the Czech republic stands on the philosophy that joint ventures should have the same rights and the same obligations as any other Czech legal entity.

CHALLENGE

The major open issue facing Czechoslovakia is the development of the state set up and the reality of splitting up the Czechoslovak federation into two independent states, with all the consequences of economic difficulties and negative impacts on economic performance of both republics, rising political instability in foreign trade and investment, etc. Current development stress out in the area of foreign trade the necessity of analysis of:

A. the export performance of both republics in foreign trade of Czechoslovakia,

B. inter-republic deliveries between the Czech and Slovak republics,

C. issues of continuation of foreign trade policy in new republics and their relationships to the neighbours, particularly relations to EC and GATT.

A. Czech and Slovak Foreign Trade Performance

The figures on foreign trade of both republics indicate that the share of the Czech Republic in the total turnover of present day Czechoslovakia amounts roughly 70.0 percent. The rest, 30.0 percent is for the Slovak Republic. But the data also show, that the trade balance of the Czech Republic closed the year 1991 with trade surplus (+24.8 billion crowns). On the contrary trade balance of the Slovak Republic in the same period was in deficit (-9.6 billion crowns).

This result follows from the fact that the share of the Slovak Republic in total imports of Czechoslovakia was 34.0 percent, but the share in exports was only 29.0 percent. The high share of the Slovak Republic in total imports was concentrated in trade with former USSR. Deficit in trade with this country amounted 74.0 percent of total Slovak trade deficit. From the point of view of imported commodities the high share of Slovakia in Czechoslovak imports is affected particularly by imports of raw-materials and fuel (just from the former USSR). Higher openness of the Slovak Republic towards the former CMEA countries and former Soviet Union is also evident in exports (deliveries of consumer goods and chemical products).

Export performance of the Czech Republic is higher than those of the Slovak Republic. Revealed differences are visible particularly in machinery, due first of all to high share of armament production in Slovakia. Moreover the Czech Republic revealed greater adaptability to new conditions in the year 1991. More than a half (55.0 percent) of exports of the Czech Republic was oriented to the western markets and only 36.0 percent to former socialist countries. Higher share of trade to area of former CMEA and lower standards of this market disadvantages, among other factors, Slovak Republic in this respect, and also jeopardize Slovakia's effort to change radically its production structure and trade flows towards western markets. Only 44.0 percent of exports was sold in the west and almost 48.0 percent in the former socialist countries. The share of developing countries in total exports was for both republics equal - 8.6 percent.

B. Mutual Deliveries

The economies of both republics are very closely interconnected by thousands of economic, financial, personal etc. relations the intensity of which is much higher than those between individual market economies in the EC. The rate of mutual interdependence is rather high in both republics and is in reverse proportion to the size of both republics. While in Slovakia the share of deliveries to the Czech Republic in total sales was 27.0 percent and the share of deliveries from the Czech Republic in total consumption of domestically produced goods more than 30.0 percent, the values of both indicators in the Czech Republic were around 10.0 percentage level. (As a base for the computation the year 1989 was taken - year of almost full employment of production capacities, at the same time the last year with reliable data.) In many key industries (metallurgy, chemical industry, machinery, pharmaceuticals, textile and clothing industry etc.) was this mutual interdependence even higher than were above mentioned averages.

The high share of economic interdependence of both republics is more evident from comparison of mutual deliveries and total exports of both republics. The volume of deliveries from the Czech Republic to Slovakia amounted (1989) roughly 80.0 percent of total exports from the Czech Republic and were almost two times higher than exports of the Czech Republic into the market economies. Deliveries from Slovakia were two times higher than total Slovak exports and almost five times higher than exports to the market economies.

C. Relationships of the Separate Republics to GATT and EC

In that moment when Czechoslovakia will split up into two new sovereign, internationally recognised states, the Czech Republic and the Slovak Republic will no longer be the member states of GATT. It is natural, with regard to the great importance of foreign trade for newly established states, that it will be of their eminent interest to re-enter GATT as soon as possible. The reason is very simple. Without multilateral most favoured nation treatment the exports of both republic will loose competitiveness in many markets, because general tariffs are often much higher than those under GATT.

There are three principal conditions which have to be fulfilled in order to re-enter GATT without, or with minimum, negative impacts on foreign trade of both countries:

(i) the split up of Czechoslovakia should be realized by agreement of the republics, which will be for world and GATT members transparent and politically acceptable,

(ii) both new states should clearly present their commitment to take over the same tariffs as original Czechoslovakia (i.e. in shape after waiver from December 1991), as well as to continue in the same trade policy in the area of non-tariff export and import measures.

(iii) negotiations with GATT and at least principal members (USA, EC, EFTA, Japan, India, Brazil) early enough before the real moment of proclamation of the new two states.

The same is valid towards the EC. On March 1, 1992 so called Interim Agreement was signed between Czechoslovakia and EC. This Agreement covers the whole trade part of Association Agreement between Czechoslovakia and EC and specifies advantageous asymmetric conditions of tariff ceilings and quotas. Situation with EC is even more complicated. Whereas in GATT case the new states should take over all the commitments of original Czechoslovakia, in case of EC in Interim Agreement specified tariff ceilings and quotas have to be divided into two new state subjects. This could be very difficult not only technically (due to number of items and location of producers of individual items either in Slovakia and/or in the Czech Republic), but also politically (both on the Czechoslovak side and from the point of view of still increasing protective policy of individual EC member states).

All the situation could be simplified by additional fourth condition:

(iv) The Czech Republic and the Slovak Republic would establish customs union, which would take over tariffs and other trade policy commitments of original Czechoslovakia.

Above outlined solution of relations to GATT and EC in the near future is an ideal one. It is evident, that such an arrangement in the form of customs union subject to limitation of willingness of both republic to give up of part their future sovereignty in the field of trade and tariff policy in favour of potential supranational authority just after that the new state had received it.

The latest development of political representations of both republics indicates the will of the republics to conclude agreement on customs union and declared this intention on the international scene by the end of October 1992, after that sign the agreement and ratify it by national parliaments by the end of November 1992 at the latest.

Political intention, is only one side of all the matter. The other side is practical functioning of the customs union. There are good conditions for functioning of the union given until now existing economic relations between the two republics in the single state. On the other hand possible different economic and social development, different economic policy (not only interest to change the foreign trade and tariff policy on the basis of different development, but also divergent evolution of exchange rate and monetary policy) can jeopardize no matter how advantageous political intention. The near future will show us the mirror.

October 1992

9

IMF FINANCED PROGRAMS IN CZECHOSLOVAKIA: TARGETS AND OUTCOMES

Jiri Jonas**
International Monetary Fund
Washington, September 1992

1. INTRODUCTION

Czechoslovakia was among the 44 founding members of the International Monetary Fund, which has been established in 1944 in Bretton Woods, USA. However, it did not enjoy the opportunity to participate in the activities of this organization for more than 10 years. As the communists seized the power in Czechoslovakia in 1948, and the economic and political system started to be adapted according to the soviet example, it became evident that despite the relatively liberal character of conditions of membership in the IMF, Czechoslovakia will not stay in this organization much longer. The differences between the IMF and communist authorities regarding the obligations of Czechoslovakia from the membership in policy conduct and data disclosure widened. In June 1953, Czechoslovakia changed without prior consultations with the Fund the par value of KCS from KCS 50 = US$ 1 to KCS 7.20 = US$ 1. This started the period of discussions, with the result that at the end 1954, Czechoslovakia was required to withdraw from the Fund.[1]

It took another 36 years before the political changes in Czechoslovakia made the option of renewed membership again realistic. Velvet revolution in November 1989 initiated deep political and economic changes that were

** Assistant to Executive Director, International Monetary Fund. The opinions expressed in this paper are the author's own and do not represent the opinion or assessment of the IMF.

[1] See Horsefield, J.K., *The International Monetary Fund 1945-1965, Volume I: Chronicle.* International Monetary Fund, Washington, D.C. 1969, pp. 359-364.

aimed at establishing democratic society with market economy. It was one of the first steps of newly appointed government to apply for the membership in the IMF and also in the institutions of the World Bank Group.[2] On the occasion of the Annual Meeting in Washington, on September 20, 1990, Czechoslovakia rejoined the IMF and the World Bank, 36 years after it left this organization. Czechoslovakia was placed into the constituency led by Belgium, with Austria, Luxembourg, Hungary and Turkey.[3] Initial quota of Czechoslovakia was set at SDR 590 mil.[4]

The paper is organized as follows. In the first section will be discussed initial economic conditions in Czechoslovakia at the time of rejoining the IMF and during first stand-by arrangement, which was approved in January 1991. Second section will analyze the conditions and preliminary results under second stand-by arrangement, which has been approved in April 1992 immediately following the first one. Third section compares the scope of financial assistance of the IMF in Czechoslovakia with other countries of central and eastern Europe (CEE), and discusses the common features and differences of outcomes under these programs.

1. LEGACY OF THE SOCIALIST SYSTEM AND FIRST STAND-BY ARRANGEMENT

The imprint of 40 years of experiments with substituting the market coordination of economic activity and private ownership of the factors of production by pretentious engineering of economic system with help of central planning and so called "socialist ownership of factors of production" became more and more manifest in the second half of the 1980s. While the symptoms of economic deformations and distortions among all centrally planned economies in the microeconomic sphere displayed many similarities, there were more pronounced differences in the degree and particular form of macroeconomic disequilibrium. The reason why there were more similarities on the microeconomic level is that the pattern of behavior of economic agents has been determined by the same characteristics of economic system: missing or extremely restricted private ownership of the factors of production; administratively formed structure of relative prices bearing little relation to the supply and demand conditions; highly monopolistic structure and distorted and to a large degree discretionary by bureaucrats determined dependence of incomes on economic performance. On macroeconomic level, due to different preferences and objectives of the authorities reflecting the concrete situation in each particular country, the similarities were less obvious. Not quite traditionally in the CEE countries, Czechoslovakia was

---

[2]This group includes International Bank for Reconstruction and Development; International Finance Corporation; International Development Agency; Multilateral Investment Guarantees Agency and International Center for Settlement of Investment Disputes.

[3]In 1992, this constituency was joined by Belarus and Kazachstan.

[4]After the Ninth review of quota, which is expected to become effective in the end of 1992, the quota of Czechoslovakia will be SDR 847 mil.

pursuing during most of the 1970s and 1980s relatively restrictive fiscal and monetary policy.[5] As a result, external indebtness did not reach levels that would cause problems with debt service (see table 1), and monetary overhang, as represented by hidden and suppressed inflation, was not significant.[6]

Table 1.

External Debt of Czechoslovakia (US$ bil)

	1987	1988	1989	1990	1991
External debt in convertib. currencies	6.7	7.3	7.9	8.2	9.9
Debt service in % of export	24.0	24.8	24.4	19.5	15.2
Official reserves in months of import	2.3	2.5	2.0	0.6	1.3

Sources: All data in this paper are either IMF calculations or data from *Statistical Yearbook of Czech and Slovak Federal Republic.*

In contrast to relatively careful macroeconomic management, however, microeconomic distortions necessarily began to show up, and serious structural problems accumulated. The structure of production did not reflect demand and cost conditions but rather, through a perverse system of bargaining, the preferences of planners and their negotiating positions vis-a-vis the managers of enterprises, this all in the context of specific role played by Czechoslovakia in the framework of CMEA. Instead of being shaped by comparative advantage, the production structure of Czechoslovak economy has been thus gradually deformed on the basis of mix of political considerations, autarkic tendencies and attempts to increase the growth of progressive industries with high content of latest technology and scientific achievements. Bias toward heavy industry and lack of specialization, as well as significant technological and efficiency gap in many industries and

[5]The degree of restrictiveness might have been somewhat lower if the fiscal balance is measured by the IMF concept of general government accounts.

[6]See Drabek, Z., Janacek, K., Tuma, Z., Inflation in Czechoslovakia, 1985-1991, Prague 1992, paper written as a part of the World Bank research project. The authors review estimates of hidden inflation, which are in the range of 0.5-3.0 percent p.a., and also discuss the magnitude of suppressed inflation, the impact of which after full price liberalization they estimate to be about 5 percentage points which it added to existing inflation.

firms, were predestined to be at the roots of future problems connected with the dissolution of the CMEA trade and payment relations.

In addition to these structural distortions, there began to accumulate in the second half of the 1980s, discrepancies between aggregate demand and potential supply. As we have indicated, the degree of macroeconomic disequilibrium was not prima facie as high in Czechoslovakia as in some other CEE countries[7], and it was not thus transformed so extensively into the increase of external indebtedness or fiscal deficits. However, as a matter of accounting identity, some components of aggregate demand had to adjust in the wake of appearing discrepancy between demand and supply. In Czechoslovakia, this adjustment in the 1980s took the form of gradually decreasing future productive potential of the economy due to attempts to keep the level of current consumption on an unsustainably high level. This is illustrated by a relatively low and still declining level of net fixed investments in the second half of the 1980s. Although this was no dramatic decline, the erosion of the stock of productive capital is well documented also by other indicators, like, for example, the increased average age of business fixed investments. Therefore, the data on net fixed investment in Table 2 and 3, underestimate somewhat the size of the problem, partially because they record only a short period of time, and also because the net fixed investment include unfinished construction, which accelerated at the end of the 1980s.[8]

Table 2.

Investment in Czechoslovakia, 1985-1989 (KCS bil)

	1985	1986	1987	1988	1989
Gross fixed inv.	168.3	170.0	176.8	186.1	184.2
Depreciat.	92.8	97.1	102.0	108.0	112.6
Net fixed invest.*	88.1	94.4	82.5	89.3	88.2
In % of GDP	13.0	13.6	11.6	12.1	11.6

* Net fixed investments plus depreciations add up to more than gross fixed investments due to loses.

[7]One of the factors explaining this difference is that Czechoslovakia did not experiment in the 20 years following the period of partial political and economic reforms during the Prague Spring 1968-1969 with market socialism, as for example Hungary. Usually these reforms entailed only relaxation of aggregate demand management, without significantly improving the supply-side response to price signals.

[8]In 1986, unfinished construction increased by 0.1 percent, in 1987 by 1.1 percent, in 1988 by 1.2 percent and in 1989 already by 3.8 percent.

Table 3.
Investments in Czechoslovakia. Index at constant prices, 1980 = 100.

	1985	1986	1987	1988	1989
Gross fixed inv.	94.6	96.0	100.2	104.8	103.8
Net fixed invest.	76.9	84.1	76.8	81.2	83.2

To sum up, the result of the microeconomic distortions and growing latent macroeconomic disequilibrium has been at the end of 1980s in Czechoslovak economy inefficient structure of production, with high cost and low quality of products; monopolistic position of many enterprises, which were inward-oriented and protected from foreign competition; and by accelerating macroeconomic disequilibrium, that was potentially exacerbated by preserving the level of current consumption at the cost of capital formation and future productive capacity of the economy. This was obviously a very short-sighted policy, because the combination of the lack of demand restriction and undermining of the potential for the increase in supply in the future could have only made the problems in the future worse.

Attempts were made to address some among the most visible distortions under the old economic system, and within its boundaries. Some reform attempts started in 1987, with greater autonomy being granted to enterprises, prices adjusted so as to reflect more the costs, and state monopoly of foreign trade weakened. But it was only in mid-1990 when the comprehensive program of reform strategy, prepared by the newly elected government, created a basis for radical change of economic system. It does not happen often in the history of mankind that majority of people support an outright change of the basic elements of economic system. The speed and relative easiness with which this occurred in Czechoslovakia, as well as in other CEE countries is an eloquent evidence of how defunct economically and politically the old system was.

At the time when Czechoslovakia became a member of IMF, in September 1990, Czechoslovak government approved a reform strategy outlined in the "Scenario of Economic Reform". In the 1990, there was yet little experience with the transformation of the system of central planning to a market based system. Serious reforms have just started few months ago in Poland and Hungary. Many proposed policy measures were inevitably a step into the unknown as there was little information about how the economic agents will respond. In Czechoslovakia, some measures were implemented in the course of 1990, including reduction of consumer subsidies and separation of central and commercial banks, as well as tightening of fiscal and monetary policy.[9] But the crucial bulk of measures was to be implemented at the beginning of 1991.

At the end of 1990, as open discussion over the scenario of economic reform continued, expectations of inflation and devaluation of exchange rate became widespread. The former caused a hoarding of goods by households and producers, the latter initiated a run on the foreign reserves of the banking system. Despite the devaluation of commercial exchange rate in October 1990 by a 35 percent, or maybe because of it, enterprises continued to stock up on imports and prepay debt obligations as much as possible. The result was that at the end of 1990, foreign exchange reserves declined under US$ 1 bil, which was sufficient to cover hardly two weeks of imports.

In October 1990, the IMF concluded first Article IV consultation[10] with the Czechoslovak authorities, and at the same time agreed with them on a Letter of Intent, which was submitted together with a request for financial assistance to the Executive Board of the IMF in January 1991.

To receive a financial assistance from the IMF, member country must usually meet two basic conditions. First, it must have a balance of payments need; secondly it must accept appropriate policy measures that address both the underlying causes of balance of payments problems and consequences of the balance of payments shocks if their primary cause is of exogenous character, unrelated to conduct of macroeconomic policy. Czechoslovakia met both these conditions easily. The need for the balance of payments support was obvious. Depletion of the foreign reserves at the end of 1990 threatened by an imminent crisis which would put under a risk one of the major pillars of the economic reform package, introduction of the current account convertibility and liberalization of foreign trade in January 1991. As far as the appropriate policy is concerned, the IMF was assured on the basis of Article IV consultation and submitted Letter of Intent that Czechoslovak authorities are prepared to make any necessary effort to remove the endogenous causes of the balance of payments problems, as well as to adjust to external shocks which hit the economy in 1990 and which were expected to continue even more vigorously in 1991.

Therefore, the request for 14-month stand-by arrangement in amount of SDR 619.5 mil was by the Executive Board of the IMF on January 7, 1991 approved. Total access of Czechoslovakia under this arrangement represented 105 percent of its member quota. Stand-by arrangement was combined with access under the oil import element of the Compensatory and Contingency Financing Facility in the amount of SDR 466 mil, which has been ultimately drawn in the course of stand-by arrangement, and contingency element of CCFF in the amount of up to SDR 147.5 mil, which was not drawn. The

---

[9]See Bijan B. Aghevli, Eduardo Borensztein and Tess van der Willigen, *Stabilization and Structural Reform in the Czech and Slovak Federal Republic: First Stage.* IMF Occasional Paper 92, p. 3-6.

[10]Article IV consultation is basic tools with the help of which the IMF performs its supervisory role.

purpose of the financial assistance under the oil element of CCFF was to help Czechoslovakia to finance increased costs of import due to the introduction of world prices in the mutual trade of former CMEA countries. The introduction of world prices led in the first line to increase in oil prices, and Czechoslovakia's terms of trade deteriorated sharply in 1991. Financial assistance to oil import helped to avoid its suppression to a level that would cause serious disruptions in production or reintroduction of administrative methods in allocating foreign reserves and conducting foreign trade policy.

The main objective of economic reform package, launched in January 1991, and financially supported by first stand-by arrangement with the IMF, was twofold. First, introduce comprehensive liberalization of prices and foreign trade; secondly, preserve macroeconomic stability by sufficiently tight fiscal and monetary policies and by accelerating structural reforms that would eventually stimulate positive supply response in a liberalized economy. This strategy was also decisive to formulating performance criteria, that were attached to the stand-by arrangement, and on the observance of which were conditional subsequent disbursements of purchases.[11] The following four performance criteria were agreed:

(A) Limits on change in net credit from the banking system to the Government, cumulative from December 31, 1990;

(B) Net domestic assets of the banking system;

(C) Change in net international reserves in convertible currencies, cumulative from December 31, 1990;

(D) Limits on contracting and guaranteeing of new external debt with maturity 1-12 years, cumulative from December 31, 1990.

Quantitative indicators for these performance criteria are showed in Table 4.

---

[11]It reflects the nature of Fund's financial assistance to speak about purchases and not loans, because the member is in fact buying the desired convertible currency with its own currency, usually in the form of promissory notes. Instead of repaying the debt, it repurchases its own currency.

Table 4.
Quantitative Performance Criteria for First Stand-by Arrangement

Criterium	1.1.-31.3. 1991	1.4.-30.6 1991	1.7.-30.9. 1991 2/	1.10.- 31.12. 1991 2/
A (bil KCS) 1/ 3/	-11.0	-11.0	-9.5	-8.0
B (bil KCS)	600.0	620.0	633.0	642.0
C (mil US$) 2/ 3/	-900.0	-1300.0	-1500.0	-1700.0
D (mil USD) 3/	1000.0	1000.0	1000.0	1000.0

1) Negative numbers mean decline. It was supposed that any disbursement of foreign loans received by the federation or the republics, and any borrowing by the federation or the republics from the domestic non-bank public would change these limits.

2) Numbers for end-September and end-December were set as indicative limits. Definitive performance criteria targets were to be set as a part of second review under the program.

Limits on net credit from the banking system to the Government had to prevent an excessive financing of budget deficit by banking system. Limits on net domestic assets of banking system were intended to influence monetary policy be guaranteeing that excessive expansion of credits does not interfere with the goals of macroeconomic stabilization and restructuring of enterprises. Minimum levels of net international reserves in convertible currencies were introduced in order to follow whether the replenishment of reserves proceeds satisfactorily. Adequate amount of foreign reserves was a necessary condition for the credibility of the fixed exchange rate policy, as the fixed exchange rate of Czechoslovak koruna (KCS) played an important role of nominal anchor against inflation. As for the limits on foreign borrowing guaranteed by the Government, this is an usual condition in most of the arrangements with the IMF. It should prevent the Government from increasing excessively its (contingent) foreign liabilities and provide in this way reasonable guarantees that the country will be in a position to repay all its obligations to the Fund.

According to the provisions of stand-by arrangement, individual purchases by Czechoslovakia were conditional on compliance with the above discussed performance criteria at given dates. Exact schedule, amounts and conditionality of disbursements is shown in Table 5.

Table 5.
Conditions For Disbursement Under First Stand-by Arrangement

Amount	SDR 221.25	SDR 99.56	SDR 99.56	SDR 99.56	SDR 99.56
Date	January 7, 1991 or after	May 15, 1991 or after	August 15, 1991 or after	November 15, 1991 or after	February 15, 1992 or after
Condition	IMF approval of stand-by	Observance of PC as of March 31 and completion of program review	Observance of PC as of June 30	Observance of PC as of September 30 and completion of program review	Observance of PC as of December 31

At the time when the request for stand-by arrangement by Czechoslovak authorities was submitted to the IMF board, it has been based on the following projections of major macroeconomic indicators for 1991. Some of these projections were stated in the form of program objectives:[12]

- decline of real gross domestic product maximally by 5 percent;
- initial jump of prices after price liberalization in the beginning of January about 25 percent;
- average unemployment rate at most 4.5 percent of labor force, which means 350,000 unemployed;
- external current account deficit US$ 2.5 bil;
- general government account surplus of 1 percent of GDP;
- maximum growth of liquidity 5.5 percent.

As soon as in February, it became apparent that at least one of this macroeconomic assumptions is erroneous. In January 1991 alone, price level measured by consumer price index jumped by more than 25 percent. Even though inflation declined sharply in subsequent months and prices were nearly stabilized in the second half of 1991, they increased in the year as a whole by more than 50 percent.

First review of stand-by arrangement took part in June 1991. All performance criteria for end-March have been observed with substantial margin, as is shown in Table 6. At the same time, performance criteria A

[12]It is necessary to distinguish between quantitative performance criteria, the observance of which is a condition for further disbursement of financial support, and broader objectives of the program, the achievements of which should be assisted by compliance with performance criteria.

change in net credit from the banking system to the Government was adjusted to take into account the takeover by the Government of export credits to the U.S.S.R., transfers from the Government to the banks to cover losses from 1990 devaluation, and some other minor transfers. Instead of original target of KCS -11.0 bil, new performance criteria for end-June was now set at KCS -27.8 bil, and for end-September, original target KCS -9.5 bil was replaced by KCS -29.5 bil. Other performance criteria remained unchanged after first review.

Table 6.

Observance of Performance Criteria, End-March

Criterion	Target	Actual
A	-11.0	-16.3
B	600	558
C	-0.9	-0.3
D	1.0	--- *

* "---" indicates zero values

Also second review, which was completed in November, showed successful compliance with performance criteria at the end of June, and the staff - as was later confirmed, correctly - projected that the end-September targets would be observed too. Comparison of actual data and targeted values for end-June and end-September performance criteria is shown in Table 7.

Table 7.

Observance of Performance Criteria, End-June, End-September

Criterion	Target June	Actual June	Target Sept.	Actual Sept.
A	-27.8	-45.6	-29.5	-42.6
B	620.0	591.0	633.4*	621.8
C	-1.1	—	-1.3	0.2
D	1.0	—	1.0	—

*End-September performance criteria net domestic assets of the banking system was adjusted against original target KCS 640 bil by KCS 6.6 bil for receipts of EC foreign loan.

As a part of second review, performance criteria A and B for end-December, which were set at the beginning of the program only indicatively, were corrected to reflect recent economic development. The adjustment was as following:

A: from KCS -16.8 bil to KCS -38.0 bil;
B: from KCS 675.0 bil to KCS 660.0 bil;

At the end of 1991, it was evident that actual macroeconomic development differed, in many respects notably, from the working assumptions of the program. The negative external shock related to the disintegration of the CMEA hit the Czechoslovak economy with more vigor than expected, and the loss of many relatively "soft" markets meant that enterprises were forced to cut their production sharply. The result was that instead of 5 percent, real GDP declined in 1991 by approximately 15 percent. On the other hand, surprisingly more positive was the development of the balance of payments: instead of projected deficit US$ 2.5 bil, it registered a surplus over US$ 1 bil.

However, the more than projected decline in economic activity negatively affected the fiscal position. Although higher price jump in the beginning of 1991 inflated profits of business sector and therefore budgetary revenues from profit taxes, these one-time gains were more than countered by weaker economic activity in the rest of the year. The result was that contrary to projected surplus of general government budget of 1 percent of GDP, it registered in 1991 a 2 percent deficit. This is also a reason why end-December performance criteria A and B were not observed (see Table 8). Underlying cause of worse than projected fiscal performance have been shortfalls in budgetary revenues, while expenditures were not as a total restrained appropriately and remained at the originally proposed level, as is illustrated in Table 9.

Table 8.

Observance of Performance Criteria, End-December 1991

Criterion	Target	Actual
A	-38.0	-17.4
B	660	674.9
C	-0.5	0.4
D	1.0	— *

* "—" indicates zero values

Table 9.

Budgetary Revenues and Expenditures, 1991 (bil KCS)

	Adjusted Target	Actual	Actual as % of target
Total Revenue	490.31	466.26	95.1
In Which: Turnover Tax	141.91	123.37	86.9
Corporate Tax	250.49	231.76	92.5
Others	97.91	111.13	113.5
Total Expenditures	482.91	482.85	100.4

Table 10.

Budgetary Balance in the Course of 1991 (Cumulative, KCS bil)

Datum	31.3	30.6	30.9	31.10	30.11	31.12
Balance	15.26	17.68	11.44	8.00	-2.70	-18.59

As was concluded by the IMF, the failure to keep the fiscal balance in small surplus has not been a result of weakening of fiscal policy stance. It was generated by large unfavorable changes in underlying macroeconomic conditions which were not correctly projected at the start of the program. For this reason, the IMF provided a waiver for non-observance of end-December performance criteria A and B, and Czechoslovakia was allowed to draw the final disbursement under first stand-by arrangement.

Czechoslovakia has thus made all scheduled purchases under first stand-by arrangement in the amount of SDR 619.5 mil, and additional purchases under the compensatory element of CCFF in the amount of SDR 466.0 mil. Total purchases at the end of first stand-by arrangement achieved SDR 1085.5 mil.

Financial assistance, provided in the course of 1991 by the IMF, as well as first and second disbursement under Structural Adjustment Loan by the World Bank in the amount of US$ 325 mil and EC financial assistance, coupled with the non-debt financing in the form of direct foreign investment has assisted in the building up of sufficient levels of foreign reserves. They increased from less than US$ 1 bil at the end of 1990 to US$ 3.3 bil at the end of 1991, which was sufficient to cover approximately two months of import. Although such a level of foreign reserves was not still fully satisfactory, especially with the prospect of eventual revival of economic activity and increase in demand for imports of investment goods, critical situation from end 1990 was warded off. Limited current account convertibility, introduced at the beginning of 1991 was maintained, as well as fixed nominal exchange rate of KCS to a basket of five currencies. Especially fixed exchange rate played an important nominal anchor, as all other nominal magnitudes in the Czechoslovak economy moved rather erratically in the wake of price liberalization.

First stand-by arrangement therefore fulfilled its role in providing financial support to the macroeconomic stabilization after comprehensive price liberalization in January 1991. It helped to institute favorable initial conditions for the third part of economic reform that was to follow after the liberalization and macroeconomic stabilization, namely structural reforms.

2. SECOND STAND-BY ARRANGEMENT

After first stand-by arrangement expired in April 1992,[13] it was immediately followed by second stand-by arrangement. Foreign currency reserves in the banking system continued to build up in the 1992 as well, and in mid-1992 exceeded US$ 4 bil. This implied that the IMF financial assistance was not as urgent at that time as it was at the beginning of first stand-by arrangement, when the reserves lingered at a dangerously low level of two-weeks export. But because it was expected that demand for import will increase rapidly after the first wave of privatization, as the new owners will start to put in effect their investment plans, the authorities agreed with the IMF that due to the still existing uncertainties with respect to balance of payments development, it is reasonable to maintain the access to the IMF resources.

Another reason why second stand-by arrangement immediately followed first one was to assure a continuity of the Fund surveillance. Usually, once the IMF approves a financial assistance, it gives an important signal that the country will follow sound macroeconomic policies and that it will try to avoid using price distortive measures and other market unfriendly policies. Although Czechoslovakia gained a reputation of a country that is fully resolved to pursue the transformation of centrally planned to a market economy, no matter how high the short-term costs may be, there are still many uncertainties lying ahead, mainly in political sphere. Willingness of

[13]It was originally bound to expire in March, because it was concluded in January 1991 for a 14-month period. However, it was decided to extend it by one month in order to provide for a continuity with new arrangement.

Czechoslovak authorities to stick to the conditions prescribed by performance criteria of second stand-by arrangement served therefore also as a signal that they do not want to give up to short-term difficulties at the costs of sacrificing the long-term strategy of macroeconomic stability.

Second stand-by arrangement was approved by the IMF on April 3, 1992, this time for a much lower amount of SDR 236 mil. Moreover, with regard to a favorable foreign reserves level, the disbursement of individual tranches was in contrast to first stand-by arrangement back-loaded,[14] as is seen in Table 12, which showed the phasing-in of disbursements and the conditions attached to it. In qualitative terms, performance criteria attached to second stand-by arrangement were similar to these in first stand-by arrangement. The small modifications were that performance criteria A, limits on change of net credit to Government by banking system, was replaced by net credit from the banking system to the Government, and performance criteria D, net external debt contracted or guaranteed, was replaced by net disbursements of external debt in convertible currencies, with subdivision for 1-12 years maturity (D1) and 1-5 years maturity (D2).

Table 11.

Performance Criteria for Second Stand-By Arrangement

Criterion	1.4.-30.6. 1992	1.7.-31.8. 1992	1.10.-31.12 1992
A (KCS bil) *	64	70	82
B (KCS bil)	732	754	781
C(US$ mil)	—	150	300
D1 (US$ mil) *	800	1000	1200
D2 (US$ mil) *	300	500	600

* Cumulative from December 31, 199

[14]Eventually, Czechoslovak authorities decided in mid-September, after the consultation with the IMF, that with regard to further increase in foreign reserves, which for the whole banking sector approached at that time US$ 5 bil, it is not necessary to make the third and fourth purchase under the second stand-by arrangement. This, of course, did not mean that Czechoslovakia will not continue to pursue the program targets, as expressed by end-September and end-December performance criteria.

Table 12.

Conditions for Disbursement Under Second Stand-By Arrangement

Amount	Date	Condition
SDR 18 mil	April 3 1992 or after	Approval of stand-by
SDR 18 mil	July 1, 1992 or after	Observance of end-June performance of criteria
SDR 100 mil	October 1, 1992 or after	Observance of en-Sept. performand criteria and completion of mid-term review
SDR 100 mil	January 1, 1993 or after	Observance of end-December performance criteria

Both macroeconomic conditions projected for 1992 and accompanying structural changes in the course of the program were different from these expected for the period of first stand-by arrangement. In contrast to 1991 program, when the major uncertainties were related to external environment, the determining source of unpredictable development during 1992 was connected with the acceleration of structural reforms. By the start of large privatization in mid-1992, profound transformation of productive assets was initiated. While there is generally agreement that the behavior of firms will change in the direction of increased efficiency with subsequent positive supply response once they will have real owners, there is no warranty that this movement will be straightforward. Furthermore, even if we are relatively assured about what will be the direction of changes, we can only estimate what will be their speed, how long will it take before the dispersed shareholders will organize themselves and establish such a managing structures that will allow them to become active owners. This all made the prediction of macroeconomic aggregates in the short-run more difficult.

Similarly as in 1991, real GDP was projected to decline by 5 percent. However, in a sharp contrast to a previous year, it is clear from the development in the first half of 1992 that the projection is not overoptimistic. Thanks to strong performance of the export sector and new private sector, it is even possible that the actual decline of real GDP in 1992 will be less than projected 5 percent.

As far as inflation rate in 1992 is concerned, the program was based on the expectations that GDP deflator will be in the range of 12-15 percent.

Again, data for the first three quarters of the year signal that actual outcome may be somewhere about 10 percent. Because there were still some price increase due to the liberalization of remaining administratively regulated prices, underlying rate of inflation was in fact even lower.

General government budget was projected to reach a deficit of 3 percent of GDP, which is slight increase in comparison to actual deficit in 1992. Current account was expected to record a deficit of US$ 1.1 bil. Development in the first half of 1992, with fiscal position on cash-flow basis on average balanced and current account in surplus by more than US$ 800 mil, it is not excluded that, despite the expected deterioration in the second half on 1992, actual 9912 outcome in fiscal and external balance may be more favorable.

Table 13.

Budgetary Revenues and Expenditures in First Half of 1992 (KCS mil)

	Budget 1992	Actual	% from 1992 Budget	Index 92/91
Total Revenues	504,806	227,460	45.1	94.5
InWhich: Turnover Tax	144,980	56,905	39.3	89.6
Corporate Tax	239,305	108,967	45.5	84.9
Total Expenditures	504,806	223,445	44.3	100.2

However, this does not imply that the current stance of fiscal policy will be sufficient to guarantee such a positive budgetary development in the future as well. Because the transition to a market economy involves short-term transformation costs in the form of higher unemployment and reduced real incomes, pressures to increase budgetary spending will continue. Additional source of pressure on budgetary expenditures comes from these groups in economy which relatively or absolutely loose as a consequence of the changes in relative prices and internal terms of trade shocks, or as a consequence of the changing criteria for the distribution of incomes.

Moreover, as the experience from other reforming countries shows [15], important fiscal implications follow from the process of privatization, which now accelerates dramatically in Czechoslovakia. It was more easy to collect, or sometimes rather confiscate, the taxes from state enterprises, which were relatively few in number and fully dependent on the state. On the contrary, as the share of private sector in the economy grows, administrative complexity of tax collection quickly increases, and consequently, its effectiveness declines. It is also much more difficult to offset eventual revenue shortfalls by changes in tax rates because private firms could be more sensitive to similar policy measures, and the outcomes could be rather perverse. Shortfalls in revenues are further aggravated by generally weak economic activity, with cyclical deficit developing.

For these reasons, it is recognized that one of the main goal of macroeconomic policy in Czechoslovakia in 1992 is to ensure that the deficit does not get out of manageable levels and that automatic stabilizers, together with the modernization of the tax system and improved tax collection capacity keep fiscal position sustainable. Judging from end-September data, this goal will be probably achieved, despite the additional complications which brings for macroeconomic management future separation of Czechoslovakia.

3. IMF-FINANCED PROGRAMS IN OTHER COUNTRIES OF CEE: COMPARISON WITH CZECHOSLOVAKIA

Czechoslovakia was not the first country in the region of CEE where the IMF became involved. Already in the beginning of the 1980's, the IMF concluded two stand-by arrangements with Hungary. Hungary, together with Poland also were the first countries which received stand-by support from the Fund after the radical political changes in the CEE countries at the end of 1980's. Later on, in 1991, together with Czechoslovakia, stand-by arrangements were also approved for Romania and Bulgaria. In 1991, Poland and Hungary continued with the Extended Financing Facility. In 1992, the IMF agreed second stand-by arrangement for Bulgaria. Review of financial scope of the Fund involvement in these countries is shown in Table 14.

---

[15] See J. Kornai, The Postsocialist Transformation and the State: Reflection in the Light of Hungarian Fiscal Problems. *American Economic Review*, Papers and Proceedings, May 1992, p. 1-21.

Table 14.

Financial Assistance of the IMF in CEE Countries by September 1992, SDR mil

Country	Membership Quota After 8th Review	Total Credits Committed by the IMF	Total Credits Actually Disbursed	Credits Disbursed as % of Quota
Czechoslov.	590.0	1321.5	1121.5	190.0
Bulgaria	310.0	490.9	428.9	138.4
Hungary *	530.7	2505.65	1819.28	343.0
Poland	680.0	1931.6	596.6	87.7
Romania	523.4	803.4	698.56	133.47

* Data for total credits committed and actually disbursed include stand-by arrangement approved in 1984 in the amount of SDR 425 mil, and stand-by approved in 1982, in the amount of SDR 475 mil. Actual disbursement was equal to committed resources in these cases.

In Hungary, if we disregard two arrangements from the beginning of 1980's, first stand-by arrangement after the serious start with reforms was approved in the amount of SDR 159 mil in March 1990. At this time, Hungarian economy was threatened by weak fiscal position and by deteriorating external position. After maintaining the budget balanced in 1988, it was in deficit by 1.3 percent of GDP in 1989. It was obvious that without immediate policy measures, it will rise much more in 1990. Convertible currency account deficit widened from US$ 0.8 bil in 1988 to US$ 1.4 bil in 1989, which represented 5 percent of GDP. There were fears that the access to external financing will be limited, and that this would put under risk either debt servicing capacity or current account liberalization. Therefore, main objective of the program was to maintain external solvency of Hungary. The program also assumed an achievement of balanced fiscal position and an increase of domestic credit not higher that 11 percent in 1990. Deficit of current account in convertible currencies was to be limited to US$ 550 mil. An assumption was adopted that real GDP will remain unchanged in 1990, and the rate of inflation will remain under 20 percent.

Despite the unfavorable external circumstances, the most pronounced success of the program was achieved on the external front, in preserving and even improving the external solvency of Hungary. Instead of programmed US$ 550 mil deficit, the convertible current account recorded a small surplus in 1990. On the contrary, the program projections for output and inflation proved to be overly optimistic. Real GDP declined by 4 percent, while the consumer price index increased by about 30 percent. External shocks that negatively affected Hungarian macroeconomic performance in 1990 were absorbed rather by declining output and increase in prices than by deterioration of external equilibrium.

Among the causes of larger than projected decline of output were negative effect of drought on agriculture, estimated at 1.5 percent of GDP, decline in ruble exports, estimated at 1 percent of GDP, and also sharp real contraction of domestic credit by 15 percent instead of programmed 8 percent.

With regard to budgetary balance, the target of balanced budget was broadly observed. Fiscal deficit in 1990 was negligible 0.2 percent of GDP.

In Poland, after the price liberalization in August 1989, monthly inflation rates moved in the range of 30 to 50 percent, and inflation rate for whole 1989 was 640 percent. Domestic financial instability therefore predetermined the main goal of stand-by arrangement with Poland, approved by the IMF in February 1990 in the amount of SDR 545 mil, which was to reduce fiscal budget from a deficit of 8 percent of GDP to a balanced position. Real GDP was projected to fall during 1990 by 5 percent; inflation was expected to reach 45 percent monthly rate in January as a consequence of price liberalization, and to fall quickly thereafter.

Actual development diverted again from projected, similarly as in the case of Hungary. And interestingly, better than projected development was again recorded on external front, while domestic indicators turned out worse than projected.

While there was expected a current account deficit of US$ 290 mil in the first quarter of 1990, Poland actually achieved thanks to a substantial revival of export to convertible currency area a surplus of US$ 1622 mil. The surplus then diminished in the rest of the year, but it still remained for the whole 1990 at the level of US$ 668 mil, instead of projected deficit US$ 3 bil. On the other side, prices jumped after the January price liberalization in this month by 90 percent, twice as much as expected. Even though the monthly inflation rates declined rapidly in subsequent months, it was still not enough to meet the original inflation projections. The price level, measured by consumer price index, increased between December 1989 and December 1990 by 246 percent.

Higher price jump in the beginning of 1990 inflated temporarily the profits of enterprises, which offset the negative impact of inflation on budget balance through the Tanzi effect.[16] The budget was during the first quarter of 1990 in surplus by 3.4 trillion zloty, instead of expected deficit of 3 trillion. This shift corresponded approximately to 4 percent of GDP. But the budget started to deteriorate in the second half of 1990, with slight deficit registered in the fourth quarter. For the whole year, the budget was in a

---

[16]Tanzi effect refers to the erosion of real tax revenues by inflation due to time lags in tax collection. See Vito Tanzi, "Inflation, Lags in Collection and the Real Value of Tax Revenues", IMF Staff Papers, Vol. 24, March 1977.

surplus by 3.5 percent of GDP on cash basis, but on commitment basis, there was a deficit of 2.7 percent of GDP.

Finally, the real GDP dropped much more than projected in 1990, by 11.6 percent. There were some doubts whether the officially measured decline of GDP reflected accurately the real decline of economic activity, with developing private sector activities largely unrecorded. However, this is a problem which is common to all CEE countries.

In general, programs of economic reforms in the CEE countries, supported by financial assistance from the IMF, were rather successful in preventing aggregate demand to exceed potential output significantly. Unexpectedly favorable has been in all countries improvement in the balance of payment position. Although this reflected to a large degree depression of import demand as a consequence of general slump in economic activity in the CEE countries and of postponement of many investment plans during the process of privatization, important factor was also the increase of export to industrial countries. The fears that import of consumption goods after the trade liberalization will shoot up because of its long-term administrative suppression also did not materialize. With the assistance of the IMF and other official creditors, the countries were therefore able to build up notably their foreign reserves.

In contrast to over pessimistic projections of balance of payments, the estimates of magnitude or price jump after the comprehensive price liberalizations were consistently overoptimistic. The reason is that there existed only approximate assessment of possible discrepancy between aggregate demand and supply in the CEE countries in the form of monetary overhang[17]. Therefore, the judgments about how large the price jump would be after allowing the suppressed inflation to take explicit form were very rough. Furthermore, it was not clear how the business sector will respond to price liberalization , which was still dominated by state owned firms, often with monopolistic position on the markets. The attempts of monopolistic producers and distributors to increase rather than output prices ultimately hit the ceiling given by demand constraint, but prices remained at higher level.

At the beginning of reforms in early 1990's, the IMF and authorities in the CEE countries obviously underestimated the output decline that would occur during the transition. This was partly due to the unexpected development in the former U.S.S.R., where the disintegration of political and economic structure negatively impacted on the reform process in other countries. The external shock also exacerbated initial price increase after the liberalization in all the CEE countries. In Czechoslovakia, it is estimated that external factors contributed by some 60-70 percents to the output

[17]See for example Drábek, Z., Janáček, K, Tůma, Z., op. cit.

contraction in 1991. Therefore, the decline in economic activity cannot be subscribed fully to the impact of economic reforms and restrictive policies.

This is can be illustrated by two findings. First, there was strong correlation between the share of foreign trade with the former U.S.S.R. in total trade and between the rate of decline of output on the CEE countries. Bulgaria, which was the country most dependent on trade with the former U.S.S.R., experienced also largest decline of production, while Hungary, which succeeded in transforming largely its exports toward western markets during the 1980's was affected substantially less. Second, Finland, which did not implement any economic reform during 1991, but which was similarly dependent significantly on trade with the former U.S.S.R., recorded a decline of GDP by some 6 percent.

In all the CEE countries, the government budgets were not a source of major problems usually only for a short period of time after the start of reforms. Later on, however, budgetary deficits began to appear or increase. In Czechoslovakia, it remained on relatively moderate level in 1991 and the authorities week to limit the 1992 deficit even more. However, deficits will probably rise to 8-9 percent of GDP in 1991 in Hungary and Poland, and prospects for 1993 are not much more promising.

There are many reasons why it is very difficult to avoid sizable fiscal deficits during the period of transition. At the start of the reforms, larger price jumps helped to attain relatively high fiscal surpluses rather than expected small deficits or balanced positions. In the very short-run, price liberalization and higher inflation spurred more budgetary revenues than expenditures, but the situation changed in the time. Weakening of economic activity, no additional one-time sources of revenue from stock revaluation and inflated profits, and at the same time increasing demand for budgetary resources due to the unemployment and other costs of transition pushed the fiscal balance in the direction of larger budget deficits.

The impact of economic reforms on fiscal balance does not provide, however, strong reasons for modification of reform strategy. If the transition of state dominated economy to a private one proceeds quickly, tax collection could be eroded for some time, due to administrative difficulties. But if the inefficient state sector remains largely nonprivatized, with implicit or explicit subsidies still largely untouched, impact on fiscal balance will be sooner or later equally negative. But in contrast to the first alternative, fiscal problems will not be in this case an outcome of administrative difficulties but of basic faults in the economic systems, and thus impossible to solve. On the contrary, potentially negative short-term implications of increasing share of private sector in the economy on budgetary balance will tend to be offset in the longer-run by positive impact of more vigorous economic growth.

Initial experience with the Fund programs in Romania and Bulgaria was similar to this in Hungary, Poland and Czechoslovakia. Actual output decline and price increase was larger than expected in the programs, while relatively more favorable was external balance development. Delays in structural reforms, especially in privatization, could, however, severely undermine the efforts of authorities in Romania and Bulgaria to achieve a degree of financial stability that would be necessary for successful realization of economic reforms.

10

TAX REFORM

Eva Zamrazilova
Institute of Economics
Czechoslovak Academy of Sciences

1. BRIEF OUTLINE OF TAX REFORM

The tax reform represents a very important part of the whole economic reform process. The tax system as it was at the end of 1989 was completely unsuitable neither for market economy nor for the period of transition and the need to integrate Czechoslovakia into the international economic system - moreover in the situation of harmonizing the tax systems in the EC. The preparation of the new tax system has started immediately in 1990; the proposed tax system is due to be introduced in 1993 and some preparatory changes have already been made in 1990 and 1991. The present tax system is therefore represented by the old framework improved by some partial changes directed in the way of the proposed system. In the first part of this report the present tax system and the proposed one will be briefly outlined with main focus being on changes that should take place.

The present Czechoslovak tax system can be characterized by following structure:

1. Taxation of companies
- Payroll tax
- Company income tax
- Profit levy (delivery)
- Depreciation levy
- Regulation and price deliveries
- Agricultural tax

2. Taxation of population
- Wages tax
- Population income tax
- Tax on income from literary and artistic activities

3. Taxes on goods and services (indirect taxes)
- Turnover tax
- Import tax

4. Other taxes
- Agricultural tax
- Housing tax
- Local taxes

1.1 Taxation of Companies

The subjects of payroll tax are almost all companies without any difference as far as the form of entrepreneurship is concerned; the exception being self employed people only. This tax is levied at a basic rate of 50% of employers` total wage bill. Some organizations (health resort organizations, organizations in culture and city transport) are charged a lower rate and therefore the actual percentage of total Czechoslovakian wages collected by the government (by payroll tax) is about 30%.

Company income tax is designed principally for non-state owned incorporated companies. The base for this tax is annual company profit defined as revenue minus the costs of inputs (including any taxes paid on wages), nominal interest payments and depreciation allowances. The first 200,000 of profits are taxed at a rate of 20%, the remainder profits at 55%. Czechoslovak companies and cooperatives involved in wholesale and retail trade, catering, hotels and tourism are taxed at a rate depending upon the ratio of profits to expenditures. These rates vary from 10% (if the ratio of profits to costs is up to 10%) and 50% (if the ratio exceeds 30%). Agricultural businesses pay a rate of 50%.

The profit levy (delivery) pay state owned companies, joint stock companies, foreign trade companies and state monetary institutions. In essence this is a profit tax at a rate of 55% (profit modified by several items again).

The rates of company income tax and profit levy are aligned. Foreign enterprises investing in Czechoslovakia are a subject of tax incentives for encouraging investment. Tax holidays up to 100% are given to newly established enterprises for the first two years. Companies are allowed to deduct depreciation from their taxable income.

After the period of tax holidays being over, enterprises are subject to a tax rate of 20% (taxable income less than 200,000) or 40% (more than 200,000) if the foreign capital share is greater than 30%, otherwise 55% like the other subjects of company income tax.

Subjects of depreciation levies are only a limited number of state enterprises with damping programme.

Regulation deliveries pay all companies exceeding the growth of average nominal wages (wage control is yet an important part of macroeconomic stabilization policy).

The system of agricultural tax consists of already mentioned payroll tax, profit tax and moreover land tax.

Although many changes have been made in taxing of companies during last two years, present system still preserves some features typical for the period of administrative management. At first the taxation of profit is very high because the former purpose was extensive redistribution - high taxation of the best companies while subsidizing worse ones. This system of taxation was directed to depriving enterprises of the profit left after having produced their output indicated by plan. Another inconsistencies are represented e.g.. by different rates of social security contributions paid by individual subjects, different possibilities of deduction items application (losses, gifts etc.), different liability for state cooperative and social organizations etc.

1.2. Taxation of the Population

Wage tax is a monthly paid tax levied on wages and salaries. The tax varies according to age, sex, family status and the number of dependents in the family. As a consequence of this differentiations there are tax bands, the illustration of which can be seen in Table 1.

Table 1

Tax paid as a proportion of income by different type of taxpayers

Yearly Wage Kcs	30,000	50,000	70,000	90,000
Single or married without children	21.8	26	27.6	28.6
2 dependents	13.6	16.2	17.3	17.9
3 dependents	9.52	11.3	12.1	12.6
4 dependents	6.8	8.1	8.6	8.9
Married 25 45	20.4	24.1	25.6	26.8
Married up to 25 over 45	18.6	22.6	24.2	25.0

Population income tax is principally a tax levied on small businesses and other self-employed workers. The base for this is entrepreneurial and private farmers incomes. The rates of taxation are shown in Table 2.

Table 2

Taxable amount		Marginal Tax rate
over	up to	
0	60,000	15%
60,000	180,000	25%
180,000	540,000	35%
540,000	1,080,000	45%
1,080,000	and more	55%

Tax on income and artistic activities is levied on total net royalties earned during the year at rates of between 3 and 33%. The marginal tax is similar to the marginal rate of wage tax, the structure being somewhat different. In comparison to other taxes these are low since they were designated to compensate for the absence of a social security system for people not in regular employment which is not the case any more. The incomes paid to citizens from health insurance, pensions etc. are not taxed.

From this very brief outline is quite obvious that tax rates represent different tax burden for the same amount of income originating from various sources. Incomes from individually performed activities fall in a category with much higher progression than wages, tax rate of the population incomes is unproportionally progressive if income exceeds CSK 60,000. As far as wage tax is concerned unjustifiable or hardly justifiable differentiation in the tax rates based upon age, sex, marital status and number of persons maintained exists with the difference exceeding 25 percentage points in extreme cases.

1.3. Taxes on Goods and Services (indirect taxes)

The turnover tax is levied on all manufactured and imported goods excluding capital equipment and goods which are to be exported. The tax is also imposed on a limited number of services. It is paid by all resident and non-resident enterprises in Czechoslovakia. The tax base is the price at which the goods is sold. It is levied at the last production level, as the goods is sold to the wholesaler.

The turnover tax was radically reformed at the end of 1990 in a move which resulted in great reduction in the number of the tax rates. Up until 1990 there existed 1506 different tax rates on manufactured and imported goods. A large number of these were subsidies (negative taxes) imposed on foods. In January 1991 however, as a preparatory step towards price liberalization, the number of tax rates was reduced from 1506 to 4 (0, 11, 22, 29). Higher rates are imposed on selected groups of goods (tobacco, spirits, gold, jewelry etc.). A per capita subsidy (negative poll tax) was introduced in

July 1990, when negative turnover tax was abolished, in order to compensate for the rise of prices. This was substantially reduced in January 1992 and is provided only to individuals who are not economically active.

The total tax revenue in 1991 amounted 466 mild Kcs and was divided by following scheme:

Profit deliveries	27.3%
Turnover tax	26.4%
Payroll tax	20.3%
Wage tax	12.1%
Company income tax	1.0%
Other deliveries	0.9%
Others	12.0%

The structure of total tax revenue is expected to change very significantly with the new tax system; in a great detail this problem will be analyzed in the final section.

Next part will briefly outline the general structure of the proposed tax system which is due to be introduced as from January 1, 1993.

The new tax system is to comprise the following:

1. Corporate income tax
2. Personal income tax
3. Taxes on goods and services
   - VAT including import taxes
   - Consumption taxes
4. Property and land tax
5. Road tax
6. Tax on inheritance and gifts
7. Tax on real estate transfers
8. Environmental taxes

The first three taxes are most important both from the viewpoint of economic reform as well as from that of revenue. They will be also principally determined at Federal level with determining of the extent of changes that might be made at lower levels of governments. The republics will be free to set other taxes at whatever levels they wish.

Next a very brief outline of individual taxes will be performed.

Personal income tax

This tax will be introduced instead wage tax, tax from the income of population and the tax from literary and artistic activities. Income taxation will be unified subjecting both individuals and unincorporated businesses to the new income tax. Pensions and other social benefits will not be taxed. Major changes to previous system can be characterized by following points:

- unification of tax rates for different types of incomes, if an individual has different sources of income, they will be considered together;
- application of unified tax allowance for each individual;
- strong reduction of social criteria (age, sex, marital status);
- payment of contributions to social funds (health, social and employment fund) separated from the tax and budget system;
- application of deductible items like gifts and social contributions.

Corporation income tax

A new corporation income tax is to replace the existing profit deliveries, company income tax and agriculture profit tax. The new tax will be levied on all incomes from corporate activities, where income is defined as being the difference between revenue and costs. Main differences over the previous system can be characterized as follows:

- unification of this tax for all entrepreneurial forms;
- enlargement of base for application of deductible items (loss that can be deducted from tax liability over a period of five years, gifts);
- abolishment of depreciation, price and wage control deliveries;
- possibility of choice between linear and degressive form of depreciation;
- abolishment of the payroll tax, corporations will pay contributions directly to three social funds.

Taxes on goods and services

The most significant tax on goods and services will be the VAT. replacing in fact the turnover tax. Introducing VAT represents principal change in taxation of goods and services. The tax applies to sales of all goods and some services including the transfer of real property and leases and will be paid by all subjects with a turnover exceeding 5,000,000 Kcs per year.

There will be two tax rates, 23% on most goods and limited number of services and leases and 5% on food and some other selected goods, the majority of services and real estate. Some services will be exempted.

The consumption taxes will be levied on selected goods (tobacco, spirits, fuel) and will be applied by fixed amounts per unit of goods.

Land and property tax

These taxes will be under control of local authorities. The land tax will be applicable to agricultural land; the rates will vary according to quality and type of land.

The property tax is payable at rates varying with both the size and location of the property.

Road tax

This will take the form of a tax on all vehicles apart from those used for personal purposes. The rates for Czech vehicles will depend upon the weight, performance and the purpose of the vehicle. Foreign vehicles will be charged according to the length of time that they are in the country.

Property transfer taxes, Inheritance and gift taxes

These two taxes will be levied on the transfers of real and moveable property. In the case of inheritances, the size of the tax will depend upon the net price of the property (liabilities and other costs of property transfers can be deducted first). If a gift is given than the tax will be depending upon the current price. The person who gives the bequest or the gift will be taxed; there will be three different tax rates which will vary according to the relationship between the original owner and the beneficiary.

Tax on real estate transfers

This tax will apply to the sale of property and as under the inheritance and gift taxes, the size of the tax will depend upon the price of property and relationship between the people involved.

The proposed tax system in the CSFR represents a major improvement over the previous one. It will make an important contribution to the development of an efficient market economy by simplifying taxes and applying them in a more consistent manner. The priority has been focused on equity principles - the implementation of similar conditions of taxation to similar economic subjects.

The new tax system is sure to have many far reaching economic and social consequences concerning both micro and macro level of the economy. Next parts of this report will therefore be devoted to more detailed analysis of three major parts of the new tax system - personal income tax, corporation income tax and value added tax with regard not only to their description but also to their economic consequences as well as social ones.

2. PERSONAL INCOME TAX

2.1. Taxpayers, Types of Incomes, Exemptions

Personal income taxpayers are persons having permanent residence in the CSFR or those staying there at least 183 days in the respective year. Other persons having incomes from the sources situated on the territory of CSFR are subject to a limited tax liability.

The following incomes will be subject to taxation:

- Wage income
- Income from independent business activity
- Income from property;
- Income from rents;
- Other income.

Incomes not being subject to PIT:

- Inherited or given real and moveable property (these incomes are to be subject to inheritance and gift tax);
- credits and loans.

Several types of incomes will be exempted, especially:

- Payments from obligatory social, health and employment insurance,
- state and social benefits provided under special regulations,
- alimony,
- compensations received for damages (restitution),
- incomes from selling real and moveable property (under certain conditions concerning mostly excluding speculations),
- payments to non-professional soldiers,
- incomes from non-obligatory insurance,
- incomes from small hydro-power stations.

If an individual owns less than 20% of a company than all income that is received by that individual is subject to personal income tax only. If more than 20% is owned, then CSK 10,000 per month will be taxed under the PIT and the remainder will be subject to corporation income tax.

2.2. The Tax Schedule

The tax base is the difference between the incomes obtained and the respective costs (in the case of wage incomes the wage) adjusted for tax allowances. The respective costs can be stated either in actual level (with receipts) or can be subtracted as a certain relative amount. This latter possibility will differ for individual types of activities:

50% in agriculture and forestry,
30% in literary and artistic activities,
20% in individual businesses, rents and other activities.

If a person will have more than one type of income - which will often be the case (e.g.. wage income and rent income) - than the tax base will be the sum of tax bases of individual types of incomes. If in some cases the tax base is not positive (the loss occurs) this will be taken into account in next years.

Simple system of allowances is characterized by:

- The single persons allowance — 20,400
- Married persons allowance (provided the wives earning is less than 20,400) — 12,400
- Child allowance — 9,000
- Disabled persons allowance (depending upon the nature of disablement) — 12,000 or 36,000
- Traffic allowance (depending upon the distance between home and job - lower level is for distances up to 30 km) — 2,400 or 3,600
- Obligatory insurance payments to social, health and employment fund. — 14% of income

All these allowances are stated an amount per year. After subtracting those tax allowances (or deductible items) following scheme of tax rates will be applied:

Marginal Personal Income Tax Rates (per year)

Over	To	Rates
0	60,000	15%
60,000	120,000	20%
120,000	180,000	25%
180,000	540,000	32%
540,000	1,080,000	40%
1,080,000	-	47%

The proposed income tax system can be interpreted as being progressive because at every point of the income schedule marginal tax rates are greater than average rates; but it should be noted that the system becomes less progressive as income rises.

The new system is therefore progressive with tax free allowances and multiple rates. Particular improvement over the old system is that the taxes for wage earners and the self-employed people have been unified and the rates structure has been simplified.

In this respect however Czechoslovak tax reform does not correspond to international trends in income tax reforms, because these trends seem to reflect two facts - that progressivity does not require a multiple rate system and that multiple rate system impose significant administrative costs and problems; Reduction in the number of different tax rates within individual systems is therefore a result of tax reforms as well as broadening and simplifying the tax base by removing or reducing special exemptions and reductions. Lowering tax rates is also quite frequent.

It should be noted that a similar degree of progression over the income range could be achieved using higher allowances and a single tax rate for all but the very rich. Theories of optimal income tax structure predict that the most efficient income tax structure is approximately linear one consisting of a tax free allowance and a single marginal tax rate. Also there are considerable administrative advantages to such a simplification.

One interesting feature of the proposed tax system is that most taxpayers will be paying income tax at the rate of 15% which is rather low by OECD standards. The reason why this rate is so low appears to be very high rate of social security contributions. The details of this are described in the fourth section, where it is shown that the overall tax rates for the highly paid become quite high indeed.

2.3. The Social Security Reform

Very important part of the reform is that social security will be separated from the tax system. It will be specified by separate law which has not been completed yet.

The pre-reform system of payroll tax is to be replaced by a scheme of contributions to three funds - social security fund, health fund, employment fund. These contributions will be compulsory for both the employees and employers.

Perhaps the most controversial issue is the actual rates that employers and employees should pay. Individual persons' contribution to these funds will represent 14% of their total tax base, corporation's contributions will be discussed in respective section.

As no lower earnings limit below which social contributions are not paid has been specified, it is assumed that all employees will be liable to pay them.

It is possible to make following comments about the reforms of social security financing. Firstly it can be inferred from the discussions that the government is to have a minimal role in the running of the funds. According to current plans, the state shall only contribute revenue to the fund on behalf of those who are earning no or low incomes (the unemployed and those in the forces for example) and it is stressed that no capital reserves will be made available. This implies that the funds will have to rely upon their current revenues to finance their activities. Whilst such a scheme that is operated independently of the government does not run the risk of increases of benefits being financed from general government revenue (thus belying on the point of contributions ear-marked for social security expenditure) it may be possible that it will be difficult to fund such a scheme. This could very well be a problem given that unemployment in Czechoslovakia is likely to rise during the early years of transformation to a market economy and the old - age dependency ratio, through predicted to be stable over the next fifteen years, is very high at 30% compared to the OECD average of 21%. The provision of old age pensions through social security is a complicated issue given that the scheme either requires a very protracted period - fifty years or more - before it reaches maturity, or a rate of contribution that is much in excess of the actual benefits promised.

A second issue, and one that has not yet been specified in government plans, relates to whether the funds are going to be run on a "strict insurance" bases or not. It would be possible to relate the amount of benefits paid out to the size of contributions as this will ensure that the funds are able to support themselves. However, such a scheme may be too rigid to cope with the wide and changing circumstances which might lead to hardships for individuals and households. Furthermore, it may not be desirable on equity grounds to have, for example a system of health care that is based on the extent of contributions rather than need.

A third point to note relates to criteria that the government establishes for giving benefits. It is evident from their commitment to contributing to the social funds on behalf of those who are unable to do so themselves that the government intend that all individuals and households should be able to sustain a minimum standard of living. If this is the case, then it is important to bear in mind that the degree of contributions will depend upon how the minimum standard is defined. If the standard is defined relatively (in reference terms to standards of the day) than contributions will have to increase at the same rate as economic growth, but if standards are defined in absolute terms, targets will be achieved relatively easily.

2.4. Economic and Social Consequences of Personal Income Tax

The average rate of wage taxation is at present 18%. According to preliminary calculations the average rate of net taxation of personal incomes will be about 6% under the new system. Together with 14% of income representing individual contribution to the funds of social security system the total relative burden levied upon the populations incomes will amount about 20%. The new legislation will therefore slightly rise the average rate of taxation of the incomes of population.

Another question is the impact of changed system of taxation of personal incomes on different types of taxpayers. Enclosed tables (Table 9 - Table16) show the present taxation of wages of selected types of taxpayers on different levels of income compared to new situation. These calculations make it possible to identify the types of taxpayers profiting under the new system of taxation as well as those whose position deteriorates. Most significant changes that will occur as far as individual types of taxpayers and different levels of income are concerned can be outlined as follows:

- Much higher taxation of high incomes (over 100,000 Kcs-high incomes represented just a very small proportion and the old wage tax in fact did not take them into account), and lower taxation of low incomes; changes are generally least significant in the group of middle incomes.
- Single persons or married couples without children are the groups of taxpayers that will profit from the new system. The new scheme will be particularly advantageous for low and middle income groups of those taxpayers.
- Position of tax payers with one or two children with working wife will deteriorate under new conditions, the difference being naturally greater for tax payers with one child. The worse off is progressive with growing income. The difference is small for low income groups and very substantial (10 - 20 percentage points) for high income groups.
- Situation of married couples with children is slightly differentiated according to whether the wife is working or not. The threshold of CSK 20 400 determining whether a tax allowance for wife can be applied or not means in fact that this allowance is oriented to non-working (or part- working) wives.
- The situation of families with identical number of children where mother works or not differs roughly in 1-3 percentage points, the difference being greatest on middle income levels.
- Dramatic change is observable at the group of taxpayers amounting about 50,000 people - taxpayers who pay alimony (fathers mostly). Their relative tax burden impose on personal income will increase very significantly. This worse off will be greater for the taxpayers with new families (children) - if there is one child in the family and one alimentated then the relative change will amount (in average according to preliminary calculations) about 10 percentage points, and with every next child there is another rise of this difference. This fact could have a negative effects on families with children that suffer first from higher taxation of families with children and second from expected behavior of fathers that will be less willing to paying alimony or raising them.

As far as the incentive aspects are concerned it is quite obvious that progressiveness of the scheme represents potential reducing of work incentives. relatively little strong evidence of incentive effects has been found, so this is not easy to state precisely how serious these potential disincentives are. However it is quite sure that the tax allowance for low income wives represents disincentive for them.

The withdrawal of allowance for wife (if her income exceed CSK 20,400) constitutes a significant disincentive for married women to work which is especially remarkable for women working part-time (for increase in hours is not supported by this scheme).

The fact is that those potential disincentive effects are not so relevant to the current circumstances of the CSFR: there is growing unemployment rather than labor shortage and there are not as many part-time workers as in OECD countries. However the tax system should be designed with a long term view. Rules introduced now can be very difficult to reverse later.

Perhaps more serious consequence of the progressivity of tax schedule is encouraging tax avoidance and evasion.

One possible form of avoidance is the use of "fringe benefits" instead of cash income. These benefits are often taxed by the personal tax system, although that is administratively difficult, but are more rarely subject to social security contributions. This can therefore be a particularly severe problem when social security contributions form such a large part of the total tax payment.

The most extensive form of tax avoidance in the present situation is such called "system Schwarz". Self employed persons employ other self employed persons on the basis of contract - the result being great amounts of payroll tax avoidance. This situation should be solved very soon by the new Employment Law.

Turning to evasion, this is much serious problem in the taxation of the self-employed as there income is much more difficult to verify. It is therefore important to realize that large social security contributions can be an incentive for the part of the labor force to become self-employed if, as in many countries, the self-employed pay insurance contributions at a lower rate than the combined employer and employee contribution.

There can be expected problems with administrative matters. The greatest problem will arise about people having more than one type of income (one of them being wage) - which will be frequent. Wage will be taxed at source, as the only income while other incomes will be most probably administered by self-assessment. The tax base is in fact represented by all net incomes minus deductible items. Because there is more than one marginal tax rate, there will be in some cases very probably used lower marginal rate for taxing wages than it should have been if all the incomes had been known before - which obviously is not realistic. Therefore perhaps some tax adjustments will be necessary after the end of year taking into account all the incomes.

The total tax revenue from PIT is expected to be about CSK 30 billion, 75% of which will be represented by taxation of wages, while the rest falls on the taxation of other incomes (individual activities, rents, etc.). This will therefore represent reducing of the incomes of the state budget by almost one half (speaking about this kind of revenue). On the other side separation of the social security system from the budget area means reducing demands on the state budget. Anyway this reduction of revenue is expected to be outweighed by indirect taxes the analyses of which will be devoted last section of this report.

2.5. Summary

The new system of personal income taxation is progressive with tax free allowances and multiple rates. In this respect Czechoslovak tax reform does not correspond to international trends in income taxation reforms aiming at reduction in the number of different income tax rates.

The system of social security will be separated from the tax system. The pre-reform system of payroll tax will be replaced by a scheme of contributions to three funds (social security fund, health fund, employment fund) paid by both employees and employers.

The average rate of net taxation will amount to 6% under the new system (which seems to be substantial lowering to previous system where the average rate of wage taxation is 18%) but which together with 14% of income representing individual contributions to three social funds will represent about 20% of average taxation of incomes. If compared to present situation when the average rate of wage taxation is 18%, the new scheme represents slight rise of the tax burden levied upon the personal incomes.

As far as changes in position of individual types of taxpayers are concerned, the single persons and married ones without children will be the ones profiting on the new system while the position of families with children will deteriorate, which will be particularly remarkable for the families with one child. Subject to much higher taxation will be the tax payers paying alimony, which unfortunately might have some negative social consequences.

The total tax revenue is expected to fall down substantially but this will be outweighed by separation of social system from the tax system and by other changes in the tax system as a whole.

The character of the personal income taxation may perhaps have some disincentive working effects as well as incentives to tax evasion and avoidance. Another problems may consist in administrative difficulties caused by multiple system of tax rates.

3. CORPORATE INCOME TAX

3.1. Taxpayers, Exemptions

Corporate income taxpayers are legal entities. Taxpayers having permanent residence in the CSFR are subject to unlimited tax liability concerning both foreign and home income while those not having permanent residence in the CSFR are subject to limited tax liability concerning CSFR-source incomes only. Corporate income tax will be levied on all incomes of Czechoslovak legal entities. Several types of incomes will be exempted, especially:

- membership fees of political parties and similar organizations
- incomes of non-profit sector from non-commercial activity
- payments for cooperative flats

- incomes from small hydro-power stations
- yielding from church collections
- incomes of state funds specified by special regulations
- Czechoslovak State Bank is exempted from tax liability.

Subject to this tax is not inherited or given property.

3.2. The Tax Base, Tax Rate, Deductible Items

The tax base is defined as being the difference between revenue and costs. The tax base does not involve:

- incomes taxed by special tax rates (see later in a more detail)
- exempted incomes,
- incomes from the difference between issued and sale price of own shares,
- incomes from buying own shares under nominal value.

Costs are deducted as proved by taxpayer and in some cases specified by the new tax law and by special regulations. The new law lists cost items. These include especially:

- depreciation allowance
- social security contributions
- financial and operating lease payments
- real estate and road taxes
- certain expenditures relating to health and safety at work and environmental protection.

The new law lists also certain categories that are specifically tax deductible:

- losses
- gifts
- shares of general partners of limited partnership companies.

Losses incurred in accounting period can be deducted from the tax liability over a period of five years. Special gifts to legal entities and municipalities can be deducted as well (at least CSK 2,000, at most 2% from yearly tax base). Reductions are provided for employers employing people with reduced work ability. The tax is reduced for CSK 5,000 for each employee with reduced work ability and for CSK 15,000 for each employee with reduced work ability and higher degree of health damage.

The standard rate of corporate tax will be 45% and will apply irrespective of whether the enterprise is subject to Czechoslovak or foreign ownership. The law permits the Czech and Slovak parliaments to raise this rate by up to 5% in these respective republics (which in today's situation is of no great importance).

Certain types of incomes will be subject to withholding taxes as follows:

- 25% on dividends, profit shares and other related distributions
- 20% on directors fees
- 15% on bank interest

It would have been willing to unify tax rates of interest, dividends and different types of savings. One obvious consequence may be the preference of individuals to deposit money in the bank instead of investments to shares. Lower tax rate of interest taxation than rate of taxation of dividends may moreover discourage investors from investments.

Subject to the provisions of relevant double taxation treaties, withholding taxes will apply to CSFR-source income and payments to non-resident taxpayers as follows:

- 25% on licence payments, royalties, rentals and operating lease payments
- 1% on financial lease payments.

The withholding tax applicable on interest payments made abroad does not appear to be specified by the new law although it is likely to remain at 25% in the absence of a double taxation treaty.

In comparison with previous taxation the introducing of corporate income tax represents lowering of tax rate concerning most taxpayers amounting to about 10 percentage points. The adverse effect is remarkable for part of companies with foreign capital, the profits of which were taxed at a rate of 40%.

A brief international comparison can be performed with the help of Table 3 where corporation tax rates for selected European countries are presented.

Table 3
Corporate tax rates in selected European countries

Country	Profit tax %	Local tax %	Social security contribution %
Austria	30	cca 15	15.85 - 16.5
Belgium	39	-	12.07
Denmark	40	-	-
Finland	23	14 - 19.5	4.85 - 6.5
France	37	16	37 - 45
Germany	50	12 - 20	18.6
Greece	46	-	22.2 - 23.6
Ireland	43	-	12.2
Italy	36	16.2	50
Netherlands	35 - 42	-	10.09
Norway	27.8	18 - 21	2.2 - 16.7
Portugal	36.5	raising of PT up to 10%	24.5
Spain	35	15	24 - 30
Sweden	30	20	39

The total level of profit taxation is very scarcely lower than 40% in European countries. It is quite obvious that Czechoslovak corporate tax being about an average of respective countries corresponds very well with international trends. The level of future taxation can therefore not be considered as discouraging economic activity.

3.3. Depreciation

A very important part of tax reform in the area of companies taxation is the change in the way of depreciation. The value base for depreciation is the purchase price of an asset - in the case of purchasing it or own costs in the case of own production.

Under the new tax system companies can make their choice whether they deduct depreciation costs, limited to a maximum of 100% from their taxable income on a straight line or a declining balance basis, although certain companies will be subject to some restrictions in their choice. After the choice being made it becomes irreversible.

As with the current depreciation system, the new law specifies a fixed life for tangible and intangible assets ranging from 4 to 50 years, depending upon the asset category. The assets will be grouped into five categories, the supposed time of depreciation for each of them is showed in Table 4.

Table 4

Life length for different groups of asset categories

Asset category	Life length (years)
1	4
2	8
3	15
4	30
5	50

Software and tools are included in group one, machinery is a part of group three and buildings belong to group five.

One obvious conclusion is that a strong incentive for companies will exist to classify equipment as tools rather than machinery. This will create problems with compliance and collection of the corporate tax.

The total economic life is the same in both methods of depreciation. The depreciation rates for both methods in individual years present Tables 5a and 5b.

Table 5a

Rates of Linear Depreciation (%)

Group	1st Year	Following Year
1	14.2	28.6
2	6.2	13.4
3	3.4	6.9
4	1.4	3.4
5	1.0	2.0

Table 5b

Rates For Declining Depreciation

Group	1st Year %	Following Year
1	4	5
2	8	9
3	15	16
4	30	31
5	50	51

Obviously the rate of linear depreciation is much lower in the first year than in the following ones. This represents some simplification of the depreciation method, for no adjustments are made according to the month of purchase. The declining method makes it possible to use almost doubled depreciation rate in comparison with the linear one in the first half of the life of an asset which is valid for all the asset categories. An example will be presented to illustrate differences between the linear and declining way of depreciation for the asset valued at CSK 1 million.

Table 6

Differences between linear and declining depreciation (example)

		(CSK)
1st Year	LD	142,000
	DD	250,000
2nd Year	LD	286,000
	DD	375,000
3rd Year	LD	286,000
	DD	250,000
4th Year	LD	286,000
	DD	125,000

Table 7

Capital Allowances For Industrial Buildings and Machinery

Country	Industrial Buildings Straight Rates of Depreciation Line or Declining Balance	Machinery Straight Rates of Depreciation Line or Declining Balance
Austria	SL/24.0 for 1 year then 4.0	SL /32.5 for 1 year then 12.5
Belgium	DB /then SL 10.0 for 7 years then 5.0, also allowance of 3-10.0	DB/then SL 40.0 for 2 years then 20.0, also allowance of 3-10.0
Canada	DB/4.0	DB/25.0
Denmark	SL/6.0 for 10 years then 2.0	DB/30.0
Finland	DB/9.0	DB/30.0
France	SL/5.0	DB then SL/35.7 for 5 years then 5.5
Germany	SL/10.0 for 4 years, 5.0 for 3 years and then 3.5	DB then SL/30.0 for 4 years then 10.0
Greece	SL/8.0	Sl/20
Ireland	SL 50.0 for 1 year then 4	DB 50.0 for 1 year then 12.5
Italy	SL/5.0	SL/17.5 for 3 years then 10.0
Luxembourg	SL/4.0	DB/30
Netherlands	DB/6.6	SL/12.5
Norway	DB/7.0	DB/30.0
Portugal	SL/5.0	DB 31.25
Spain	DB/7.5	DB/20
Sweden	SL/3.3	DB/30.0
Switzerland	DB/8.0	DB/30.0
UK	SL/4.0	DB/25.0
CSFR	SL/2.0	SL/6.9

The important issue is the international comparison again. Table 7 compares the proposed capital allowances in Czechoslovakia with those effective in the OECD. The rate of 2% for buildings is within the range of typical depreciation rates , although most countries tend to have those rates a little higher. For machinery the rate of 7% straight line is lower than that in most countries where straight line tend to be between 12.5 and 20%. An important question to be raised is whether the depreciation rates for machinery are too low. Economic theory suggests that in conventional corporate tax systems the most appropriate depreciation rate is the actual rate at which an asset depreciates. This is not easy to estimate but the best available estimates are around 12% for machinery and 3-5% for buildings. These figures, at first sight, seem to indicate that depreciation over 15 years for machinery is probably closer to the true value that prevailing in the OECD.

One important factor that influences these conclusions will however be inflation. The new Czechoslovak system is to depreciate assets on the basis of their cost price - i.e. no adjustments will be made for inflation. This is in line with international practice. However it leaves companies very vulnerable to inflation. Depreciation of assets is essential because there is no profit unless a company is capable of replacing the assets used in generating earnings. With inflation, the costs of replacing business assets are increasing, but if depreciation is only offered on the original costs of the asset, then the value of the depreciation allowances is being eroded.

The effects of inflation on the real value of allowances can be very substantial. The importance of inflation effect depends on the rate of inflation. The closer the inflation being to zero, the smaller the effect. The rate of inflation of 10% would affect the value of allowances very seriously.

The depreciation allowances should ideally be indexed for inflation. The alternative is to allow depreciation at a rate which exceeds true depreciation, in order to offset the effects of inflation. This approach is less precise - if inflation is above or below the expected level, depreciation allowances are worth too little or too much, so either discouraging or encouraging investments

The problem of inflation is closely connected with the choice of the form of financing. Nominal interest payments will be tax deductible in Czechoslovakia as in most countries. When a return is paid to the bank, it in fact is not taxed at the corporate level. This is not true for finance provided by retaining earnings or by issuing new equity , as dividends are paid out of past tax income, and any earnings reinvested by the company are also taxed at the corporate tax rate, there is also a strong incentive to use debt to finance investments. The higher is inflation the higher are interest rates, so the greater is the amount of tax "avoided" by paying banks a return in the form of an interest payments. The question as to whether this is desirable or not is often discussed.

Over reliance on debt finance makes companies vulnerable to changes in interest rates, use of equity finance leaves them more flexibility over dividend payments. The extent to which heavy use of debt finance matters depends on how corporate governance in Czechoslovakia develops.

Since the new corporate income tax represents reduction of tax rate for most taxpayers, it is only natural that the total revenue is expected to fall down by about 10%. Some compensation may be represented within the whole complex of the new tax system, especially by introduction of VAT.

3.4. Summary

Introduction of corporate income tax represents important change in the terms of equalizing taxation conditions for different types of taxpayers. The tax rate of 45% means reduction of tax burden (amounting to about 10%) for almost all companies, the only exception being companies with foreign capital participation, the profits of which were taxed at a rate of 40%.

Future corporate taxation in CSFR is within the range of taxation effective in most European countries. Czechoslovak tax rate represents roughly an average level of taxation. The level of future taxation can therefore not be considered as discouraging economic activity.

Substantial changes in the depreciation systems are important part of the tax reform in this area. Under the new system companies can make their choice between linear and declining system of depreciation, the choice once being made becomes irreversible. the declining method makes it possible to use almost doubled depreciation rate in comparison with the linear one in the first half of the life of any asset.

The depreciation rate for buildings is a bit lower in comparison with most European countries while that for machinery is substantially lower.

As assets will be depreciated on the basis of their original price - no adjustments will be made for inflation, the effect of inflation on the real value of allowances can be very substantial.

The total revenue of corporations taxation is expected to fall down by about 10% under the new system, with some compensation for state budget based mainly upon introducing VAT.

4. VALUE ADDED TAX

4.1. Taxpayers, Registration, Exemptions

The taxpayers of VAT are legal entities as well as individual persons performing taxable activities/deliveries of goods and services concerning their economic activity. Subject to tax liability are only those entrepreneurs the turnover of which exceeds CSK 1.5 mil in three succeeding calendar months. Those entrepreneurs are obliged to ask for registration at the financial authorities not later than until the 20th day of the month following after the threshold being crossed. The entrepreneurs with lower turnover are exempted from the tax liability but they can register at their option.

Preliminary estimates indicate that the number of taxpayers will amount to 500,000.

The beginning of registration is 1.7.1992, the final dates are as follows:

- 30. 11. 1992 for entrepreneurs with turnover exceeding CSK 56 million in 1991
- 20.12. 1992 for those with turnover exceeding CSK 6 million the first nine months of 1992
- 20. 1. 1993 for those with turnover exceeding CSK 6 mil in 1992.

The registration can be abolished if the conditions for exemption are fulfilled. The law permits to apply for this abolishment not sooner than one year after registration. This one year term means a prevention against speculations about registration aimed at the tax avoidance.

Subject to VAT are all entrepreneurial activities with no difference concerning the form of entrepreneurship. The new tax law moreover lists following activities being exempted from tax liability the reasons for their exemption consisting not only in administrative difficulties with appropriate setting of the tax base but predominantly in social aspects:

- postal services
- insurance
- financial services
- transfer and rent of lands and buildings
- education
- health goods and services
- social activities
- lotteries
- deliveries of packages
- sales of enterprises
- non-profit activities (foundations)

The taxpayers realizing these activities are not entitled to refundation of VAT paid on the inputs(see later in a great detail).

4.2. The Tax Base, Tax Rates, Refundation

The tax base is represented by the price of taxable activity (predominantly goods or service) without tax unless the law specifies other price. If taxable activity is a subject to consumption tax or other taxes under special regulations, the price includes it. In the case of price not being specified in the contract or being lower than under usual conditions, the tax base is the usual price. For financial leasing the tax base is represented by the price stated in the contract. If the price of the goods exceeds CSK 1 mil., the tax base is the amount of financial activities.

Two basic rates of VAT will be effective: the rate of 23% on goods and 5% on services. The law specifies the list of goods taxed at a reduced rate of 5% (basic foodstuff, fuels with the exception of driving ones) as well as the list of services taxed at a rate of 23%(most of repairing services, road carriage of frights traffic accommodation services etc.).

There is a potential possibility of tax avoidance or tax reduction in the case of separating some price of services performed on goods (and than taxing it separately at a reduced rate) from the total price of goods. Therefore a specific category of "industrial services of productive nature" that are taxed at a rate of 23% was introduced (their list is also specified in the law) to avoid this possibility of reducing the appropriate amount of tax.

A very important point in the VAT law is the refundation of tax. The taxpayer is entitled to refundation of VAT paid in the input if purchased taxable activities are used for economic activity under specific conditions. This entitlement for refundation must be proved by tax document (see above in a more detail).

The regulations for refundation are tightly connected with the choice whether to register as a voluntary VAT taxpayer or not. The incentive for being a voluntary VAT taxpayer originates in fact that the registered VAT taxpayers are entitled to refundation of VAT paid in inputs. Exempted entrepreneurs have to include VAT into costs and if selling their goods or services to their subscribers it means disadvantage for those subscribers. VAT in this case is not refundable and represents in fact higher price for inputs. This moment can be very important in decision making whether to register as a VAT taxpayer or not, because naturally all the entrepreneurs will prefer purchases of inputs from VAT taxpayers. Those effects therefore must be very deliberately calculated. Another incentive for voluntary registration represents the fact that starting a business is in many cases connected with investments charged with substantial amounts of VAT and the refundation is possible for VAT taxpayers only.

In the situation of two tax rates a special situation can come to an existence, when VAT charged on the input exceeds the VAT charged on the output, an excessive refundation appears. The VAT taxpayer than does not pay the tax and moreover can claim the value of excessive refundation from financial authorities.

Purchases of cars are not entitled to VAT refundation unless the activity of the taxpayer consists in sales or rent of cars. Taxpayer performing financial leases are entitled to refundations of VAT imposed on goods being the subject of the lease.

The system of VAT imposes the tax on the value of the goods or service being the outcome on each part of the productive/distributive process. This means that the value of the goods or service is taxed repeatedly. The mechanism of VAT however insures that the taxpayer pays only the VAT imposed on that part of the product that he has added himself. the rate is specified according to the final nature of the product.

The chain of the transfer of VAT is finished at the final consumer who purchases the product or service with the aim of personal consumption not for the purpose of any economic activity. Final consumer therefore pays the total amount of VAT. Financial authorities receive the total sum of VAT from the entrepreneurs but the real payer is the final consumer.

The principle of evidence is not very difficult . Each taxpayer must keep files of the VAT paid to his subscribers as well as the tax charged to his customers. The tax declaration must than contain the difference of those two items (see Part 4 for more detail).

4.3. Export, Import

All export realized by VAT taxpayers will be exempted from VAT liability and will be entitled to VAT refundation as well. Since this exemption is valid for VAT taxpayers only the tourists are not entitled to VAT refundation (as is the case in Austria, Germany and other countries).

The basic condition for being entitled to refundation is the acknowledgment about the final transport abroad, the tax document being the written proposal for customs procedure.

All imports are subject to VAT. The tax law unifies conditions for all economic subjects (entrepreneurs being and not being VAT taxpayers, individual persons).In the case of import the imposing of VAT will be tightly connected with imposing of duty. The novelization of constitutional law has been made so the customer institutions can perform the management of VAT as well as the Consumer goods tax.

The origin of the tax liability will be connected with the customs (coming into existence in the moment that goods comes under the customs control). The same entity (person) will be obliged to pay the VAT that manages the customs procedure under the customs regulations and no problems about the entity charged to pay the tax can arise as is the present case (with the turnover tax).

4.4 Tax Control, Tax Documents, Penalties

System of VAT should theoretically prevent the most frequent forms of tax avoidance and evasion that are effective nowadays (the practical management will of course be another question). The state institutions have some control tools. The calculation of the amount of the tax paid (the difference between own tax liability and the tax paid in the inputs) will have to be based on actuarial documents. When paying the amount of tax the taxpayer is simultaneously obliged to present tax declaration to tax authorities.

The basic role in the control of the correctness of the tax paid amount will play the tax documents. The form of tax documents is not strictly specified by the new tax law but basic requirements are presented . The tax document must contain basic identification data of both taxpayers (the realizing as well as the purchasing one) and the identification of the taxable activity and its price with and without tax . The taxpayers are obliged to issue the tax document not later than 15 days after realizing the transaction.

The liability to pay the VAT comes into existence in the day of the tax document being issued. The basic tax period is one calendar month if the yearly turnover does not exceed CSK 10 mil or three months in other cases. The tax must be paid not later than 15 days after finishing the tax period and in the same time the tax declaration must be submitted to tax authorities.

All the tax documents mused be saved for 10 years which is period significantly longer than the Calculation law states. This long period should rise the effectiveness of the tax system as well as rise the possibility of tax evasion discoveries.

The basic data on tax documents must be the price with and without VAT, that must be extra stated. The financial institutions can then perform the cross control - the tax liability of the suppliers represents the refundations for the subscriber. The tax documents are of great importance since the entitlement for refundation must be proved by the documents from the supplier.

It is obvious that management of VAT will be extremely demanding, because it can be performed with a rather extensive system of tax documents. It can be only stressed by the fact that evidence and saving of these documents with the use of computers will probably be rather an exception than as a rule.

The evidence and issuing of the documents is of vital importance because the penalties for non correctly paid tax are quite hard. The penalties are stated as a percent from the tax owed or by fixed amount. If the tax paid is incorrectly stated, the penalty is 100% of the difference in the case of being discovered by the financial institution and 20% in the case of being discovered by the taxpayer himself.

If the tax is not paid in time the penalty represents 0.1% from the tax owed for each day of the delay. If the tax declaration is not presented in time the penalty represents 10% of the tax, at least CSK 5,000. If the taxpayer is not registered in time he can be charged a penalty at least CSK 5,000, at most CSK 1 mil.

Effective administration of the VAT imposes great demands on administrative resources. This must be stressed in the situation where VAT is principally a new tax being introduced together with other changes in the whole tax system. Great problems can therefore be expected with managing of VAT at least in the first year of the reform. Perhaps it would have been much better to exempt (at least temporarily) some necessities from the tax liability and apply a single tax rate to all other goods and services. Unfortunately this has not been the case so the tax evasion can be expected to be very substantial due to administrative bottlenecks. The estimates originating from the experiences from the countries where VAT was introduced indicate that the losses of VAT collected amounts to 50 - 60% in the first year.

4.5 Some Economic Effects of VAT

Introducing of VAT will affect both sides of state budget. The nowadays revenue of the turnover tax including consumption taxes amounts about CSK 123 billion in 1991. The estimated amount of the revenue of VAT plus consumption taxes is about CSK 190 billion in 1993. This rise of revenue can be considered quite substantial as to offset the reduction of direct taxes revenues as was mentioned in previous parts. On the other side the budget expenditures will grow as well due to enlargement of the range of taxpayers involving non entrepreneurial subjects.

Introducing of VAT represents a significant intervention to a market environment that can be compared to that of price liberalization in 1991. Similar behavior of households and firms can be therefore expected. Some preliminary calculations have been made to estimate the possible movements of price level caused by the introducing of VAT. The estimated rise of the price level amounts to 7%. This rise is not caused mainly by the effective tax rates but can be attributed to enlargement of the range of taxed activities in comparison with the present situation. About one third of the estimated price movement can be attributed to combination of VAT and consumption taxes concerning alcohol , tobacco and fuels. The rise of prices can be even higher, partly due to the fact that the entrepreneurs are going to anticipate this price movement and will form wider space in their price policy than would be adequate to the rise of the price of inputs. Some other economic effects can be expected concerning the changes in the demand structure resulting consequently to changes in price structure, the preliminary calculations of these effects have not been finished yet.

These price movements will for sure have far reaching social consequences and their effects will differ according to different groups of population. These effects must be deliberately considered from the viewpoint of complex tax reform (see later for a detail).

The VAT will be completely neutral as a factor of competitive ability of individual entrepreneurs because the VAT that each entrepreneur is to pay to financial authorities is added to the price of the product and the VAT paid in the input is entitled to reclaiming.

Brief international comparison has been made to illustrate the position of Czechoslovakia in international context from the viewpoint of VAT. Since there are differences in number of tax rates and their structure, the best possibility is to compare the average level of VAT rates. This was not possible to calculate for all relevant countries (as was the case in the comparison of PIT and CIT) so the comparison was concentrated on Germany, France and the UK. The results are presented in Table 8.

Table 8

Comparison of average VAT rates

	CSFR	Germany	France	UK
Average VAT Rate	17%	11.5%	17%	8.5%

Although the calculation for CSFR is rather orientative yet it shows that the average rate of VAT is going to be relatively high.

4.6. Summary

The VAT represents general tax liability concerning all entrepreneurial economic activities, the exemptions being a limited number of specified activities. Subject to tax are also all imports, exports are exempted (if certain conditions are fulfilled).

The VAT is imposed (from the point of view of individual entrepreneur)on the part of value that is added to the product or service. This tax should be completely neutral as a factor of competitive ability.

Subject to tax liability are these entrepreneurs the turnover of which exceeds the threshold of CSK 1.5 billion in three succeeding calendar months. These entrepreneurs are obliged to ask for registration at the financial authorities, the others are exempted from tax liability but can register at their option. The choice whether to be or not to be the voluntary VAT taxpayer of VAT must be deliberately considered and will depend on specific conditions of each entrepreneur. The substantial difference in comparison to present system of turnover tax is general liability of the tax payment on purchase. The range of taxable activities is much wider in comparison to present situation, this enlargement is connected mostly with taxation of services including such activities as the transfer of rights and financial leasing.

Two tax rates will be effective: the rate of 23% on most goods and 5% on most services. The law specifies the list of goods taxed at a reduced rate as well as the list of services taxed at a rate of 23%. Illustrative international comparison has been made that indicates that the average rate of VAT in CSFR is relatively high.

Administration of VAT will be extremely demanding on administrative resources, because VAT is principally a new tax in Czechoslovak tax system. This can be only stressed by the fact that the tax control can be performed only with an extensive system of tax documents the evidence and saving of which with the use of computers will not be very frequent in present situation. Penalties for non correct fulfillment of tax liability are relatively very hard.

The fiscal revenue of VAT will be much higher compared to the revenues of the present turnover and consumption taxes. This rise of revenue should offset the reduction of direct taxes revenues.

The introducing of VAT will effect the price level and structure, the estimated rise of price level amounting to at least 7% which for sure will have some social consequences as well..

5. CONCLUDING REMARKS

One of the preliminary intentions of the Czechoslovak tax reform was to reduce the total tax burden. According to preliminary calculations the contrary will be the case. The total tax burden (ratio of taxes to GDP) will probably slightly rise.

Another question is future structure of taxation. In this area very substantial changes can be expected. The main feature of Czechoslovak tax reform is change of the tax structure characterized by growing of the significance of the direct taxes together with the reduction of direct taxes. The reduction of direct taxes is considered to be a very important factor to encourage the economic activity.

The tax reform is therefore sure to have far reaching consequences concerning the income structure of the budget system. While in 1991 the turnover tax and consumption taxes (indirect taxes) represented only a quarter of total tax revenue, in 1993 completely different situation can be expected. The VAT plus consumption taxes should represent more than half of the revenue. These two numbers cannot be compared exactly because of other changes (mainly the separation of the financing of social security system from state budget and setting it on insurance base), but the difference is very substantial in any case. Simultaneously will of course occur changes in relative contribution of direct taxes.

The main problem arising in this context consists in similar conditions and consequently the income side of the state budget on the one side and in completely different conception on the side of expenditures. In this area the problems of the amount of state participation in national economy and social insurance have not been solved yet.

It is not clear so far neither which activities will be financed from the state budget nor the amount of this financing and which activities will be fully financed by the individuals.

The tax reform can be probably expected to have some positive effects on economic activity, which means that the entrepreneurs will take some advantages while the burden of the tax reform will be levied upon the population. In the first part of this study preliminary estimates concerning the changes in position of average taxpayer as well as individual groups of taxpayers have been presented involving the changes of the system of personal incomes taxation.

It is quite evident that these estimates are of only orientative character because for complete analysis of the impacts of the tax reform on population many others aspects must be considered too. The range of incomes that will be taxed is much broader - the interests, dividends, selected insurance benefits etc. the rise of indirect taxes that will be reflected in the rise of price level will afflict the population. Some substantial changes concerning inheritance tax, gift tax and housing tax will represent additional changes in tax burden for individuals.

It is quite evident that the estimates of social consequences of the tax reform can be only very preliminary but the rise of the tax burden will obviously arise the necessity of compensation of selected social groups.

It can be concluded that the tax reform in fact reflects the problems of economic reform as a whole - there is an urgent need of the economic growth (which is source demanding) as well as that of sufficient social security system. In the situation of very limited sources some trade off must be accepted between these two aims.

Table 9

Single Taxpayer or Married One without Children

Income	Old system	New system		Difference
	Wage tax %	PIT %	Total %	% points
30,000	21.8	1.5	15.5	6.3
40,000	24.3	4.4	18.4	5.9
50,000	26.0	6.1	20.1	5.9
60,000	26.9	7.2	21.2	5.7
70,000	27.6	8.0	22.0	5.6
80,000	28.2	8.6	22.6	5.6
90,000	28.6	9.1	23.1	5.5
100,000	28.9	9.5	23.5	5.4
150,000	30.0	12.2	26.2	3.8
200,000	30.5	14.2	28.2	2.3
300,000	31.0	17.9	31.9	-0.9
400,000	31.2	20.4	34.4	-3.2
500,000	31.4	21.7	35.7	-4.3
1,000,000	31.7	27.0	41.0	-9.3

Table 10
Married Taxpayer with One Child and without Dependent Wife

Income	Old system	New system		Difference
	Wage tax %	PIT %	Total %	% points
30,000	13.6	0.0	14.0	-0.4
40,000	15.2	1.0	15.0	-0.2
50,000	16.2	3.4	17.4	-1.2
60,000	16.8	5.0	19.0	-1.2
70,000	17.3	6.1	20.1	-2.8
80,000	17.6	6.9	20.9	-3.3
90,000	17.9	7.6	21.6	-3.7
100,000	18.1	8.1	22.1	-4.0
150,000	18.7	10.9	24.9	-6.2
200,000	19.0	13.0	27.0	-8.0
300,000	19.4	16.9	30.9	-11.5
400,000	19.5	19.6	33.6	-14.1
500,000	19.6	21.2	35.2	-15.6
1,000,000	19.8	26.6	40.6	-20.8

Table 11

Married Taxpayer with One Child and with Dependent Wife

Income	Old system	New system		Difference
	Wage tax %	PIT %	Total %	% points
30,000	13.6	0.0	14.0	-0.4
40,000	15.2	0.0	14.0	+1.2
50,000	16.2	0.0	14.0	+2.2
60,000	16.8	2.0	16.0	+0.8
70,000	17.3	3.5	17.5	-0.2
80,000	17.6	4.7	18.7	-1.1
90,000	17.9	5.6	19.6	-1.7
100,000	18.1	6.3	20.3	-2.2
50,000	18.7	9.4	23.4	-4.7
200,000	19.0	11.5	25.5	-6.5
300,000	19.4	15.6	29.6	-10.2
400,000	19.5	18.6	32.6	-13.1
500,000	19.6	20.4	34.4	-14.8
1,000,000	19.8	26.1	40.1	-20.3

Table 12
Married Taxpayer with Two Children and without Dependent

Income	Old system	New system		Difference
	Wage tax %	PIT %	Total %	% points
30,000	13.6	0.0	14.0	-0.4
40,000	15.2	0.0	14.0	1.2
50,000	16.2	0.7	14.7	1.5
60,000	16.8	2.7	16.7	0.1
70,000	17.3	4.2	18.2	-0.9
80,000	17.6	5.2	19.2	-1.6
90,000	17.9	6.1	20.1	-2.2
100,000	18.1	6.8	20.8	-2.7
150,000	18.7	9.8	23.8	-5.1
200,000	19.0	11.9	25.9	-6.9
300,000	19.4	15.9	29.9	-10.5
400,000	19.5	18.9	32.9	-13.4
500,000	19.6	20.6	34.6	-15.0
1,000,000	19.8	26.3	40.3	-20.5

Table 13

Married Taxpayer with Two Children and with Dependent Wife

Income	Old system	New system		Difference
	Wage tax %	PIT %	Total %	% points
30,000	13.6	0.0	14.0	-0.4
40,000	15.2	0.0	14.0	1.2
50,000	16.2	0.0	14.0	2.2
60,000	16.8	0.0	14.0	2.8
70,000	17.3	1.6	15.6	1.7
80,000	17.6	3.0	17.0	0.6
90,000	17.9	4.1	18.1	-0.2
100,000	18.1	5.0	19.0	-0.9
150,000	18.7	8.2	22.2	-3.5
200,000	19.0	10.4	24.4	-5.4
300,000	19.4	14.7	28.7	-9.3
400,000	19.5	17.9	31.9	-12.4
500,000	19.6	19.8	33.8	-14.2
1,000,000	19.8	25.8	39.8	-20.0

Table 14
Taxpayer with One Alimony

Income	Old system	New system		Difference
	Wage tax %	PIT %	Total %	%points
30,000	13.6	1.5	15.5	-1.9
40,000	15.2	4.4	18.4	-3.2
50,000	16.2	6.1	20.1	-4.1
60,000	16.8	7.2	21.2	-4.4
70,000	17.3	8.0	22.0	-4.7
80,000	17.6	8.6	22.6	-5.0
90,000	17.9	9.1	23.1	-5.2
100,000	18.1	9.5	23.5	-5.4
150,000	18.7	12.2	26.2	-7.5
200,000	19.0	14.2	28.2	-9.2
300,000	19.4	17.9	31.9	-12.5
400,000	19.5	20.4	34.4	-14.9
500,000	19.6	21.7	35.7	-16.1
1,000,000	19.8	27.0	41.0	-29.2

Table 15
Taxpayer with One Child and One Alimony

Income	Old system	New system		Difference
	Wage tax %	PIT %	Total %	% points
30,000	9.6	0.0	14.0	-4.4
40,000	10.6	1.0	15.0	-4.4
50,000	11.3	3.4	17.4	-6.1
60,000	11.8	5.0	18.0	-6.2
70,000	12.1	6.1	20.1	-8.0
80,000	12.3	6.9	20.9	-8.6
90,000	12.5	7.6	21.6	-9.1
100,000	12.7	8.1	22.1	-9.4
150,000	13.1	10.9	24.9	-11.8
200,000	13.3	13.0	27.0	-13.7
300,000	13.6	16.9	30.9	-17.3
400,000	13.7	19.6	33.6	-19.9
500,000	13.7	21.2	35.2	-21.5
1,000,000	13.9	26.6	40.6	-26.7

Table 16
Taxpayer with One Child and Two Alimony

Income	Old System	New System		Difference
	Wage Tax %	PIT %	Total %	% Points
30,000	6.9	0.0	14.0	-7.1
40,000	7.6	1.0	15.0	-7.4
50,000	8.1	3.4	17.4	-9.3
60,000	8.4	5.0	18.0	-9.6
70,000	8.6	6.1	20.1	-11.5
80,000	8.8	6.9	20.9	-12.1
90,000	8.9	7.6	21.6	-12.7
100,000	9.0	8.1	22.1	-13.1
150,000	9.4	10.9	24.9	-15.5
200,000	9.5	13.0	27.0	-17.5
300,000	9.7	16.9	30.9	-21.2
400,000	9.8	19.6	33.6	-23.8
500,000	9.8	21.2	35.2	-25.4
1,000,000	9.9	26.6	40.6	-30.7

11

CREATION AND DEVELOPMENT OF A SOCIAL SAFETY NET

Marie Frydmanova and Hana Zelenkova
Institute of Economics
Czechoslovak Academy of Sciences

SUMMARY

The article deals with one of the most important prerequisites of successful economic reform in the CSFR - creation and development of a social safety net. Basic objectives and function of the social safety net are characterized within introduction. After a brief description of present welfare system, its most important components - social security and state social support are analyzed. Issues on poverty level which most of the social benefits are derived from are elaborated separately. Based on existing problems of the social safety net some changes and new measurements, as a reaction to the progress of economic transformation, are drafted. They are designed to take new market phenomena into account, and to reach objectives of economic and social policies.

1. INTRODUCTION

Transformation of the Czechoslovak economy brings about many new economic and social situations. Realities like decline in economic activity, growth of unemployment, inflation, drop of real incomes, consumption structure changes and decline in personal consumption and most of all, a significant fall of the standard of living of certain groups of population may cause or cause social tensions [1].

To provide the public with truthful information on economic development and its social impacts, on unemployment and social costs is a precondition for confidence to outweigh social demagogy and to lessen social tension. Importance for the society of social impacts raised by transformation from the centrally planned economy into a market one needs an adequate reaction of the state/government in the form of a social safe net.

2. SUBSTANCE OF THE SOCIAL SAFETY NET

In a simplified way, a social safety net can be defined as a system of state measures guaranteeing people they will not find themselves in a situation neither without means to finance fundamental needs nor without medical care and basic education. This should be guaranteed by the state in every situation.

The state takes on the most decisive role in setting social minimum, minimum wages, minimum rent, unemployment benefit and social benefits. The state also - this time outside the social safety net - protects a citizen employee against a citizen employer by stating maximum working hours, minimum vacation and other limitations (for example working contents of female and youngsters or legal protection of tenants).

The biggest trouble is a loss of a job, therefore the social safety net focuses on unemployment insurance and active measures towards creation of new job opportunities, retraining.

The public has to be informed what part of living standard decline will be at the expense of population and what part can be compensated by the state. It is generally agreed that primary measures should be taken by the state, namely measures against unemployment, providing unemployment benefits and active employment policy, subsequently increase of pensions and help for those in social need.

Population can react on price increase by reduction of consumption, qualitative change of consumption structure or by putting durables purchases off, but only up to some limit that we can name a social tolerance limit. However such a limit approaches zero for those groups of population whose living standard has become at present partly or wholly dependent on social incomes, filling the gap between their wages and other incomes and the social minimum stated by the state.

When compensating price and other effects, the state should proceed so that proportions among different kinds of income were preserved in a way that working incomes did not lose their motivation function and social incomes retained their level sufficient to cover living costs and not going beyond possibilities of the state budget.

In this sense the social safety net is being formed and an indexation mechanism of social benefits and wages to living costs moves. A task is to keep stable real value of benefits supplementing income of socially weak groups of population to hinder anybody getting into poverty which would mean satisfying fundamental needs (housing, nutrition, and other personal needs) in an undesirable way from the social point of view. Certainly beware inflationary financing of these benefits.

There are three functions imposed on the social safety net. Active ones are: (1) to help to create new job opportunities having on mind fast return of the labour force into economic activity; (2) to maintain labour force ability before reentering working activity through unemployment insurance and retraining, The third (passive) function is to provide social security to old and handicapped people and temporarily even in cases where an active role of the net failed.

Social benefits for people within lowest income range are very sensitive to price moves of fundamentals; these are therefore indexed on living costs changes. A number of participants of the social safety net is influenced by the labour market situation and the rate of inflation. Thus a reaction of the social safety net to these phenomena has to be flexible.

The whole system of the social safety net is in a straight relation to efficiency of an economy. When an economy grows and so do real incomes of population then growth of expenditures on the social safety net may be slowed down and the social safety net takes care only after a limited number of people, for a limited time. In a recession, the social safety net becomes more important and its components are a source of financial and material means for quite a large number of applicants.

Components of the social safety net are based on minimum levels and to reduce their real value would originate serious conflicts. Institutional working and financial supply is an unavoidable task of the state and a necessary precondition for economic reform to be pursued, economic growth to be started and for the net itself to be reduced in the future. Much effort is made to base forming of the social safety net and of an indexation mechanism (of wages and social incomes to living costs changes) on social consensus represented by tripartite agreements that are supposed to reflect an economic situation in our country.

The social safety net is a complex of interconnected measures and activities and it can work efficiently only if all components work. If any component is neglected other components cost more. If personal and technical questions are not solved quickly it may cause social conflicts as well as other unnecessary costs.

3. POVERTY LEVEL

A prime building stone of Czechoslovak social system is a poverty level set for various life situations. Other minimum social benefits are derived from it. For example a level of a pension that is the only source of income and the bottom level of an unemployment benefit are fixed on a poverty level and minimum wages are roughly by 10% higher.

The Law on Poverty Level that came into effect in November 1991 sets minimum amounts needed in a certain period for securing essential personal needs of individual members of a household and amounts needed for covering vital household expenses; the amounts are differentiated based on the age of children and on the size of a household. At the same time, the law also includes a mechanism for indexation. When living costs of families with employed people in a low income range increase by 10 %, the amounts of the poverty level will be increased in such a way that in principle the ratio of these amounts to average net monetary incomes will remain the same.

The poverty level is an aggregate of goods and services expressed in value, calculated on the basis of statistical data, consented by social partners and approved by the Parliament, that enables a household of a certain size and composition to provide for its needs at a modest level. Currently, the following amounts are considered essential for an individual (1 USD = approximately 29 CSK):

- CSK 900 for a child under 6 years;
- CSK 1,000 for a child between 6 and 10 years;
- CSK 1,200 for a child between 10 and 15 years;
- CSK 1,300 for a child between 15 and 26 years;
- CSK 1,200 for other individuals.

In addition, the following amounts are considered essential for a household:

- CSK 500 for a one-member household;
- CSK 650 for a two-member household;
- CSK 800 for a household with three or four members;
- CSK 950 for a household with five and more members.

The poverty level, as a socially acknowledged minimum standard of income for a family of any type, can serve as a base for the creation of a new system of state social support. In the framework of that system a flat allocation of benefits will be targeted on the most needy households in such a manner that the more needy households will be eligible for higher benefits. On the other hand, the transfer must however be implemented in such a way that it will not interfere with the system of social assistance.

4. PRESENT SHAPE OF THE SOCIAL SAFETY NET

Here is presented a summary of main financial allowances, benefits and supports that are provided by the social safety net.

State benefits:

- parental benefits
- state compensatory grant
- state contribution to loans for newly-married couples
- allowance for families of draftees in military service, for using an army apartment, etc.

Health insurance:

- sickness benefit
- family care benefit
- maternity benefits
- compensatory allowance in pregnancy and maternity
- funeral grant
- birth grant
- child allowance, supplementary child allowance
- spa treatment.

Pensions security:

- old-age pension
- disability pension
- widower and widow pension
- orphan pension
- social pension
- child allowance and supplementary child allowance for pensioners.

Social care benefits:

- benefits for families with children
- benefits for heavily handicapped people and old people
- benefits for people in need of special assistance and for socially unadaptable people.

Unemployment benefits:

-unemployment benefits.

Empirical data on expenditures within the social safety net from which a stabile increase in expenditures can bee seen are in Table 1.

5. CHANGES IN SOCIAL SECURITY SYSTEM

Changes in a social security system are a reaction to the progress of transformation of the national economy. Modifications of until now working social security system are getting ready. Changes in an institutional structure and in a way of financing in state employment policy, new system of state support, all this is aimed at reaching objectives of economic and social policies.

Present social security arrangement is still based on a socialist economic system and state social paternalism. It does not take new market phenomena into account, most of all a new set-up of economic activity and income sources of people, a new role of a state and responsibility of an individual for social security of his own. Expenditures on social benefits are fully covered from the state budget. Neither employees nor employers pay taxes and fees directly addressed to social benefit system.

This system fails most in addressee determination and transparency, in giving a feeling to insurance payers that it is them who accumulate resources for themselves and fellow-citizens. On the contrary, it intensifies an impression that the state is responsible.

A new concept of a social benefit system getting ready at the Ministry of Labour and Social Affairs on a republic level leads to compatibility with systems in developed market economies in Europe. The new conception of social benefit system is to be carried out in several steps.

Subsequently to a new tax system starting on January 1, 1993, it is of prime importance to change a system of fund raising for social security and health insurance through implementation of insurance paid by employees, firms and self-employed people because a new tax system does not consider incomes for these expenditures any more.

A second step in the social security system transformation during 1993 is a change of its present state execution and implementation of General Social Insurance Company as a person at law with the executive bodies of its own and with financing through funds. At the same time, social insurance companies at a level of industries and enterprises can be established.

The third step, supposedly in 1994, has to restructure conditions and benefits of social security and health insurance of people aiming at public legal structure with the state guarantee supplemented with a system of collective and individual additional insurance possibilities. Ministry of Labour and Social Affairs of the Czech republic worked out a Draft Law on Social Security Insurance and on Participation in State Employment Fund and on Changes and Amendments of Organisation and Performance of Social Security [2]. A purpose of the law becoming effective on January 1,1993 is mainly following:

- to make employees, employers and self-employed persons obligatory pay social security and health insurance and participate in state employment fund;
- to set a body that will be collecting money;
- to expand a range of operation of Czech Social Security Administration.

Amounts and conditions of social security insurance in the draft are such to cover expenditures on social security and sickness benefits that are derived from incomes of economically active people within a present state of law. It matters for pension, widow pensions, orphan pensions, pensions for handicapped people, sickness benefits, family care benefits, maternity allowance, compensatory allowance in pregnancy and maternity.

In the case of benefits where using insurance principles is not reasonable (see part 6), state budget will cover the expenditures from its own resources.

At present, state employment policy is fully funded from the state budget and executed by state administration bodies in each republic. In the year 1992 expenditures on unemployment benefits and active employment measures are covered from the federal budget, active measures like retraining, new jobs creation, allowances for employers providing special training for graduates and youngsters without qualification or employment of people with lower ability to work. Operational and investment expenditures are covered from budgets of each republic.

Full payment of labour expenditures from the state budget and institutional building-in of bodies working in labour services, necessary in the first years of labour market existence, is not anticipated in the economic reform for the future. A scenario of the reform and a tax system assume therefore that social partners themselves will be raising funds for smooth labour market working and representatives of employees, businessmen and of the state will be administrators of institutions handling the money.

According to the new concept, a fee into the state employment fund should reimburse both expenditures on unemployment benefits and expenditures on active employment policy. The amount of unemployment insurance and a fee into the employment fund is supposed to cover expenditures of the Czech Social Security Administration and Labour Offices.

Czech Social Security Administration and its territorial offices should be competent for collecting insurance premiums and other administrative acts. A prerequisite for this solution, administratively simpler and less costly, is to specify the same range of rate-payers and of the qualification base for unemployment insurance and fee into the fund.

According to budget rules, collected insurance premiums will be recorded separately in the state budget and all expenditures on social security and employment will be covered through a budget chapter of the Ministry of Labour and Social Affairs of Czech Republic.

In the range of rate-payers, there are all employees who pay health insurance obligatory because of their working contract and persons on the same level with incomes originating in the dependent work, there are cooperative peasants and self-employed people liable to social security insurance by law. The range of rate-payers equals a range of persons entitled to get corresponding social security benefits.

A qualification base for employees insurance will be an income from the dependent work reduced by a few items not included in the health insurance qualification base. This reduction serves to system unification of the qualification base for insurance calculation and of the base for calculation of sickness benefit and wages reimbursement for legal labour purposes. An employer pays insurance from a sum of qualification bases of his employees.

A proposal for the amount of social security and health insurance paid by an employee is 8% and for the unemployment insurance 1% of the qualification base. A proposal for an employer is 24% of the qualification base for the social security and health insurance and 3% for the unemployment insurance. Together 32% for the social security and health insurance and 4% for the unemployment insurance, i.e. 36% in total. For self-employed people qualification base is set in such a way so that the insurance percentage paid by an employer together with an employee was the same, i.e. 36%.

6. STATE SOCIAL SUPPORT

A task of the social support realized in the form of state allowances is to partially cover expenses of persons that are not yet earning any income and to solve social situations that cannot be overcome without external assistance to families. At the beginning of April 1992, a draft of principles of a law on state social support including a system of support for families with children as well as childless families was submitted to the Government of the CSFR [3]. Within that system, the support is targeted on needy families, but unlike the system of social assistance this system focuses on families whose incomes are above the poverty level.

The draft of principles changes the existing concept of state allowances to families, in particular the concepts of the child allowance and the state compensatory grant. The system introduces new benefits responding to situations that have not yet been dealt with, and for most benefits the system is based on a poverty level multiple for the purposes of determining eligible recipients and it is based on a ratio of the poverty level for the determination of the amount of a benefit.

The draft presumes the introduction of a child allowance differentiated according to age. The allowance will be provided to families with incomes of a certain amount. Social allowance to families with children will be determined based on total incomes in families that are in an agreed income range lower that the income range within which the child allowance will be provided. The higher the income the lower the social allowance. At the same time, other situations worsening the economic status of families with children will be considered in the framework of the social allowance.

Parental allowance for a parent caring for a child under 3 years of age, or under 7 years of age provided the child has a long-term health handicap, will be equal to the poverty level amount (received by a citizen in order to provide) for his/her personal needs.

Housing allowance will cover a part of housing costs of a person or a family provided that his/her/their income does not reach a certain multiple of the poverty level. The allowance will apply to childless families, too. It is assumed that the allowance will be provided to families with incomes lower than those qualifying for a social allowance.

The state support to families with children includes, besides the above-mentioned, an allowance paid upon childbirth, an allowance for families of draftees serving in the arm forces, foster-parent benefits, a single allowance to families with very low incomes to cover increased living costs, and an allowance if caring for a child with a serious long-term health handicap. Furthermore, in the framework of other state social support benefits an allowance if caring for a relative that is partially or completely dependent and a funeral grant are also proposed. Loans to young couples and students with an advantageous interest rate are also included.

Effective from January 1993, it is proposed, in conjunction with the new tax system that considers number of children in a family, to implement the first stage of this concept by transforming children allowances into a new system that considers the age of a child. Under the new system the amount of the benefit per child increase with increasing numbers of children in a family as it has been up to know.

Practically the whole concept of state social support benefits is derived from the poverty level. The poverty level, as a state acknowledged minimum amount needed for securing personal needs of individual household members and needs of operating a household may be used for:

- setting income limits up to which a certain benefit will be provided;
- determining the amount of benefits paid.

By combining these two principles, a fundamental tool for determining state social support benefits is created that is in relation to total financial sources of a household, (at the same time with the possibility to consider certain social situations), on the other hand with regard to the state economic resources and to future social policy.

The following are fundamental determinants that served as a basis when a reconstruction of the state social support tools was considered:

- the necessity to unify benefits representing state support to individuals and to families with children;
- introduction of new benefits which will respond to situations that have never been dealt with before (high housing costs, students welfare, one-time increase of living costs, and so forth);
- the need to find new forms for the most important benefits - the child allowance and the state compensatory grant introduced in connection with the liberalization of prices;
- maximum effectiveness and targeting of the new system;
- principle of redistribution organized by the state - from the rich to the poor and from childless families to families with children;
- versatile solutions (with regard to the possibilities and the extent of means testing and the amount of financial means for benefits);
- harmony with the proposed income tax, which introduces a different type of preferential treatment to families with children in that deductions are dependent on the number of children and independent of the level of income;
- the necessity to find relevant criteria for individual benefits in relationship to recipients.

7. CONCLUSION

Since 1990, the CSFR has introduced a number of new basic economic measures that set the foundations for market economic system in the country. So far, the pace of social policy reform has been slower and changes less comprehensive than that of economic reform. In most cases, social policies must compensate for initial hardships associated with economic reforms while operating under fiscal restraining resulting from the process of transformation. While social policies respond to needs of citizen created in part by economic reforms, they will also continue to influence the course of economic reforms and help determine the future of economic development.

In the period of economic transition, a number of provisional social policy measures have been prescribed to offset the initial ill-affects of economic reforms. They partially buffer population from inflation rates higher than those during the previous period, rising unemployment, decreasing real incomes, and growing tendency for families to fall to a living standard below the poverty line.

A brief overview of the present the social safety net shows that it is a very generous one. But on the other hand, it has a number of deficiencies and faults in relation to contemporary state of economic development and progress of economic reform. In order to secure social policy objectives adequate to the period of economic transition, three relatively independent systems are currently being created: social insurance, state social support, and social assistance. In close connection with that a qualitatively new employment policy including a new system of uniform fund management is being created, as well as new wage and income policies. The main aim is to constitute a universal and uniform welfare system.

This innovative social safety net will, under the conditions of a uniform labor market be composed of (1) allowances on the basis of obligatory insurance and voluntary additional insurance with the aim to preserve an achieved standard of living, (2) social support realized in the form of state allowances provided to partially cover expenses of persons that are not yet earning any income and to solve social situations that cannot be overcome without external assistance to families, (3) state social support provided in case a citizen or a family is not able to secure basic living needs by themselves.

Table 1
Social Transfers in the CSFR
(in billion of CSK)

Year	1990	1991	1992 (expected)	1993 (forecast)
Total Expenditures	71.4	91.3	104.8	116.3
Pensions	45.5	56.1	65.0	74.7
Child Allowances	0.3	0.3	0.3	0.3
Social Pensions	0.1	0.1	0.1	0.1
Funeral Grants	0.1	0.1	0.1	0.1
Total Pension Security	46.0	56.6	65.5	75.2
Sickness Benefits	6.9	7.3	8.0	8.5
Family Care Benefits	0.7	0.6	0.6	0.6
Maternity Benefits	1.4	1.4	1.5	1.8
Birth Grants	0.3	0.3	0.3	0.4
Funeral Grants	0.1	0.1	0.1	0.1
Child Allowances	10.2	9.8	9.8	9.7
Total Health Insurance	19.6	19.5	20.3	21.1
State Compensation Grants	4.2	12.1	13.7	13.6
Parental Benefits	1.5	3.0	4.0	4.3
Benefits for Draftee's Family	0.1	0.1	0.1	0.1
Total State Benefits	5.8	15.2	17.8	18.0
Administration			1.2	2.0

Source: Ministry of Labor and Social Affairs of the Czech Republic.

REFERENCES

1. K. Janáček et al.: *Macroeconomic and Social Analysis*: Spring 1992. Prague, Institute of Economics, Czechoslovak Academy of Sciences, 1992.

2. *Draft Law on Social Security Insurance and on Participation in State Employment Fund and on Changes and Amendments of Organisation and Performance of Social Security*. Prague, Ministry of Labor and Social Affairs of the Czech Republic, 1992.

3. *Draft Law on State Social Support*. Prague, Federal Ministry of Labor and Social Affairs, 1992

4. *Market Economies and Social Safety Nets*. Stirin, Institute for East-West Security Studies, 1992.

12

ECONOMIC TRANSFORMATION AND THE PRODUCTIVITY GAP

Stanislava Janáčková
The Institute of Economics
State Bank of Czechoslovakia

Political transformation of the post-communist countries toward a democratic system can only succeed if their economic performance is improved substantially. Economic transformation - transition toward the market - is not an aim in itself: it is meant to increase productivity, quality, and the technological level of production. Along with more freedom, a growth in living standards is expected by the population. For an economist, the test of success will be an improvement in international comparison - doing away with the growing backwardness, and a turn toward closing the gap behind advanced economies. This long-term test of success will be decisive for both of the new states which are to emerge from today's Czechoslovakia.

In the past, international comparisons of Czechoslovakia's macroeconomic performance were difficult - in GDP per head, labour productivity, or total factor productivity trends. Official statistics of national production covered only the "material sphere" (roughly, the primary and secondary sectors), bringing figures on Net Material Product, but no data on GDP. Expressing national production in dollars or other foreign currency brought additional problems.[1] Total factor productivity calculations were confronted with further practical obstacles (like estimation of the weights of individual production factors in this specific economic system). Moreover, an attempt to calculate total factor productivity required complicated explanations of the relation of this concept to the Marxist concept of production factors and

[1] A very good survey of problems of assessing GDP per head in dollars for Czechoslovakia see Dlouhý, V. 1987.

value.[2] International comparability, even of long-term trends in productivity, was further limited by distorted prices and hidden inflation.[3]

In spite of this, studies of total factor productivity were elaborated by Czech authors in the 1980s.[4] Attempts were made to compare the growth rates of total factor productivity with those of some OECD countries. The results are presented in Table 1. The studies proved a long-term slowdown of productivity growth since the sixties; if hidden inflation is taken into account, productivity has actually been falling since the second half of 1980s. International comparison also showed that in the whole post-war period, Czechoslovakia was lagging more and more behind the advanced market economies.[5]

Before transition toward a market economy started in 1989, Czechoslovakia's GDP per head (according to U.N. estimates) amounted to about 52 % of West German, and 44 % of U.S. level.[6] The lag in labour productivity, however, was even bigger, as Czechoslovakia had longer work-hours and a higher women work participation. Still wider was the country's gap in total factor productivity.[7] The gap was verified also by some microeconomic data, according to which labour productivity in manufacturing firms was, in 1988, at about 35 % of West German, and 47 % of Austrian level.[8]

---

[2]See, e.g., Janáčková, S., Overall efficiency, 1990.

[3]A study of different forms of inflation in Czechoslovakia in the 1980s has been written by Z. Drábek, K. Janáček, Z. Tuma, 1992.

[4]Major contributions in this field were made by M. Toms, M. Hájek, 1987, O. Dědek, V. Nachtigal, 1987.

[5]After the First World War, the western part of Czechoslovakia belonged to the most economically advanced territories in Europe. It is estimated that in the 1920s, the territory if Bohemia and Moravia, inhabited by approximately 20% of population of the former Austro-Hungarian Empire, concentrated 60% of the industrial potential of the former empire.

[6]United Nations, 1990, see also *The Economist*, May 26, 1990.

[7]Though no reliable figures on the comparative level of total factor productivity exist in the Czech literature, analysis of the diverting long-term trends shows the magnitude of the gap. See Hájek et al. , 1991.

[8]Kolanda, M. Kubišta, V. , 1990, p. 45-6.

Table 1

Growth of Total Factor Productivity (K,L) in Selected OECD Countries and in Czechoslovakia[a]
(Average annual percentage change)

Country	1960-73	1973-79	1979-88
United States	1.6	-0.4	0.4
Japan	6.4	1.8	1.8
Germany	2.7	2.0	0.7
France	3.9	1.7	1.5
United Kingdom	2.2	0.5	1.9
Austria	3.4	1.4	0.7
Switzerland	1.6	-0.9	0.2
Finland	3.4	1.7	2.3
OECD	2.9	0.6	0.9
OECD Europe	3.3	1.5	1.2
Czechoslovakia			
-based on official data	2.6	2.2	0.3
-adjusted for			
hidden inflation	1.3	0.9	-1.0

Note: a) OECD - business sector, Czechoslovakia - national economy.

Source: OECD Economic Outlook, No. 46, December 1989, p. 116; Hájek, M. - Janáčková, S. - Nachtigal, V., *Total Factor Productivity Trends in Czechoslovakia: A Comparison With Advanced Market Economies*, EU CSAV, Prague 1990, p. 12.

SHORT-TIME EFFECT OF THE FIRST STAGE OF TRANSFORMATION ON PRODUCTIVITY

As was to be expected, the start of economic transformation brought no quick turn toward a productivity catch-up. The opposite was true: in 1990 and 1991, productivity in Czechoslovakia decreased even more than would be explainable by the long-term trend - and the gap further widened. Labour productivity has been falling also in the first half of 1992, but the fall slowed down.

The additional productivity slump was caused by two intertwined groups of factors. First, there was a deep fall of production, due to decreased domestic demand after the liberalization of prices, to the breakdown of C.M.E.A. market, but also due to first signs of cutback of inefficient activities; GDP fell by 15.9 % in 1991 and by 13 % in the first half of 1992, industrial production by 21.2 % and 20.2 %, respectively. As employment was not falling in the same proportion, labour productivity declined. Second, the Czechoslovak economy is still a hybrid economy, with a large state sector, and with the bulk of enterprises going through the first stage of privatization. The enterprises are highly mutually indebted, many of them insolvent. Financial infrastructure is underdeveloped; and there are other factors that preclude efficient allocation of resources.[9] That forms an important obstacle to productivity growth.

In the first half of 1992, first signs of economic revival could be observed, and the fall of labour productivity was slowing down. According to preliminary data of the Czech Ministry of Economic Policy and Development, labour productivity in Czech industry - if compared with the same period of 1991 - fell by 28 % in January 1992, but only by 8 % in June 1992. The June 1992 fall against June 1991 was 10.7 % in the state sector, and 2.9 % in the private sector.

Obstacles of a faster improvement of productivity are numerous: a still high share of the state sector, the fact that enterprises are only in the first stage of privatization, the persistent high enterprise indebtedness and widespread insolvency, the slow improvement of financial infrastructure - in short, all that hinders free flow of resources from inefficient to efficient activities.

Before a decisive turn for the better can come, a wave of bankruptcies is to be expected which will cut off hopelessly inefficient enterprises and reallocate the production factors to better uses. As in all post-communist economies which had highly distorted relative prices, enterprises exist in Czechoslovakia which add no value by their production, or even consume value: if expressed in world prices, the value of their output would be lower than the value of used-up materials and other inputs. (A study published by the E.C. estimated that the share of such enterprises in the Czechoslovak economy, in 1987-1989, was as high as 20% [10]). Other enterprises produce goods of low quality and technical level, which are uncompetitive even with low costs and at low prices.

Opening the economy to international competition and the emergence of more rational price relations has revealed the inefficiency of many enterprises. Unfortunately, indebtedness and insolvency is not limited to non viable producers; it hits also enterprises that are potentially viable. Insolvency has a number of causes - from frozen assets in the former Soviet Union to old patterns of behaviour of enterprise management.[11] The multiplicity of causes calls for differentiated cures - but neither the market

---

[9]Compare Janáčková, S., 1992.
[10]Hare, P., Hughes, G., 1991.
[11]Janáčková, S., 1992.

nor the government posses the ability to distinguish between inborn inefficiency, and financial crisis caused by external or temporary factors.

With the existing long chains of mutual indebtedness and secondary insolvency among enterprises, the fall of inefficient producers could provoke a chain process of bankruptcies killing the potentially viable producers as well, and devastating a large part of the economy. This is why the insolvency problem is passed there and back between the government and the commercial banks, without a fast solution being in sight. Though the law on bankruptcy has been passed, the force of some of its articles is being postponed by the government and the parliament, with the result that in most cases, only commercial banks could initiate bankruptcies of highly indebted enterprises. In principle, the government suggests that commercial banks have most of the information needed to decide who are the losers, and which enterprises can go bankrupt without causing a disastrous chain reaction. The banks retort that in the case of large enterprises, bankruptcy is also a political decision where the government must share the responsibility.

However, an emerging third partner should soon take part of the responsibility. Some of the causes of the insolvency problem lie in the behaviour of managers of state-owned enterprises. In the pre-privatization period and during the first stage of privatization (before the new owners can take control), goods are being produced which are already known to be unsalable, and supplies to insolvent buyers go on, financed by failing to pay past debts or by taking new credits; with such "strategy", bankruptcy is prone to be the only outcome. But new owners that will emerge from the first wave of privatization - especially the investment funds who are biggest owners - will be motivated to look for better production strategies than this.

From January 1993, the problem of indebtedness and insolvency will acquire a new dimension, as Czechoslovakia is to be divided into two states and part of mutual enterprise debts and bank credits will have to be settled within a mechanism of international settlement. Existence of a special bilateral monetary system is highly probable in the first stage after separation, and mutual enterprise indebtedness provides an additional reason for such solution. Its sustainability, however, will depend on the degree of convergence of fiscal and monetary policy in the two new states. Potential dangers of mutual indebtedness and insolvency for a fast disintegration of existing economic links, with adverse effects on production, employment and productivity, will be high. This could cause for both divided economies a new shock, not dissimilar to the one incurred by the breakdown of the C.M.E.A.

LONG-TERM CAUSES OF THE PRODUCTIVITY GAP

On the whole, the problems of productivity decline and productivity gap in Czechoslovakia are to be seen in two perspectives - as both short-term and long-term problems. Above, some of the short-time aspects of the productivity decline have been discussed. They hang together with the first stage of transformation of the economy, the fall of productivity being part of the necessary price to be paid for the fundamental systemic change. In specific transitional situation, a wide complex of factors influence productivity in the short run.

In the long run, the chief factor of productivity growth is technological change; this must stem predominantly from the internal forces of the market. Indeed, this paper suggests that the long-term trend of more than three decades of declining and, finally, negative rates of productivity growth was, in Czechoslovakia, predominantly caused by the existence of the command economy. The intricate forces which induce technological change and productivity growth in a market system, did not work in the centrally directed economy, with enterprises owned by the state and run by state bureaucracy.

The historical experiment of communist economies offers a lot of lessons for economic science: the strong link between technological progress and a well-functioning market may be the key lesson to be learned from this painful experience. Market pressure for innovation - the ability of a market economy to generate technological change from within - is a feature which is absolutely vital for the modern history of advanced economies.

This feature is often neglected by economic theory, which focuses rather at the short-term virtues of the market - the ability to foster efficient allocation of resources under the existing state of technology. One of the reasons for this bias may lie in the fact that theoretical models have shown that endogenous technological change can lead to increased returns to scale and thus destroy competitive markets. In fact, however, it is only perfect competition in its traditional concept which is infringed upon - the concept of perfect competition that was predominantly static, and concentrated on analyzing the situations within a single industry.

In a realistic, dynamic market economy, competition is never perfect - but as long as competitive pressures exceed some "critical mass", the market possesses the vital ability to induce innovation, to induce technological change. Technological change, in turn, fosters competition; even if innovation limits competition in one segment of the market, it simultaneously reinforces competitive pressure in other segments. First, competition works across the borders of industries: even the most diverse goods compete with each other to some degree, as each product fights to get a higher share of total consumer demand. Second, product innovation limits the life cycle of any product, continuously reinstalling competitive pressures. Third, innovation has led to globalization of markets, giving competition a new scope.

Though economic theory is still unable to define rigorously the link between technological change and the market system, historical evidence of a close link is being offered by the very comparison with command economies. True, not every market economy is able to achieve fast technological progress; but for command economies, as a rule, very limited ability to induce technological change has been proven by practical experience. The examples of the two German states, of North and South Korea, or of Austria and Czechoslovakia speak for themselves. This is why, in Czechoslovakia, transformation toward a market economy is seen as a necessary condition of productivity catch-up.

Yet it is clear that reducing the technological gap will be a long-term task, and the success will depend on a number of additional conditions.[12] Productivity catch-up will be difficult for both parts of today's Czechoslovakia - harder probably for Slovakia than for the Czech Republic whose territory between the Wars belonged to industrially most developed regions of Europe. Several authors have profoundly analyzed the long-term trends of productivity convergence, or divergence, among market economies. In a world divided into the groups of advanced and backward economies, the problem of catch-up is far from being an academic question.

PRODUCTIVITY CONVERGENCE IN RETROSPECT

In the long run, the existence of a distinct catch-up process and mutual convergence of productivity levels can be proved only for a limited group of about 15 countries - those which can be now characterized as advanced market economies. In this group, mutual convergence of labour productivity levels has existed since 1870. Around 1890, the U.S. has become the technological leader and has kept this position up to the present time. The catch-up process was interrupted by the second world war, but since the fifties it went on with much more speed. (See Table 2).[13] After the second world war, Japan has been very successful in reducing its technology gap, and a new group of countries - the so-called new industrialized countries - joined the catch-up club. But the rest of the world has been, on the contrary, lagging more and more behind in productivity levels in the seventies and eighties.[14] The same, alas, was true also for the Czechoslovak economy.

In a 1990 study[15], the author of this paper has expressed an opinion that there may have existed a certain "catch-up threshold", given by the original degree of backwardness, i.e. by the level of productivity and GDP per capita at the start of a period characterized by productivity convergence. Around 1970, this threshold apparently was connected with the preceding participation of countries in the first phase of industrialization. Countries which around 1970 were already above a certain level of GDP per head, had a very good chance to start catching up with Australia and United Kingdom (then technological leaders) and even to overtake them. For countries above

[12]Within this context we do not see it necessary to discuss the differences between technological change and productivity growth; let us just recall that technological change can support economic prosperity also in ways that are not measurable by productivity data. Compare, e.g., Janáčková, S., 1990.

[13]Detailed data can be found in Maddison, A., 1987, 1989. Both sets of figures in Table 2 show a convergence of productivity levels; the newer figures, however, indicate a somewhat lower degree of productivity catch-up achieved. For more data, see Abramowitz, M., 1990, Baumol, W.J., 1986, Baumol, W.J., Wolf, E.N., 1987, Wolf, E.N., 1987, Christensen, L.R., Cummings, D., Jorgenson, D.W., 1981, Landes, D.S., 1990.

[14]Baumol, W.J., Wolf, E., 1987; Maddison, A. 1989.

[15]Janáčková, S. Technological Gaps, 1990.

the threshold, being a laggard even in some sense was an advantage - it gave an opportunity to profit from the experience and the knowledge potential of the leader. In countries which were below the threshold, a successful catch-up process was an exception and required unique favourable conditions.[16]

Similar situation probably existed after the second world war. In that time, by the level of GDP compared to West-European countries, Czechoslovakia definitely was "above the threshold" - in other words, it had, like them, a potential opportunity to profit from a catch-up process, with U.S. as the technological leader. That did not work - partly because of the political division of the world which prevented the access of countries of the Soviet bloc to technology transfer from the U.S. or other advanced economies. But the main cause of failure was the inability of Czechoslovakia's command economy to create an innovative climate. Moreover, the country was locked within the group of C.M.E.A. economies suffering the same problem, where the superpower - the Soviet Union - was unable to take the role of technological leader.

[16]A "catch-up threshold" is difficult to be defined exactly. Rather, its existence is suggested by the fact that as countries which originally were poorer are added to the analyzed group, less and less convergence of productivity levels can be observed (compare Baumol, W.J., Wolf, E.N., 1987.

Another cause of a "catch-up threshold" might lie in the fact that in each historical period, productivity growth is driven by some leading technology (the steam machine, electronics). A country which fails to start in time with this technology (e.g. because it s comparative advantage lies in other fields) may soon find itself below a threshold - the gap becomes qualitative.

Other authors have come to conclusions which support the idea of threshold effects in productivity growth, with divers causes. See Barro, R.J., 1991, De Long, J.B., Summers, L.H., 1991.

Table 2

Comparative Levels of Labour Productivity, 1870-1986 (U.S. = 100)

	GDP per hour worked		GDP per man hour				
	1870	1984	1900	1913	1950	1973	1986
France	54.7	97.5	41	41	38	67	89
Germany	58.9	90.5	49	48	29	64	79
Japan	19.3	55.6	16	17	13	40	51
Netherlands	105.2	97.2	72	67	51	78	84
U.K.	110.9	80.6	82	74	54	64	75
5 country average (excluding U.S.)							
	70.5	84.3					
U.S.	100.0	100.0	100	100	100	100	100
Australia	94	87	64	68	73		
Austria	47	46	26	57	70		
Belgium	63	58	40	62	90		
Canada	61	76	76	85	89		
Denmark	52	56	42	61	63		
Finland	30	31	30	55	65		
Italy	39	43	33	66	74		
Norway	39	41	42	64	84		
Sweden	41	41	46	72	76		
Switzerland	53	53	58	70	73		
15 country average (excluding U.S.)							
	52	52	43	65	76		

Sources: Data on GDP per hour worked - Maddison, A., "Growth and slowdown in advanced capitalist economies: techniques of quantitative assessment", *Journal of Economic Literature*, 1987, VI., p. 651. Data on GDP per man hour - Maddison, A., *The World Economy in the 20th Century, OECD Development Center*, Paris 1989, p. 89.

POTENTIAL SOURCES OF PRODUCTIVITY CATCH-UP

Though analyses of market economies cannot pinpoint persuasively any single factor guaranteeing successful catch-up, individual authors tend to stress one or other condition as being crucial. The factors most often cited as decisive are sufficient capital formation and investment, opening of the economy and avoiding anti-import strategies, ample support of research and development, and investment in human capital - education. In Czechoslovakia, most of these factors (except one) were present over the last forty years - yet the country's productivity gap has been growing. The vital question is whether the country will be able better to use some of the factors of productivity catch-up in future, under the market system.

The analysis done by Wolff has pointed out the importance of sufficient capital formation for productivity catch-up - the more so, the bigger the original backwardness. Other authors see investment as crucial, too.[17] For the Czechoslovak economy, investment rates under the command economy were traditionally high. For example, in an international comparison based on data of Planecon and C.I.A., Czechoslovakia's average share of investment in GNP during the 1980s was estimated at 21.1 %.[18] In the country's history, this was no exception. The figures for the investment rate were perhaps somewhat biased upwards by hidden inflation which was higher in the investment sector; but the main problem was that investment was never used efficiently. Most of it was sucked into a huge sponge of "production for production" - over dimensioned production of materials and capital goods, supporting a very high material and capital intensity of production, with little final effect for the consumer. In a "shortage economy" so well described and analyzed by J. Kornai, there was always lack of capital. Equipment in existing plants was used to the limits of its physical life, and capacities were multiplied by building new plants with essentially unchanged technical level. As a result, the economy now suffers from a high degree of obsolescence of capital equipment.

The present lack of capital, combined with a lack of technological know-how, will be a serious obstacle of future productivity growth. Domestic capital will have to be mobilized in a much more efficient way, with preference to equipment investment.[19] But the country is so decapitalized that the ability to attract foreign capital will also be crucial (preferably, capital should come in forms combined with an inflow of technological, organizational and managerial know-how). On the world capital markets, there are signs of a possible general shortage of capital. On the other hand, the share of Czechoslovakia in total world demand for capital is so low that it probably would not be a problem, with appropriate policies, to attract a larger inflow. Factors stimulating foreign capital flows often respond to unique historical events. Transformation of East- and Central-

---

[17] Wolf, E.N., 1987, De Long, J.B., Summers, L.H., 1991, Levine, R., Renelt, D., 1992.
[18] Jefferson, G.H., Petri, P.A., 1990.
[19] See De Long, J.B., Summers, L.H., 1991.

European countries into market economies - seeking integration with the rest of Europe - can bring into life new factors influencing capital, production and trade flows. If sufficient political stability is achieved and kept over some period of time, strategically thinking western firms will come to get hold of the new area for economic activity which is offered here.

In Czechoslovakia, the inflow of foreign capital is only starting. In 1990, foreign direct investment to Czechoslovakia amounted to $ 200 billion, in 1991, it was over $ 600 billion, and in the first half of 1992, almost $ 450 billion. Joint ventures were the most frequent form of foreign investment. Total number of joint ventures with foreign capital was 2901 at the end of May 1991 (2235 in the Czech Republic, 666 in the Slovak Republic), with total capital of over 36 billion CSK, and invested foreign capital over 10 billion CSK[20] (the sum of total committed foreign capital would be higher). The largest amount of capital came from West Germany, and 76 % of the total came from the E.C. countries.

There were more joint ventures were in trade and services than in production and construction; in the volume of foreign capital invested, however, production had a high lead, followed by trade. An analysis of the number of joint ventures, and their size distribution, leads to the conclusion that the entrepreneurial, managerial and organizational know-how brought by foreign capital is dispersed over the economy - as there is a high number of small joint ventures. Most of the total sum of capital invested, on the contrary, is concentrated in a narrow group of largest joint ventures. As the transfer of technology and technological know-how within joint ventures is probably closely tied to the volume (size) of foreign capital invested, one may conclude that most of the transfer of technology, and technological know-how, is also concentrated in the biggest joint ventures.

Czechoslovakia, especially the Czech Republic, can offer some favourable conditions for foreign investors. The country has relatively low foreign debt, a sound balance of payments, and good prospects to avoid further devaluation of the currency. In a longer perspective, its territory can serve as a gate to Eastern Europe, including countries of the former Soviet Union; Czech and Slovak firms have experience and long-term contacts with this region.

The Czech republic is a territory with an old European culture, not differing substantially from West European traditions and way of life. That makes both production, and marketing, much easier. Czech and Slovak consumers, as those in other communist countries, are hungry for goods approaching western quality standards, but produced with cheaper domestic labour and offered for a somewhat lower price. And Czechoslovak labour is substantially cheaper in comparison to any West-European country (now even cheaper than in the former GDR). It is, at the same time, relatively highly skilled; the combination of cheapness with relatively high skills applies not only to blue-collar workers but also to some groups of technicians and

[20]Data from the Federal Ministry of Finance.

R&D staff. What is missing is knowledge of latest technologies, and the managerial and entrepreneurial know-how.

As will be shown below, the lower productivity of Czechoslovak labour was not caused by lack of general education or skill (as is true of many other less advanced countries also offering cheap labour); in Czechoslovakia, low productivity was mainly a result of the centrally planned economy, undermining any initiative and innovation, and neglecting investment in new technology. This could be a very important difference for prospective foreign investors.

Of course, making use of such potential advantages will not be simple. Success will depend on political stability, speed of the privatization process, reasonable macroeconomic policy, and favourable external conditions. At present, the key factor discouraging foreign inventors is political instability connected with the expected breakup of the Federation.

Technology transferred from abroad could be used as a starting point for a chain of domestic innovations. Here, the Czech and Slovak Republic could learn from the experience of new industrialized countries, and of the relatively less-developed follower countries within the E.C.

The decisive source of innovation however, must be own invention, domestic research and development. Here again, Czechoslovakia has invested a lot in the last four decades, without the desired effect for productivity and competitiveness. The obstacle was not lack of invention: it is an almost unknown fact that in the post-war period, Czechoslovakia has made an important contribution to the world stack of commercially-used knowledge. For example, the soft material for contact lenses which later made them a world-wide success was first discovered in Czechoslovakia. The same is true of the jet spinning machine which revolutionized the textile industry. In neither case, the country was able to make proper use of the discovery - to commercialize it.

Indeed, the problem was not invention but innovation. The chief dilemma of every inventor or research team was where to find a producer: in most cases, no state-owned enterprise was willing to jeopardize the fulfillment of planned targets by trying out something new, risky, and unplanned. On paper, many large enterprises had their own research teams; in fact, they often refused even projects for innovation offered to them free of charge by institutes financed by the Academy of Sciences, or by the sector ministries.

Another factor which more and more economists see as having a close link with productivity growth is the level of education.[21] Though the secondary school (college) and university enrollment rates in Czechoslovakia were somewhat lower than in the neighbouring Western European countries in the last decades, the level of education was relatively very good, especially in mathematics, technical disciplines, and natural sciences. Also, the country had a well-organized apprenticeship system which was practically comparable to secondary education, and (for about three decades) compulsory.

[21] There are very interesting empirical data on the importance of education for productivity growth in a recent study by Barro, R.J., 1991. Compare also Romer, P.M., 1990, Murphy, K.M., Shleifer, A., Vishny, R.W., 1991.

As far as education was concerned, Czechoslovakia indeed had no reason to lag behind in productivity.[22] But even education is only a necessary condition, not a sufficient one: decisive is the motivation and freedom to use knowledge in production - to transform knowledge into quality of production, into initiative, entrepreneurship and innovation.

There are many reasons why innovation activity of state-owned enterprises in a command economy was low. The omnipresence of planned targets, endless shortages of materials and labour, redistribution of profits of good enterprises over the state budget to support loss-makers seen as "needing help", the soft budget constraint which undermined any economic incentive, prices set arbitrarily from the center, lack of competition, and a secure perspective that the hungry domestic market will take even goods of low quality. And, after all, there were always other C.M.E.A. countries with equally hungry markets, with consumers who had no other choice.

TRADE LIBERALIZATION: NOT A UNILATERAL TASK

This brings us to another important factor of productivity growth - opening the economy to international trade, inviting foreign competition, and using the advantages from access to larger markets.[23] Among the proposed explanations of a lag in productivity growth, artificial closing of the economy is the only one that, without doubt, applies to Czechoslovakia. Growing isolation from the broader world markets went hand in hand with forced integration into a trade block with other low-productivity countries. Within this block, the Soviet Union was a leading power whose market, always hungry for low-quality imports, in fact worked as an inhibitor of rapid technological change within the block.

In Czechoslovakia, artificially imposed political barriers to trade with Western markets led to lagging productivity - and lagging productivity, step by step, undermined the competitiveness of Czechoslovak industry in exports to advanced countries. In the sixties, average yearly growth of kilogram prices in Czechoslovak exports to the European Community still equaled 95 % of kilogram price growth in other countries` exports to this territory; in the seventies, it was only 71 %, and, in the eighties, only 17 %.[24] In 1988-9, only 0.4 % of Czechoslovak firms achieved exports per worker comparable to the average exports per worker of firms in West Germany, Austria or Sweden. Of Czechoslovakia's exports to hard currency regions, 93 % were attributable to a narrow group of 210 enterprises (out of 866 enterprises

---

[22]This can be confirmed by international comparison. See Unesco, *Statistical Yearbook 1989*, Paris 1989.

[23]R. Baldwin has recently pointed out the importance of opening the economy, predicting a very positive influence of the Maastricht Agreement on productivity of European firms, *The Economist*, January 4, 1992. Other authors, stressing this factor are Rivera-Batiz, L.A., Romer, P.M., 1991, Levine, R. Renelt, D., 1992. Compare also World Development Report, 1991.

[24]See Kolanda, M., 1991.

existing in manufacturing). Four out of ten enterprises had practically no experience with exports to exacting markets.[25]

Liberalization of trade and the introduction of internal convertibility (convertibility of the CSK for trade transactions of Czechoslovak enterprises) in 1991 created potential conditions for opening of the economy. After a short fall in the first quarter of 1991, exports to OECD markets started to grow. The originally very low share of market economies in the country's exports has, by the second half of 1992, grown to 78%. Czechoslovakia considers the growth of trade with E.C. countries to be an especially crucial factor of economic recovery in the short run, and of catch-up in the long run.

At present, owing to political instability in Central and Eastern Europe (but also owing to internal problems within the EC, and to resentment of many West European firms toward competition of Eastern goods produced by cheaper labour), a growing reluctance is observable in the organs of the European Community in relation to possible future full integration of Center-European countries. There are proposals that these countries should, instead, form their own regional block. The breakdown of C.M.E.A. is being criticized as premature and too fast; a feeling is growing that many goods which these countries are trying to export to Western Europe should, instead, be sold in Eastern markets.

The critics of a too fast breakdown of the C.M.E.A. disregard, however, both the political aspects of this process, and the economic consequences which the forced orientation on mutual trade brought for the structure, quality, and technological level of production in the C.M.E.A. countries. The system in which these countries were supplying each other with low-quality goods unsalable at other markets just cannot go on any longer, if there is to be any hope for future prosperity and stability in this part of Europe. To expose the domestic producers to competition of products from advanced countries, and to world prices, is the only way toward restructuring and economic recovery. Liberalization of imports, however, cannot be one-sided. In the case of Czechoslovakia, imports from EC countries have to be paid for by increased exports, if the stability of the currency is to be maintained. At present, a moderate current account surplus is desirable to build up the country's reserves and foster its credibility.

Producers in EC countries now see mainly the potential competition by imports from Central Europe. But in restructuring of post-communist economies, a moment will necessarily come when demand for imports of sophisticated investment goods will grow significantly - and Western Europe is the most feasible supplier. Restructuring will require new technology and know-how. At present, an investment upsurge based on Western technology is being hindered by the decapitalization of post-communist economies. But, in the longer run, EC countries could play, for Central Europe, the role of technological leader - as the U.S. did for Western Europe after the War.

---

[25]See Kolanda, M., Kubijta, V. 1990.

It should be recalled that this follower-leader relation was advantageous for both parts. For Europe, it enabled a much faster absorption of new technology. As Maddison wrote in 1987: "If the follower countries follow an appropriate policy mix and are not disturbed in the convergence process by war, they should be able to increase productivity at a faster pace than the lead country. They enjoy "opportunities of backwardness", which means that over a considerable range of technology they can emulate the leader and get a given amount of growth with less expenditure on research and development. They can push the rate of capital formation per worker faster without running into diminishing returns, and structural change is rapid."[26] Analyses of other authors have confirmed these conclusions, stressing that both embodied and disembodied technological progress can be faster in the follower countries.

On the other part, the role of technological leader of Western Europe which was ripe for a catch-up process (and of japan and, later, of the Newly Industrialized Countries) provided the United States with secure markets for their technically advanced industries. This had a positive feedback - it fostered in the U.S. growth of production, and further technological advance. Technological leadership also made the position of the dollar stronger, and gave the U.S. more freedom in fiscal and monetary policy. Now the U.S. is very distressed by the prospect that the country may lose its leading position - that the role of technological leader within the existing "catch-up club" is shifting toward Japan. In contrast, the E.C. countries do not seem to appreciate fully the chance of becoming technological leaders in economic restructuring and revival of post-communist European countries.

REFERENCES

Abramowitz, M., The catch-up factor in postwar economic growth, *Economic Inquiry*, January 1990.

Barro, R.J., Economic growth in a cross section of countries, *Quarterly Journal of Economics*, May 1991.

Baumol, W.J., Productivity Growth, convergence and welfare: What the long-run data show, *American Economic Review*, December 1986.

Baumol, W.J., Wolff, E.N., *Is international productivity convergence illusory*, C.V. Starr Center for Applied Economics, New York, 1987.

Christensen, L.R. - Cummings, D., Jorgenson, D.W., Relative productivity levels, 1947-1973. An international comparison, *European Economic Review*, 1981, V, p. 72-83.

[26]Maddison, A., 1987, p. 650.

De Long, J.B. -Summers L.H., Equipment investment and economic growth, *Quarterly Journal of Economics,* May 1991.

Dêdek, O. - Nachtigal, V., Dezagregace tempa souhrnné hospodár-rnosti, *Politická ekonomie,* 1987, No. 2.

Dlouhÿ, V., HDP a ekonomická úroveñ Çeskoslovenska I, II, *Politická ekonomie,* 1987, No. 4, 6.

Drábek, Z. - Janáček, K. - Tûma, Z., *Inflation in Czechoslovakia 1985-1991,* World Bank Working Paper, 1992 (forthcoming).

Hájek, M. - Janáčková, S. - Nachtigal, V., *Total Factor Productivity Trends in Czechoslovakia: A Comparison With Advanced Market Economies,* Institute of Economics of the Czechoslovak Academy of Sciences, Prague, 1990.

Hájek, M., et al., *Inovace a vÿzkum v Çeskoslovensku,* Institute of Economics of the Czechoslovak Academy of Sciences, Prague 1991

Hare, P., Hughes, G., *Competitiveness and industrial restructuring in Czechoslovakia, Hungary and Poland,* Center for Economic Policy Research, London 1991 (also European Economy, Special Edition, No. 2, 1991).

Jefferson, G.H., Petri, P.A., From Marx to Markets, *Challenge,* September/October 1990.

Janáčková, S., *Overall efficiency and total factor productivity - theoretical basis for comparisons,* Czechoslovak Economic Papers, No. 28, Prague 1990.

Janáčková, S., *Technological Gaps and Productivity Convergence - Lessons for Czechoslovakia,* Institute of Economics of the Czechoslovak Academy of Sciences, Prague 1990.

Janáčková, S., *Microeconomic Aspects of Transformation,* Prague Economic Papers, No. 3, 1992.

Kolanda, M., Kubičta, V., *Náklady, vÿkony a chování podnikû çs. zpracovatelského prûmyslu na svétovÿch trzích v 80. letech,* Institute of Forecasting of the Czechoslovak Academy of Sciences, Prague 1990.

Kolanda, M., *Ke strategii dalçího zapojování ÇSFR do mezinárodní dêlby práce v príčtích letech,* Institute of Forecasting of the Czechoslovak Academy of Sciences, Prague 1991.

Landes, D.S., Why are we so rich and they so poor?, *American Economic Review,* May 1990.

Levine, R. - Renelt, D., A Sensitivity analysis of cross-country growth regressions, *American Economic Review,* September 1992.

Maddison, A., Growth and slowdown in advanced capitalist economies: techniques of quantitative assessment, *Journal of Economic Literature,* 1987, VI.

Maddison, A., *The World Economy in the 20th Century,* OECD Development Center, Paris 1989.

Murphy,K.M., Shleifer, A., Vishny R.W., The allocation of talent: implications for growth, *Quarterly Journal of Economics,* May 1991.

OECD Economic Outlook, No. 46, December 1989.

Rivera-Batiz, L.A., Romer, P.M., Economic integration and endogenous growth, *Quarterly Journal of Economics,* May 1991.

Romer, P.M., *Are Nonconvexities Important for Understanding Growth,* American Economic Review, May 1990

Romer, P. M., Endogenous technological change, *Journal of Political Economy,* 1990, No. 5.

The Economist, May 26, 1990, January 4, 1992.

Toms, M. - Hájek, M., The measurement of overall efficiency, *Czechoslovak Economic Papers,* No. 24, Prague 1987.

UNESCO, *Statistical Yearbook* 1989, Paris 1989.

United Nations Development Programme. "Human Development 1990", see *The Economist,* May 26, 1990.

Wolff, E.N., *Capital Formation and Long-Term Productivity Growth: A Comparison of Seven Countries,* New York University, July 1987

13

COMPETITION POLICY IN CZECHOSLOVAKIA

Alena Zemplinerová
Institute of Economics
Czechoslovak Academy of Sciences

SUMMARY: The heritage of centrally planned economy /CPE/ consists not only of highly concentrated market structures but also of a legal and institutional framework directed towards the creation of monopolies.

This contribution examines the problem of demonopolization as well as the policy for support of competition during the transition to the market economy.

Two different demonopolization concepts are discussed:

a) Demonopolization by means of removing barriers to entry
b) Demonopolization by means of breaking-up the corporations.

Special features of the monopoly in the command economy, dilemmas of the antimonopoly policy as well as the problems of its implementation in ex-CPEs are discussed.

1. INTRODUCTION

Monopolization was an immanent and basic feature of the command economy. Not only there existed numerous barriers to entry and single producers in most of the markets,[1] but monopolistic market structures have been consolidated also by autarkic policies and isolating domestic markets by the means of the state protectionism.

The existence of monopoly in centrally planned economies was directly connected with centralized coordination of economic activities. The causes,

[1] Level of monopolisation was substantially higher in final products than in the case of products that are characterized as semi-finished articles (such as parts, accessories, aggregates, components).

institutional preconditions as well as the background motivating the existence of monopoly have to be therefore discussed both on macro- and micro- levels.

Such an approach makes it possible to reveal specific features of monopoly in a centrally planned economy as compared to monopoly in liberal market economy. Such an approach is also important with regard to the evaluation of conditions and prerequisites necessary for a transition to market-based functioning of economic subjects and for effectual demonopolization of the economy.

In socialist countries, in compliance with the set of political and economic tasks and under the impact of existing ideas on management in a socialist economy, there was carried out a vast integration of small and medium enterprises. Big "national enterprises" were created from them. These administrative measures were put into practice with a high degree of consistency in Czechoslovakia in two respects simultaneously.

On the one hand, the private sector was completely liquidated[2] and, on the other hand, the total number of enterprises was drastically reduced. Several hundred thousand of enterprises which existed in Czechoslovakia after the World War II were squeezed into approximately 588 state industrial enterprises, 600 cooperatives and enterprises controlled by local authorities in 1989. An average size of enterprises active in Czechoslovak industry, measured by the number of employees, has thus become most probably the largest in the world.

Small businesses did not exist in Czechoslovak economy. Firm size distribution in developed market economies is characterized by a great differentiation of sizes; there is a high number of small and medium enterprises on one side, and a low number of very big enterprises on the other. Size distribution in CPEs had fully opposite characteristic.

The general distortion of the concentration of the industry in Czechoslovakia can be illustrated by the comparison of Hirschmann-Herfindal index for West Germany and Czechoslovakia.

[2]Private sector was practically non-existent in Czechoslovakia in 1987 its share in the total number of employees amounted to a mere 0.6 per cent. Estimation of the share of private sector on Net material product of CSFR in 1990 is 0.38 per cent.

Table 1.

Hirschmann-Herfindal index (x 10 000)	Share of Industries	
	Germany	CSFR
3 000 and more	6.3	68.1
2 500 - 3 000	3.7	8.6
2 000 - 2 500	6.0	4.4
1 800 - 2 000	3.7	2.9
1 500 - 1 800	4.3	3.8
1 250 - 1 50	6.7	3.6
1 000 - 1 250	6.0	3.2
750 - 1 000	8.0	3.1
500 - 750	13.7	1.3
250 - 500	20.3	1.0
less than 250	21.3	-

Source: Monopolkommission Germany, FSC CSFR, 1989. Computations by F. Ventura

Deformation of the particular market structures can be proved also by the computations of the concentration ratios. Although Germany is about four time bigger country (as for number of inhabitants) the respective concentration ratios were much higher in Czechoslovakia but the number of enterprises in all market is lower in order. Involvement of the import into the analysis, as it is showed in the appendix, would not change the picture much.

Table 2.

	Share of three biggest producers on the total output CSFR	Total number of enter-prices in the industry CSFR FRG	Share of three biggest producers on the total output	Total number of enter-prices in the industry FRG
Flat glass	100.0	1	80.9	18
Wash machines	100.0	2	79.4	21
Refrigerators and freezers	100.0	2	73.0	16
Stocking goods	98.0	7	45.0	44
Underwear garments	79.0	5	28.4	91
Lights fittings	78.1	9	17.2	264
Textile machines	75.2	2	32.4	21
Leather shoes	69.0	6	23.9	158
Printing paper	64.0	9	52.8	25
Yarn	52.0	10	51.6	120
Woven clothing	44.0	33	10.0	1151
Wood furniture	41.0	26	7.0	906
Knitted clothing	40.0	18	13.6	237

Sources: Hauptgutachten der Monopolkommission 7, Baden-Baden: Nomos, Verl.-Ges. 1988, Materials FSC 1989.

There existed a great divergence between enterprise and plant concentration. Thus monopolistic or oligopolistic positions of the state industrial enterprises, have been caused by organizational concentration in the prevalent number of industries. Economic arguments favouring creation of big enterprises were based on a hypothesis of continuously growing concentration of production capacities and on presumed economies of scale. Enterprises were fused on the basis of the criterion of product similarity, which resulted necessarily in concentration of organizational structure of branches.[3]

On the other side technical concentration in most of manufacturing industries stayed on low level, because during the "socialist industrialisation" very little have been invested to the traditional manufacturing industries as cars, textile, glass, shoes, leather, wood processing, etc.[4]

On the other side heavy machinery, iron, steel and heavy chemicals are technically highly concentrated. Most of the centralised finance means have been invested into these industries, especially in 1950s and became obsolete. Level of depreciation of machines and equipment in the manufacturing in 1990 was 56.4% for the whole CSFR, 55.9% for the Czech Republic and 58.4% for the Slovak Republic.

It was the state that contributed a major share to establishing and continuous maintaining of monopolies in centrally planned economies. Institutional framework of the economy functioning and its organizational structure have been tuned to the centrally planned model of economic management.

Such policy had no doubt its origin in the mono-party political system. The political monopoly generated monopolies in all fields of the social life and the economy was no exemption. The directive measures which are mentioned above and which led to great distortion of size structures in CPEs were a direct consequence of rejecting market as a mean of ensuring economic equilibrium, and of accepting instead a doctrine of direct links along the central planning hierarchy.

At he same time, a multi-tier system of vertical management was being created. The organizational structure constructed in such a way was to enable the central authorities to control, by directives and operative management, the entire national economy. For the same reason, the development of organizational structures in local (the so-called communal or municipal) and cooperative industries developed along analogical patterns. The integration tendencies in local economy have been even more pronounced than in the centrally managed industry. Large, territorial monopolized enterprises have been created.[5] Gradually, markets have been administratively divided between the enterprises of local industry, cooperative enterprises and centrally managed enterprises (controlled by branch ministries). It was very difficult for the production cooperatives and local industry enterprises to enter industries reserved for centrally managed enterprises.

---

[3]In Czechoslovakia, the average number of plants for an enterprise is 10.6 (in local industries average 17 plants). Analogical indicators are 1.25 and 1.38 for Austria and Great Britain respectively.

[4]For instance, the capacity of the production line of the Skoda car factory was 180,000 cars in 1990. After creation of joint ventures with Volkswagen the capacity will increase to 450, 000 cars per year in 1997. In the textile enterprise Mosilana, yearly capacity of yarn was 3,000,000 meters per year. The optimal capacity of comparative enterprise is 25,000,000 meters per year etc.

[5]The structural hierarchy of management, characterized by an up to 6-tier management, was the central body being the Ministry of Interior.

By the end of 1989, when Czechoslovakia has embarked upon a course of principal economic transformation to a system functioning on the principle of the competitive market.

On January 1, 1991, the key macroeconomic elements of the Czechoslovak economic reform were put into place: the majority of prices were liberalized, the currency was declared to be "internally convertible," and foreign trade was liberalized. These policies were complemented by continuation of macroeconomic austerity.

Table 3.

Relation between concentration, price and output index according to the industries, CSFR first Quarter of 1991 over first Quarter 1990

	Share of produced by single enter-price first quarter 1990	Wholesale price index first quarter 1991 over first quarter 1990	Percentage output over first quarter 1991
Wood processing	2.8	150.5	96.1
Food	6.2	126.1	82.9
Clothing	6.7	143.7	71.1
Printing and publishing	14.3	172.3	88.0
Paper and cellulose	15.0	172.0	106.0
Iron metallurgy	17.1	167.7	84.6
Textiles	27.4	167.4	83.8
Machinery	28.9	148.4	89.3
Leather industry	30.7	174.0	81.3

Sources: Materials FSC, own computations

Price liberalization, which was realized as of the January 1,1991 led to and an increase of consumer prices in average by 34% during the first quarter of 1991 as compared to the December 1989 and to the sharp decline of the industrial output in prevalent number of industries (see table No 3). At the same time profitability of many state industrial enterprises increased by 300-320% as compared to the same period of 1989. Such behaviour can be ascribed to the monopolistic situation of the most of enterprises.

What can be done with big state enterprises, which possess big power and are able to survive by virtue of monopolistic position, state protection and artificial barrier to new entry?

This study examines two questions connected with demonopolization:

- When to carry out the demonopolization (i.e. prior to, simultaneously or after the privatization.
- How to perform the demonopolization (i.e. how fast, by which instruments and in which measure and in which industries).

In dependence on general philosophy to the economy transformation and role of state in the economy, two difference concepts of demonopolization can be adopted. First one relies on indirect participation of the state and gives preference to the progressive removal of existing barriers to entry into the industry. Second one consider the direct participation of the state authorities in the break up of the big state organizational concentrated enterprises.

2. DEMONOPOLIZATION THROUGH THE ENTRY BARRIERS BREAK UP

Government economic policy, adopting the first approach to demonopolization, doesn't consider direct state interventions into the enterprise sphere, but changing the rules of towards the creation of equal rules of all economic agents. The state enterprises are exposed to competition. Domestic competition is supported through the removal of entry barriers, deregulation and price liberalization and through foreign competition by virtue of foreign trade liberalization and introduction of the crown convertibility, which would allow for increased domestic competition via imports. New starts-up are promoted , establishment of new enterprises stimulated. Expected effect of such policy is the frequent spontaneous break-up of or liquidation of existing state enterprises and subsequent arising of industrial structure based on the market criterion. A constituent component of this approach is the creation of a new legal and institutional framework suitable for a competitive market economy.

Such an approach is naturally a long term process. Society thus bears the costs of monopoly and have to tolerate the monopolistic behaviour for a relatively long time.

In the government economic policy of Czechoslovakia this approach prevails but it is not consequent. Substantial restriction on foreign trade remain. Nevertheless development of the structures of some industries give evidence in favour of this approach. During a six month period in 1990 the number of enterprises increased rapidly as it is showed in Table 4.

Most of these break-ups have been in response to requests from plants and units to become an independent enterprise. There exists a certain pressure for and movement towards the independence of particular plants or parts of existing enterprises. Indications of this independence movement were seen in the opposition to unqualified decision making and resource redistribution in the framework of existing state enterprises, as well as to the possibility of acquiring property rights to these parts of enterprises in the future during privatization.

Table 4

Growth of the number of the enterprises in selected sub industries, CSFR, January - June 1990

SUB INDUSTRY	1/90	4/90	6/90
Manufacture of machinery and equipment for heavy industries	53	77	79
Manufacture of machinery and equipment for agriculture, trade and service-producing industries	49	58	60
Manufacture of high-tension products for industrial purposes	9	16	17
Manufacture of low-tension products for industrial purposes	22	30	31
Manufacture of metal products for industrial purposes	18	21	25
Manufacture of flat, building and technical glass	5	14	15
Printing and publishing production	6	30	30
Fish, game and small animal products	14	15	22
Building industry	28	49	65
Inner trade, restaurants	128	170	177

Sources: Materials of Federal Statistical Office, own computations.
Only state enterprises are involved into the survey.

The strength for independence is often motivated by the entrepreneur intention and based on good knowledge of the plant or part of the enterprise. Usually only technically well-furnished plants which have a good chance for economic prosperity are requesting independence. More pure and weaker plants and enterprises endeavour to associate with the larger enterprises, relying on power based on size, and open hand of the state.

Unfortunately these processes of spontaneously breakups and de concentration based on economic calculation have been held up by the decision of the government.[6]

[6]The reason for such a decision was the fear of the total collapse of the functioning of basic supplies for inhabitants. Government intended to quash an uncontrolled elementary process of privatization by the was of creation of the private joint stock companies or in cooperation with foreign firms. Low experience and qualification of existing managers is typical for these transactions. The managers pursue their own aims selling the enterprises at a very low price. It

Space for renewal process of natural breakup of state enterprises provide process of privatization. Privatization projects (proposals) can be prepared and submitted by each plant, unit or part of the state enterprise.[7]

It should release entrepreneurial activity, this time not only Platonic, but along with a clear definition of property rights. It is expected that in this way the spontaneous demonopolization of many industries could be achieved.

Industries which are not capital intensive, especially services, took a clear course to de concentration. There are for instance about 2600 travel agencies registered, the number of enterprises in building and construction is higher in order. As of late February 1991 there were already about 2000 foreign firms operating in Czechoslovakia as joint-ventures, several hundreds of new small cooperatives have been established. More than a half million of private entrepreneurs have been registered in the Czech republic alone.

These are symptoms of thriving competition.

Small scale privatization which is realized through public auctions enables demonopolization of the retail distribution net and together with restitution to bridge the existing technical barriers entry in the form of the lack of space for entrepreneurship. Demonopolization of the banking and finance network is going on, about 430 investment funds and the stock exchange have been established. These are assumptions of the stock market development.

Nevertheless the biggest problem in demonopolization are the big industrial state enterprises, which often operate in capital intensive industries and are not capable of changing their productions in a program flexible manner. It is often asserted, that demonopolization of these industries is connected with considerable social risks and thus also with political destabilization. But the contrary is true: the longer is the existence and maintenance of monopolies in the economy the higher are the social losses from these monopolies. Social and political commotions will thus be stronger and longer, if the monopolies will be artificially protected and retained by the state for a longer time. The liquidation of the state monopolies by the means of shock therapy is also not acceptable. In the GDR there has been a collapse of the major part of the economy. The state is for this reason forced for a certain limited time to pursue a protectionist policy towards the domestic resident enterprises.[8]

To compensate the lack of qualified entrepreneurs managers the government hired in foreign consulting firms elaborating of the conception of reconstruction and privatization in the particular industries. Recommendation

---

was also argued that from the ethical point of view, it is unfair that the same people who profited from their position in the communist era can again realize their privileges.

[7]Law on big scale privatization, February 1991.

[8]For instance, in the paper industry the original 12 enterprises have been spontaneously, on their own request broken up into 23 independent enterprises. A foreign consulting firm in its study suggests the creation of three big capital, powerful enterprises by the mergers of all of the existing enterprises. The firm BATA asked, in the first proposal, for state protection of the inner shoe market for foreign competition for several years. The attempt to monopolize the whole distribution network of building materials can be further examples.

of these firms as well as the revealed preference of potential foreign partners and investors. Often prefer big enterprises. Foreign enterprises intend to buy the whole market, and naturally they prefer monopolized market to competitive one.

The decision of the government during the privatization will consist in a trade off between the price of the sale of the monopoly and the amount of the social losses from the privatized monopoly.

3. DEMONOPOLIZATION THROUGH THE ENTERPRISE BREAK-UP

Dismantling of monopolistic structures without any state intervenes as well as privatization without using the free state property voucher system would probably be a very long-term process.

De concentration or breakups of state enterprises through the state authority would increase the number of enterprises in the industries much more quickly. Unfortunately, none of the transforming state-owned economies until now have realized a radical de concentration of the state owned enterprises on the base of state directives.

Dissolution as well as merger of enterprises is relatively simple and quick operation [9],nevertheless this variant is connected with certain risks as well.

Organizational concentrated enterprises are composed by factories and plants which differ substantially in their levels of efficiency. Cross-subsidization takes place very often between the plants which made up an enterprise. Liberalization of prices, enables to distinguish effective and non-effective enterprise, but the measure of cross-subsidization between the operational units of the enterprise remain hidden. After the enterprise is broken up, an inefficient factory which had been subsidized by the rest of the enterprise would be apparent and such a factory could not - without other assistance - avoid bankruptcy or the required restructuring.

The single radical decomposition of the state enterprises would likely increase the number of enterprises /as it was already mentioned one state industrial enterprise has in average 5-7 plants or local and technological separate units). Many of these new independent enterprises would go bankrupt, but what would be positive that these bankruptcies would concern only inefficient units, while when the big integrated enterprise go bankrupt many potential effective units would be liquidated at the same time.

The other fear or risk consists in the fact that the government decision about the enterprise division could be mistaken as well as the decision about the forced merges integration of enterprises in the framework of the CPE.

---

[9]The technical obstacles to decomposition are not so insurmountable as one often judges. Separate plants or factories are keeping accounting practices parallel with the whole enterprise. Also loans and debts are usually held separately. As further subsidiary criterion could be used, local and technological separability of particular factories, plants and other operational units as it is already the case during the small scale privatization.

Again trade off between costs on such a decision and costs on the surviving of the monopolies have to be considered. Big enterprises often have big political power. De concentration would no-doubt lead to decreasing of their power in bargaining with the government. An oppressive heritage of a directive system is not only highly concentrated monopolistic structure of the enterprise sphere, but also in the structure of an economic centre, created for the needs of the CPE. Along with newly established institutions that signal gradual adjusting of central bodies to a pattern typical for liberal market economies the old patterns survive. In considering of this variant the inertia of the surviving institutions of CPE as well as social values inherited from the command type of economy have to be taken into the account. The ministries and government agencies remained quite numerous, often changed only the names. They adjust to the new style of work and role of the state only very slowly.

The changes concern only the pyramid's top of hierarchical structures and surviving hypertrophied foundations can represent strong and concentrated power capable of efficiently preventing changes and rising competition.

There exist another objective against performing the instantaneous break-up of enterprises. In spite of decomposition of big state enterprises, the firms which have resulted from the breakups of large monopolies need not exhibit competitive behaviour. The reason can be seen in maintenance and surviving of barriers to entry to the industry due to legislative lag. In connection with this fact parallel implementation of deregulation will play a decisive role.

4. DILEMMAS OF ANTIMONOPOLY POLICY IN EX-CPE

Demonopolization has from the beginning of 1991 its concrete institutions in Czechoslovakia. January 30, 1991 parliament passed the Competition Protection Act[10]. Originally there have been established three Offices for the protection of economic competition - two on the republic's level and a federal one. In the meantime there exist only two - the Czech and the Slovak one. They are supposed to serve as watchdogs of the starting competition (by illicit restriction of competition, controlling the mergers etc., which is the classical function of these institutions in developed market economies. They should fulfill also the specific - temporal function, which consists in active liquidation of the inherited monopolies.

The main dilemma of these institutions will be the choice to which of the variants of demonopolization described above to choose or prefer. Antimonopoly committees or offices in market economic usually deal with tens of cases yearly. Some of cases have to be decided by the court and last years.

According to the Law on the protection of the competition "Dominant position in the market is held by an entrepreneur who supplies the relevant

[10]No 63/1991 Coll. of Law

market in the course of the calendar year with at least 30% of supply of identical, comparable or mutually commutable goods".[11]

It gives the Offices responsibility to perform de concentration already prior to privatization. These Offices should also approve each privatization project from the point of view of possible de concentration during the privatization.

The Offices should apply the indirect method of demonopolization as well and care about competition by removing of existing entry barriers, crating of the climate for fair competition i.e. equal conditions and rule for all enterprises.

5. CONCLUSIONS

In 1989 there were only 430 industrial state enterprises in the Czech republic. By August 1992 have been registered by the Czech Statistical Office already 2258. This number includes both new entry and parts of former state enterprises.

Former large state enterprises are being restructured, divided into several independent units,[12] new private enterprises created.

Number of small enterprises increases sharply after 1989 and continue to grow. Czech industrial enterprises size structure is thus gaining the usual shape we can meet in the developed market economies.

Table 5

Czech industrial enterprises according to the size

Enterprise according to the number of employees	1989	1990	1991	1992
25 - 99	–	–	–	549
100 - 149	–	–	129	216
150 - 299	–	–	397	522
300 - 599	48	459	394	409
600 -1199	84	207	348	260
1200 -2499	175	250	383	195
2500 -4999	74	74	137	78
5000 and more	49	29	29	29
Total number	430	1019	1750	2258

Source: *Statistical Abstracts and Statistical Information*, CFU

[11] Article 9, Law on the protection of competition

[12] For example, form one of the companies interviewed, AERO, four plants separated from the enterprise in 1991 and became the independent enterprises.

Share of the private sector increases. As for the structure of industry according to the ownership forms, the decisive share on the industrial output as by September 1992 and the whole CSFR still have state enterprises (74.8%), share of private firms is 16.2% and international ones 3.9%. Cooperatives produce 1.5% from the total output.[13]

Most of the private firms are small and medium sized. The smallest size category was the only one in which industrial output grew during 1992 (by 23.3%).

Share of the private sector on the total output in the industry was in Czech republic during first quarter of 1992 7.3% and in second quarter already 26.8%. In the construction, trade and services the shares were even higher.

The number of joint ventures increased from 1 600 in 1990 to more than 8,000 at 1991.[14] Inflows of foreign investment rose from zero to almost $0.6 billion in 1991 and to $1.2 billion by the end of the first half of 1992.

Protectionism and tariffs are still often argued in highly concentrated industries. For instance car industry.[15]

Nevertheless the only way of demonopolisation is to open the economy and import foreign cars.

Competition Protection Act became effective in February 1991, Offices of the Economic Competition have been established and started to operate. Nevertheless Law as well as the Office for support of competition seem to be weak vehicle and institutions to demonopolisation. Approval of mergers is formal, applying of the law bureaucratic.

Anti-monopoly policy is a delicate issue. On one side it is one of the means of threat to enterprises not to abuse monopolistic position. On the other side too active anti-monopoly office can repeal foreign investment. Also delays caused by the long approval process can repeal investors.

The government competition policy should be and in fact is a compromise of both described approaches.

---

[13]Comp. Aktualni statisticke informance: Prumysl, September 1992, Federal Statistical Office.

[14]Uneven tax regulations encouraged the establishment of a lot of "fake" joint ventures in order to save tax. Profit tax was 55% for Czech firms and 40% for joint ventures with at least 30% foreign participation. This regulation should be abolished in 1993.

[15]The monopolistic behaviour of Skoda-VW is allowed by the protection of domestic market. Legal units have to pay import duty on the cars (19% or 15.2% in cases of EC production) plus import surcharges of 10% plus turnover tax according to the turnover tax tariffs.

In addition, it is prohibited to import second hand cars produced after 1985. The car industry is thus well protected against foreign competition and can increase prices or maintain the quality of the cars.

Appendix 1

Concentration ratios and Shares of imports in selected sectors, Czechoslovakia 1990

Sector	Share of the biggest producers on the total output of the sub-industry	Share of the four biggest producers on the total output of the sub-industry	Share of the import on the total output of the industry
Basic metallurgical products from iron and steel	20	67	1
Manufacture of chemical consumer goods	39	84	10
Manufacture of pharmaceutical products	23	69	26
Manufacture of rubber-asbestos products for industrial purposes	24	66	10
Processing of plastics	26	69	5
Manufacture of machinery and equipment for energy industries	32	76	13
Manufacture of machinery and equipment for heavy industries	13	34	24
Manufacture of machinery and equipment for manufacturing industries	7	26	36
Manufacture of machinery and equipment for agriculture, trade and service-producing industries	27	44	16
Manufacture of means of transport for industrial purposes	17	41	7

(continued on the following page)

Appendix 1

Concentration ratios and Shares of imports in selected sectors, Czechoslovakia 1990

(continued)

Sector	Share of the biggest producers on the total output of the sub-industry	Share of the four biggest producers on the total output of the sub-industry	Share of the import on the total output of the industry
Manufacture of means of transport for non-industrial purposes	62	91	10
Optics and fine mechanics industry	19	55	51
Manufacture of measuring instrument and equipment	28	98	23
Manufacture of high-tension products for industrial purposes	8	24	6
Manufacture of high-tension products for non-industrial purposes	48	-	22
Manufacture of low-tension products for industrial purposes	19	40	38
Manufacture of low-tension products for personal consumption	62	92	28
Manufacture of lumber, joiner and carpentry products	11	38	1
Manufacture of wood furniture	16	53	4
Manufacture of wood-fabrication consumer goods	59	-	6
Simple engineering products	24	61	3
Manufacture of joint chains and bearings	46	77	10

(continued on the following page)

Appendix 1

Concentration ratios and Shares of imports in selected sectors, Czechoslovakia 1990

(continued)

Sector	Share of the biggest producers on the total output of the sub-industry	Share of the four biggest producers on the total output of the sub-industry	Share of the import on the total output of the industry
Manufacture of metal products for industrial purposes	17	51	5
Manufacture of metal products for non-industrial purposes	10	36	14
Engineering manufacture from plastics	40	100	7
Manufacture of paper and cellulose	15	47	1
Manufacture of flat, building and technical glass	38	77	6
Manufacture of technical and medical ceramics	33	100	4
Manufacture of glass consumer products	17	52	1
Manufacture of utility chinaware and ceramics	99	-	17
Processing of textile raw materials	30	75	24
Manufacture of fabrics and piece textile goods	8	23	5
Manufacture of knitted goods	14	38	13
Manufacture of apparels	13	50	9
Manufacture of hat goods	100	-	-
Tanning production	35	-	69
Footwear manufacture	48	92	7
Manufacture of leather fancy goods	28	95	9

(continued on the following page)

Appendix 1

Concentration ratios and Shares of imports in selected sectors, Czechoslovakia 1990

(continued)

Sector	Share of the biggest producers on the total output of the sub-industry	Share of the four biggest producers on the total output of the sub-industry	Share of the import on the total output of the industry
Fur production	100	-	9
Printing and publishing production	9	34	2
Fish, game and small animal products	13	40	2
Products from fruits, vegetable and forest products	13	47	15
Dairying and egg products	16	55	-
Manufacture of fats and oils	32	74	5
Milling, paste and baking production	13	34	6
Sugar refining production	44	80	6
Confectionery	36	100	5
Manufacture of malt and brewing	20	47	-
Wine, spirits and starch production	28	85	12
Freezing and refrigerating	72	-	24
Manufacture of tobacco products	64	-	25

Source: Materials of the Federal Statistics Office 1990 -own computations.

14

MICROECONOMIC CLIMATE IN CZECHOSLOVAKIA - FIRM'S BEHAVIOR DEPENDING ON METHOD OF PRIVATIZATION

Jiří Hlaváček
Faculty of Social Sciences
Charles University, Prague

1. INTRODUCTION

Profit maximizing is not necessarily a self-evident characteristic in the behavior of producers even in market economies. When the owners and employees are the same individuals, wages and probability of survival of the firm are higher and profit is smaller : owners operate with low profitability because of higher transaction costs. Similarly, the behavior of a firm in which the owners also play the role of managers differs from profit maximizing *homo oeconomicus* : manager's wages are higher to the detriment of profit, probability of bankruptcy is considerably increased.

Thousands of new firms have been and are being created in Czechoslovakia in 1991-1993. Only a portion of these firms are organized in the standard way, with different lists of owners, managers and employees. As far as objective functions and future behavior of firms are concerned, one can expect great differences between firms established in the standard way and those established in alternative ways.

One of most interesting questions concerned economies of Czechoslovakia and other post communist countries is the following : what economic climate will prevail in next years, and what changes and what dynamics in the changes in firms' behavior can be expected?

Because of the heterogeneity of firms mentioned above one cannot answer this question without somehow categorizing these firms. The most useful criterion for establishing these categories, in my opinion, would be the method used to create the firm, i.e. the form of privatization.

Czechoslovak law allows for a few ways to found new private firms. Before we speak about these various privatization methods we will describe (in section two) the initial economic climate, i.e. economic climate with prevailing state ownership of enterprises.

In section three of this paper, the various methods of privatization will be discussed, and in section four we will predict typical behavior of firms depending on the method of privatization. In the section five, taking certain data into consideration (number of firms and share of state property privatized by various methods), we will forecast the economic climate and its dynamics in next several years.

2. ECONOMIC CLIMATE BEFORE PRIVATIZATION

There were only two sorts of firms in centrally planned economy of Czechoslovakia before the year 1990 : state firms and co-operatives. In contrast to Poland there was practically no private sector even in Czechoslovak agriculture. In 1986, about 96.7 of Czechoslovak net national product was produced by state sector. Czechoslovakia alongside East Germany and Soviet Union, had the highest percentage of state production among communist countries.[1]

The difference *de iure* between state enterprises and co-operatives did not lead to any differences in their economic conditions and in their behavior, because all firms were dependent on allocation of sources, prices and plan targets laid down by the center. As a result, their behavior was identical. Their main criterion of success was not profit but rather satisfaction of the central planning authority . This effort was the only way to "survive," or, in other words, for the director to remain in his position.

The planning authority,under the pressure of political leaders who had been feeling in danger because of the increasing difference between efficiency of centrally-planned and of market economies, had been trying to increase the efficiency of enterprises.

The position of the planning center in centrally planned economies of Soviet type was very difficult. The center guaranteed the structural proportionality of the economy in such conditions where the capital market was missing, and where prices were administered and reflected no real information about the efficiency of producers and about the relation between

---

[1]For comparison: East Germany 96.5 % (in 1982)
Soviet Union 96.0 % (in 1985)
Poland 81.7 % (in 1985)
China 73.6 % (in 1984)
Hungary 65.2 % (in 1984)
Source : Milanovi((1989)

supply and demand. There was only one possibility to solve the proportionality problem : to construct a plan by multiplying all inputs and outputs on all levels in the plan hierarchy in the previous year by one constant (a number usually between 1.01 and 1.03). This number was called plan index, and this method, the planning index method. This type of planning led to paradoxical situation for firms: the more effective their production, the tighter their plan (more difficult or not possible to fulfill) for next year. In other words : a firm's effective behavior was, in fact, risk behavior.

This planning index method led to reserve maximizing behavior of firms : in order to protect themselves from tighter or unfulfillable plans in future, the firms preferred those production situations with the maximum difference between their production possibilities and their output. Typical firm in a centrally planned economy of Soviet type did not work as efficiently as possible, but as efficiently as necessary. This anti-efficient self-securing behavior was named *Homo se assecurans* in contrast to profit maximizing *Homo oeconomicus* (see J. Hlavácek (1986)).

This economic (or anti-economic) climate could not encourage efficient use of inputs in firms. In addition, when we consider evident inefficient allocation of resources including labor, it is no wonder that communist economies (before the transition to a market arrangement) were in the situation of zero unemployment in despite of low inflation. (In Czechoslovakia, the average consumers' price index was 0.28 % in 1971-1975, 2.11 % in 1976-1980, 2.02 % in 1981-1986, 0.55 % in 1986-1989. Source : Z. Tůma (1992)). Inputs were used at a maximal rate of only 60-70 %, leading to a general shortage of resources, including labor.[2]

After the revolution in November 1989, rapid changes in firms' objective functions and efficiency, resulting from the abandonment of central planning and the radical reduction of the role of the center as far as the price control was concerned. However, the surviving economic climate proved to be surprisingly persistent.

This persistence is explained by the slow changes in manager mentality. In my opinion, the surviving paternalism of the center is the true culprit. The long-discussed Bankruptcy law, which should have started the process of eliminating firms in October, 1992, will most likely be postponed and will come into force only after at least six months. Mr. Klaus, the head of economic reform in the Czech republic, had said that this law could be modified to some "non-standard form". One can speculate that the expression "non-standard" implies the resumption by the center of some form of paternalistic role. The center will probably help some firms, protecting them from bankruptcy by direct or mostly indirect subsidies, such a credit

---

[2]This situation was nicely explained by this joke from communist years: A western economist visiting Prague wants to know how unemployment in Czechoslovakia can be zero. His colleague from Prague explains : " The working hours are eight hours like in the West, it is true, but workers work only four hours, idleing four hours left. That is why there is work enough for all of them "."But ", asks the foreigner again, " when workers work four hours and are paid for eight hours, it has to lead to inflation, doesn't it?" "You are wrong", explains Czech economist, " they are paid only for two hours ! "

preference (the banks are strongly influenced by government). Because of "principal - agent" dialogue profit maximizing is once again not the optimal strategy for state-supported firms: they draw a profit from false information about their production capabilities, they tend falsely represent their inability to cover their costs and their need of higher subsidy or credit.

It has been a commonplace that only rapid privatization will lead to substantial changes in the economic climate. But one cannot assume that the producers' objective functions will be changed into "neoclassical" profit maximizing in a short time. No stable capital and labor markets will exist at least through 1993. Let us ask the question : what objective function of producers will indeed prevail ? The answer depends - in my opinion - on which method of privatization is used, a choice which predetermines the firm's behavior. The future economic climate could be guessed with taking into consideration the percentages of firms, privatized by various methods.

3. MAJOR METHODS OF PRIVATIZATION

The original ideas of Czechoslovak economic leaders in the first quarter of 1990 concerning privatization differ from the reality of autumn 1992. At the beginning, the "small-scale" privatization was prepared, along with voucher privatization. The lack of money in the hands of Czechoslovak citizens was taken into consideration. Because of great difference between the value of factories and the total savings of households, only small, service sector firms were presumed to be sold for the beginning of privatization. The other firms, especially large firms (i.e. majority of state property) were assumed to be given to Czechoslovak citizens practically free of charge through voucher privatization.

This conception had to be changed because of laws accepted by Members of Parliament in November 1991, above all the Restitution Act and the Large-Scale Privatization Act.

According the Restitution Act, property nationalized after the communist coup of 1948 should be returned to the original owners or their heirs.[3]

This law has complicated and protracted the process of privatization of large firms. On the other, small-scale privatization was accelerated as a result of these restitutions.

The Large-Scale Privatization Act has enabled additional methods of privatization of state property. The methods, so called "standard methods", are the following:

- direct sale
- public tenders and auctions
- commercialization into joint-stock structure
- unpaid transfer to municipalities, banks etc.

[3]This Act refers to individual and partners ownership only, it does not concern share ownership in companies.

Foreign investors are permitted involvement in privatization projects, even 100 % foreign privatization projects are allowed, but when a foreigner takes part in a privatization project, the price is higher. Domestic investors pay book value, foreigners, market value).

Cooperatives are transformed into companies, where the identical people play the role of owners along with the role of employees or managers.

A great percentage of managers tries to buy their firm with 100 % of price covered by credit.[4]

Obviously, there is a wide spectrum of firms being created. Because of the various methods of privatization, there are great differences in the connections between owners, managers and employees, and in the goals of these groups . These groups mostly share individuals. The firms will differ in their economic criteria and behaviors, in investment activity, in tendency towards discharging from work, in wage policies, etc. One could say that method of privatization influences the "genetic code" of a firm.

If we want to predict dynamics of economic climate, we must discuss the objectives and behavior of firms *per partes*, in separate sections dealing with groups of firms categorized by their distinct methods of privatization.

4. EXPECTED BEHAVIOR OF FIRMS DEPENDING ON METHOD OF PRIVATIZATION

4.1 Firms Arising Through the Voucher Privatization

About 40 % of firms and 50 % of state property has been privatized by voucher privatization. The state property is being put to citizens and privatization funds in the iteration process, substituting capital market. Vouchers, distributed to citizens almost free of charge (for small administrative charge 1000 Koruna, i.e. average wage of worker per week), are used in this iteration process instead of money.

To assist the citizens, who are not able or willing to cope with the iteration process of voucher privatization, privatization founds were established. They are closed-end funds, organized as joint-stock companies, which are allowed to collect voucher points from the public (The vouchers are not allowed to be sold). Some of these funds are private, and some were established by banks (which at present remain in state ownership). There are about 420 privatization funds, but the top ten of them obtained about 56 % of the points received by all funds combined, i.e. 40 % of the total number of voucher points).

Despite the initial intentions to have mostly individual investors, privatization funds have dominated the voucher privatization. Such funds

[4]About 45 % of proposed privatization projects (4905 of 10949) propose direct sale to predetermined buyer, in the majority of these cases to the mangement of a privatized state firm. Source : M. Mejstřík J. Burger (1992).

have received about 72 % of the total available voucher points. One can expect these giant funds to dominate future joint - stock companies.[5]

These funds will be in financial trouble one year after the end of voucher privatization. To obtain voucher points from the public, they promised to pay (on demand) 10 - 15 thousands Koruna to each of their shareholders. At least one half of shareholders of these funds, according to my estimate, took part in voucher privatization (and paid administrative charge 1000 Koruna) because of this promise. Hence, the funds will have to gain a lot of cash to be able to pay promised amounts . One can expect these funds to sell large numbers of some obtained shares, potentially causing dramatic decrease in prices on the capital market.

This situation will likely be favourable for many managers. If they misrepresent production possibilities and possible profitability of company, its price would be far bellow the book value of their firm, and they could, in partnership with foreigners, buy firm cheaper than they would be able to in large-scale privatization. Such dealings will slow down the changes in the microeconomic climate ; one cannot expect profit maximizing behavior to prevail in these firms. On the contrary : managers will increase wages and payments to those private firms in which they have their interests.[6]

Because these firms would have no genuine interest in decreasing costs, there will be no increase in employee lay-offs. On the other side, one could apprehend inflationary pressures arising in discussed group of firms.

4.2 Firms from Small-Scale Privatization

The small-scale privatization is based on laws, accepted by parliament in the autumn 1990: on the Restitution Act and on the Small-Scale Privatization Act. Wherever possible, property nationalized after communist coup 1948 should be physically returned to the previous owner(s). The Small-scale Privatization Act is based on the idea of auctions. The first wave of then was closed to foreigners.

These firms have got standard genetic code, they maximize their profit. Because of bad estimates, the auctioned prices were often too high. Banks provided credits in first stage as a "political task", without taking into account a solvency of clients. This bank support is way about 30 % of those firms (the starting number of them was about 22,000 firms, with book value of 23.6 billion Koruna, which was increased in auctions 1.5 times) have been closing till now. When we compare these numbers with the book or market value of firms privatized in large-scale privatization, the influence of small privatization on microeconomic climate could be passed over.

---

[5]Each of the top ten funds has got more than 100 billion voucher points, i.e. (aproximately) more than 300 millions Czechoslovak Koruna in shares. Source : M. Mejstřik,, M. Sojka (1992).

[6]A law concerning comflict of interests has not yet been accepted by MPs (maybe because of their commertial and privatizing interests). Even ministers have taken part (and have won, of course) in privatizing competition .

4.3 Firms with prevailing foreign capital

There are three options for foreign investors interested in penetrating into Czechoslovak economy: first, through the official privatization process; second, as an unofficial sleeping partner in small-scale privatization, third, by the purchase of the restitutioned property. Foreign capital, some officially acknowledged, began flowing into the Czechoslovak economy even before acceptance of Large Privatization Law and Restitution Law in October 1991.[7]

There are two possible reasons for the purchases of Czechoslovak firms by foreign investors (mostly from Germany). The first is to draw a profit from the many times cheaper, yet similarly skilled, workers in Czechoslovakia. The second reason could be the an attempt to liquidate competitors on the international market. Taking into account the quality of Czechoslovak products and its insignificant percentage from world economy, the second possibility could be passed over.

The producers discussed in this section, will behave in a standard market way, given by their genetic code, by their market origin. Therefore, one can expect that these firm will discharge from work all redundant employees.

Because of the considerable influx of unofficial capital from abroad, it is not possible to estimate its weight in the Czechoslovak economy. The influence of such capital is probably low, but it will increase after the decisions are made regarding the problem of splitting Czechoslovakia, currently the most significant reason for foreign investors' hesitation.

4.4 Direct Sales in Large-Scale Privatization

Direct sales to predetermined[8] buyer has a 19 % share of the total number of privatization projects (524 project out of 2795), but only a 3.3 % share as far as total property is concerned. These numbers will substantially increase, because voucher privatization proposals have been decided first, in order to start the first wave of voucher privatization on schedule.

Relatively small enterprises (with about 50 - 150 employees) are mostly privatized by direct sales. The majority of them will start with 100 % of their property in debt. Considering that every year they will have to pay about 20 - 25 % of the starting debt (mostly 20 - 25 % of initial book value) out of their profit, they will be under strong pressure to make profit.[9]

---

[7]The total value of capital inflow into Czechoslovakia in the year 1991 was 607 mil. US dollars. Most important capital inflows were :

Skoda - Volkswagen (Germany), 383.2 mil. US dollars
Sklo Union Teplice - Glaverbel (Belgium), 292 mil. US dollars
Rakona - Procter & Gamble (Germany)
Technoplyn - Linde (Germany), 17.3 mil. US dollars

[8]By Ministry of Privatization with approval of Czech (Slovak) government.

[9]And pay tax, of course, which is important for income side of state budget.

Therefore, one could expect :

- profit maximizing (excluding those firms making a net profit of more than 25 % of the initial book value. The number of such firms will be close to zero).
- relatively low wages
- high risk of bankruptcy
- frequent strikes (what will increase the threat of bankruptcy)
- very low (or no) investment activity

In these firms, the same people will play the roles of both owners and managers. As a result, after the last installment has been paid, after about four or five years, their behavior will change radically. Managers' wages will rapidly increase, costs such as new cars for managers or other tax avoidances will increase, profit will decrease, and employee wages will increase.

4.5 Firms Privatized By Public Auctions and Public Tender

The new Czech and Slovak governments elected in June 1992 prefer (according to their declarations) competition privatization methods (probably to avoid corruption of civil servants and to increase incomes of the state).

The difference between auction in small or large - scale privatization and public tender will be eliminated by currently preferred "envelope method" of buyer selection. All interested people or firms will have to print their bids and hide them in envelops. All such envelops will be opened at the same time and place, and the buyer who has written the highest amount will be chosen.

New owners will descended from :

- upstarts from illegal activity money laundering schemes),
- risk preferring people

After the bankruptcies of these firms, which will probably afflict the majority of them, one can expect, in general, standard profit maximizing behavior of firms founded by public auction or tender.

4.6 State Firms and Firms Privatized by Unpaid Transfer to Municipalities, Pension Funds Etc.

There is no reason to suppose a change in behavior of these firms. They will behave in the way described in the second section of this paper. The owner (state, municipalities) will not be able to compel managers to efficiency and as a guarantor of the survival of the firm he will have to subsidize them .

If the policy declared by the current Czech government is not changed, the number of these firms will be radically decreased in next two years, and, as a result, their influence on the economic climate will weaken.

5. ECONOMIC CLIMATE AT PRESENT AND EXPECTED IN THE UPCOMING YEARS

The contemporary economic climate is given by shares of the producers described in section four. The following table provides information about these shares for the Czech republic (June 30, 1992, source: M.Mejstřik, J.Burger (1992)):

Approved method of privatization	number of bus.	share units	total value of property (mil.Koruna)	share of property %
Public auction and tender	365	13.06	8602.8	1.99
Direct sale (state owned joint stock comp.including)	701	25.08	140803.8	32.57
Voucher privatization	943	33.74	229364.2	53.05
Unpaid transfers	786	28.12	7395.3	1.71
Property for restitutions			650.4	0.15
Property written off as unusable			10047.6	2.33
Small privatization			1177.1	0.26
Expected earnings from stock sale			427.2	0.10
Total	2795	100.00	423318.4	100.00

The economic climate in next several years will not be stable. Some changes will run smoothly and gradually, some will occur in jumps.

The gradual changes will be caused by higher risk of bankruptcy for firms privatized by non-standard methods.

The first jump, the first rapid change can be expected one year after the end of the first wave of voucher privatization, i.e. in the winter of 1993-1994. At this time, privatization funds will have to pay the promised money to their shareholders, prices in the capital market will decrease, and many firms will be purchased by new owners, mostly with standard (profit maximizing) behavior.

The second jump could be expected in the years 1996 - 1997. At that time, the majority of firms privatized by standard methods will be paying the last installment of their starting debts, and they will radically increase their costs.

A standard economic climate could be expected at the end of century, when the owner, manager and employee role will usually be played by different individuals. Until that time, the outcomes of neo-classical microeconomic theory can only be used for the Czech and Slovak republic only in a limited way.

REFERENCES

Burger J., Mejstrík M., First Round of Voucher Privatization Ends: 30 % of All Shares Sold. *Privatization Newsletter of Czechoslovakia,* Number 7, Prague 1992

Hlaváček J., Homo se assecurans. *Politická ekonomie 6,* Prague 1986

Hlaváček J., Mejstrîk M., Precondition for Privatization in Czechoslovakia in 1991, 1992. In: Earle J., Frydman R., Rapaczynski J. (ed.), *Studies of Privatization in Eastern Europe.* Central Europian University, Prague 1992

Mejstrík M., Sojka M., *Privatization and Regulatory Change: The Case of Czechoslovakia.* Faculty of Social Sciences, Charles University, Prague 1992

Milanović B., *Liberatization and Enterpreneurship Dynamics of Reform in Socialism and Capitalism.* Armonk, M.E., Sharpe, New York 1989

Tuma Z., *Inflation in 1985-1991: Case of Czechoslovakia.* Institute of Economics, Prague 1992

15

BARGAINING STRUCTURE AND WAGE DEVELOPMENT IN CZECHOSLOVAKIA[1]

Alena Buchtíková and Vladislav Flek
Institute of Economics
State Bank of Czechoslovakia

1. INTRODUCTION

Both from standard macroeconomic and microeconomic argumentation[2] follows the necessity of consistent conceptual approach within the creating of wage bargaining system (including the role of the state) also in the case of transformation of former central command economies toward market oriented ones. As usual for these economies, the current organizational structure of the trade unions is strongly concentrated, especially at the central and branch levels.

It is important to note that only the wage rate - and definitely not the level of employment and/or prices - is subject to explicit bargaining in Czechoslovakia. In other words, there are intuitively felt reasons for the existence of trade union monopoly power and its consequences to be regulated (Flek 1992).

While the necessity of "competition policy" in the post communist countries is quite often expressed, it is explicitly or implicitly understood mainly in connection with products and services markets (Izák 1992). It should be more discussed if there is the same necessity in connection with the

---

[1]The authors are research fellows in the Institute of Economics, State Bank of Czechoslovakia. The views expressed are those of the authors and do not necessarily represent those of the State Bank. We also wish to than A. Kotulan and J. Krovak for a lot of helpful comments on the earlier draft version of this study.

[2]See Oswald 1985, Pencavel 1985, Calmfors and Driffil 1988, Layard and Nickell 1990, inter alia

specific production factor market - on the by trade unions influenced labor market (Svejnar 1991).

There is so far a lack of analytical literature concerning given topic. So far, other transition issues are more popular. However, some important partial analyses exist (Burda 1991, Klacek et al. 1991, Janáček et al. 1992).

Therefore, a more detailed analysis of all relevant levels of trade unions - employers - government relations is needed. A quantitative analysis of wages, (un)employment and labor productivity developments since 1989 is needed as well.

We start from an overview of the institutional structure of wage bargaining in Czechoslovakia. Then we analyse wage development in Czechoslovakia during the investigated period with a help of empirical data.

2. WAGE BARGAINING STRUCTURE

The process of the affection of working conditions starts in the basic production units: in the factories and plants. The application of the norms, agreed upon at the higher levels of negotiations, are there concretized as well.

First we shall consider the character of workers' representation at this particular level and its influence on general non-wage working conditions.

Even at this stage of the analysis it is possible to point out a principal item of knowledge about the Czechoslovak structure of bargaining: there is no authentic (i.e. non-union) representation of the current staff that were independent of the trade unions. In other words, there is no institution which equals that of work council ("Betriebsrat" in German terminology).

The plurality of the trade union representation is accepted formally in each enterprise. Nevertheless, there is an essential differentiability between legitimate successors of the previous - now non-existent- communist trade unions(now Czechoslovak Confederation of Trade Unions - CSKOS) and those newly arisen, and often more radical trade unions.

The different attitudes concern the property, the membership and the fact that the government is negotiating in a centralised tripartite body exclusively with CSKOS.

The standard rights of European workers' representations can be classified as follows: right for information, right to be given a hearing, right to control, right to preliminary consultation of certain managerial decisions and veto power (Mitbestimmung 1980).

The most important fact is that the key condition of inevitable agreement, i.e. workers' representation veto power does not actually exist. This absence can be seen in Czechoslovakia just in the areas on which the concept of social partnership is based: agreement of the workers' representation with the rationalization measures, organisational and structural changes and with dismissals.

The possibility for wage bargaining at the plants themselves is considerably limited. The lower limit is usually defined by a generalized branch wage scale and the upper limit is given by the governmental wage regulation. The wage bargaining is realized by the enterprise trade union, led on behalf of all the workers irrespective of whether they are members of the trade union or not (unless there were more trade unions in the enterprise).

In addition, the reform of obsolete branch wage scales is realized slowly and we assume there are no terms for the coordination of this reform in particular branches. On the contrary, the limits of the governmental wage regulation are unified for all the enterprises of all branches. The consequences of this state will be more studied later.[3]

Now we shall investigate to which extent the workers' representation affects the top-management decision making. According to § 55 of the appropriate Czechoslovak law dealing with (state-owned) joint-stock companies, the delegates of the workers (i.e. of the trade unions) are entitled to one third of the staff of the supervisory boards on condition that the number of employees exceeds 200 workers.

The analogical law from 1990 dealt with the state-owned enterprises (which have not been converted into the form of state joint-stock companies) assumed the establishment of a special body of parity composed of the so-called founder (mainly the branch ministry) and the delegates of trade unions.

If the body such as a supervisory board possesses minimal formal rights as a whole, the same applies to the delegation of the trade union in this body. Only a third of trade union participation in the supervisory board is then of no significant importance. The appropriate body of the state-owned enterprise bore the similar feature when having only the right to be listened to by a founder and to recommend the change of the top-management.

An international comparison (Mitbestimming 1980, Niedenhoff 1990, Hoerr 1991) suggests that the trade unions are not the exclusive actors of representation of workers in the supervisory board (e.g. with the exception of Sweden). This particular form of workers' participation is more associated with the social partnership at the corporate level which is not necessarily mediated by the trade union (Fitz Roy 1988, Hoerr 1991).

The result of the analysis is similar to the level studied before: prevailing trade union monopoly for the representation of all workers and at the same time there are formally declared rights under the standards of social partnership. Neither can we conceptually identify these relations in Czechoslovakia as purely decentralized industrial relations: enterprise trade unions are incorporated into the hierarchical structure which over branch levels leads to the centralized national and/or federal tripartite. Besides,

[3]Since 1989 the difference between the average wage in the manufacturing and non-manufacturing sector has been diminished. However, the wages in health services, judiciary and science are below the average wage rate in Czechoslovakia: the wage in the fuel industry is 75% higher than those in culture and 55% higher than those in education and 42% higher than in health services. The salaries of doctors are equal to agrarians' salaries in the state farms (Janáček et al., 1992, p. 25).

the trade union right to participate in supervisory boards is guaranteed by law, which is not usual for the decentralized industrial relations such as in the UK or USA.

In Czechoslovakia there is not such a strong concentration of industrial trade union, as can be found in Germany, Austria or Sweden. Nevertheless, the hierarchical structure of the negotiations is given and also collective agreements of a higher type are obligatory for subordinate trade union organisations: both for members and non-members of the trade union.

On the one hand there is a relatively strong structure of the branch (industrial, professional) trade unions which has been actually established. On the other hand, due to the present governmental wage regulation and the lack of large private employers in the industry, this structure has not started to function so far considering all its standard consequences. This is the reason why the trade union activities were more oriented to unofficial actions with disputable legality. Thus the (branch, industrial, professional) trade union exert the pressure on the personnel composition of the top-management, on the removal of ministers unwilling to cooperate according to trade union requirements, on influencing of governmental subsidy-, structural- and price policy.

In 1991 and in the beginning of 1992 the number of the pressure actions rose (railway and bus transport, mining, agriculture, air traffic controllers etc.). The aims, the ways of the declaration of these actions and their legality were disputable and as was repeatedly illustrated they have not been agreed clearly by the plenary basis of trade union.[4] The legal controversy of these actions is reflected even in the publications which present opinions close to those of trade unions. It is stated hereby that the strikes held up-to-now are not supported by any law: "The common denominator of these actions is the disagreement with state ministries ... The strike by law ... has not held so far or there has not been any threat" (Subrt 1991. p. 31).

The rising strength of the trade unions thus can be seen mainly in the area of non-wage requirements. The general unwillingness to follow the law caused that the law proved to be an inefficient instrument of regulation: "In most plants the strike was called by the branch-centre of the trade union" (i.e. without previous agreement of the staff of the enterprises - A.B.,V.F.) "The most of enterprises paid the full wages to the strikers" (Bulletin FSO, No. 7, 1992, p. A 16).

The tripartite approach is based on the centralized level of the cooperation of the state, trade union and employers.

---

[4]By law, the strike must be approved by at least a half of the staff of each enterprise and the strike can be called only to reach the collective agreement for the upcoming period. These conditions were not fulfilled by the trade unions at all, as well as others were not respected. In Article 18, paragraph 1 of the Collective Bargaining Law there are namely the following statements: "The strike is the extreme means in the dispute how to reach the collective agreement." It is stated in § 22: "The strike is illegal in case there were no further negotiations in presence of arbitration... or after achievement of the collective agreement" (letter b), "is exclusively of political nature" (letter h), "it is solitary" (letter j).

The analogy of the Czechoslovak system with these rules - considering their original rather than present form - is also confirmed by the studies made abroad, even if they suggest implicitly the controversy of the chosen solution:

> "The tripartite approach along the lines of Austria or Sweden has been adopted as a collective bargaining model ... Unions enjoy little popularity, especially at the national level "(Burda 1991, p. 120).

In any case, the anti-inflationary wage regulation accompanied by a significant fall of real wages for 1991 was the only tangible outcome of the Czechoslovak tripartite system. It could be understood as a part of the general governmental anti-inflationary policy as well as the sign of the achievement of the consensus with the trade unions about this policy.

Czechoslovak tripartite body declared by itself and very ambitiously the general obligation of its statements for the entire economy: "The negotiating parties will assure the fulfillment of the obligations accepted for all the employers and employees" (the General agreement for 1991).

Particularly the part III. of this agreement stated that the contractory parties should have dealt with the partial adjustment of nominal wages and should have adjusted the federal unified minimum wage to the development of the cost-of-living index (CLI), too.

The initial consensus about the wage regulation for the year 1991 was reflected by Czechoslovak government in its Direction No. 15/1991, which was adopted on 3rd January 1991. The status of this direction can be compared to that of law. In this way there has been established the construction according to which every enterprise except small private enterprises was forced not to exceed the maximum permissible wage level (WM) without being sanctioned.

The basis for the calculation of WM was created by three items: the unified federal limit (WG) of nominal wage growth allowable for (single quarters) 1991, given structure of branch wage tariffs (WT) being mainly approved in the period before 1989 and finally the percentage share of bonuses in the wage bill (WBS) (excluded the bonuses paid from profit) in every enterprise according to 1990:

$$WM_{91} = WT_{89} * \frac{100 + WG91}{100} * \frac{100 + WBS90}{100} \qquad \text{(i)}$$

In addition to the given quarterly percentage limits of nominal wage growth there was another 3% range for further growth which was free of sanctions. The excession of the given wage maximum by more than 3% would be sanctioned: if the enterprises exceeded WM by 3 up to 5%, the sanction would represent 200%, and in case of the excession over 5% the sanction would be 750%.

The basis for the establishment of the amount of sanctions was the following relation: the actual quarterly wage bill / WM * 100%. In 1991 the wage regulation included the bonuses paid from the profit, too. Simply said, the total wage bill including bonuses paid from profit (WA) was not allowed to exceed the amount of WM + 20%. Industrial data of FSO were as follows:

Table 1

CLI, WG and WA: the development in 1991 (the percentage growth in comparison with 1990

	I.Q.	II.Q.	III.Q.	IV.Q.	91/90
CLI	44.41	54.65	58.11	61.12	54.32
WG *	9 /12/	22 /25/	29 /32/	32 /35/	23 /26/
WA **	4.72	13.58	13.83	35.12	16.38

* the maximum admissible % growth of nominal wages except the bonuses paid from profits
** the actual nominal wage growth including bonuses paid from profits

It is characteristic for the whole construction that the payment of the maximum possible volume of wages with the use of centrally fixed WG for single quarters was in 1991 in fact dependent on the ability and/or willingness of each enterprise to pay these wages. Therefore, it was only the possibility at issue, and not the wage claim. And thus the development of magnitudes given in Table 1 is explained.

Presumably this important nuance was not consulted enough when signing the General agreement for 1991. And thus this fact became the subject of the misunderstanding from the side of trade unions and therefore they attempted to call a general strike (mainly in Slovak Republic).[5]

Trade unions insisted on the recognition of the maximum admissible nominal wage growth according to WG as a wage claim. A similar problem arose in the case of the federal unified minimum wage which should have been adjusted "irrespective of the professional classification, the activity performed, the results obtained and the solvency of the employer" (the General agreement for 1991).

This principle was declared in the article 10 of the appropriate part of the General agreement, but it could not be abode by the government for quite clear economic reasons. Minimal wage was initially set for a level of 2,000 CSK a month and it was partially adjusted only once: up to 2,200 CSK without full respect to the dramatic growth of CLI. It is important to note

[5]Only some Slovak enterprises recorded the data from 1991 about strikes in their official statistics. According to these dates, there were 48,860 striking workers in 7 large enterprises. FSO states that in the first half of 1992 there were 45 Czech enterprises on strike with 1,800 workers, besides 15,000 bus drivers.

that the average nominal wage rate was 3,292 CSK for 1990 and 3,782 CSK for 1991 (Bulletin FSO 1/92, p.A18). According to the official data dealing only with Czechoslovak industry, following wage development of average nominal wage rate was stated: 3,456 CSK for 1990, 4022 CSK for 1991 (Monthly Statistics of Czechoslovakia, 12/91, 5/92).

And thus it is evident that in the case of a permanent obligatory valorization of minimum wage it would lead to the destruction of the whole system of wage tariffs. Minimum wage could exceed in the case of its permanent adjustment even the level of the average nominal wage rate.

Czechoslovak tripartite body also dealt with the reading of nearly all the laws concerning the economic and social area and, of course, the strategy of the economic transformation was discussed there, too.

However, this "cooperation" was not supported by real and namely constitutional power to make the key decisions concerning the strategy and norms of the economic reform. Anyway, the trade unions were practically not able to change the governmental "suggestions" and/or to refuse them at all.

After finding the actual results of wage regulation during 1991 the initial consensus concerning this measure was dissolved very fast.

The crystallized preferences of the trade union leaders and their prospective attitudes to the centralized tripartite system can be illustrated by the following statement of the top trade union leader in Czech republic, V. Petrus, quoted in the publication: "Trade unions are of the opinion that wage regulation actually represents an anti-reform measure, which is not consistent with market economy, because ... it conserves overemployment..." (Mladá fronta Dnes, 14. 4. 1992, p. 1).

Considering all these facts the question of further duration of wage regulation for 1992 was hotly debatable. Its future has not been clear nearly for the whole first half of the year, namely because of the disagreement of trade unions. The signing of the General agreement for 1992 has been continuously postponed, too.

Essentially there were no rules available about the limits referring to the wage growth for the first half of 1992. The enterprises, however, either for this reason, or for not having more money did not substantially exceed the limits of wage regulation from 1991. According to our preliminary data, the industrial average nominal wage rate has increased in comparison with the end of 1991 by some 10%, while in case of the real industrial wage by some 3%. The absence of the agreement about wage regulation for 1992 caused that the government began to warn the trade unions of the bare fact that the direction of wage regulation is in their exclusive legal competence after all.

The government originally was considering about the average nominal wage rate growth for 1992 by 12%. It corresponded to the expected inflation. Due to the attitudes of the trade unions a more substantial wage differentiation has been approved: the enterprises were divided into several groups with different rules of wage regulation according to actual profit/production cost ratio achieved. Anyway, the expected 12% growth for 1992 has remained. It is generally supposed that for 1993 the wage regulation will be abolished totally.

Finally the Federal government introduced the rules of wage regulation by its Direction No. 260/1992 in a more liberal form in comparison with the year 1991. These rules are to be kept only in the enterprises, where the share of state represents more than 50%.

On the contrary, the rules of wage regulation do not refer to a private sector, cooperatives, and newly arisen production units (with the exception of re-organized ones) and also in the enterprises where the share of foreign investors represents at least 30%.

The construction of wage regulation for the rest of 1992 is created by the actual volume of the regulated wages paid to the workers during the aliquot basic period in 1991 (WBP 91) and taking into consideration the changes in the employment between the basic period and the present one, too (L_{92-91}).

There have been established three ranges of the percentage nominal wage growth (WG) in dependence on profit/production costs ratio:

Entrepreneurial subject	WG
a) banks	0 %
b) others	
- p/p.c. ratio up to 12%	10(12) %
- p/p.c. ratio over 12%	15(17) %

The sanction rates for the excession of limits are analogous to those in 1991. The construction of maximal admissible wage growth is as follows:

$$WM_{92} = WBP_{91} * \frac{L/92\text{-}91/}{100} * \frac{100 + WG92}{100} \qquad \text{(ii)}$$

While the results of standard bargaining between employers and trade unions have the character of wage claim, the governmental wage regulation implies the whole process as a "possibility" again.

In addition, it appears to make it advantageous for the enterprises which in the period 1991 exhausted as high wage bill within the wage regulation as possible.

As the wage regulation for 1992 in comparison with 1991 is much more liberal, the same applies to the reading of the General agreement for 1992. The agreement does not even include any rules or, at least, consensus concerning the wage regulation for 1992. It decrees only such obligations of the government, which would have to be fulfilled in any case: the due respect for the internationally binding social norms, the active employment policy, the guaranty of unemployment benefits etc.

From the range of codetermination rights, the trade unions are again given only the very elementary ones: the right for information and the right for consultation of certain decisions without veto power. Nevertheless, the General agreement does not even include any specific obligations from the side of the trade unions.

3. THE DATA

The general picture characterizing the results of prevailing wage regulation was outlined. However, there is a need of description of the database used for computations. The official source of the given database "Industrial Companies" is Federal Statistical Office (FSO). The data are originated from Profit and Loss Accounts and Balance Sheets of Czechoslovak industrial enterprises which are obliged to fill in these accounting formulas and send them for processing to statistical bodies. Firms employing less than 100 persons are excluded from this scheme. Therefore, the database is not complete - but it is perhaps the best available source of data about companies that can be found in Czechoslovakia now (Buchtíková, Capek and Macourková 1992, Křovák, Buchtíkova and Macourková 1992).

This database includes 1702 industrial companies for 1989, 2016 companies for 1990-1991 and 2355 companies for 1992*.

Data	Formula/Source
L^{**} -numberof employees	database "Industrial Companies"
w^{**} -total year wages	database "Industrial Companies"
w_a -average nominal wage rate	w/(12*L) for 1989-1991 w/(6*L) for 1992
OG^{**} -output of goods at const. prices 1989	database "Industrial Companies"
LP -labor productivity	OG/L for 1989-1991 2*OG/L for 1992
CLI -cost-of-living index	BULLETIN FSO 1/92, 7/92
w_r -average real data wage rate	w_a/CLI
p^{**} -profit	database "Industrial Companies"
VA^{**} -value added	$w+p^{***}$
d.s.**** -distribution share of wages in value added	w/VA
w_i -relative wage of branch	$w_a(1\text{-}5)/w_a(\text{all})^{*****}$

* - for 1992 the data for the first half of 1992 were used

** - these data were computed for branches as aggregates of original data from the database "Industrial Companies"

*** - we are aware of the possible shortcomings of this formula, but we hope that it is sufficient for our purpose, i.e. to show the proportions of distribution between profits and wages

**** - for the first half of 1992 the data about profit were available only for 921 companies; the d.s. obtained is then estimated to be the same for all companies.

***** - w_a(1-5) - average nominal wage rate of branch

w_a(all) - average nominal wage rate of all branches

For the purpose of our analysis it is possible to create four basic tables (see Tables 2-5). To take the officially published industrial data of statistical bodies into account, available data of the FSO dealing with the entire industry are introduced, too. The potential differences are caused by our desegregation at the branch levels which is different in comparison with given official source. Moreover, as specified further, our investigation does not include all branches of Czechoslovak industry consequently.

We are dealing with following branches:

1 - fuel & energ. - includes fuel industry and production of electric power and heat;

2 - heavy ind. - includes iron and steel industries, non-ferrous metallurgy and chemical and rubber industries;

3 - eng. & electr. - includes engineering and electrotechnical industry;

4 - light ind. - includes woodworking industry, metalworking industry, pulp and paper industry, glass, china and stoneware industries, textile industry, clothing industry, leather, boot-and-shoe and furrier industries and printing industry;

5 - food & tobac. - includes food industry and cooling and tobacco industries.

Table 2

The Development of Variables*

Branch	average nominal wage rate - W_a (CSK)				number of employees - L				Labor productivity - LP (Thous. CSK/1 employee)			
	1989	1990**	1991	1992	1989	1990**	1991	1992	1989	1990**	1991	1992
1-fuel and energy	4285.50	4346.18	5249.65	5868.09	313020	270345	250232	232760	334.25	312.11	318.11	310.51
2-heavy ind.	3689.14	3801.04	4585.56	5129.88	396798	382070	343296	311417	594.90	545.20	455.85	467.17
3-energy and electricity	3199.57	3354.95	3840.27	4420.54	925905	875643	755218	677672	257.38	253.29	199.19	174.79
4-light ind.	2899.62	3040.83	3489.54	3855.51	703673	682238	595707	565701	245.42	250.09	198.88	199.59
5-food and tobacco	3024.73	3144.91	3825.24	4230.53	211981	198763	178634	162629	836.51	808.24	750.59	701.81
all	3311.69	3430.65	4027.22	4464.29	2551377	2409059	2123087	1950179	363.40	351.07	301.01	288.82
FSO	3332.00	3428.00	4022.00	4448.00	2623200	2533700	2230600	n.a.	350.00	349.00	298.60	n.a.

Table 3

The Development of Variables

Branch	average real wage rate - W_r (CSK)				distribution share of wages in value added - d.s.				relative wage - w_i			
	1989	1990	1991	1992	1989	1990	1991	1992	1989	1990	1991	1992
1-fuel and energy	4285.50	3954.67	3106.30	3196.13	0.52	0.40	0.20	0.15	1.29	1.27	1.30	1.31
2-heavy ind.	3689.14	3458.64	2713.35	2794.05	0.53	0.47	0.39	0.37	1.11	1.11	1.14	1.15
3-energy and electricity	3199.57	3052.73	2272.35	2309.66	0.64	0.62	0.60	0.60	0.97	0.98	0.95	0.95
4-light ind.	2899.62	2766.91	2064.82	2099.95	0.62	0.57	0.52	0.57	0.88	0.89	0.87	0.86
5-food and tobacco	3024.73	2861.61	2263.46	2304.21	0.57	0.56	0.33	0.33	0.91	0.92	0.95	0.95
all	3311.69	3121.61	2382.97	2431.53	0.59	0.53	0.40	0.33	1.00	1.00	1.00	1.00

Table 4
% Change of variables

Branch	w_a			LP			L		
	90/89 **	91/90	92/91	90/89 **	91/90	92/91	90/89 **	91/90	92/91
1-fuel & energ.	1.42	20.79	11.78	6.62	1.92	-2.39	13.63	-7.44	-6.98
2-heavy ind.	3.03	20.64	11.87	8.35	-16.39	2.48	3.71	-10.15	-9.29
3-eng & electr.	4.86	14.47	10.42	1.59	-21.36	-12.25	5.43	-13.75	-10.27
4-light ind.	4.87	14.76	10.49	1.90	-20.48	0.36	3.05	-12.68	-5.04
5-food & tobac.	3.97	21.63	10.60	-3.38	-7.13	-6.50	-6.24	-10.13	-8.96
all	3.59	17.39	10.85	-3.39	-14.26	-4.05	-5.58	-11.87	-8.14
FSO	2.90	17.30	n.a.	-0.3 ***	-14.40	n.a.	-3.40	-12.00	n.a.

*) Building materials industry and "not specified" small industrial branches are there not included as well as construction, transport etc. which are not counted into the "industry" in the Czechoslovak statistic system.

**) Above all other mentioned reasons, the differences between our database and official source (FSO) are for 1990 caused by the following problem : There are two available sets of data concerning 1990. The first one was derived from database 1989/1990, and, on the contrary, the second one from 1990/1991. To achieve the compatibility with further years, the second database is used by authors, while the first one by FSO.

***) In our investigation, labor productivity is computed from the output of goods consequently. However, for 1989, the official source computed LP from gross output.

Table 5
% Change of variables

Branch	w_r			d.s.			w_i		
	90/89	91/90	92/91	90/89	91/90	92/91	90/89	91/90	92/91
1-fuel & energ.	-7.72	-21.45	2.89	-23.08	-50.00	-25.00	-1.55	2.36	0.77
2-heavy ind.	-6.25	-21.55	2.97	-11.32	-17.02	-5.13	0.00	2.70	0.88
3-eng & electr.	-4.59	-25.56	1.64	-3.13	-3.23	0.00	1.03	-3.06	0.00
4-light ind.	-4.58	-25.37	1.70	-8.06	-8.77	9.62	1.14	-2.25	-1.15
5-food & tobac.	-5.39	-20.90	1.80	-1.75	-41.07	0.00	1.10	3.26	0.00
all	-5.74	-23.66	2.04	-10.17	-24.53	-17.50	0.00	0.00	0.00

4. THE ANALYSIS OF WAGE DEVELOPMENT

In this Section we try to characterize wage development under wage regulation at the same time accompanied by a lack of wage bargaining in the usual sense.

Figure 1
The development of d.s. in the branches and at the industry level (1989-June, 1992).

branch d.s. industry d.s.

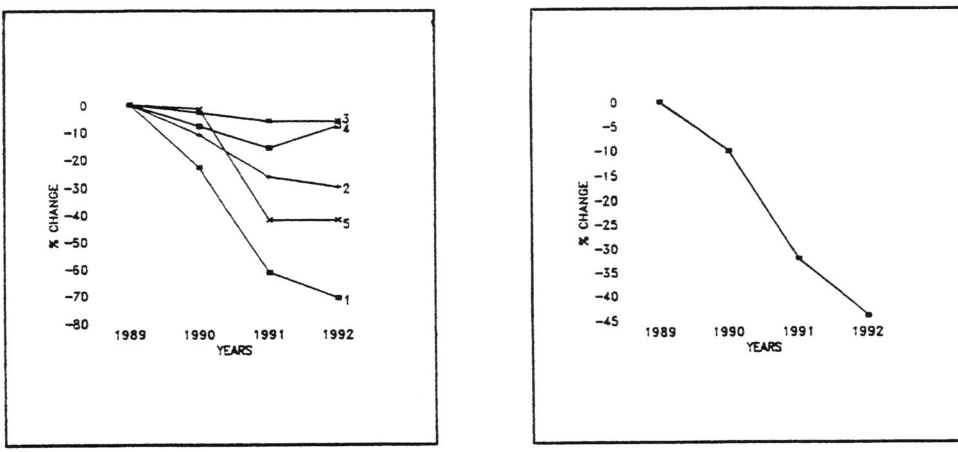

BRANCH 1 - fuel and energy
BRANCH 2 - heavy industry
BRANCH 3 - eng. and electr.
BRANCH 4 - light industry
BRANCH 5 - food and tobacco

Figure 1 describes the actual development of d.s. during the investigated period. It is possible to verify the intuitively felt finding: during the practically full price liberalization and parallel wage regulation in Czechoslovakia, the share of wages in value added has been lowered dramatically, too. It was to happen in all branches of Czechoslovak industry as well as at the entire industry level.

But it is necessary to underline that the (full) adjustment of d.s. is neither realistic nor acceptable in the current Czechoslovak conditions, especially in a short run. But the extent of the fall of d.s. could be relevant for an international comparison.

The governmental wage regulation has been accompanied by "undesirable" redistribution between wages and profits from the point of view of (rational) trade union.

The lowest decrease of d.s. was recorded in branch 3: eng. & electr., i.e. from 0.64 in 1989 to 0.60 in 1992. On the contrary, the highest one in branch 1: fuel & energ., i.e. from 0.52 to 0.15. For the entire industry the following decrease of d.s. was stated: from O.59 in 1989 to 0.33 in 1992.

Figure 2

The development of real wages in the branches and at the industry level (1989-June, 1992).

branch w_r industry w_r

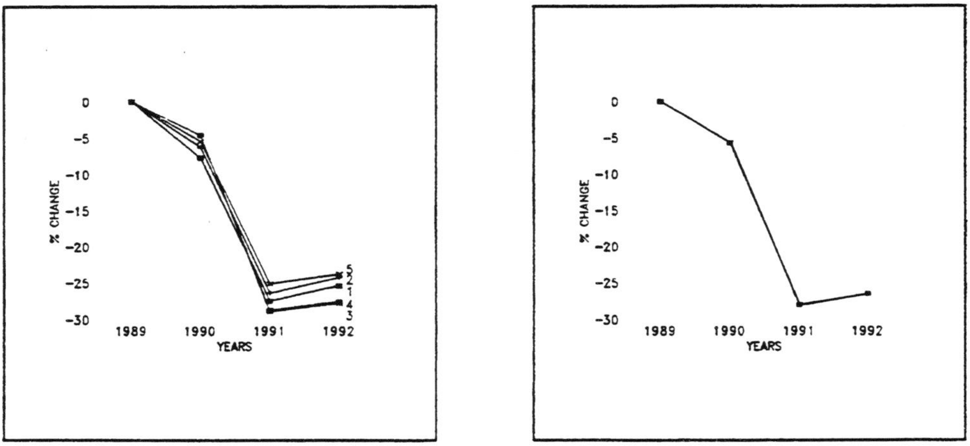

BRANCH 1 - fuel and energy
BRANCH 2 - heavy industry
BRANCH 3 - eng. and electr.
BRANCH 4 - light industry
BRANCH 5 - food and tobacco

Figure 2 illustrates the development of real wages at the branch levels as well as at the entire industry level. The level of real wages has been lowered dramatically, too - with an exception of (June) 1992. On one hand, the recent development in 1992 might be regarded as a sign of certain success of the reform strategy in connection with wage development. Due to the expected price increases in the second half of 1992 and tax reform in 1993, the real wage stabilization might so far not to be judged as a long-term phenomenon, on the other hand, especially in connection with prevailing overemployment and decreasing labor productivity. However, the increase of real wage for 1992 is officially expected by some 7-10%.

The most significant real wage decrease was observed in branch 3: eng. and electr., i.e. from 3200 CSK in 1989 to 2310 CSK in 1992 (27.81%). The lowest, on the contrary, was this decrease in branch 5: food and tobacco, i.e. from 3025 CSK to 2304 CSK (23.82%). The decrease of w_r by some 27% was recorded at the entire industry level during the given period (i.e. from 3312 CSK to 2432 CSK).[6]

---

[6]It is not quite usual to introduce the development of real wage in CSK. It means that for each year the current average nominal wage rate is divided by the appropriate CLI where 1989 is the basic period.

The key task of the governmental wage regulation, as a part of its general anti inflationary stabilization policies during the transitory period, was fulfilled "successfully". Perhaps only the high extent of real wage decrease can be in doubt.[7]

The relative wage was at strongest decreasing in branch 4: light industry (from O.88 in 1989 to O.86 in 1992). The opposite development was at most significant extent present in branch 5: food and tobacco (from O.91 to O.95). Therefore, no dramatic change in the structure of branch relative wages was recorded.

Figure 3

The development of relative wages within the Czechoslovak industry (1989-30.6.1992).

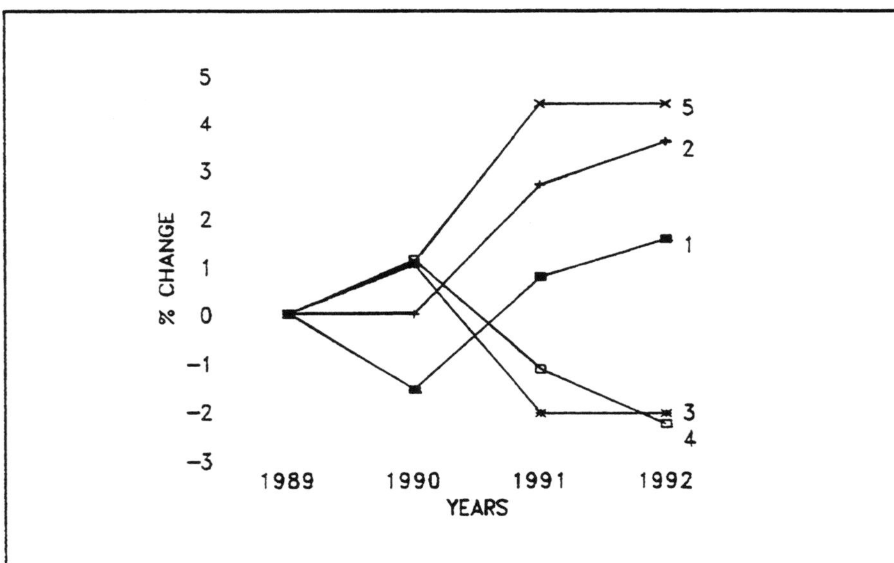

In other words, the structure of relative industrial wages has not been changed substantially due to the governmental wage regulation implemented during the transitory period in Czechoslovakia.

[7] "The current relative strength of government as well as the weakness of unions and employers should allow the government to engineer a significant real wage reduction. At the same time the support for the government in its role will be crucial." (Burda 1991, p. 120).

Table 7 describes the development of percentage change of average nominal wage rate ($\%\Delta w_a$) as well as the development of employment ($\%\Delta L$). We are aware of the fact that the analysis of nominal wage development has no significant economic meaning for analysis. It is introduced only to achieve the complete picture. Anyway, the nominal wage is an outcome of wage bargaining after all.

Table 7

The development of w_a and L (percentage changes) in Czechoslovak industry (1989-June, 1992) :

	% growth of w_a		% decrease of L
$w_{a(90/89)}$	+3.59	$L_{90/89}$	-5.58
$w_{a(91/90)}$	+17.39	$L_{91/90}$	-11.87
$w_{a(92/91)}$	+10.85	$L_{92/91}$	-8.14

The opposite development of both variables is most significant in branch 5: food & tobacco ($\%\Delta w_{a(92/89)}$ = +39.86%; $\%\Delta L_{92/89}$=-23.28%), while the most "close" one in branch 4: light industry ($\%\Delta w_{a(92/89)}$ = +32.97%; $\%\Delta L_{92/89}$ =-19.61%). At the entire industry level the differences between the development of both variables were as follows: $\%\Delta w_{a(92/89)}$ =+34.80%, $\%\Delta L_{92/89}$ =-23.56% (Figure 4).

Different wage-employment relation is obviously recorded if the development of real wage is taken into account (Figure 4). At the industry level, $\%\Delta w_{r(92/89)}$ =-26.58%, while $\%\Delta L_{92/89}$ =-23.56%.

The validity of relation: $\%w_{r(92/89)} < \%\Delta L_{92/89}$ is present in all branches with only one exception (branch 1: fuel and energy) where $\%\Delta w_{r(92/89)}$ =-25.42%, while $\%\Delta L_{92/89}$ =-25.64%.

Table 8

The development of w_r and L (percentage changes) in Czechoslovak industry (1989-June, 1992) :

	% change of w_r		% decrease of L
$w_{r(90/89)}$	-5.74	$L_{90/89}$	-5.58
$w_{r(91/90)}$	-23.66	$L_{91/90}$	-11.87
$w_{r(92/91)}$	+2.04	$L_{92/91}$	-8.14

It is possible to argue that during the period of the governmental wage regulation the fall of real wages was deeper than the decrease of employment.

Figure 4

The development of average nominal wage rate (w_a), real wage rate (w_r) and employment (L) in the branches and at the industry level (1989-June 1992).

BRANCH 1 - fuel and energy

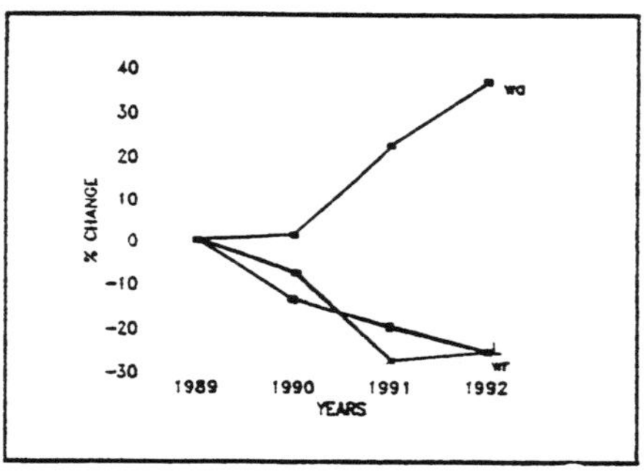

BRANCH 2 - heavy industry

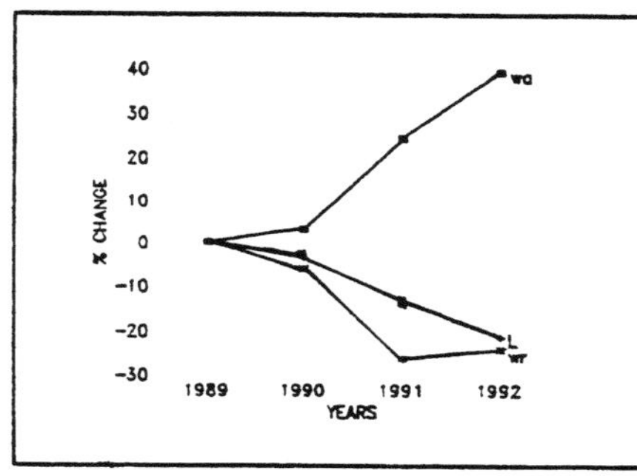

BRANCH 3 - eng. and electr.

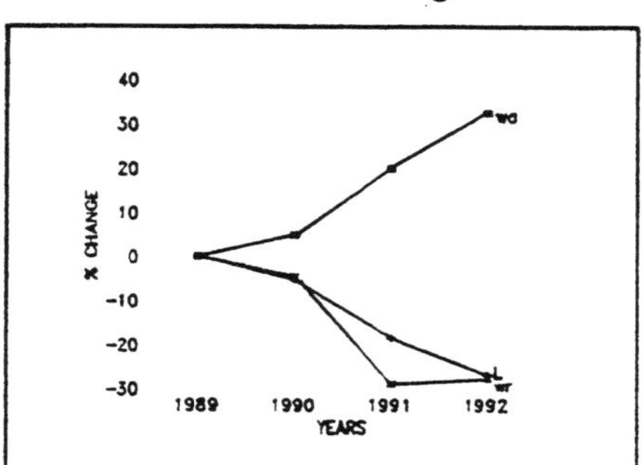

BRANCH 4 - light industry

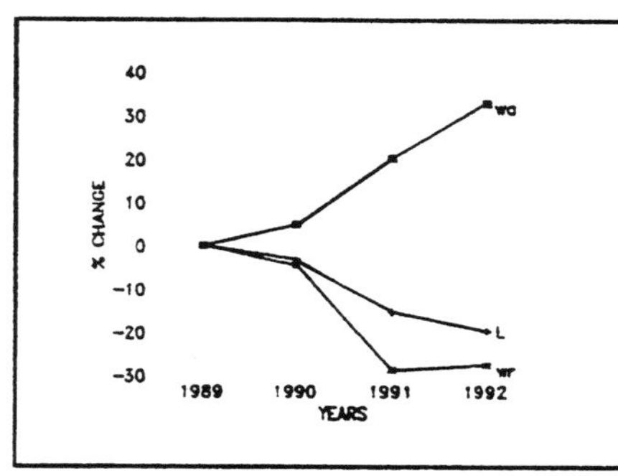

BRANCH 5 - food and tobacco

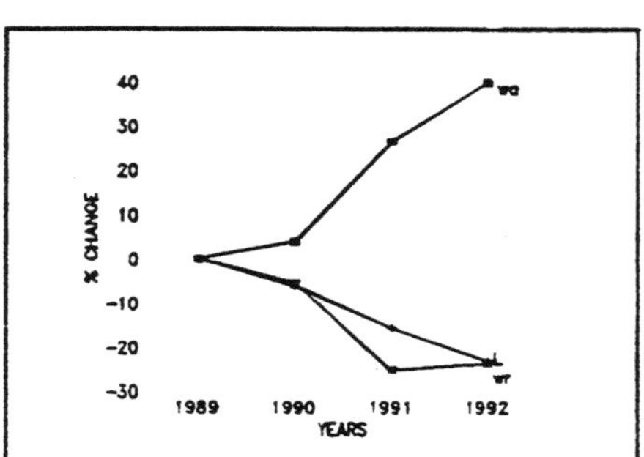

INDUSTRY

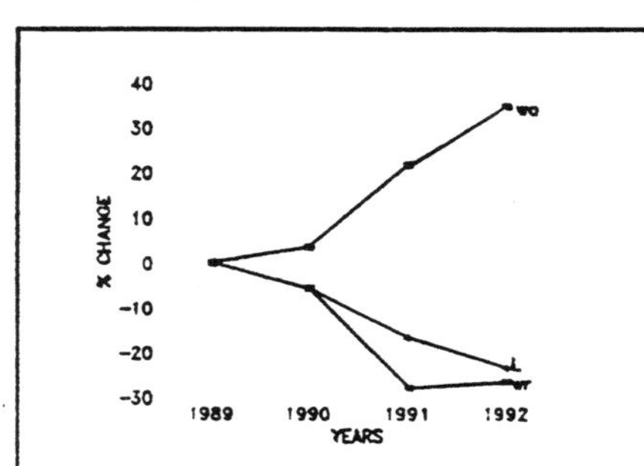

It is necessary to compare also the wage development with that of labor productivity (LP). At first, w_a (current) and LP (deflated) are compared:

Table 9

The development of w_a and LP (percentage changes) in Czechoslovak industry (1989-June, 1992) :

	% growth of w_a		% decrease of LP
$w_{a(90/89)}$	+3.59	$LP_{90/89}$	-3.39
$w_{a(91/90)}$	+17.39	$LP_{91/90}$	-14.26
$w_{a(92/91)}$	+10.85	$LP_{92/91}$	4.05

The gap between these variables is growing (Figure 5). It means that the larger mass of money wages is paid for the smaller comparable amount of the goods produced by current staff during wage regulation.

This gap is the largest in the branch 3: eng. & electr. ($\%\Delta w_{a(92/89)}$ = +32.53%; $\%\Delta LP_{92/89}$ =-32.09%), while the "smallest" one in the branch 1: fuel & energy ($\%\Delta w_{a(92/89)}$ = +36.93%; $\%\Delta LP_{92/89}$ =-7.10%). At the entire industry level the results are as follows:

($\%\Delta w_{a(92/89)}$ = +34.80%; $\%\Delta LP_{92/89}$ =-20.52%)

Figure 5

The development of average nominal wage rate (w_a), real wage rate (w_r) and labor productivity (LP) the branches and at the industry level (1989-June, 1992).

BRANCH 1 - fuel and energy

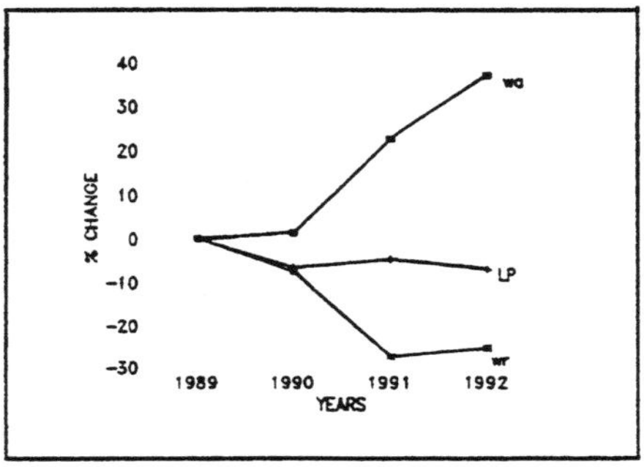

BRANCH 2 - heavy industry

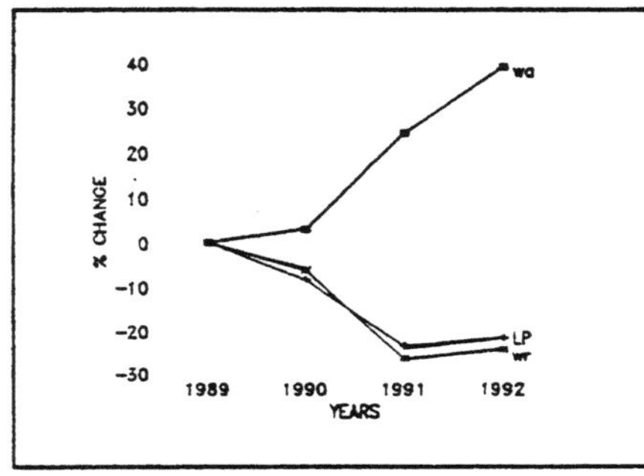

BRANCH 3 - eng. and electr.

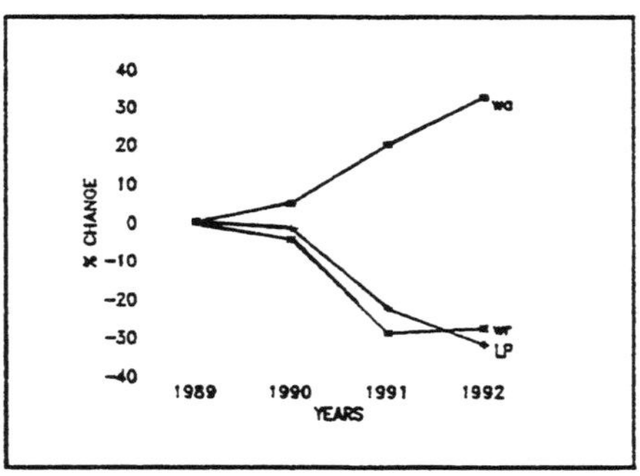

BRANCH 4 - light industry

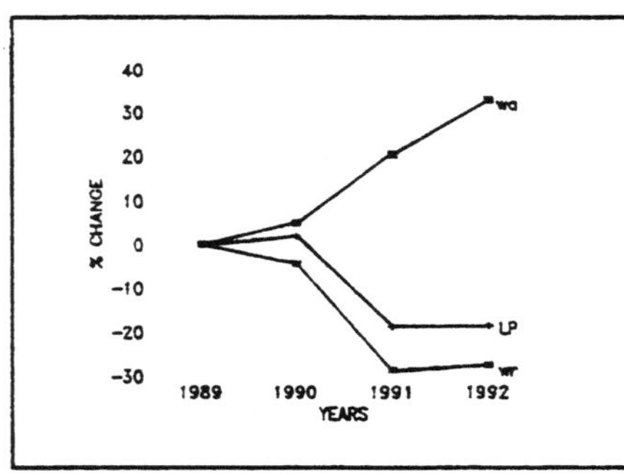

BRANCH 5 - food and tobacco

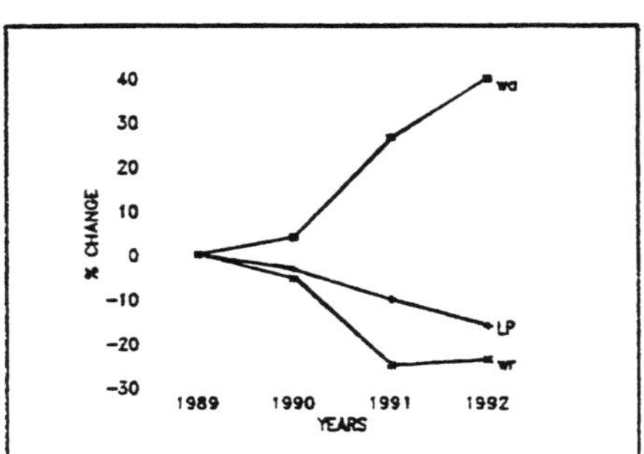

INDUSTRY

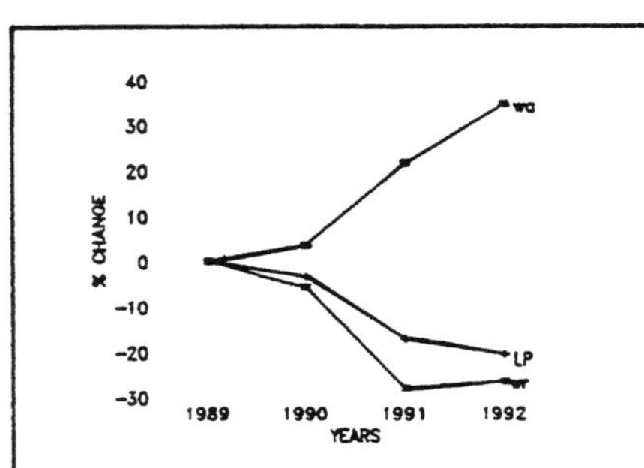

Table 10
The development of w_r and LP (percentage changes) in Czechoslovak industry (1989-June, 1992) :

	% change of w_r		% decrease of LP
$w_{r(90/89)}$	-5.74	$LP_{90/89}$	-3.39
$w_{r(91/90)}$	-23.66	$LP_{91/90}$	-14.26
$w_{r(92/91)}$	+2.04	$LP_{92/91}$	-4.05

Looking at these data, we see that the decrease of real wage was faster than the decrease of labor productivity (LP) during the period of the governmental wage regulation (with exception of branch 3: eng. and electr.).

At the entire industry level $\%\Delta w_{r(92/89)}$ = -26.58%, while $\%\Delta LP_{92/89}$ =-20.52%. The most different development of both variables can be observed in the branch 1: fuel & energy ($\%\Delta w_{r(92/89)}$ = -25.42%; $\%\Delta LP_{92/89}$ =-7.10%), while the most common one in the branch 2: heavy industry ($\%\Delta w_{r(92/89)}$ = -24.26%; $\%\Delta LP_{92/89}$ =-21.47%).

The relations of d.s. with L and LP are remaining to be judged. Unfortunately, there is so far a lack of available data about the development of the value added at constant prices. Our LP constructed according to output of goods at constant prices 1989 is not suitable for this purpose.

We can only state that the d.s. has been lowered dramatically during the governmental wage regulation - this development is characterized even with higher dynamics than the parallel decrease of employment (with exception of branch 3, where $\%\Delta d.s._{92/89}$ = -6.25% and $\%\Delta L_{92/89}$ = -20.81% and branch 4, where $\%\Delta d.s._{92/89}$ = -8.06% and $\%\Delta L_{92/89}$ = -11.54%.

The gap between the dynamics of d.s. decrease and L decrease is at higher extent to be observed in branch 1 (fuel & energy) where $\%\Delta d.s._{92/89}$ = -71.15%, while $\%\Delta L_{92/89}$ = -25.64%. The most "common" development of both variables, on the contrary, is present in branch 2 (heavy industry), where $\%\Delta d.s._{92/89}$ = -30.19%, while $\%\Delta L_{92/89}$ = -21.52%. The gap at the industry level is as follows: $\%\Delta d.s._{92/89}$ = -44.07%; $\%\Delta L_{92/89}$ = -23.56%

Table 11
The development of d.s. and L (percentage changes) in Czechoslovak industry (1989-June, 1992) :

	% decrease of d.s.		% decrease of L
$d.s._{90/89}$	10.17	$L_{90/89}$	-5.58
$d.s._{91/90}$	24.53	$L_{91/90}$	-11.87
$d.s._{92/91}$	17.50	$L_{92/91}$	-8.14

5. CONCLUSION

The main results obtained through our analysis of the wage development are as follows:

1/ The so far governmental wage regulation was accompanied by a strongly negative development of the share of total industrial nominal wages in the industrial value added ($d.s._{89} = 0.59$, $d.s._{92} = 0.33$);

2/ the wage regulation was accompanied by a recent decrease of the industrial real wage ($w_{r(89)}$= 3312 CSK, $w_{r(92)}$ = 2432 CSK);

3/ the development of relative wages within the industry was practically neutral to the current wage regulation;

4/ the dynamics of the industrial real wage decrease was higher than the dynamics of the parallel decrease of employment ($\%\Delta w_{r(92/89)}$ =-26.58%, $\%\Delta L_{92/89}$ = -23.56%);

5/ the dynamics of the industrial real wage decrease was higher than the dynamics of the parallel decrease of labor productivity, too ($\%\Delta w_{r(92/89)}$ = -26.58%, $\%\Delta LP_{92/89}$ = -20.52%);

6/ the share of the total industrial nominal wages in the industrial value added has not only been lowered dramatically : the dynamics of this development was higher than the dynamics of the decrease of employment ($\%\Delta d.s._{92/89}$ = -44.07%; $\%\Delta L_{92/89}$ = -23.56%);

Both achievements reached by government (preventing the wage-push inflation as well as the shock of massive unemployment) are under threat in the near future due to the expected abolishing of the wage regulation. To face such a threat it might be necessary to continue the restrictive macroeconomic policies probably longer than originally expected, partially owing to the newly arisen problem of wage pressures. Obviously, an adjustment of the Czechoslovak wage bargaining system according to standard European rules is needed, too.

REFERENCES

1. Buchtíková, A., Capek, A., Macourková, E.: *Statistical analysis of the privatization projects*. Institute of Economics of the Czechoslovak Academy of Sciences, Prague 1992

2. *Bulletins FSO* No.1/92, 7/92, Monthly Statistic of Czechoslovakia No. 12/91, 5/92

3. Burda, M.C.: Labour and product markets in Czechoslovakia and the ex-GDR: a twin study. In: *European economy. The path of reform in Central and Eastern Europe.* Commission of the European Communities, Special edition No. 2, 1991

4. Calmfors, L., Driffil, J.: Bargaining structure, corporativism and macroeconomic performance. *Economic Policy*, 1988,(6)

5. Fitzroy, F.R.: The modern corporation: Efficiency, control and comparative organisation. *Kyklos*, 1988,(2)

6. Flek, V.: Wage bargaining in the period of transition to the market economy. *Politicka ekonomie*, 1991,(9-10)

7. Flek, V.: Marketisation, demonopolization and nature of Czechoslovak firms. *Workshop and Conference ACE EC*. Leuven, June 1992

8. Generálni Dohoda ze dne 28. 1. 1991. *Hospodářské noviny*, 30. 1. 1991 (The General Agreement for 1991)

9. *Generální Dohoda na rok 1992*. Práce, 5. 5. 1992 (The General Agreement for 1991)

10. Hoerr, J.: What should unions do. *Harvard Business Review*, 1991, May - June

11. Izák, V.: *Current problems of monopoly power.*Institute of Economics of the Czechoslovak academy of Sciences,Prague 1992.

12. Janaček, K. et al.: *Macroeconomic and social analysis* : Spring 1992. Institute of Economics of the Czechoslovak Academy of Sciences, Prague 1992

13. Klacek, J. et al.: *Economic reform in Czechoslovakia : Current evaluation.* Institute of Economics of the Czechoslovak Academy of Sciences, Prague 1991

14. Křovák, J., Buchtíková, A., Macourková, E.: *Enterprise sector behaviour and performance.* Workshop ACE EC, Prague 1992

15. Layard, R., Nickell, S.: Is unemployment lower if unions bargain over employment? In.: *Advances in the theory and measurement of unemployment.* (Weiss, Y., Fishelson, G. - eds.) London, Macmillan 1990

16. Mitbestimmung. In: *Handwörterbuch der Wirtschaftswissenschaften* (HdWW). Stuttgart, New York, Tübingen, Göttingen, Zurich, G. Fischer, J.C.B. Mohr, Vandenhoeck & Ruprecht 1980

17. Niedenhoff, H.U.: *Produktionsfaktor und soziale Errungenschaften.* EG-Magazin, 1990,(3)

18. Oswald, A.J.: The economic theory of trade unions: An introductory survey. *Scandinavian Journal of Economics,* 1985,(2)

19. Pencavel, J.H.: Wages and employment under trade unionism: Microeconomic models and macroeconomic applications. *The Scandinavian Journal of Economics,* 1985,(2)

20. Svejnar, J.: *Microeconomic issues in the transition to a market economy.* CERGE, Working Paper No.1. Prague, July 1991

21. Subrt, B.: O právu na stávku. *Práce a mzda,* 1991, d. 12 (Towards the right for strike)

22. O akciových společnostech. *Hospodářské noviny (příloha č. 18),* 1990 (Joint-stock Company Law)

23. *Zákon o kolektivním vyjednávání a kolektivní smlouvě* (návrh). Práce, 31. 8. 1990(Collective Bargaining and Collective Agreement Law)

24. Zákon o státním podniku. *Hospodářské noviny (příloha č. 17),* 1990 (State-owned Enterprise Law)

16

ECONOMIC DISCONTENT AND POLITICAL BEHAVIOR[1]

How an Economic Reform Jeopardizes the Political Stability of a Federation in Which Two Speeds of Economic Development Are at Work

Lisbeth Yancis[2]
The University of Texas at Austin

SUMMARY: Between the Velvet Revolution and today, two national general elections took place in the country. It is the purpose of this report to relate the evolution of the economic conditions in the Czech and Slovak republics to the voting behavior of the irrespective citizens during the 1990 and 1992 general elections. In particular, it is found that the way the governing party handles the economy, the belief that some specific party will best take care of the economy, and the evaluation of the economic reforms were all very relevant to the voting behavior of the Czechoslovak people in 1992. Similarly, collective economic judgments, mixed with views about the political situation before the Velvet Revolution, explained much of the political attitude in 1990.

---

[1]The author is grateful to the Public Opinion Research Institute of Prague and the Department of Economics of the Czechoslovak Academy of Sciences for their guidance and provision of economic and political data. The author also owes a heavy intellectual debt to Prof. Brian Roberts of The University of Texas at Austin.

[2]At the time of writing this paper, the author completed a graduate education in Government Studies at the University of Texas at Austin. She can be contacted in Belgium at Rue de Nalinnes, 7, B-5651 Thy-le-Chateau.

1. INTRODUCTION

Since Czechoslovakia chose democracy as an alternative to communism during the "Velvet Revolution" of 1989, many aspects of the daily life of its people have changed. Contributing to these changes, far reaching economic reforms have been implemented to convert the former command economy into a full-fledged market economy. Economic liberalization and stabilization programs were quickly followed by waves of privatization. The transition is still under way.

If Czechoslovakia is now one of the most advanced emerging market economies in Eastern Europe, reforms have brought a fair degree of uncertainty, and economic hardship settled progressively in some parts of the country. Unemployment has risen and real income has dived, more dramatically so in the Slovak republic than in its Czech counterpart. The political climate became less stable.

The opinions of the two republics clearly diverged on the adequate economic reforms program to adopt. If, in a survey held by the Public Opinion Research Institute in October 1991, people largely mentioned the economic reforms and the social conditions as the major problems that they were facing, a significantly larger discontent was expressed in the Slovak republic. 78% of the Slovak respondents were unsatisfied; 54% in the Czech republic. As reasons for their discontent, respondents cited mainly the following: concerns about new personal financial constraints (increase in living costs and rent, low income),disappointment about the conduct of economic policy in Czechoslovakia (nothing being solved, uncertainty about the future), and the general economic conditions. Unemployment was slightly more emphasized in Slovakia.

The aim of this article is to analyze the relationship between economic discontent and political behavior in the Czech and Slovak republics since the Velvet Revolution of 1989.

More accurately, we will compare the political behavior of the Czech and Slovak respondents. Since the recent economic reforms in Czechoslovakia have, admittedly, been felt more painfully in the Slovak part of the country, we will verify if, accordingly, the impact of economic discontent on the respondent's voting behavior is more pronounced in the Slovak republic than it is in the Czech lands.

After a short description of the sample in the next section, we will undertake three sets of analyses. Two of these are common in the Economic Voting literature[3]: The study of the influence of personal economic grievances,

---

[3]For methodological information about the distinction between personal economic discontents and collective economic judgments, see for example Kinder, Donald R. and D. Roderick Kiewet, "Economic Discontent and Political Behavior: The Role of Personal Grievances and Collective Economic Judgments in Congressional Voting", American Journal of Political Science, vol. 23, nx3, Yale University, August 1979.

and the study of the influence of collective economic judgments. For this study of Czechoslovakia, I have selected a third locus of research, to be found more scarcely in the literature, which aims to determine the impact, on election outcomes, of the voter's assessment of the economic competence of political parties.

2. DATA AND METHODOLOGY

All sets of analyses rely on ordinary least square multiple regression models. The dependent variable in the models relates to the respondent's vote choice for the elections of the federal parliament and of the national councils.

The statistical work is based on survey data provided by the Public Opinion Research Institute (P.O.R.I.). Located in Prague, the Institute collects opinion information on a regular basis and is involved in various areas of research, including political, social and economic opinion research.

Pre-election survey data have been obtained from the Institute. These data relate to the first two general elections which took place in Czechoslovakia since the Velvet Revolution. These elections were held on the 8th and 9th of June, 1990, and on the 5th and 6th of June, 1992. In order to carry out these surveys, P.O.R.I. sent about 2000 questionnaires to Czech and Slovak citizens in proportions consistent with the respective population of each republic. Approximately 2/3 of the questionnaires went to Czech citizens and 1/3 to Slovak citizens.

We face a minor methodological difficulty, however: the 1990 survey differs from that of 1922. The questionnaire of the former emphasizes the political aspect of the respondent's life, while the latter focuses to a larger extent on attitudes concerning the current economic situation in Czechoslovakia. Since the 1990 survey does not provide a great variety of information related to the economic situation in Czechoslovakia, I have measured the impact of the respondent's views about the old regime on his/her political behavior.

To construct the dependent variable, each political party has been placed on a linear scale, within three possible categories: left-wing, center, and right-wing parties. The scale results from a consensus of Czechoslovak political analysts.[4]

---

[4]See Hudecek, Jaroslav "Pokus o Identifikaci Stran na"Levo-Pravm" Kontinuu, Politick Spektrum v Cesk Republice v Roce 1991" (An attempt at the Identification of Parties along the "Left-Right" Continuum, the Political Spectrum in the Czech Republic in 1991), Sociologicky Casopis, Vol. 28, nx2, pp. 275-283. Praha, 1992.) Dr. Libor Kudlacek also helped me to determine the political orientation of the 1992 parties. This taxonomy, as well as the list of the parties which are used in this analysis, can be found in Yancis, L., "Economic Discontent and Political Behavior: How an Economic Reform Jeopardizes the Political Stability of a Federation in which

To select the sample from the 1990 data, I have included those Czech and Slovak respondents who said that they will or may vote, that they were undecided, or that they may not vote. This excludes only those who said that they will definitely not vote. This choice--which may seem exaggeratedly lax at first glance--is justified by the fact that the turnout in 1990 was very high. Around 95% of the Czechoslovaks voted.

The 1992 survey, unlike that of 1990, distinguishes between the votes for the federal parliament elections, and those for the elections to the national councils. The respondent was asked for which party he/she would vote at these different levels. In order to construct the dependent variable, I refer to the same question as in the 1990 survey. Here, however, are excluded from the sample all respondents who said that they do not have the right to vote or that they will not vote.

The number of respondents who remain in the 1990 sample is 1237 in the Czech republic and 547 in the Slovak republic. The 1992 samples contain 845 Czech and 499 Slovak respondents for the elections to the federal parliament, and 524 Slovak and 834 Czech voters for the elections to the national councils.

We will first focus on the impact of personal economic grievances on voting behavior, and see if a model representing personal grievances performs consistently in accounting for the results of the elections to the federal parliament and to the national councils in the Czech and the Slovak republics. We will then direct our attention to collective economic judgments. Finally, we will focus on the evaluation, by the voters, of the economic competence of the different parties.

3. PERSONAL ECONOMIC GRIEVANCES AND THE CZECHOSLOVAK ELECTIONS

One of the economic grievances that is believed to have a major effect on political behavior is a diminution of the voter's income. In the 1992 P.O.R.I. survey, the respondent was asked to answer the following question: "How is your present financial situation in contrast with your situation in 1989? Better/ the same / worse / hard to say?"

This does not allow us to consider recent (i.e. over a six-month span) changes in income, as is commonly done in this type of analysis. A comparison of the respondent's financial situation in 1992 with that of 1989 is however most adequate in the case of Czechoslovakia. People in 1989 had indeed high expectations about their future; for many of them, unfortunately, the actual financial situation deteriorated.

---

two Speeds of Economic Development are at work", Thesis, The University of Texas at Austin, 1992.

Information concerning the evolution of the respondent's financial situation were not available in the 1990 pre-election survey.

Our second variable about personal economic grievances relates to the employment status of the respondent at the time of the survey. The same question appeared in the 1990 and 1992 questionnaires: "What is your current job?"

Almost all Czechoslovak citizens were able to keep their job immediately after the Velvet Revolution. The unemployment rate[5] in Czechoslovakia at the end of the third quarter of 1990 was only 0.6% of the active population. However, as we mentioned earlier, social conditions deteriorated thereafter. The unemployment rate rose to 5.2% of the active population in June 1992, although in an unbalanced fashion. The rate of unemployment was 2.7% in the Czech republic, whereas it reached 11.3% in the Slovak republic. Hence, it is likely that the conditions of the job market play an important role in explaining the results of the 1992 elections in Slovakia.

Another typically important determinant of voting behavior is partisanship[6] In order to analyse the effects of the attachment to political parties, I have included in the models, whenever practical, a variable which defines the political identification of the voter.

I am also interested in the possible impact of the living environment of the respondent at the time of the elections. This would shed some light on whether people living in rural and urban areas have different patterns of political behavior. The question survey underlying the construction of this variable is "What is the density of population in the city where you live?".

The Model

With the 1992 data, we are able to test two important hypotheses. The first holds that voters who find themselves financially worse off in 1992 than in 1989 vote for a political party with an orientation different from that of the governing party: they prefer center or left-wing to right. The second hypothesis is that people who experience unemployment at the time of the elections also vote against the governing party.

These two hypotheses cannot be tested on the 1990 sample. The data related to the respondent's financial situation in 1990 are not available. Moreover, there was no unemployed in that sample. The variables associated with unemployment and income will therefore lack in all studies based on the 1990 sample.

---

[5]Source: Federal Ministry of Labor and Social Affairs, Prague.

[6]See, for example, Campbell A., W.E. Miller, and D.E. Stokes, "The American Voter", John Wiley, New York, N.Y. 1960.

Formally described below is the linear regression model which tests the impact of personal economic grievances on voting behavior in 1992:

PARTY92 = a + b1 URBAN + b2 PARTYID + b3 UNEMPL + b4 INCOME + f

Specifications of the Variables

The dependent variable, "PARTY92", takes the value (-1) if the respondent supports a left-wing party, the value (0) if the respondent intends to vote for a party which is in the center, and the value (+1) if the respondent prefers to elect a right-wing party.

The first independent variable, "URBAN", describes the location of the respondent in the country. This variable takes the value (+1) if the respondent lives in a village, or in an area dominated by rural activities (less than 5,000 inhabitants),and the value (+2) if the respondent lives in a city (more than 5000 inhabitants).

The second variable, "PARTYID", stands for the partisan identification of the voter. The respondent places himself/herself on a 9-point scale which represents the political tendencies from left to right. Respondents who did not answer are excluded from the sample.

Left								Right
-4	-3	-2	-1	0	+1	+2	+3	+4

The next two explanatory variables reflect the respondent's personal economic grievances. The variable "UNEMPL" takes the value (-3) if the respondent is currently unemployed, and the value (+1) if the respondent has a job. The choice of the coding coefficients is based on the assumption that unemployed people will be opposed to the political party in power, more strongly than employed people would support the political party in power.

The variable "INCOME" is re-coded (1) if the respondent thinks that his/her current financial situation has improved since 1989, (0) if the respondent thinks that he/she is in the same financial situation as in 1989 (or if it is hard for him/her to say whether his/her financial situation has changed during the period), and (-1) if the respondent finds that his/her situation has become worse.

Interpretation

The regression output for the model, is reproduced in Table 1. The results show that partisanship and personal economic discontents account for roughly 30% in the explanation of the political behavior during the 1992 elections to the Czech and the Slovak national councils, and to the federal parliament. The relatively large b2 coefficients simply account for the fact that voters who politically position themselves to the left, in the center, or to the right are likely to vote for a party which has the same political orientation as theirs. The remaining variance is explained by other factors.

The model seems to imply that, in the 1992 elections, changes in a respondent's financial situation have influenced his/her voting behavior. The interpretation of the b4 coefficients is the following: A positive coefficient means that an increase in the respondent's discontent concerning his/her income raises the support for center or left political parties.

The current experience of unemployment appears to be insignificant in the development of the respondent's political behavior.

Based on the 1992 survey data, around 40% of the Czech people, and 60% of the Slovak citizens, felt that their financial situation had worsened, while the others felt that their situation had not been affected, or had improved, since 1989. Moreover, around 50% of the Czech people declared themselves of right-wing political orientation, while in Slovakia only 30% are right-wing oriented. It is interesting to see how these facts read in the model: In the Czech republic, the impact of partisanship on the voting behavior of the respondent dominates the influence on the model of the evolution of incomes;meanwhile, the explanatory power of the model for the Slovak republic is due more to the income evolution than to the partisanship of the voters.

The results claimed by the model coincide with what actually happened during the 1992 elections: The winners of the 1990 elections, "Public against Violence" and the "Civic Forum", both right-wing political parties, have been replaced by a right-wing party, "Civic Democratic Party" in the Czech republic, and by a center-left party, "Movement for a Democratic Slovakia" in the Slovak republic.

We will now turn our attention to variables reflecting amore global conception of the economy: The so-called collective economic judgments. This analysis will allow us to determine if voters take into account only their personal situation, or if the evolution of the general economic conditions -which affect others as much as, or maybe more than, them- are the main matter of concerns.

4. COLLECTIVE ECONOMIC JUDGMENTS AND THE CZECHOSLOVAK ELECTIONS

Collective economic judgments are the voter's opinions on the general economic situation of his/her country and on the economic competencies of the governing party.[7] The data in all samples allow us to test their impact.

The 1990 Model

The first independent variable in our 1990 elections model relates to the question: "Are you satisfied or dissatisfied with the general situation of Czechoslovakia?". This question may refer to all aspects of life in Czechoslovakia but it is clear that, in answering this question in 1990, the respondent could not make abstraction of the general economic conditions. The inflation rate[8] in June 1990 was 16.2%, and real income dived.

The second variable related to the collective economic judgments describes the opinion of the respondent concerning the benefits of a market economy. The respondent had to approve or disapprove with the following statement: "Market economy paves the road to better standards of living". In 1990, citizens who thought so were generally dissatisfied with the way the socialist government handled the economy. A complete revision of the Czechoslovak economic system was desired by most of the people.

The last independent variable of the 1990 model refers to the political situation in Czechoslovakia before the Velvet Revolution. The respondent must give his/her appreciation on the following statement: "Since 1948, there was no freedom and it was the time of darkness." In a country where the collapse of the communist regime was welcome, it is likely that the citizens will firmly reject left-wing political parties. This variable is obviously not a collective economic judgment, but is included in the model because, in 1990, people worried at least as much about the political situation of their country as about its economic future.

Our 1990 Model reads as follows:

$$\text{PARTY 90} = a + b1\ \text{URBAN} + b2\ \text{SATISFACTION} + b3\ \text{MARKET} + b4\ \text{FREEDOM} + \mu$$

The variable "SATISFACTION" takes the value (-1) if the respondent is dissatisfied with the general situation in Czechoslovakia, and the value

[7]See, for example, Kinder and Kiewet, Op. Cit.
[8]Source: Federal Statistical Office.

(+1) if he is satisfied. The respondent who has no position on this issue is excluded from the sample.

A large value of the variable "MARKET" means that the respondent is favorable to a market economy. It is re-coded (-2) if the respondent believes that a market economy does definitely not pave the way to better standard of living,(-1) if he believes that, perhaps, a market economy does not lead to better standard of living, (+1) if he believes that, perhaps, it does, and (+2) if, for the respondent, a market economy will definitely lead to a better standard of living.

The variable "FREEDOM" is re-coded from (+2), if the respondent thinks that, since 1948, there was definitely freedom and that it was definitely not the time of darkness, to (-2) if the respondent thinks that there was definitively no freedom and that it was definitively the time of darkness. In short, a large value of this variable means that the respondent was favorable to the communist regime.

The 1992 Model

In the 1992 model, I also refer to two categories of collective economic judgments: The government's general performance on economic affairs, and the assessment of general business conditions. Moreover, I am interested in the way the respondent assesses the recent economic reforms.

The question which underlies the government performance variable is "How are you satisfied with the outcome of the 1990 elections concerning the Czech (or the Slovak) economy?" In order to construct the variable related to the business conditions, I refer to the question "What type of possibilities do people have today to achieve their goals?" If people have abroad array of possibilities, that means that the business conditions are favorable, and conversely.

In 1992 Czechoslovakia, there was a cleavage between those who approved the economic reforms and those who were opposed. Positions were often extreme, and the trend was different in each republic. Figures 1 illustrates this fact, based on monthly surveys from P.O.R.I. It is interesting to look at the impact of such polarization on voting behavior. Accordingly, a variable related to the following question "What do you think of the economic reforms?" is included in the model.

Our 1992 model is:

$$\text{PARTY92} = a + b1\ \text{URBAN} + b2\ \text{PARTYID} + b3\ \text{UNEMPL} + b4\ \text{INCOME} + b5\ \text{ECON REFORM} + b6\ \text{ACHGOAL} + b7\ \text{GVTPERFORM} + \mu$$

The variable "ACHGOAL" takes values from (+1), if the respondent finds that people have little chances of achieving their goals today, to (+4), if the respondent finds that people have good chances to achieve their goals.

The variable "GVTPERFORM" has been defined as follows: (-2)if the respondent is very unhappy with the development of the Czechoslovak economy since 1990, (-1) if he is rather unhappy with it, (0) if he does not know, (+1) if the respondent is rather happy, and (+2) if he is very happy.

The variable "ECON REFORM" has been re-coded (+2) if the respondent thinks that the economic reform goes slowly and should be speeded up, (+1) if the respondent thinks that the economic reform goes quite well, (0) if the respondent does not know, (-1)if the respondent finds that the economic reform should be reconsidered, (-2) if the respondent believes that it should be stopped because the situation in Czechoslovakia changes, and (-3)if the respondent finds that the economic reform was not good from the beginning.

We test the hypotheses that voters expressing negative collective economic judgments on business conditions or on the performance of the government vote for a party which is significantly distinct from the governing party on the point of view of its political orientation.

Interpretation

Table 2 shows that, in the 1992 elections, the respondent's partisanship, its views on the economic reform, and collective economic judgments explain between 23% and 42% of the political behavior of voters, according to the sample.

Partisan identification plays a decisive role in explaining the political behavior of voters. The coefficient b2 in the 1992 models is relatively large and is significant at the 0.01 level. Personal economic grievances do no longer contribute to the explanation of the voting behavior of the Czechoslovak citizens. The coefficient of the variable "INCOME", which played an important role in the previous model, is insignificant here. This result suggests that the influence of the personal economic discontents on the respondent's voting behavior is negligible compared to the impact of the collective economic judgments.

Collective economic judgments account indeed for a large part of the variance of voting choice in the 1992 elections. A belief that the conduct of the economic policy was outstanding made people favorable to the political orientation of the governing party, for instance the right-wing "Civic Forum". On the contrary, a belief that the government did not well handle the economy made the citizens vote for a party of political orientation opposed to that of the governing party.

The respondent's appreciation on the economic reforms also influenced his/her political behavior. The coefficient of the variable related to this topic (b5) is significant at the 0.01 level. A favorable opinion on the economic reforms seemed to favor the political orientation of the governing party in 1992, and conversely.

Based on the 1992 survey, we have seen that as much as 50% of the Czech people and only 32% of the Slovak citizens were right-wing oriented. In 1992, 50% of people in the Czech lands also found that the economic reforms worked quite well or even that they had to be speeded up. On the other hand, only 22% of Slovak people had the same opinion. Moreover, only 10% of people in Slovakia, and as much as 33% in the Czech republic, were happy or rather happy with the economic developments in Czechoslovakia. Negative economic judgments strongly dominated in Slovakia, while a rather positive opinion on the economy prevailed in the Czech republic.

Our 1992 model reflects fairly accurately the outcome of the 1992 elections in each republic. The Czech republic, where most people were relatively enthusiastic about the developments of the economy, elected a right-wing party which promoted the continuation of rapid economic reforms. On the other hand, the Slovak republic, where the economic reforms admittedly caused more hardship than in the Czech lands, elected a center-left party which vowed to fundamentally revise the reform program by slowing down privatization, restoring a system of state subsidies, and broadening the social safety net.

In the 1990 elections, collective economic judgments, political judgments about the former communist regime, and the region of origin together accounted for roughly 25% in determining a respondent's political behavior (Table 2).

The political situation which prevailed before the Velvet Revolution of 1989 exerted a strong influence on the voting behavior of Czech citizens. The coefficient b4 in the 1990 model is highly significant, up to the 0.01 level. Its negative sign confirms that the less the respondent supported the ante-1989 political situation, the more likely he or she was to vote for aright-wing party.

Collective economic judgments played a great role in the 1990 elections as well. We see in Table 2 that the more favorable a Czech respondent is to a market economy, the more likely he is to vote for a right-wing party. We will test this hypothesis on our 1990 and 1992 sets of samples.

5. JUDGMENTS ON PARTY COMPETENCE AND THE CZECHOSLOVAK ELECTIONS

In 1990, the majority of Czechoslovak people (95% in the Czech lands and 91% in Slovakia) were rather enthusiastic about the realization of a market economy. Moreover, we observe that increased satisfaction with the general situation in Czechoslovakia seemed to induce people to vote for a more right-wing oriented party.

Since Czech and Slovak citizens hold different opinions about the way the economy should be handled, one can assume that the perception of the economic competence of parties would contribute to determine voting behavior. In the 1990 and the 1992 elections surveys, the respondent had to determine which political party will the best take care of the economy. To test our hypothesis, we add this variable to our model. The formal representations of the adapted 1990 and 1992 models read as follows:

PARTY 90 = a + b1 URBAN + b2 SATISFACTION + b3 MARKET +
b4 FREEDOM + b5 PARTYCPT + f

PARTY 92 = a + b1 URBAN + b2 PARTYID + b3 UNEMPL +
b4 INCOME + b5 ECON REFORM + b6 ACHGOAL +
b7 GVTPERFORM + b8 PARTYCPT + f

The variable "PARTYCPT" is the new independent variable in our models. Like the explained variable, it is re-coded (+1) if the respondent thinks that a right-wing party will best take of the economy, (0) if he/she thinks that a party in the center will best handle the economy, and (-1) if the respondent believes that a left-wing party is more capable.

Interpretation

We see in Table 3 that the 1990 and the 1992 models respectively explain roughly 40% and 55% of the political behavior of the respondent. Our observations from the previous analyses still hold, but the Table 3 results stress the importance of judgments related to the economic competence of parties in Czechoslovakia.

The explanatory power of the 1990 and the 1992 models is due largely to the respondent's appreciation of the party competence. The coefficient of the corresponding variable is indeed large and significant at the 0.01 level. If a respondent identifies aright-wing party as being the best party for handling the economy, he or she is likely to vote for a right-wing party. In 1992, around 62% of the Czech population, but only 30% in Slovakia, preferred a right-wing party. In 1990, both republics largely favored a right-wing party: 75% and 68% in the Czech and the Slovak republics respectively.

In 1992, unlike in 1990, the coefficient of "PARTYCPT" is significantly larger in the Slovak republic than in the Czech republic.

There are two other interesting differences between the republics in 1992. In Slovakia, as opposed to the Czech lands, the government performance ("GOVPERFORM") in handling the economy is very significant. Also, in the Czech republic, unlike in its Slovak counterpart, the conduct of the economic reforms("ECON REFORM") is significant. By looking back at the construction of these two variables, one comes easily to the conclusion that Slovaks have been largely influenced by past economic performances, while Czech tended to concentrate on the future of the economy. The recent economic history of each republic may fully explain this divergence of focus.

6. CONCLUSION

After having applied three sets of analyses (personal economic grievances, collective economic judgments, and opinions on the economic competence of parties), we can sum up by saying that the last two factors, and especially the latter, bear most of the explanatory power of our models. Personal economic grievances, like in many other countries, are not a good predictor of the vote choice of individuals.

We have mentioned, on several occasions, that the outcome of the elections were fairly well represented by our models. It should be remembered however that these models have been regressed on data obtained from pre-election surveys. This has two important implications.

First, that the study of pre-election data in Czechoslovakia--or, in the future, in the Czech and Slovak independent republics-- allows the scholar to identify important trends and determinants of the elections outcomes. Secondly, our study seems to indicate that the survey data gathered by the Public Opinion Research Institute of Prague is a reliable source of information.

Of course, further study will be needed to confirm these preliminary assessments. Research would be fertile on other matters as well.

During a survey that was held in March 4-9, 1992 by P.O.R.I., most of the respondents said that they somewhat feared inflation. In the Czech republic, 22% of the respondents had little fear and 62% had great fear, while in the Slovak republic, 13% had little fear and 67% had great fear. However, there was a much stronger confidence about the effectiveness of the stabilization policy in the Czech republic, 47%, than in Slovakia, 23%. The perceived impact of a future increase in the rate of inflation on the political behavior of the respondents would be an interesting subject of research, but the P.O.R.I. elections surveys so far do not include this kind of questions.

The elections of June 5th and 6th, 1992 split power along national and ideological lines. The results of the elections revealed an accentuation of the ideological differences between the pro-reform, anti-communist Czechs and the Slovak anti-reform, nationalist left. This political polarization has been an important handicap to the formation of a workable federal government and to the design of a coherent economic program.

This report demonstrates that the diverging political orientations taken by each republic are in part related to the progress or the defeat of the economic reforms, such as it was experienced by the citizens of Czechoslovakia.

The 1992 elections polarized Czechoslovakia. Voters in the Czech republic elected the Civic Democratic Party led by Vaclav Klaus. While Czechs supported the continuation of rapid economic reforms and saw a future for the federation, Slovaks had confidence in the Movement for a Democratic Slovakia led by Vladimir Meciar, who proposed to slow down economic reforms and to declare the sovereignty of the republics. The period after the election was eventful. The Czech right-wing party and the Slovak left-wing party did not reach a compromise which would keep the federation together. The republics will be independent in 1993.

Figure 1

Attitudes Towards Economic Reforms

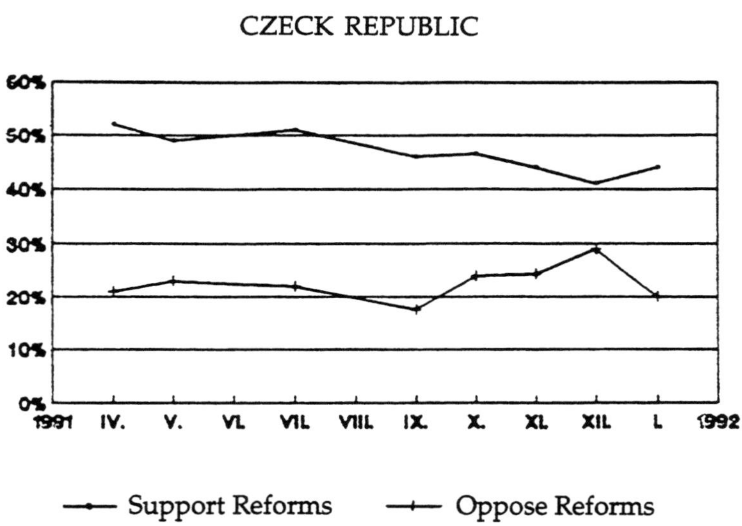

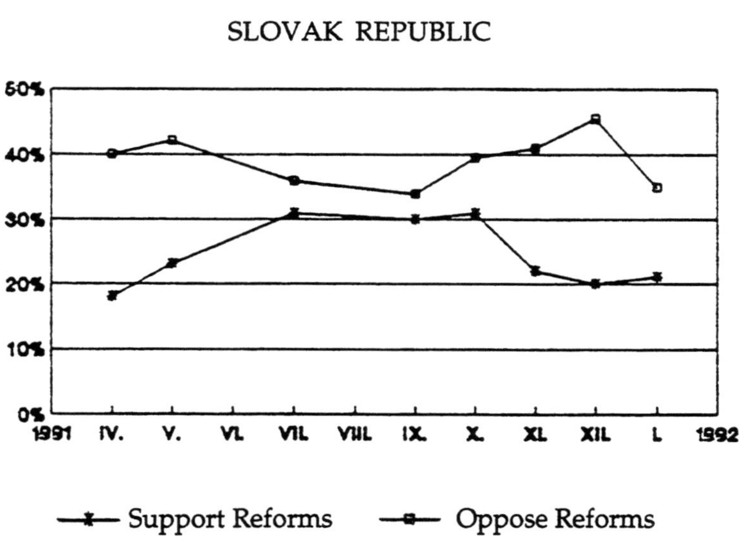

Table 1

The Effect of Personal Economic Grievances and the Voting Behavior of Czech and Slovak Citizens in 1992

	1992 Elections			
	National Councils		Federal Parliament	
	Czech Republic	Slovak Republic	Czech Republic	Slovak Republic
Intercept	0.2417** (0.1065)	-0.0834 (0.1216)	0.2465** (0.1041)	-0.1527 (0.1316)
Urban	0.0017 (0.0541)	-0.1132 (0.0680)	0.0117 (0.0528)	-0.0662 (0.0736)
Partisanship	0.2250* (0.0134)	0.1955* (0.0188)	0.2293* (0.0131)	0.1523* (0.0203)
Personal Economic Discontents:				
Unemployment	-0.0741 (0.0467)	0.0243 (0.0425)	-0.0698 (0.0459)	0.0418 (0.0461)
Income	0.1172* (0.0387)	0.2270* (0.0537)	0.1541* (0.0377)	0.2209* (0.0582)
Adj. R-square	0.3255	0.2642	0.3501	0.1781
N	784	476	93	56

* Significant at the 0.01 level
** Significant at the 0.05 level

Table 2

Collective Economic Judgments and the Voting Behavior of Czech and Slovak Citizens in 1990 and 1992

	1990 Elections		1992 Elections			
			National Councils		Federal Parliament	
	CR	SR	CR	SR	CR	SR
Intercept	0.1736 (0.1098)	0.3405** (0.1459)	0.1960 (0.1248)	0.1441 (0.1690)	0.2410** (0.1206)	0.0178 (0.1810)
Urban	-0.1555* (0.0553)	-0.1418 (0.0880)	-0.0294 (0.0536)	-0.1020 (0.0671)	-0.0077 (0.0518)	-0.0495 (0.0724)
Partisanship			0.1781* (0.0146)	0.1796* (0.0193)	0.1790* 0.0141)	0.1334* (0.0206)
Personal Economic Discontents:						
Unemploy-ment			-0.1024** (0.0482)	0.0315 (0.0419)	-0.0971** (0.0469)	0.0421 (0.0455)
Income			-0.0231 (0.0421)	0.0824 (0.0580)	0.0206 (0.0407)	0.0433 (0.0635)
Collective Economic Judgments:						
Satisfaction	0.0982* (0.0277)	0.1593* (0.0455)				
Market	0.0899** (0.0364)	0.0681 (0.0477)				
Freedom	-0.2808* (0.0217)	-0.2347* (0.0315)				
Economic Reform			0.0947* (0.0173)	0.0733* (0.0249)	0.1049* 0.0166)	0.1111* (0.0271)
Achieve Goals			0.0775** (0.0324)	-0.0529 (0.0470)	0.0501 (0.0311)	-0.0306 (0.0507)
Government Performance			0.0845* (0.0248)	0.1451* 0.0435)	0.0964* 0.0238)	0.1277* (0.0475)
Adj. R-sq	0.2410	0.2102	0.3830	0.3131	0.4199	0.2347
N	952	398	741	456	750	436

* Significant at the 0.01 level
** Significant at the 0.05 level

Table 3

The Economic Competence of Parties and the Voting Behavior of Czech and Slovak Citizens in 1990 and 1992

	1990 Elections		1992 Elections			
			National Councils		Federal Parliament	
	CR	SR	CR	SR	CR	SR
Intercept	-0.0073 (0.1053)	0.3294** (0.1599)	0.0667 (0.1275)	0.1018 (0.1202)	0.2015 (0.1605)	
Urban	-0.0863 0.0525)	-0.1767 (0.0945)	-0.0085 (0.0532)	-0.1422** (0.0579)	0.0064 (0.0499)	-0.1025 (0.0616)
Partisanship			0.1082* (0.0155)	0.0914* 0.0169)	0.1147* (0.0145)	0.0415** (0.0179)
Personal Economic Discontents:						
Unemploy-ment			-0.0835 (0.0533)	0.0086 (0.0357)	-0.0835 (0.0502)	0.0435 (0.0372)
Income			-0.0091 (0.0408)	0.0305 (0.0511)	0.0524 (0.0383)	-0.0434 (0.0522)
Collective Economic Judgments:						
Satisfaction	0.0495** (0.0258)	0.1717* (0.0482)				
Market	0.0487 (0.0346)	0.0199 (0.0509)				
Freedom	-0.1920* (0.0212)	-0.1759* (0.0353)				
Economic Reform			0.0503* (0.0180)	0.0009 (0.0227)	0.0550* (0.0170)	0.0322 (0.0244)
Achieve Goals			0.0553 (0.0321)	0.0189 (0.0428)	0.0247 (0.0299)	-0.0379 (0.0455)
Government Performance			0.0330 (0.0244)	0.1059* (0.0386)	0.0255 (0.0227)	0.0972** (0.0413)
Party Competence	0.4795* (0.0308)	0.3325* (0.0516)	0.455* (0.0359)	0.5866* (0.0372)	0.4810* (0.0337)	0.6458* (0.0402)
Adj. R-sq	0.4090	0.3166	0.5341	0.5923	0.5930	0.5621
N	809	312	577	374	580	358

* Significant at the 0.01 level
** Significant at the 0.05 level

SUBJECT INDEX

90 0591781 3